Inclusion Strategies That Work!

Research-Based Methods for the Classroom

AT A GLANCE

Contents

SECOND EDITION

Inclusion Strategies
That Work!

Research-Based Methods for the Classroom

TOBY J. KARTEN

CORWIN
A SAGE Company

For information:

Corwin
A SAGE Company
2455 Teller Road
Thousand Oaks, California 91320
(800) 233-9936
Fax: (800) 417-2466
www.corwin.com

SAGE India Pvt. Ltd.
B 1/I 1 Mohan Cooperative
    Industrial Area
Mathura Road, New Delhi 110 044
India

SAGE Ltd.
1 Oliver's Yard
55 City Road
London EC1Y 1SP
United Kingdom

SAGE Asia-Pacific Pte. Ltd.
33 Pekin Street #02-01
Far East Square
Singapore 048763

Printed in the United States of America

Library of Congress Cataloging-in-Publication Data

Inclusion strategies that work!: research-based methods for the classroom/Toby J. Karten.— 2nd ed.
    p. cm.
Previous edition cataloged under Karten, Toby. J.
Includes bibliographical references and index.
ISBN 978-1-4129-7937-5 (pbk.)
    1. Children with disabilities—Education—United States. 2. Teenagers with disabilities—Education—United States. 3. Inclusive education—United States. I. Karten, Toby J. II. Karten, Toby J., Inclusion strategies that work!

LC4031.I527 2010
371.9'046—dc22   2009047381

This book is printed on acid-free paper.

10 11 12 13 14 10 9 8 7 6 5 4 3 2 1

Managing Editor:	Jessica Allan
Acquisitions Editor:	David Chao
Editorial Assistant:	Sarah Bartlett
Production Editor:	Libby Larson
Copy Editor:	Teresa Herlinger
Typesetter:	C&M Digitals (P) Ltd.
Proofreader:	Theresa Kay
Indexer:	Terri Corry
Cover and Graphic Designer:	Michael Dubowe

Inclusive Activities and Worksheets for Teachers and Students

Preface

Teachers and students are sometimes caught up in the special education paradigm, with a San Andreas Fault separating effective research practices from classroom implementation. This book hopes to facilitate learning for students with and without disabilities by jump-starting teachers with research-based strategies for inclusive classrooms. As you proceed through the chapters and activities, please note that I often italicize the base word *abilities* in the word dis*abilities* to highlight that it is not about what students *cannot* do; instead, the focus in inclusive classrooms must be on students' strengths—what they *can* do. Educators owe students the opportunity to achieve their maximum potential. This need not be a complicated process if professionals are trained and equipped with the right tools that focus on students' abilities. Step-by-step practices are explained in each chapter, with guided student and teacher activities to internalize strategies. This text explains what research says about inclusion of children as well as inclusive content, focusing on achievement of productive student outcomes in diverse classrooms. Knowledge is retained by *doing,* so the words in this text leap off their pages with activities for inclusive classrooms, as shown below. A goal of this book is to help you tackle your list of inclusionary concerns.

Prior Inclusion Confusion

Historical Sample of Inclusionary Concerns	*My List of Inclusionary Concerns*
1. What's inclusion?	
2. I won't do inclusion.	
3. I don't know how to do inclusion.	
4. Who's included?	
5. Can I have training for inclusion?	
6. I need more planning time.	
7. It's not working.	
8. More direct skill instruction is needed.	
9. What's differentiated instruction?	
10. When do I retire?	

The first chapter begins by establishing the reason for inclusion. Research and legal considerations are detailed and examined with text and cooperative assignments to help readers understand more about the impact of the Individuals with Disabilities Education Act (IDEA) amendments with response to intervention (RTI) entering classrooms. Classroom impacts of the Americans with Disabilities Act (ADA) and Section 504 of the Rehabilitation Act of 1973 are also investigated. The second chapter explains some of the special terminology along with the negative effects that labeling has on students with and without disabilities. Simulations and resources for more dis*ability* awareness are experientially included. The third chapter delineates how knowledge of special education strategies benefits students with and without exceptionalities. Expansive interactive strategies and techniques ask the reader to process strategic concepts through varied activities.

The text moves onward to discuss the individualized education program (IEP), demystifying the document with practical guidelines that include basic IEP elements and ways for teachers to provide and document goals with classroom modifications that accommodate and honor individual needs. The text also addresses social issues as an integral part of the curriculum, including ways for teachers to improve student behavior. Emotional intelligences, self-advocacy, functional behavioral assessments, and interpersonal reflections are all major components of successful inclusive classrooms, as shown with academic and social connections.

None of these inclusive principles would work without teachers coplanning structured lessons with clear-cut objectives, UDL (universal design for learning) principles, and thinking about assessments with UbD (understanding by design). Sample collaborative classroom dilemmas are examined. The chapter on coteaching tries to blur the lines between special and general education teachers, to merge the sometimes separate worlds. The longest chapter in the book, Chapter 7, is about using the three R's of reading, 'riting, and 'rithmetic, with an abundance of student templates that focus on teaching the basics. Content areas of physical education, art, music, science, and social studies complement this chapter along with thematic interdisciplinary lessons. Learning more about study skills is next, along with retention, comprehension, and accountability issues with assessments. Teachers can reflectively examine classroom scenarios, questioning whether fair translates to equal and how effort, progress, and achievement factor into the grading and overall assessment process.

Chapter 10 focuses on how parents and families need to be part of the inclusive team, communicating and working together with teachers. Parents, families, and guardians are teachers' allies who should be valued as members of the school planning team. Establishing an ongoing system of home–school communication benefits all.

The technology chapter includes sample classroom activities and resources that teachers and students can use to maximize inclusive performances. Examples include how technology assists students with varying disabilities to lead more productive lives, and how technology does not replace but augments curriculum topics.

The last chapter of the book reiterates the benefits of revisiting concepts to ground learning in memory. Reflections direct educators to plan lessons with clear-cut objectives in which they teach, move onward, and then review. Reviewing is not taking a step backward, but cementing or concretizing student learning. Educational mirrors benefit all!

At the end of the book, readers are given descriptive, clear, and informative dis*ability* tables that delineate possible causes, characteristics, and educational strategies of many disabilities, from attention-deficit/hyperactivity disorder to autism, physical disabilities, emotional disorders, and more. A compilation of acronyms is given for quick reference. There are also many organizations and references offered in the bibliography to seek out for further investigation.

Inclusion Strategies That Work! Research-Based Methods for the Classroom, 2nd edition offers updated research-based practices and connects them to inclusive classrooms to reflect ongoing changes in the special education (SE) and general education (GE) fields. It is no ordinary book that is intended to collect dust on your shelf. It is a book whose binding will be well-worn, since it is meant to be used and reused. Existing materials touch upon many of these topics, but this compilation of materials houses not only the characteristics and dynamics of dis*abilities*, but also vital and feasible strategies that teachers of all students can use in their classrooms. The text pragmatically explains how research meshes with inclusion, with prepared teachers at the helm.

Acknowledgments

I would like to acknowledge all of my colleagues, friends, and family who answered countless questions and offered endless encouragement to complete this text.

Specific acknowledgment is given to the teachers whose dedicated collaboration is making inclusion a successful reality for all very *abled* students!

More specifically, thanks to Marc and Adam, the two sources of my personal inspiration and the rocks I can lean on. Life has purpose with the two of you by my side. Zelda and Al, I love you as well, and always will.

Thanks to all the professionals at Corwin who are part of the production team, as well as to the peer reviewers at distinguished universities who carefully scrutinized the text. The first edition was made possible with the assistance of Julia Parnell, my production editor, along with Jingle Vea and Candice Ling who meticulously and skillfully helped prepare the 400-plus pages of this manuscript for publication.

Technology should also be acknowledged, since the East Coast met the West Coast as emails drifted through cyberspace between my copyeditor, Teresa Herlinger, and myself. Perhaps one day we will formally meet, so I can properly thank her. Thanks to my first editor, Robb Clouse, who read an electronic query and *tastefully* acted upon it, and much appreciation to Allyson Sharp, David Chao, Sarah Bartlett, Jessica Allan, and Libby Larson, my current Corwin liaisons.

PUBLISHER'S ACKNOWLEDGMENTS

Corwin gratefully acknowledges the contributions of the following individuals:

Joyce Bergin, Assistant Dean,
  Professor of Special Education
College of Education
Armstrong Atlantic State University
Savannah, GA

Debi Gartland, Professor
Department of Special Education
Towson University
Towson, MD

Nicole Guyon, Learning Specialist
Community Preparatory School
Providence, RI

Rick Maloney, School Administrator;
  Math, Physics, English, and
  Psychology teacher
Highline School District
Burien, WA

Vicki McFarland, Special
  Education Director
Learning Matters Educational Group
Glendale, AZ

Joseph Staub, Resource
  Specialist Teacher
Thomas Starr King Middle School
Los Angeles, CA

About the Author

 **Toby J. Karten** is an experienced educator who has worked in the field of special education since 1976. She has an undergraduate degree in Special Education from Brooklyn College, a master's degree from the College of Staten Island, and a supervisory degree from Georgian Court University. Being involved in the field of special education for the past three decades has afforded Ms. Karten an opportunity to help many children and adults from elementary through graduate levels around the world. Along with being a resource teacher in New Jersey, Ms. Karten has designed a graduate course entitled *Skills and Strategies for Inclusion and Disability Awareness.* She has presented at local, state, national, and international workshops and conferences. Ms. Karten has been recognized by both the Council for Exceptional Children and the New Jersey Department of Education as an exemplary educator, receiving two "Teacher of the Year" awards.

Ms. Karten is married and has a son, as well as a few dogs. She enjoys teaching, reading, writing, artwork, and—most of all—learning. As the author of this book, she believes that inclusion does not begin and end in the classroom, but is a philosophy that continues throughout life. Hence, inclusion is not only research-based, but life-based as well!

*This book is dedicated to all of my
students throughout the years.*

Together we have learned so much.

*The world awaits, welcomes, and applauds your
brilliance and perseverance to succeed.*

Examining the Research Base and Legal Considerations in Special Education, and the Reasons for Inclusion

DISABILITY LEGISLATION

Legislation has changed the way society thinks about disabilities and has also driven research to find better ways for schools to deliver appropriate services to children in the least restrictive environment. Basically, students have rights to a free, appropriate public education that addresses their diverse needs. Teachers must understand what legislation and research say about students with differing abilities in regard to the curriculum, instruction, assessment, and daily living skills. In addition, there is thankfully now a huge emphasis upon improving both the academic and functional outcomes of students with disabilities with research-based interventions. Legislative information, standards-based reforms, and strategic research about disabilities are detailed in this chapter, along with the reasons why we need to do inclusion.

INTRODUCTION: WHY DO INCLUSION?

Affective Comparison

Directions: Think of a time when you were excluded from an academic or social activity as a child or an adult. List the emotions you experienced as a result of this exclusion. Contrast this experience with a time when you were included or allowed to participate with others, and list those emotions as well under the appropriate heading.

| Inclusion Versus Exclusion ||
Inclusion	Exclusion

The primary reason for inclusion is the list of positive inclusive emotions. The Latin root of inclusion is *includo,* meaning to embrace, while the Latin root of exclusion is *excludo,* meaning to separate or shut out. Unfortunately, in the beginning haste to include students, administrators in some school districts created the impression that inclusion is just a way to save money, with the unintended outcome that it only burdens teachers. All educational players now realize that inclusion will not succeed without the proper scaffolding. Most teachers are skeptical because there is no script or template to follow for inclusion. Even though inclusion has been in the forefront for a while, it is still in its infancy and will continually evolve. Simply stated, inclusion is a way of life and a preparation for adulthood. It supports the civil rights of all learners. Inclusion may not be the most appropriate placement to meet all students' needs, yet it should be considered as the first viable option. Now think of teaching a student who has similar exclusionary emotions to the ones you listed under the Exclusion column, and how he or she would feel about school. How could you learn, if you were experiencing these exclusionary emotions?

Any moral here???

ESTABLISHING LEGISLATIVE KNOWLEDGE

Courting Issues

Laws were designed to protect people with disabilities by giving them access to the same societal opportunities as those accessible to people without disabilities. Segueing to a more detailed examination of the special education laws and research, answer the following "true or false" questions.

True or False?

____ 1. Eighteen percent of the school-age population has a disability.

____ 2. Cooperative learning is a competitive teaching strategy.

____ 3. Right angles of learning refers to measuring the classroom.

____ 4. About 5–6% of the school-age population has a learning disability (LD).

____ 5. Section 504 of the Rehabilitation Act has been in effect since 1983.

____ 6. FAPE stands for Federally Approved Programs for Education.

____ 7. IDEA is an educational program that protects children ages 5 to 21.

____ 8. Teachers can call for a new IEP meeting anytime they need additional support.

____ 9. A student who is not classified can be considered for Section 504 protection.

____ 10. There are 13 specific disability categories under IDEA for students from ages 3 to 21.

____ 11. ADA protects individuals with physical or mental impairments that may limit a major life activity.

____ 12. People with mental retardation, e.g., developmental or cognitive disabilities, or intellectual impairments, are more likely to have children who are also cognitively impaired. (The term *mental retardation* has a negative connotation and should be avoided, even though it is still a formal classification under IDEA.)

Inclusion Web

Special education laws demand that the general education classroom be looked at as the first placement option and the least restrictive environment for students with disabilities. The web below outlines more inclusive particulars about inclusion.

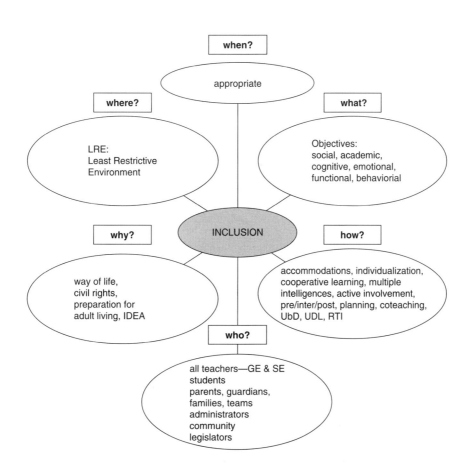

The "true or false" activity might have been frustrating if you did not have background knowledge about special education or the laws. Compare it to the spelling pretest given to students who have no prior knowledge of the words. Teachers sometimes begin a content area, assuming children have prior knowledge.

Moral: All students do not have the same background knowledge or experience. Learning should be at an optimum, while frustrations are kept at a minimum since they only interfere with and thwart the learning process. Ascertaining what students know before the lesson proceeds then helps to guide instruction. (See page 5 for answers to the true or false statements.)

Research about cooperative learning affirms that it confers both social and academic advantages (Jenkins, Antil, Wayne, & Vadasy, 2003; D. Johnson & Johnson, 1975; Kagan, 1994; Slavin, 1990). Socially, positive interactions increase as students work collaboratively toward a common goal. Academically, students are willing to spend more time learning from each other rather than from the teacher, resulting in better products with often challenging curricula. Cooperative communication also bridges schools to adulthood, since it is a prerequisite for future employment relationships. Getting along with others is a skill that schools can foster through cooperative learning. Team skills, increased self-esteem, improved peer interaction, and higher task completion with learning assignments are some of the benefits that are yielded when structured cooperative groups heterogeneously work together in classrooms. Overall, cooperation is a functional skill for educators and peers in inclusive classrooms to repeatedly foster and model.

Special education (SE) services are provided without cost to the students and families under all three laws of IDEA, ADA, and Section 504, with the least restrictive environment being the first option unless the severity of the disability prohibits that placement. The intention of this next legislative review is to increase the knowledge of SE laws and to *walk the cooperative talk.*

Jigsawing Reading

To review the basic terminology and legislation in the field of special education, cooperative groups equitably divide the legislative readings on the following pages to collectively share knowledge and then answer 6 out of 10 listed questions under the heading Cooperative Legislative Review. This jigsaw technique is a cooperative learning strategy, where teachers direct students to learn and share content with each other. Having choices of which questions to answer empowers the student under the teacher's auspices. Teachers monitor learners and drift to different groups, clarifying questions and concerns, while addressing individual and group thought processes. The following readings summarize pertinent facts about legislation, along with past/present/future concerns about special education and the rights of people with disabilities.

Cooperative Division

1. Everyone reads the IEP/ADA/504 comparison.

Then, equitably divide the following:

2. Details about the least restrictive environment

3. Description of 13 disability categories under IDEA

4. History of the ADA

5. Civil rights for people with disabilities

6. Past, present, and future concerns

Answers to true/false

1. F—Approximately 9% of all children and youth ages 3–21

2. F—Noncompetitive

3. F—It's a hierarchy of learning objectives.

4. T—Students falling under the LD category vary from state to state, e.g., low of 2.2% in Kentucky, 7.7% in Iowa and Oklahoma.

5. F—1973

6. F—Free and Appropriate Public Education

7. F—Ages 3 to 21 (students with developmental delays from birth to age 3 are eligible for services under IDEA Part C, e.g., physical development, cognitive development, communication, social or emotional development, or adaptive [behavioral] development)

8. T

9. T—Examples include a child with asthma (staff trained to administer EpiPen), diabetes (glucose monitoring with trained personnel, access to water, bathroom), food allergies (safe snacks available), juvenile arthritis (word processor, scribe), AD/HD (modified schedule, homework decreased, reduced or minimized distractions). Review this site for more 504 ideas: http://special-children.about.com/od/504s/qt/sample504.htm.

10. T

11. T—Life activities include walking, speaking, working, learning, caring for oneself, eating, sleeping, standing, lifting, bending, reading, concentrating, thinking, and communicating.

12. F—Children can be affected by the limitations, but their mother's illnesses during pregnancy and use of drugs and alcohol are major contributors.

Sources:

About.com: Special Needs Children, http://specialchildren.about.com/od/504s/qt/ sample504.htm.

Holler, R., & Zirkel, P. (2008). Section 504 and public schools: A national survey concerning "Section 504-only" students. *NASSP Bulletin*, 92(1), 19–43.

IES National Center for Education Statistics: Participation in Education. (n.d.). *Indicator 8: Children and youth with disabilities*. Retrieved May 3, 2009, from http://nces.ed.gov/programs/coe/2009/section1/indicator09.asp.

National Center for Educational Statistics (2003), Institute of Education Sciences, U.S. Dept. of Education. 1990 K Street, NW, Washington, DC 20006, (202) 502–7300, http://www.nces.ed.gov.

National Center for Learning Disabilities, http://www.ncld.org, as cited in http:www.ideadata.org.

National Dissemination Center for Children with Disabilities, http://www.nichcy.org/Laws/IDEA/Pages/BuildingTheLegacy.aspx.

IDEA 1990 & Individuals with Disabilities Education Improvement Act (IDEIA 2004)	American with Disabilities Act of 1990 (ADA) Americans with Disabilities Act Amendments Act of 2008 (ADAAA)	Section 504 of the Rehabilitation Act of 1973/ Impact of ADAAA 2008
Children ages 3 to 21 with disabilities listed below are eligible for a free and appropriate public education in the least restrictive environment (LRE). IDEA is a statute that funds special education programs under the following categories: • Autism • Deafness • Deafness–Blindness • Hearing Impairments • Mental Retardation • Multiple Disabilities • Orthopedic Impairments • Other Health Impairments • Emotional Disturbance • Specific Learning Disabilities • Speech or Language Impairments • Traumatic Brain Injury • Visual Impairments States may choose to add a 14th category of developmental delay for students ages 3–9 who exhibit significant physical, cognitive, behavioral, emotional, or social differences in development, in comparison with children of the same age and for students from birth to age 3, under IDEA Part C. The IDEA defines an Individualized Education Program (IEP), which lists written statements of current academic and functional levels. Long-term and short-term objectives are required	Civil rights antidiscriminatory law that protects people with disabilities from discrimination in public services, if reasonable accommodations can be provided there by state and local governments Physical or mental impairment has to substantially limit one or more life activities (walking, breathing, seeing, hearing, speaking, learning, working, caring for oneself, eating, sleeping, standing, lifting, bending, reading, concentrating, thinking, and communicating) A word such as *concentrating* qualifies a student with attention issues such as a child who may have a diagnosis of AD/HD. Disability determinations are made without regard to mitigating measures, e.g., medication, appliances, medical supplies, low-vision devices (not eyeglasses or contacts), prosthetics, hearing aids, and mobility devices. Person must have a record and be regarded as having such an impairment. This does not include transitory or minor disabilities that have a duration of 6 months or less. Prevents employment discrimination against individuals with disabilities who meet other job qualifications	Civil rights law that stops discrimination against people with disabilities in public and private programs/activities that receive financial assistance Services under 504 protection include special education and general education with appropriate related services, accommodations, and aids. ADAAA extended more eligibility for K–12 students under Section 504. Before ADAAA, students with 504 plans comprised about 1.2% of national school-age children. That number is expected to increase, e.g., to incorporate those with AD/HD, diabetes, food allergies (Holler & Zirkel, 2008). Similar to IDEA, but can include students and staff of all ages who may not be covered under IDEA classifications Disability has to limit student's ability to learn or perform other major life activities Students who use illegal drugs are not eligible for 504 plans. Lists mitigating measures, e.g., low vision (except contact lenses or eyeglasses), hearing aids, cochlear implants, assistive technology Includes reasonable accommodations and modifications

IDEA 1990 & Individuals with Disabilities Education Improvement Act (IDEIA 2004)	American with Disabilities Act of 1990 (ADA) Americans with Disabilities Act Amendments Act of 2008 (ADAAA)	Section 504 of the Rehabilitation Act of 1973/ Impact of ADAAA 2008
for students who take alternate assessments. Accommodations, modifications, and evaluation criteria are listed for each child.

Present levels of academic achievement and functional performance are written in students' IEPs as snapshots of each child's current status and progress achieved. The word *functional* refers to routines of everyday living that are nonacademic, to better prepare students with disabilities for postschool adjustments.

Implementation of early intervening services by LEAs (Local Education Agencies) to include professional development for educators and for related staff to deliver scientifically based academic and behavioral interventions, e.g., literacy, services, supports

Limitation of related services for devices that are surgically implanted, e.g., cochlear implants

Supplementary aids and services are provided in general education classes as well as extracurricular and nonacademic settings.

IEPs are based on each child's individual and unique needs. | Helps to ensure public access to transportation and communication

Can include special education students who are involved in community jobs or those people with disabilities visiting schools

Can refer to private, nonsectarian schools

OCR (Office of Civil Rights) enforces Title II of the ADA, which extends the prohibition against discrimination to public schools, whether or not they receive public funding.

Expanded definition of *substantially limited* rather than mandating a *severe* or *significant* restriction

The definition of *major life activities* says that the impairment only needs to limit one major activity in order to be considered as an ADA disability, although it may limit more as well.

Amendments of ADA affect 504 plans in forms and procedures, increasing the eligibility of students in K–12 grades protected under Section 504. | Limited amount of money a school district can spend if the services are too costly, since unlike IDEA, there are no provisions that districts are reimbursed

State and local jurisdictions are responsible.

Requires a plan with a group that is knowledgeable about the unique needs of the student

Specification of educational benefits, aids, services, class, and assessment modifications, e.g., reading test questions aloud, behavior intervention plans, preferential seating

Periodic reevaluations

Like IDEA, local education agencies must provide impartial hearings for parents who disagree with the identification, placement, or evaluation.

Do not need both an IEP and a Section 504 plan, if student qualifies for services under both, since one way to meet 504 requirements is to comply with IDEA

General education teachers must implement provisions of Section 504; their refusal would mean district can be found to be noncompliant. |

Least Restrictive Environments

According to IDEA, FAPE (free appropriate public education) must be provided in the least restrictive environment (LRE), which considers the general education classroom setting as the first option for academic and nonacademic benefits along with the effects of that placement on other children. Special education services are then linked to both academic and functional goals in what is then deemed as the LRE. The assumption under the law is that every child with a disability is educated in the general education classroom; if this is not the case, then the school district must provide documentation for why this should not occur.

A continuum of some alternative placements is determined on an individual basis with planning, interventions, and documentation of effectiveness merited in all environments. The LRE includes the following:

Least Restrictive Environment Options

- *General education classroom* with moderate support, e.g., consultation periods, in-class support by a special education teacher or other trained personnel for part of the day; or perhaps two teachers, general education (GE) and special education (SE), coteaching and coplanning lessons for all children in the classroom. The two teachers (GE+SE) may work together in an inclusion setting to help students with response to the curricula through strategic planning, specified interventions, and data that monitors ongoing benchmark assessments.
- *Pull-out programs* to support or replace some subjects that may be taught in a resource room. Academic subjects such as reading, language, science, social studies, or mathematics may be taught or supported in another setting within the school. The student fully participates in all other classroom content areas and activities with peers and follows the rest of the class schedule, with maximum social integration. This combination of services allows for periods of direct skill instruction, along with social and academic inclusion with peers.
- *Special education classroom* in a neighborhood school with the possibility of mainstreaming for certain subjects with academic and social goals delineated and adequate supports provided in the general education classroom and all settings. Special class placement can also be self-contained.
- *Special school* if education cannot be provided in the neighborhood school.
- *Home instruction* if the student's needs cannot be met in the school due to social, academic, physical, or medical issues.
- *Residential placement* that is provided in a setting other than the neighborhood school or home, which can include instruction in hospitals or residential institutions. Even though a placement such as a hospital is considered one of the most restricted environments, it may actually be the least restrictive setting for someone who may have a mental illness, if it is deemed the most appropriate one to service that individual's needs.

IDEA has four parts, with these inclusive elements:

Part A: General Provisions. This part includes purpose of special education law, definitions of terms, and congressional findings.

Part B: Assistance for Education of All Children with Disabilities. This part includes state formula grant program, eligibility, evaluations, IEP, funding, procedural safeguards, and preschool grants.

Part C: Infants and Toddlers with Disabilities. This part delineates early intervention programs for infants and toddlers with disabilities, along with findings and policies.

Part D: National Activities to Improve Education of Children with Disabilities. Included here are discretionary programs, state improvement grants, supporting and applying research, personnel preparation, parent training and information centers, technical assistance, technology development, and disseminating information.

When IDEA was reauthorized in 2004 as IDEIA, Individuals with Disabilities Education Improvement Act, major reauthorization points involved a focus on linking goals with academic and functional outcomes connected to research-based response to interventions (RTI). There was also an allowance to remove benchmarks and short-term objectives from a student's IEP unless that student is participating in an alternate assessment, e.g., usually a student with a severe cognitive impairment who responds markedly differently to stimuli, cannot solve problems, or has overall difficulties in communicating or providing a response. States may include benchmarks, but it is not federally mandated. Some states include benchmarks for subjects for which students are receiving replacement instruction, rather than the subjects where students have full inclusion, since the curriculum standards and objectives in the general education curriculum are then looked at as those students' goals. Overall, as with IDEA, parents, guardians, families, school personnel, and students are integral collaborative players in this process who must always consider and focus on matching all students' strengths with appropriate IEP services.

Some examples of appropriate services can include the following:

- Braille for a student with blindness or visual impairment
- Positive supports and intervention plans for a student with behavioral issues
- Communication and language supports for a student with deafness or hearing impairment; a student who is nonverbal; or a student who may have articulation, receptive, or expressive language needs
- Appropriate assistive technology services and devices *needed* by the student, though not always required by the district; e.g., a portable word processor or an instructional assistant serving as a scribe for a student with dysgraphia, although beneficial, may not be part of every school district's standard procedure
- Occupational or physical therapy for students with gross or fine motor needs, e.g., improvement with gait, balance, handwriting

As always, the present level of performance reflects how a child's disability impacts both his or her participation and progress in the general education curriculum. To qualify for services, a child's educational performance must be adversely affected as a result of the disability. The levels of academic achievement and functional performance are the crucial foundations for the development of the IEP, since they drive the appropriate services needed to address, improve, and remediate the impact of a disability on a student's performance. Families are notified of student progress through periodic reports, e.g., quarterly intervals. Most important, IDEA 2004 directs IEP teams to implement instructional programs that have proven track records based on peer-reviewed research that gives merit to a program's effectiveness in both academic and behavioral domains. That means that schools are not arbitrarily using a program, but rather there is a research-based reason for that choice.

Appropriate accommodations for standardized assessments should not modify or alter test results, but provide valid assessments that truly yield information on what the test is intended to measure. Thus, appropriate testing accommodations may include but are not limited to extra time, smaller testing group, different format, or familiar examiner. If a child has an alternate assessment based upon academic achievement standards (AA-AAS), it most likely indicates that the grade-level curriculum is not appropriate, e.g., if the student has a severe cognitive disability. An alternate assessment based upon modified achievement standards (AA-MAS) is still aligned with grade level standards with some modifications such as simpler language, fewer choices, or even less clutter. The frequency, location, and duration of all services are stated in the IEP, indicating how often, where, and for how long the services should be given.

Supporting high-quality, intensive professional development for personnel who work with children with disabilities, including training related services personnel and paraprofessionals or instructional assistants, is essential. The use of technology to maximize accessibility for children with disabilities, e.g., NIMAS (National Instructional Material Accessibility Standards; see http://nimas.cast.org) provides accessible instructional materials such as digital textbooks. Braille or text-to-speech formats are mandated for those students who would require such services. Use of transition services within a results-oriented process to the maximum extent possible to facilitate movement from school to post-secondary activities includes further recommendations for continuing education, independent living, and community participation. Transitional plans are federally required at age 16, and offered earlier if warranted.

The overall philosophy is to help students with disabilities meet challenging state academic achievement standards and at the same time yield high functional achievements. Services for the homeless, foster children, children with disabilities in the military, and the needs of English language learners (ELLs) are also addressed. Reducing misidentification of children with disabilities by encouraging direct skill instruction is something that IDEA 2004 strongly advocates.

Highlights of IDEA 2004 include the following:

- Awarding attorney fees to local education agencies if parent's case is determined frivolous or improper based on legal precedents. Law is written in such a way as to put most of the liability on the parent's attorney for pursuing a frivolous suit. There is also a 2-year time limit to file, starting from the date the local educational agency (LEA) knew of the issue in question, with information kept confidential.

- With reference to learning disabilities, IDEA says discrepancy between achievement and intellectual ability is not the sole indicator for LD classification. It allows for a process that determines if the child is responding to classroom interventions (RTIs). This targets students who are functioning below classroom standards to receive help, even though no discernible discrepancy may be revealed between tested intelligence and school performance. It focuses on early identification with assistance for early intervention services, without the specific determination of a learning disability. It includes monitoring, assessing, modifying classroom programs, and intervening, instead of referring students for automatic LD identification, giving merit to the provision of appropriate early intervention services in natural environments to meet the needs of individual children. RTI is implemented differently in many states, with a problem-solving approach that includes these overall three tiers of interventions:

1. Core (whole class) receives instruction and monitoring to determine needs and effectiveness of instruction

2. Targeted (small groups) with students who need more strategic interventions identified

3. Intensive (small groups, 1:1) for students with more chronic needs who require frequent monitoring of rigorous interventions

- Excusing IEP team members from attending meetings if all agree attendance is deemed unnecessary beforehand, with IEP team obtaining that member's input prior to the meeting, e.g., parent or guardian signs off with LEA agreement that the member's area of the curriculum or related services are not being modified or discussed in the meeting
- Trying to consolidate meetings, such as combining reevaluations with IEP team meetings
- Federal timeline of 60 days allowed for evaluation, unless states have enacted other timelines or parent or guardian enrolls the student in another school district, or does not produce the student for evaluation
- Changes to a child's IEP do not require another meeting if the LEA and parent or guardian of the child agree.
- IEP can be amended or modified without redrafting the entire IEP.
- Alternative means of meeting participation and communication, such as video conferences, conference calls, and email; e.g., parent(s) and guardian(s) must give informed consent prior to an initial evaluation, with email as an acceptable mode.
- Families have the right to obtain one free independent evaluation for each school evaluation (or reevaluation) if they believe that the evaluation conducted by qualified school personnel was inappropriate. If a school district does not agree to pay for an independent evaluation, then a hearing officer is obtained to determine whether or not another evaluation is warranted. If a private evaluation is conducted, the school district considers the findings, but does not necessarily have to agree with or implement the recommendations.
- Reducing paperwork burdens on teachers by conducting reviews of processes, forms, and expanding use of technology in IEP process
- Reducing number of times copy of procedural safeguards is given to parents or guardians, now only required once a year, unless parents request them again
- Use of positive discipline and other behavioral assessments and classroom approaches to prevent emotional and behavioral violations from reoccurring
- Change in discipline code on a case-by-case basis to ensure the safety and appropriate educational atmosphere in the schools under the jurisdiction of

the local educational agency, allowing schools to expel students without first determining whether the behavior was linked to the child's disability. Students can be removed for up to 45 school days with instruction in another setting (IAES, interim alternative educational setting).

- Recording the incidence, duration, and type of disciplinary actions, and determining if misbehaviors were the result of a failure of the IEP
- Setting up procedures that require the state educational agency (SEA) to develop a model form to assist parents in filing a complaint, and a due process complaint notice
- Delaying due process hearing while all parties attempt to meet to resolve problems, and not allowing parties to raise issues at due process hearings that were not raised in original complaint
- LEA conducts a Child Find to ensure and provide equitable services to children with disabilities who attend private schools within the LEA, without regard to where the children may reside (Office of Special Education Programs, 2005). Part C of IDEA refers to children from birth to age 3.
- Strengthening the role and responsibility of parents, and ensuring that families have meaningful opportunities to participate in the education of their children at school and at home

Resources for Further Updates

Council for Exceptional Children—www.cec.sped.org

Legislative information from the Library of Congress—http://thomas.loc.gov

U.S. Department of Education, No Child Left Behind—http://www.ed.gov/nclb/landing.jhtml

Wrightslaw, information about special education laws—www.wrightslaw.com

American Recovery and Reinvestment Act of 2009—www.ed.gov/policy/gen/leg/recovery/factsheet/idea.html

U.S. Department of Education, Building the Legacy: IDEA 2004—http://idea.ed.gov

Response to Intervention (RTI) and Literacy Collaborative—www.lcosu.org/documents/PDFs/RtI_in_Literacy_Collaborative_Schools.pdf

PACER Center: Champions for Children With Disabilities—www.pacer.org/about/index.asp

DISABILITY CATEGORIES UNDER INDIVIDUALS WITH DISABILITIES EDUCATION ACT (IDEA)

In order to receive funds under Part B of IDEA, states must assure that a free and appropriate public education (FAPE) is provided to children within 13 disability categories, at no cost to the parents, guardians, and families, in conformity with the individualized education program.

Exact classification language of each state is decided after it looks at federal regulations and does its alignment. As the United States Department of Education points out, the federal role in education is limited as per the 10th Amendment. Education policy is determined at state and local levels. School districts across the United States have many interpretations and implementations of federal disability laws. Sometimes states use different terms, but it is not the label that is important; it is matching the criteria under that disability category. Labels are just for eligibility. There is an enormous disadvantage for students when certain words and a condition title are needed to describe and convey a *disability,* rather than a person. Again, some states use different terms, as words develop negative connotations, but criteria remain the same and are aligned with federal regulations, with varying state interpretations and school applications.

IDEA Categories

Autism

A developmental disability significantly affecting verbal and nonverbal communication and social interaction, generally evident before age 3, that adversely affects educational performance. Added to IDEA in 1990.

Deafness

A hearing impairment so severe that a child is impaired in processing linguistic information through hearing, with or without amplification, resulting in adverse effects on educational performance.

Deaf-Blindness

Simultaneous hearing and visual impairments, the combination of which causes such severe communication and other developmental and educational problems that a child cannot be accommodated in special education programs solely for children with deafness or blindness.

Hearing Impairment

An impairment in hearing, whether permanent or fluctuating, which adversely affects a child's educational performance but is not included under the definition of "deafness."

Mental Retardation

Significantly sub-average general intellectual functioning, existing concurrently with deficits in adaptive behavior, manifested during the developmental period, which adversely affect a child's educational performance. Mental retardation is still listed as a category under the federal law, but some states have chosen other titles due to the associated negative connotation, e.g., intellectual, developmental, cognitive disability.

Multiple Disabilities

Simultaneous impairments (such as mental retardation/blindness or mental retardation/orthopedic impairment), the combination of which causes such severe educational problems that the child cannot be accommodated in a special education program solely for one of the impairments. The term does not include children with deaf-blindness.

Orthopedic Impairment

A severe orthopedic impairment that adversely affects a child's educational performance. The term includes impairments caused by a congenital anomaly such as clubfoot, or absence of a limb. Impairments caused by disease include poliomyelitis or bone tuberculosis, and impairments from other causes such as cerebral palsy, amputations, and fractures or burns that might cause contractures (loss of joint motion).

Other Health Impairment

Having limited strength, vitality, or alertness, due to chronic or acute health problems such as attention deficit hyperactivity disorder, heart condition, tuberculosis, rheumatic fever, nephritis, asthma, sickle cell anemia, hemophilia, epilepsy, lead poisoning, leukemia, diabetes, and Tourette syndrome (listed as a chronic or acute health problem under IDEA 2004), which adversely affects a child's educational performance.

Emotional Disturbance

A condition exhibiting one or more of the following characteristics over a *long period* of time and to a marked degree, which adversely affects educational performance:

a. An inability to learn that cannot be explained by intellectual, sensory, or health factors

b. An inability to build or maintain satisfactory interpersonal relationships with peers and teachers

c. Inappropriate types of behavior or feelings under normal circumstances

d. A general or pervasive mood of unhappiness or depression

e. A tendency to develop physical symptoms or fears associated with personal or school problems

The term includes children who have schizophrenia. The term does *not* include children who are socially maladjusted, unless it is determined that they have a serious emotional disturbance.

Specific Learning Disability

A disorder in one or more of the basic psychological processes involved in understanding or using spoken or written language, which may manifest itself in an imperfect ability to listen, think, speak, read, write, spell, or do mathematical calculations. The term includes such conditions as perceptual disabilities, brain injury, minimal brain dysfunction, dyslexia, and developmental aphasia. The term does *not* include children who have learning problems that are primarily the result of visual, hearing, or motor disabilities; mental retardation; emotional disturbance; or environmental, cultural, or economic disadvantage.

Speech or Language Impairment

A communication disorder such as stuttering, impaired articulation, a language impairment, or a voice impairment that adversely affects a child's educational performance.

Traumatic Brain Injury

An acquired injury to the brain caused by an external physical force, resulting in total or partial functional disability or psychosocial impairment, or both, which adversely affects educational performance. The term does *not* include brain injuries that are congenital or degenerative, or brain injuries induced by birth trauma. Added to IDEA as a category in 1990.

Visual Impairment, Including Blindness

A visual impairment includes both partial sight and total blindness, which even with correction adversely affects a child's educational performance.

Source: National Dissemination Center for People With Disabilities, http://www.nichcy.org.

The following is a mnemonic to help you remember all 13 IDEA disabilities:

All very determined students deserve many more opportunities than school has ever offered.

All (autism)

very (visually impairment)

determined (deafness)

students (speech and language impairment)

deserve (deaf-blindness)

many (mental retardation)

more (multiple disabilities)

opportunities (orthopedic impairment)

than (traumatic brain injury)

school (specific learning disability)

has (hearing impairment)

ever (emotional disturbance)

offered (other health impairments).

HISTORY OF THE AMERICANS WITH DISABILITIES ACT (ADA)

The Americans with Disabilities Act (Public Law 101–336), passed in 1990, was designed to prohibit discrimination against people with disabilities by state and local governments and provide equal opportunities in the following areas:

- Public accommodations
- Employment
- Transportation
- Telecommunications
- State and local governments

ADA's intent was to afford people with disabilities the same opportunities as everyone else to lead full and productive lives. Its goal was to break down barriers for people with disabilities that stop them from achieving emotional and social independence. As a civil rights act, its enforcement enables our society to benefit from the skills and talents that people with disabilities have always possessed, but have been thwarted from demonstrating. The overall goal in schools is to offer reasonable accommodations for students with disabilities to achieve the same results and be given the same benefits as students without disabilities.

The ADA Amendments Act (ADAAA) of 2008 defines *disability* as an impairment that substantially limits major life activities such as breathing, seeing, hearing, speaking, learning, caring for oneself, working, eating, sleeping, bending, lifting, communicating, thinking, reading, and concentrating. Included here are examples of major bodily dysfunctions that directly impact major life activities, related to the circulatory, respiratory, digestive, and reproductive systems, along with the functions of neurology, brain, cell growth, immune system, bowel, and bladder. If the impairment is temporary, such as a non-chronic condition of a short duration, then that person is not covered under ADA. For example, someone with a broken leg would not qualify. Disabilities that are 6 months or less in duration do not qualify. In addition, ADA states that a person must have a record of an impairment, thereby including someone recovering from a chronic or long-term impairment such as mental illness or cancer. The definition expands further by including someone who is regarded as having such an impairment. This involves how others regard or look at someone with a disability. ADA would protect someone who might have a facial disfigurement such as cleft palate from being denied employment because of workers' reactions. It would also allow an individual who has motor impairments due to cerebral palsy to perform a job that someone might incorrectly assume he or she cannot cognitively perform due to the person's discriminatory perception of the individual. The U.S. Equal Employment Opportunity Commission (EEOC) and the Supreme Court had made many decisions that are reversed by the ADAAA in terms of how to define "substantially limits," with ADAAA being less rigorous. In addition, the conditions are looked at without regard to the ameliorative effects of medication, medical supplies or equipment, prosthetics, assistive technology, reasonable accommodations or auxiliary aids, or behavioral or adaptive neurological modifications. This means that the underlying impairment is looked at without considering the effects of the extra devices; just the disability itself is addressed.

An individual is deemed "qualified" for a job position if he or she possesses the skills, education, or other job requirements of the position, with or without reasonable accommodation. This basically prohibits discrimination against individuals with disabilities in the private sector. Court systems are currently interpreting this law on an individual basis.

Examples of reasonable accommodations include the following:

- Modifying a work schedule
- Providing menus in Braille, or a waiter reading the menu to a customer who is blind (the former allows for more independence)
- Installing numbers in Braille in office or hotel elevators and outside rooms
- Allowing seeing-eye dogs in public facilities
- Providing a sign interpreter at theater performances, if the theater is given sufficient notice by someone with a hearing impairment
- Providing assistive listening devices
- Training personnel to administer insulin to people with diabetes
- Removal of existing barriers, if it is readily achievable and can be done without much difficulty or expense. For instance, if a ramp or elevator could not be built because the business is not profitable enough, curbside service could be provided to people with disabilities. However, not every building or each part of every building needs to be accessible.
- Accommodations could be as simple as lowering a paper towel dispenser, widening a doorway, or providing special parking spots.

Courts levy penalties against a business if it shows bad faith in complying with ADA. Acts of bad faith might include deliberately ignoring a person's request, hostile acts, or refusing voluntary compliance. The Justice Department considers the size and resources of individual businesses before civil penalties are issued. Complaints must be valid. For example, refusing employment to someone because he or she suffers from depression, has AIDS, or has a history of alcoholism would be discrimination based upon societal stereotypes, not the person's ability to perform a job. However, someone with myopia or hypertension is not covered by ADA because the condition is correctable (e.g., with eyeglasses and medication). If a person needs to use a seeing-eye dog, the owner of a restaurant cannot arbitrarily deny admittance to the dog and the patron who is blind. Similarly, if the venue is given ample notice, sign language interpreters must be provided at theaters and other public gatherings for people who cannot hear.

Court cases continually wrestle with the meaning of the word *disability*. In 1998, a golfer with a birth defect in his right leg, Casey Martin, was allowed to ride a golf cart instead of walking the course in tournament play. At the time, the PGA thought that Mr. Martin would have an unfair advantage over other golfers, but the Supreme Court determined that a golf cart was a reasonable accommodation, since Casey Martin suffered from fatigue, and walking the course would have been an additional burden for him. In May 2004, the Supreme Court allowed a man in a wheelchair—George Lane, who was a defendant ordered to testify—and Beverly Jones, a court reporter with a mobility impairment, to sue the state of Tennessee for monetary damages since they needed to appear in a second-floor courtroom in a building without elevators. In this ruling, it was determined that there was a failure to provide people with disabilities access to the courts. Other cases concern seniority issues being honored (e.g., person with a disability cannot take the job of a worker without a disability who has higher seniority), whether someone's health might be impacted by a certain job (e.g., working with chemicals if you have a preexisting medical condition), being granted testing accommodations on a graduate level, claiming too much noise interfered with passing a nursing exam for someone with a mental impairment, or whether someone who has chronic fatigue syndrome can adequately perform a job. Topics also include the possibility of granting indefinite periods of leave or open-ended schedules.

Reasonable accommodations mean that with the accommodation in place, the person is otherwise able to perform all of the job requirements. Safety is sometimes a mitigating factor; for example, someone who is blind cannot successfully claim discrimination because he or she is not hired as an airline pilot. ADA enters school settings by guaranteeing that staff, parents, families, and students with disabilities have access to school plays, conferences, graduation ceremonies, and more. It translates to guaranteeing the same access to students with disabilities as peers without disabilities have, e.g., a librarian assisting a student in a wheelchair so he or she has access to books on higher shelves or allowing a student who has cerebral palsy to be a cheerleader. There are no special education rules in ADA; however, it does have an impact on education as well. Overall, as a civil rights act, ADA protects persons with disabilities in the private sector and school settings by guaranteeing reasonable accommodations, services, aids, and policies, as it works in alignment with other state and federal laws.

CIVIL RIGHTS FOR STUDENTS WITH DISABILITIES UNDER SECTION 504

Section 504 of the Rehabilitation Act of 1973 generally refers to adjustments in the general education classroom, but can include other educational services as well. It states the following:

> No otherwise qualified individual with a disability in the United States . . . shall, solely by reason of her or his disability, be excluded from the participation in, be denied the benefits of, or be subjected to discrimination under any program or activity receiving Federal financial assistance. (http://www.ed.gov/about/offices/list/ocr/docs/placpub.html. The regulation implementing Section 504 in the context of educational institutions appears at 34 C.F.R. Part 104.)

Public school districts, institutions of higher education, and other state and local education agencies are required to provide the protections found in Section 504. Both ADA and Section 504 are enforced by the Office for Civil Rights (OCR), while IDEA is enforced by the Office of Special Education and Rehabilitative Services (OSERS), which are both components of the U.S. Department of Education. ADA does not limit the rights or remedies available under Section 504. Students with IEPs may also have 504 plans, while students with 504 plans do not necessarily have IEPs.

For a person to be classified as having a disability, he or she must have a record of a physical or mental impairment that limits one or more major life activities, and be regarded as having such an impairment. A life activity includes functions such as caring for oneself, performing manual tasks, walking, seeing, hearing, speaking, breathing, learning, and working, along with the amended additions from ADAAA 2008, which include eating, standing, sleeping, lifting, bending, reading, communicating, thinking, and concentrating. In addition, other life activities not included in 504 can also be protected. Trained personnel who have particular knowledge of the strengths, abilities, and unique needs of the students conduct the evaluation of students with disabilities to determine placements. The information is not solely based upon one assessment, and must assess the student's need, not the impairment. For example, a student with blindness cannot be asked to count the number of hands raised, but would need to be given an alternate kinesthetic accommodation to test the child's ability to actually count, not his or her ability to see the hands. Placement decisions come from varying sources, including teacher recommendations along with aptitude and achievement tests, and they must take into account cultural, social, physical, and adaptive needs.

Like IDEA, Section 504 states that every effort must be made to educate students with their nondisabled peers, if the academic and social needs can be met there. Appropriate education for a student with a disability might include placement in a general or special education class with or without supplementary services or related services. Specific recommendations must include strategies and delineate accommodations. Disability documentation needs to be provided, and necessary accommodations must be requested. Individuals who qualify for Section 504 protection can fall under any of the 13 IDEA classifications or others such as the following examples; this is not an exhaustive list:

AD/HD	Diabetes
AIDS	Emotional/Psychiatric Disability
Arthritis	Epilepsy
Asthma	Hearing Impairment/Deafness
Cancer	Learning Disability
Cerebral Palsy	Visual Impairment/Blindness

Strategies, names of implementers, monitoring dates, and general comments are examples of elements included in 504 plans. If a student qualifies for services under IDEA, that student does not need both an IEP and a Section 504 plan. The reason is that one way to meet 504 requirements is to comply with IDEA. General education teachers must implement provisions of Section 504, or that district may be found to be noncompliant with the federal law. Again, the general education teacher needs to review the 504 plans of students to effectively implement appropriate educational services. School districts must properly identify and evaluate students with disabilities who need services, supplying an educational plan under Section 504, which is then protected by procedural safeguards. In this scenario, teachers also need proper instruction and preparation to meet an individual child's needs if that child has a 504 plan. Parents and guardians, building administrators, teachers, support staff, and the Section 504 coordinator are involved in developing the plan. The coordinator may be a principal, guidance counselor, special education director, supervisor, or another appointed qualified staff member. A 504 plan can be as simple as including strategies that break down long-term projects into smaller sequential steps, sending home a duplicate set of texts, or maybe sitting a child nearer to the center of instruction— e.g., chalkboards or interactive whiteboards. It may also include training staff how to use an EpiPen (to inject emergency allergy medication) or allowing a child with diabetes more frequent breaks or access to unlimited water. Overall, health and learning plans are determined and outlined in 504 plans.

Section 504 laws apply to elementary, secondary, and post-secondary schools. Trained personnel who assess the needs, not the impairments, must conduct evaluative procedures in order to determine placement. Placement decisions consider the maximum extent to which the student can be educated with his or her peers without disabilities. This may be accomplished with and without supplementary and related services, but must be subject to periodic reevaluations. Parents and guardians are informed about all placement and evaluation actions, and may examine their child's records. Students may not be denied access to any nonacademic activities, such as clubs, transportation, athletics, and counseling, based upon their disability.

PAST, PRESENT, AND FUTURE CONCERNS

Special education was not always accepted in the larger school community. Before the passage of Public Law 94-142 (Education of the Handicapped Act) in 1975, students with disabilities did not receive the most appropriate services. After the act was passed, students were entitled to receive a free and appropriate public education, designed to meet their unique needs. The result of this law was the development of specialized programs and services. However, nowhere does the law explain what *appropriate* means, or use the word *inclusion*. Approximately 20 years later, it was discovered that these separate programs were actually excluding students with disabilities from exposure to the general education curriculum and not preparing them for successful community integration. IDEA 1997 advocated people-first language— looking at the student first, and then the disability. After all, students should not be defined by what they cannot do, but rather their strengths should be highlighted. IDEIA 2004 now mentions RTI as a part of the evaluation for identification of a student with a specific learning disability. RTI is not mandated, but offered as an option, instead of solely using the discrepancy model, which involves a discernible discrepancy revealed between tested intelligence and school performance. Therefore, more accountability is now placed upon the types of instruction, programs, and interventions offered. Yes, students have differences, but now classrooms must proactively offer appropriate interventions before automatic student labeling. Sometimes it's the instruction, not the disability, that's the culprit of lower performances.

Today's thrust is upon inclusion and improving student outcomes with appropriate interventions, but new concerns are already becoming evident. Debates between teachers and administrators include topics such as time for planning and collaboration, types of supports and assessments given, modifications of curriculum, how to divide instructional time to equally provide learning for all groups of learners, behavioral concerns, and accountability issues. Often teachers are so overwhelmed by their busy days that they are unable to preplan, evaluate, and assess lessons with cooperating teachers. In the ideal world, common planning time should be allotted in both general and special education teachers' schedules, giving them the time to design and evaluate lessons. Consistent constructive review of both successful and unsuccessful teaching methodology is an integral inclusionary factor. Response to interventions has entered classrooms, but just who determines what constitutes an effective intervention and assessment is still an issue in its infancy, morphing with each new report and study. Reliability and validity of programs require further determination.

Teachers are seldom unwilling to include students, but some lack the training or experience regarding what strategies, programs, or academic or behavioral scaffolding need to be provided, without sacrificing any one group of learners. State and national curricula further complicate these issues and cause concern about taking time away from instruction of much-needed skills, as well as concerns about individuality of instruction. Accountability of student performance raises the following question among teachers, students, parents, administrators, and learners:

> "Does fair mean equal?"

Outcomes and delineated standards for all students have become our nation's goal. Standards have now been applied to all students, with no one taken out of the accountability loop as with past SE practices. Several studies (Mostert & Crockett, 2000; Norris & Schumacker, 1998; Skiba et al., 2008) have revealed that in the past, schools have disappointed former special education students with ineffective interventions. Now, research highlights that aligning the content standards with assessments and appropriate instruction results in higher learning outcomes for all students, those with and without disabilities (Browder, 2006; Thurlow, 2003; Wiener, 2005).

Special education teachers face further challenges as they try to balance and align the standards with students' IEPs and the assigned curriculum. Educators feverishly think of ways that students with disabilities can achieve mastery or progress toward those standards. The curriculum is not diluted for any group of students, but taught in sub-skills that reflect the standards in smaller, more palatable bites. Individual strategies, materials, and accommodations are geared toward achieving higher outcomes for all students. As the years progress, hopefully assessments and accountability systems will highlight weaknesses in school systems, not in students.

This will require both GE and SE teachers to have a greater knowledge of the curriculum, content standards, and the strengths of students with dis*abilities* who are now expected to achieve those standards. Educators of students with more severe cognitive disabilities also take steps to help their students achieve strides toward the curriculum standards. Ignoring improvements toward achievements is simply not an option for any group of students. Inclusion is marching onward, with everyone honoring abilities and ways to increase academic, behavioral, social, emotional, and functional levels in all domains. Overall, the SE trend is now moving from access to accountability (Chambers, 2008). Thankfully so!

Unfortunately, at times, an abundance of paperwork has scared away many teachers from continuing in the field, since quite often their time is deducted from much-needed student instruction in order to comply with writing IEPs and data reports, attending meetings, and keeping on top of changes in legislation. In the attempt to "get it right," families, general and special education teachers, and all students can be frustrated by the sometimes confusing system, which makes it harder to focus on helping students with disabilities achieve academic and social successes. Some of the revisions in IDEA 2004 address that—e.g., reducing the number of meetings, allowing revision consent by email, combining meetings.

Inclusion is a fabulous concept, but the pragmatics involved do not always result in its proper implementation. Inclusion has sometimes actually resulted in *ex*clusion. Students with disabilities who are included in a general classroom are at times overwhelmed by the pace, complexity, and amount of work they are expected to do, and prior knowledge they are assumed to have. Special educators should be integral members of the larger school community, but this is often not the case. Special educators and students possess the ability to make integral, productive contributions to the classroom. All students and teachers need to be treated as equals both in the general classroom and across the whole school district. As delineated in Chapter 6 on collaboration, special education and general education teachers can work as partners to instruct all students in shared classrooms with ability levels ranging from nonverbal with autism to gifted.

The educational goals of students with disabilities are just as valid as those of other students. High expectations need to be developed for all students in the classroom, but without proper supports, children and teachers can become lost and frustrated by the system. Sometimes, wonderfully conducted research offering promising techniques seems difficult or impossible to pragmatically translate into classrooms composed of students with mixed abilities.

General education teachers want all students to succeed, but they need more direction and training on how to differentiate instruction without sacrificing any one group of students. Inclusion has sometimes dangerously erased direct skill instruction that was formerly given in separate classrooms. Public Law 94-142, the grandmother of IDEA, originally called the Education of All Handicapped Children Act, which was passed by Congress back in 1975, was designed to provide services to students whose academic needs were not being met in the general education classroom. Today, unless the dynamics of the general education classroom are changed, these academic, social, cognitive, and emotional needs will still not be met. RTI can and should be used to monitor progress and adjust interventions accordingly, yielding benefits for all learners who are struggling with the curricula, not just those learners who receive special education (Chambers, 2008). Interventions are offered in general education classrooms first, before students are assumed to require special education services. The thinking here is that perhaps it is the instruction that is the issue, rather than the student who is disabled. Many families, administrators, educators, related staff, and students have concerns and sometimes diverse desires, interpretations, and ways to think about both general and special education deliveries, services, and interventions.

Somewhere in *edutopia,* a happy balance needs to be achieved with interventions to determine what kind, what extent, how, where, and who will deliver the interventions.

Special education is headed in the right direction. With more fine-tuning, this transitional stage will effectively ride the current turbulent waves. Education never worked well with a one-size-fits-all philosophy. Inclusion is a great idea, if it is properly implemented, but should not be considered the only option if the child's academic and social needs are not being met by placement in the general classroom. Accountability, along with appropriate identifications and interventions, is essential. Special education is an *evolutionary,* not a *revolutionary,* process. Significantly reducing the bureaucracy, paperwork, and litigiousness that too often springs from disagreements over implementation of the law; settling school discipline issues; and figuring out how to continually and appropriately fund IDEA and just which academic and behavioral interventions are appropriate ones are not simple issues. Education is a complex issue for parents, guardians, teachers, administrators, all staff members, and children of all abilities. However, always keep in mind that the ultimate goal is successful outcomes for all!

COOPERATIVE LEGISLATIVE REVIEW

Directions: As a review of these readings, choose either Option 1 or Option 2.

Option 1: Cooperatively answer 6 of the following 10 questions on a separate piece of paper. Circle the question numbers you will be answering. Each person should write down the answers (true cooperative learning).

Option 2: If your group has access to multiple computers, cooperatively divide, complete, and then share questions and answers to the Legislative Web Quest (Questions 1–5) instead.

Rationale for collaborative options: Choosing questions or assignments to answer or complete empowers learners. Questions are teacher-guided, but students gain some control and responsibility as self-regulated learners. Within your classrooms, these types of choices can be offered from early grades onward to continually develop and foster independent learning and increased student responsibility. In addition, completing assignments collaboratively fosters interpersonal and team skills.

Option 1:

1. Describe three laws that protect persons with disabilities.
2. List the 13 IDEA categories.
3. Who can benefit from a 504 plan?
4. Think of a disability scenario that the ADA is protecting.
5. Compare and contrast the benefits and pitfalls of inclusion.
6. If you could amend any of the laws, what changes would you make?
7. Where do you see special education going in the next 10 years?
8. Tell how children with disabilities can benefit from inclusion.
9. How can general education teachers influence a child's classroom success?
10. Do you think special education is going in the right direction?

Option 2 **Legislative Web Quest**
1. Identify and briefly describe three major disability laws that affect students in school settings.
2. Name the elements of an IEP.
3. Briefly describe two court cases and their implications for inclusive environments. (Possible choices from 18 below)
4. Identify the elements listed in a student's transitional plan.
5. What rights do families have in formulating IEP documents?
Use these Web sites for your responses: www.wrightslaw.com, www.cec.sped.org, www.nichcy.org, http://IDEA.ed.gov

Court Cases	Main Concepts
1. *Pennsylvania Association for Retarded Children v. Commonwealth of Pennsylvania,* 1972	Students with disabilities are not excluded from appropriate educational opportunities
2. *Mills v. Board of Education of the District of Columbia,* 1972	Need to provide whatever specialized instruction will benefit the child, with due process and periodic review (precursor of IDEA)
3. *Board of Education of the Hendrick Hudson Central School District v. Rowley,* 1982	FAPE (Free Appropriate Public Education)
4. *Brookhart v. Illinois State Board of Education,* 1983	Passing state tests to receive HS diplomas
5. *School Board of Nassau County, Florida v. Arline,* 1987	Defenses under 504—reasonable accommodations
6. *Honig v. Doe,* 1988	Suspension & expulsion
7. *Timothy W. v. Rochester, New Hampshire School District,* 1989	Proof of benefit not required, there is zero reject

Court Cases	Main Concepts
8. *Sacramento City Unified School District, Board of Education v. Rachel H.*, 1994	LRE (Least Restrictive Environment)—educational & nonacademic benefits weigh in as well, e.g., social, communication
9. *Gadsby v. Grasmick*, 1997	States to ensure compliance with IDEA
10. *Sutton v. United Airlines, Inc.*, 1999	Disability defined with corrective devices
11. *Cedar Rapids v. Garret F.*, 1999	Related services
12. *Toyota Motor Manufacturing, Kentucky, Inc. v. Williams*, 2002	Substantial limitation in major life activity under ADA
13. *AW ex rel. Wilson v. Fairfax County School Board*, 2004	Manifestation determination—*Did the disability impact the student's ability to control the behavior?*
14. *Schaffer ex rel. Schaffer v. Weast*, 2005	Burden of proof in a due process hearing on party seeking relief
15. *Arlington Central Sch. Dist. Bd of Ed v. Murphy*, 2006	Entitlement to parents to recover fees paid to expert witnesses if they prevail
16. *Winkelman v. Parma City School District*, 2007	Parents who act as their child's lawyer in IDEA actions, if they are not licensed attorneys
17. *Board of Ed of City of New York v. Tom F.*, 2007	Reimbursement for private education if student was not enrolled in public school
18. *Forest Grove School District v. T. A.*, 2009	Reimbursement for private special-education services when a public school fails to provide FAPE, free appropriate public education

IMPLICATIONS OF THE ELEMENTARY AND SECONDARY EDUCATION ACT (ESEA)

Let me begin this section with a few questions before we delve into the *meaty* implications of ESEA. When George W. Bush reauthorized ESEA as NCLB, No Child Left Behind, at the turn of the millennium, panic permeated throughout school districts, with teachers asking a question such as

If my students fail the standardized tests, will I be fired?

A decade later, teachers asked a question such as

How many times do I have to administer this benchmark test?

In the future, teachers may ask,

Whatever happened to the good old days when we had time for things other than tests, such as fun learning activities?

Now let's review the history of NCLB before we return to those three questions. In its legislative infancy, NCLB was ESEA, the Elementary and Secondary Education Act of 1965. In the years 2001 to 2002, ESEA was updated and signed into law by President George W. Bush, with the intention that it would provide a better education for all children. Schools are now held more accountable for results, while families are given additional school selection options. In addition, methods of teaching and teacher qualifications are more heavily scrutinized. NCLB focuses on improving the academic achievement of all students, allowing everyone access to future progress and lifelong achievements, including those from the highest- to the lowest-income schools. The expanded definition includes the application of rigorous, systematic, and objective procedures to obtain reliable and valid knowledge relevant to education activities and programs (in the amended Section 9101-37 of ESEA). This includes rigorous data analysis with multiple measurements, observations, controls, and designs. Peer-reviewed academic journals are valued over educator magazines or practitioner journals. Instead of snapshot approaches with short-term results, assessments now involved longitudinal data that reveal and advocate more accountability, which impacts the selection of instructional programs. The data and results are viewed as valuable information and tools that yield improvements. Annual reading and math assessments are in place, with achievements made in *adequate yearly progress* (AYP). Children with disabilities are included in district testing, allowing for a small percentage of students with more significant cognitive impairments to receive *alternate assessments based on modified academic achievement standards* (AA-MAS). The Department of Education designates a status label for assessment systems in its effort to both enforce the act and realize the intricacies involved with the development, compliance, and implementation of valid standards and assessments. Under ESEA, school report cards are provided, indicating annual progress from state, district, and individual schools. Federal money is available to recruit more qualified teachers and be put toward targeted needs. Teachers are encouraged to look at *what* is taught, and *how* it is taught, using research-based and scientifically proven methods. Choices are given to parents and students with access to supplemental educational services for those students attending failing schools, along with sanctions levied for schools that do not comply with the legislation.

As this book is going to press, the ESEA act, which is also known as NCLB, will again be reauthorized, with talk of not only content changes but a name change as well. The goal is to strengthen the act with more overall accountability and pragmatic school connections. The following represents some recommendations for improvements in the act from educational organizations:

Sample of American Association of School Administrators (AASA) recommendations:

- Establishing evaluation scales to measure success/failure in working toward performance standards
- Use of accountability systems with either growth or status models to judge school successes
- Targeting assistance to students with highest needs with tailored accountability systems, e.g., students with disabilities, English language learners (ELLs)

- Ongoing improvement and alignment of state standards to match knowledge and skills schools expect students to master
- Focus on helping improve achievements among highest-poverty students

American Federation of Teachers (AFT) recommendations include the following:

- Allowing credit for system's progress or proficiency, e.g., school not solely judged upon strict percentages in each labeled subgroup if it already starts with a larger number of students who are academically behind
- Not sacrificing other subject areas outside those being tested, but the integration of content areas with other subjects, e.g., reading, math, science involved across disciplines, including continual focus on lessons that involve art, music, social studies, world cultures, physical education, alongside the reading, math, science, and more
- Data accumulated should be disseminated in a timely fashion, e.g., before the onset of the next school year, to be appropriately applied to classrooms
- Modified tests and appropriate guidelines for students with disabilities and English language learners, allowing students appropriate assessments and accommodations, e.g., guided by IEPs, linguistically modified
- Allowing schools to receive interventions and continued financial support to foster and maintain improvements
- Establishing a learning environment index that relates to students' achievements, e.g., gauging professional supports available, materials, safe conditions

Sources: http://www.ed.gov/policy/elsec/leg/esea02/index.html, http://www.ed.gov/nclb/landing.jhtml, http://www.thefreelibrary.com/AASA+responds+to+NCLB+commission+report-a0162242259, http://www.aft.org/topics/nclb/downloads/NCLBRecommend060606.pdf

Now, back to those original questions and some answers:

If my students fail the standardized tests, will I be fired?

No, but the types of programs, instructional strategies, accommodations, frequency, duration, and location of interventions, assessments, and evaluations will be reviewed and revised to determine just why the learning gaps exist. The focus needs to address how to better deliver targeted curriculum standards—not pointing fingers, but promoting remediation.

How many times do I have to administer this benchmark test?

It's not about how many times a benchmark test is given, but what that benchmark test reveals in terms of instruction and curricular focus. It's better to have more formative assessments, rather than being surprised by one giant summative evaluation! Benchmark tests hopefully reveal the effectiveness of strategies and interventions, with students' responses telling administration and staff what standards need to be addressed or what deliveries require fine-tuning.

*Whatever happened to the good old days when we had time for
things other than tests, such as fun learning activities?*

With creativity, perseverance, and diligence regarding the curriculum standards, teachers will realize that assessments do not replace *fun*, but accompany tangible learning results. The distribution of time to concentrate on learning does not translate to the deletion of other activities, but must correlate with the standards and all subjects. Then the message is transmitted to students that learning is fun and not just about the test! Accountability is crucial, but can only be accomplished if it accompanies higher student motivation.

Accountability Questions to Ponder

- How is increased accountability for students with disabilities a step in the right direction?
- What is the impact of reauthorization of NCLB in individual students from different ability groups?
- Can a revised ESEA/NCLB eventually replace IDEA?
- What impact will sanctions have on schools with students with disabilities?
- Will teachers teach to the test, or can all subjects be equally balanced?
- What will the educational picture look like in the next few decades?

(Answers can and will vary.)

TRANSLATING RESEARCH INTO LEARNING STRATEGIES THAT WORK

Researchers and Professional Literature Say the Following:

- Structured, well-delivered, research-based interventions positively influence student performance within inclusive environments, honoring high expectations and best practices for all students (Beattie, Jordan, & Algozzine, 2006; Damasio, 2003; Karten, 2007b; LeDoux, 2002; McNary, Glasgow, & Hicks, 2005; Sousa, 2007).
- Successful quality inclusion programs involve team approaches with collaborative efforts from schools and families, allowing for flexibility to perceive when something works well and adaptation to change it when it does not work (Willis, 2009).
- Social skills do not come naturally to students with autism and must be directly taught if they are going to be mastered, e.g., what to explicitly do and say in each situation (Baker, 2005).
- The stages of backward design—or *understanding by design* (UbD)—involve identifying the desired results first, determining acceptable evidence, and then planning experiences and instruction accordingly. This includes the acquisition of important information and skills, making meaning of the content, and then effectively transferring that learning beyond the school (Wiggins & McTighe, 2005).

- Teachers must understand the role of culture in human development and schooling in order to make good decisions about classroom management and organization (Rothstein-Fisch & Trumbull, 2008).

- "A teacher can be ten times more effective by incorporating visual information into a classroom discussion. . . . Our brains have more receptors to process the images coming in than the words we hear" (Burmark, quoted in Association for Supervision and Curriculum Development [ASCD], 2002, n.p.).

- Teachers need to present new information in smaller chunks and offer strategic stopping points for demonstration, descriptions, summarization, discussion, and predictions. Teachers also need to take steps to establish and communicate learning goals and track student progress as they interact with that new knowledge (Marzano, 2007).

- "Students need to know that they're accepted. I had one student with a learning disability; everyone told him what was wrong with him, but no one tried to help him realize what was good in him" (Tomlinson, quoted in ASCD, 2002, n.p.).

- "Students need multiple opportunities to meet standards, and those opportunities should include differentiated instruction, accommodations and modifications, and opportunities for advanced learners" (Harris, quoted in ASCD, 2002, n.p.).

- Teacher efficacy (thinking that you will influence students' successes), collaborative relationships, mentoring/advocacy, and community building are essential components of inclusive classrooms (Cramer, 2006).

- The people who work in the school building, e.g., principal, assistant principals, educators, instructional assistants, and all staff, along with their families, are the actual *inclusive experts* who know the students the best (Hammeken, 2007).

- "Traditionally special education legislation has focused on compliance with the procedure for providing special services described in the federal and state laws. However, the philosophy and the mandates contained in the 1997 Individuals with Disabilities Act (IDEA) shifted that accountability to focus on how students are meeting the new standards, thus increasing expectations for students with disabilities" (U.S. Department of Education, 1998, n.p.).

- IDEIA 2004 includes RTI, response to interventions, a different way to identify students with disabilities and intervene with instruction and assessments for students who may be struggling (www.nasponline.org/advocacy/rtifact sheets.aspx).

- Schools who do not have forward-thinking programs for students with special needs are usually the ones with families who do not advocate for their children (Tramer, 2007).

- The absence of interventions in the early school years has a negative impact on academic, emotional, social, and behavioral growth of students with reading and behavior disorders (Cybele, 2003; Levy & Chard, 2001; Trout, Epstein, Nelson, Synhorst, & Hurley, 2006).

- Universal design of curriculum and instruction offers learning alternatives to students with and without disabilities and provides a framework to both create and implement lessons that value flexible goals, methods, and assessments (Pisha & Stahl, 2005; www.cast.org).

- Discussions, communications, connections, and learning in context help learners in inclusive classrooms develop better literacy and numeracy competencies along with higher cognitive skills (Chorzempa & Lapidua, 2009; Graham & Harris, 2005; Hyde, 2007; Karten, 2009; Steen, 2007).

- "The public wants schools to hold kids accountable, but they also want schools to recognize that kids are kids" (J. Johnson, 2003, p. 37).

- "Teachers who were involved in inclusive school programs felt that the students with disabilities could benefit from the curriculum of the general education classroom if two basic changes in classroom practice were made . . . modifying the curriculum to enhance the relevancy for each student and modifying instructional techniques. . . . Teachers' interviews felt that the curricular and instructional changes were made possible by collaborative relationships developed, as teachers worked together to determine methods that could be used to best meet the needs of all learners. . . . Specific difficulties that impeded effective teaming included problems with scheduling and uncooperative teachers. The teachers commented that having enough time for planning is a critical aspect of effective teaming" (McLesky & Waldron, 2002, p. 53).

- Coteachers who work together in inclusive classrooms collaboratively improve student outcomes with the mastery of the curriculum standards and emotional growth (Friend & Cook, 2003; Karten, 2007b; Nevin, Cramer, Voigt, & Salazar, 2008).

- "The way to ensure that alternate assessment provides a vehicle for learning new skills is to include students in the construction, monitoring, and evaluation of their own portfolio work. Not only will this process reduce the burden on teachers, but students will have greater ownership of their own learning as they develop important component skills to the essential, long-term outcome of self-determination" (Kleinert, Green, Hurte, Clayton, & Oetinger, 2002, p. 41).

- Learning that is associated with students' interests and experiences is more likely to be retrieved from students' prior knowledge (Allsopp et al., 2008a; Karten, 2007b, 2008a, 2009).

- "Having opportunities to make choices in academic tasks can provide the environmental predictability needed to minimize inappropriate behaviors of students, while strengthening appropriate responses and increased levels of engagement. . . . For students with EBD [emotional behavioral disability], predictability and control may be critical concepts and skills that are necessary for appropriately coping with the environment" (Jolivette, Stichter, & McCormick, 2002, p. 24).

- Research-based instruction yields information on how children learn and how teachers need to teach with continual screening of essential skills, early interventions, progress monitoring, and data-driven decisions (Russo, Tiegerman, & Radziewicz, 2009).

- "We must still go a long way toward defining what curricular access means for *all* students. *We must also become more strategic* and more committed to designing professional development for general and special educators that promotes mutual understanding of standards and curricula and of how diverse students learn. Instructional planning must result in more than a sequence of lesson plans: it must become a road map for bringing a group of students on *different routes to some common destinations"* (McLaughlin, 2000, p. 31, emphasis added).

- Students with special needs require academic and social support with effective accommodations, modifications, and guidance to achieve educational and emotional gains in inclusive settings, e.g., differentiation of instruction, honoring individual student strengths, needs, and potentials (Beattie et al., 2006; Karten, 2008a, 2009; Littky, 2004; McKinley & Stormont, 2008; Salend, 2005; Tomlinson, 2008).

My Pragmatic Research Investigation

My research says . . .

Source:

INCLUSION AND THE STUDENT WITH DIS*ABILITIES*

When *inclusion* replaced the word *mainstreaming,* many teachers and professionals embraced the idea while others thought if they resisted it enough, it might go away. Mainstreaming had students included in classrooms for subjects they were more prepared for. Inclusion says, let's include the students and make it work. There are no guidelines, but listed on the next page are several ways students, teachers, and peers can fit in. As the book progresses, all of these will be delineated further, with specific curriculum classroom applications.

Activity: Each person puts his or her name on an index card or Popsicle stick that is then randomly pulled from a hat, can, or jar to read the numbered inclusion ideas listed below. Each number on the list can also be clapped to focus attention, thereby adding a musical/rhythmic component. This procedure establishes equity in the classroom and stops the *ooh-ooh child* from volunteering to read everything or answering all of the questions. It also wakes up sleepers. In the classroom, sensitivity and variation can be used to help students with reading difficulties; e.g., have students with and without reading difficulties select the Popsicle sticks to be part of the activity, instead of to determine who reads, or intermittently ask some students to paraphrase statements instead so they are not embarrassed by reading words that are too difficult in front of the class. Always mix it up by also asking the best readers in the class to do non-reading activities as well.

Eighteen Inclusive Principles

1. Ask for help.

2. Differentiate content (what you are teaching) from process (how you teach—delivery and strategies).

3. Work with specialists as a team to modify and adapt the curriculum to meet the special needs of students while allowing for flexibility in scheduling.

4. Teach students how to learn by offering lessons in study skills along with the curriculum.

5. Get the whole class involved so that everyone is working together to help each other by establishing a team mentality.

6. Use cooperative learning and let peers work together to develop friendships.

7. Know when to change course.

8. Increase your own dis*ability* awareness.

9. Be aware of the physical classroom setup.

10. Provide directions in written form for children with auditory problems and in verbal form for those with visual difficulties.

11. Teach to strengths while avoiding weaknesses to minimize frustrations; e.g., honor students' favored intelligences after informal inventories.

12. Help students with methods to organize their written work.

13. Collect files containing additional higher-level materials and activities for students who require more challenges.

14. Allow students to work on various assigned tasks.

15. Be aware of multiple intelligences.

16. Value opinions of families and community.

17. Model appropriate behavior.

18. *Believe in yourself and your students!*

INCLUSION IS . . .

> *Directions for Inclusion Acrostic Activity:* Write a word that describes inclusion next to each letter below. You can use whatever words you desire, but a suggestion for one of the Ns is the word *naturally.* Hopefully, including others can become something automatic and "natural"— a way of life.

Acrostic writing is sometimes used to focus thoughts and enhance creativity.

I

N

C

L

U

S

I

O

N . . . aturally

Success Stories

Whatever happened to that kid? Remember the one who wouldn't sit still in class and kept jumping around from activity to activity, without completing the specified requirements? Well, that child grew up and became the dancer who loves to express herself through body movements. Or that child might be the CEO who supervises others, multitasking and delegating the details to subordinates. Whatever happened to that child who doodled all day in class? Well, that child may now be the renowned architect or engineer who just designed that incredible building or new prototype for that ingenious car. Maybe the fidgety child who could never sit still learned to work with his hands, create sculpture, be a chef, or even work as a sign language interpreter. Maybe the child who had trouble making friends is now a guidance counselor or child psychologist. Maybe the child who has Down syndrome is now gainfully employed and has learned to live independently. Maybe the child who couldn't stop talking is now a lawyer or a journalist. What about the child who could barely read at grade level? Well, that child now loves audio books and has figured out how to decipher the written word by using different learning strategies. That child also went on to college. Sure, the child might have needed a remedial reading and writing course, but with strong perseverance and support from friends, educators, and family, that child never gave up on her goals. That child graduated with a college diploma and is now gainfully employed. Maybe that child never went to college, but is now taking adult education courses to learn more. Maybe that child learned a trade and is now a whiz with computers, or maybe that child is an electrician or a plumber. Maybe that child learned to focus on her strengths and abilities. Maybe that child was helped by a teacher who successfully found a way to include her in the classroom. Maybe that child was included in society, not because it was the law, but because it was the right thing to do. Legislation and research support inclusion, but educators are the ones who must support the *child* by turning the rhetoric into successful classroom practice.

Understanding Complicated Special Education Terminology

The purpose of this chapter is to investigate how others view and treat people with disabilities. Through the years, children and adults with disabilities have had to overcome the "handicapping" attitudes of society. Varying societal acceptance of differences can either thwart or foster academic and social development. This chapter offers more knowledge about special education labels and gives practical activities that teachers can use to help themselves and others to better view people with exceptionalities as valuable individuals. Experiential activities to increase understanding of learning, sensory, emotional, and physical differences are included, along with ample reflections for both teachers and students. Overall, those with disabilities should be treated as people first; the student is thereby not defined by what he or she cannot do, but by his or her strengths and potentials.

DIS*ABILITY* INTROSPECTION

Before we begin our DA (dis*ability* awareness) journey, it is vital to continually emphasize the importance of introspection for both teachers and students. *Self-awareness and accurate reflections are incredibly effective catalysts to personal, social, academic, and cognitive growth.* You need to know where you've been before you can continue onward. Including students means understanding them as well.

Defining Normal

Normal Journal Entry

Describe a normal teacher interacting with a normal child. Please note that interpretations of this assignment will vary, depending upon individual definitions of the word *normal*.

What Exactly Is Normal?

Normal food _____

Weird food _____

Normal clothes _____

Weird clothes _____

Normal book _____

Weird book _____

Normal movie _____

Weird movie _____

Normal music _____

Weird music _____

Normal hobby _____

Weird hobby _____

Normal teaching _____

Moral or question for discussion: "Who or what defines the word *normal*?"

Some of Webster's definitions for normal include words such as *conformity, average, regular,* and *usual.* A *norma* is actually a carpenter's square for measuring right angles. Later on, we'll discover some "right angles" teachers can use to help students learn.

BEING TREATED DIFFERENTLY

Spinach Helped Popeye: How It Feels to Be Special

A waitperson who serves spinach to a child would most likely be greeted with a grimace as opposed to a smile. If the spinach was replaced with ice cream, then the scenario would be quite different. Even though the child may never have tasted spinach, the reaction is strongly negative. Attitudes toward people with disabilities are a little like spinach—strong and sometimes based on misunderstandings.

People need to know how it feels to be *special* and how being treated differently can lead to attitudinal barriers and the internalization of negativity.

No matter how great one's self-worth, individuals are constantly influenced by how others perceive and act toward them. Some members of society fear diversity or think it might rub off on them or their children. Society is not born in an instant, but influenced by varying factors such as movies, books, and magazines that frequently portray *perfect people* in a *perfect world*. Sometimes one must gradually acquire a taste for spinach, in order to fully appreciate it. Didn't it make Popeye strong? The following questions have no answer key, but consider how you would respond.

Disability Reflections:

1. Is physical beauty important in our culture?

2. Do young children think disabilities can be cured?

3. How do the media portray people with disabilities?

4. Do adults and children feel uncomfortable around someone with a disability?

5. Do attitudes toward those with disabilities need improvement?

Moral: Even though someone with a disability *forgets* about it, others remind him or her through sometimes careless unintentional remarks and unwelcoming stares. It's often not just the words themselves but the manner of delivery that can also be hurtful. People with a disability can be aware of not only their disability but the associated stigma as well. Attitudes toward children in inclusive settings are no exception.

Viewing Differences in Movies and Books

The following is a list of many movies and books that portray people with disabilities. Adults and older students can view and critique these. The objective is to understand that people with disabilities can and do lead successful and productive lives.

Adam	*Brian's Song*
Rainman	*Midnight Cowboy*
The Elephant Man	*Coming Home*
Something About Mary	*Born on the Fourth of July*
Little Man Tate	*Butterflies Are Free*
Cat's Got My Tongue	*Mercury Rising*
Patch Adams	*Sneakers*
Nell	*Contact*
Lorenzo's Oil	*Young Frankenstein*
Dangerous Minds	*Awakenings*
Dominick and Eugene	*Forrest Gump*
Moby Dick	*What's Eating Gilbert Grape?*
F.D.R.—Sunrise at Campobello	*Edward Scissorhands*
Something for Joey	*Children of a Lesser God*

The Heart Is a Lonely Hunter
Of Mice and Men
Charly (movie)
Flowers for Algernon (book)
As Good as It Gets
One Flew Over the Cuckoo's Nest
Sling Blade
Johnny Belinda
Scent of a Woman
The Miracle Worker
Gaby
Educating Peter
Mask
Gigot
Catcher in the Rye
Beethoven Doesn't Live Upstairs
Mr. Holland's Opus
My Left Foot
The Point (cartoon)
F.A.T. City (Frustration, Anxiety, Tension): Last One Picked, First One Picked On
The Ugly Duckling
Dumbo
The Boy Who Could Fly
Stand by Me
Radio Flyer
Ice Castles
Untamed Heart

The Other Sister
Philadelphia
Immortal Beloved
Being There
A Beautiful Mind
Beauty and the Beast
I Am Sam
Hairspray
Simon Birch
The Dive From Clausen's Pier
The Man Who Mistook His Wife for a Hat
An Anthropologist on Mars
Still Me
Nothing Is Impossible
The Curious Incident of the Dog in the Night-Time
Emergence, Labeled Autistic
Deaf Child Crossing
Riding the Bus With My Sister
First Person Plural
The Quiet Room
Don't Worry, He Won't Get Far on Foot
The View From Saturday
Disability Joke Book
Radio
Finding Nemo
Snowcake
Including Samuel
Daniel Isn't Talking

Disability Awareness Program for Elementary Student (videotape). National Easter Seal Society. (1990). Chicago: Friends Who Care. (800) 221–6827. Updated 2009 version available at http:// www.easterseals.com/friendswhocare.

In Vogue: Wind-Blown Education— Negative Connotations of Words

There are many trends within the field of education. As the wind blows in, a new term is created, and then often thrust upon classroom teachers. Thank goodness we have come a long way from the early 1900s when the *Ugly Laws* existed, which did not allow people who were considered to be deformed in some way—e.g., a person with a physical disfigurement—to be seen in public, lest they be fined. No one today would argue that those *prettier people* who made and enforced the laws were truly the ugly ones! Society evolves, and positive changes result. Special education in particular undergoes continual changes. Through the years, the use of certain words is no longer in vogue or fashionable, since eventually the words develop a negative connotation. The names of classifications, syndromes, disorders, and existing strategies are constantly being altered. Perhaps as this book is revised, the names will again change, but the following describes former and present *special* terminology.

Trends in the field of special education include new classifications with an educational pendulum that is continually shifting back and forth. Current emphasis is to replace the word *handicapped* with the word *impaired* or *disabled*, and *retarded* with the words *cognitively* or *developmentally and intellectually limited or challenged*. Some thought the word *handicapped*, derived from "cap in hand," as in someone who begs, was derogatory, and it has dropped out of common use. Even the Arc (formerly Association for Retarded Citizens) and NICHCY (formerly National Information Center for Children and Youth with Handicaps, now the National Dissemination Center for Children with Disabilities), who kept their acronyms due to familiarity, do not want to be associated with the words *retarded* or *handicapped.* The public seems to catch on to these words as the terms change. *Retarded* at one time just meant slow, and now it has a negative connotation. Even the word *special* can be condescending when used to describe someone with a disability.

In a book entitled *Quirky Kids,* authors Klass and Costello (2003) try to deemphasize the commonly used classifications and place more attention on individual children's areas of strengths and weaknesses. They think *quirky* is a less branding term than a formal diagnosis such as AD/HD. If the word *deviance* is given a positive spin such as differing strengths, then the negativity is minimized and not internalized, and it will not propagate a self-fulfilling, defeatist, stigmatizing philosophy. Kranowitz, author of *The Out-of-Sync Child* (1998), uses the term *out-of-sync* to describe sensory integration dysfunction (SI or SID), in which a child is out of sync with his or her environment, such as being under- or oversensitive to noises and touch. Other people might diagnose the same child with central auditory processing deficits or some type of attention disorder such as AD/HD. Many of the experts in the field want to abandon the traditional medical, psychiatric, and neurological terms since they share overlapping characteristics, with sometimes a fine line separating one from the other. And so the list of names arising out of differing schools of thought and trends will probably grow. Outdated special education words, no longer in vogue, follow. Think of other more positive terms you can replace them with, before using words such as these.

moron	imbecile	crippled
idiot	handicapped	victim
retard	mongoloid	afflicted

Moral: Some of the names have been changed to protect the innocent.

MERITS OF INDIVIDUALITY

Another *special* trend is "people first" language in which the child, not the disability, is the focus. For example, rather than saying "the autistic kid," it's preferable to say "the child with autism." The difference might seem semantic, but the key point is that the disability should not scream at you. It is only one component of a person's makeup.

The disability does not define a person. People are much more than their disability!

Former Terms	Current Terms
idiot	challenged
moron	quirky
imbecile	sensory integration dysfunction
retard	impaired
crippled	cognitive impairment
lame	attention-deficit/hyperactivity disorder
socially maladjusted	autism spectrum disorder
culturally deprived	disabled
educable, trainable	special needs
mild, moderate, severe, profound	eligible for special education
minimal brain damage	differently abled
childhood schizophrenia	exceptional
handicapped	developmental or intellectual disability
	_____

We're All Individuals: Plotting Strengths and Weaknesses

Directions: Rate your personal strengths and weaknesses on this graph (with 10 being the highest), and then connect the dots to form your profile.

	Singing	Writing	Spelling	Dancing	Being a Friend	Drawing
10						
9						
8						
7						
6						
5						
4						
3						
2						
1						

Physically Seeing That Differences Exist

To further understand this concept, move to stations by posted signs in the room numbered 1 to 8. Continue movement to different stations, noting one another's similarities and differences. Descriptors can be varied to match interests of learners in Grades K–12.

Station # 1 Anyone who loves chocolate	**Station # 2** Anyone who is great at sudoku	**Station # 3** Person who easily remembers directions
Station # 4 Anyone who has glasses or contacts to see better	**Station # 5** People who speak 2 or more languages	**Station # 6** Anyone who is part of a book club
Station # 7 Someone who has a pet	**Station # 8** Anyone for whom 3 or more descriptors fit	

Moral: We're all different!

DIS*ABILITY* AWARENESS CLASSROOM SUGGESTIONS

1. Develop positive and sensitive attitudes about all students.

2. Understand that there are different types of disabilities:
   - *Visible*—Someone using a wheelchair, sign language, hearing aids, or looking different in physical appearance
   - *Hidden*—Someone with a learning disability, emotional difficulties, epilepsy, a heart condition, asthma, diabetes, sickle cell anemia, or another disability not easily seen by looking at the person

3. Focus on what individuals *can* do, instead of the disability alone, making everyone handi-*capable,* not handicapped! Be aware that people and the environment itself can transform a disability into a handicap.

4. Emphasize that a disability might mean that some students *learn and see things differently.*

5. Use "people first" language: "I know someone who has difficulty with _____" (seeing, hearing, learning, walking). Do not say "the deaf kid" or "the blind girl," since the disability should not define the person.

6. People with disabilities like to be *accepted and included by their peers,* such as receiving a birthday or holiday party invite or even going shopping together.

7. Contact family and individual disability organizations to provide more information about particular disabilities. Invite guest speakers when appropriate.

8. Do not assume that people with a disability cannot do something. *Let them be the judge of their own capabilities.* Ask first.

9. Don't be afraid to be yourself. *Treat someone with a disability with the same respect that you would want.* You can be friends with someone with a disability if you like the person, not because you feel you have to just because the person has a disability.

10. You can ask someone about his or her disability, but it is the person's choice to talk about it or not.

What I Need to Know About Dis*abilities*

(Use the following list with your younger students.)

- Everyone has differences.
- We should treat someone with a disability the same way we would like to be treated.
- Don't be afraid to be yourself!
- You can be friends with someone with a disability if you like the person, not because you feel you have to just because the person has a disability. Pity helps no one!
- People and places can be the handicaps for someone with a disability.
- Our kind attitudes will make a difference!
- Disabilities do not define people. The disability is just a small part of the whole person, like a petal on a flower.
- Focus on strengths, what people can do, their abilities!

Learning Flowers: Classroom Garden

Directions: Create your own *special* flower with unique characteristics, including *positive* statements about students with differences, or personalize your flower to tell something about yourself. Samples are shown below. Collectively, the flowers comprise a garden, just like children who can bloom all year. Remember that each flower represents a complex person, and if the person has a disability, it is only one petal of the entire flower. With the right strategies planted, inclusive education can bring sunshine and growth to all.

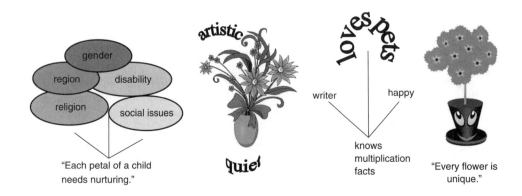

My Flower

Simulated Activities

(Always keep safety issues of foremost importance and exercise reason regarding which activities best suit the maturity levels of your students.) The Native American expression, "You can better understand what someone is saying by walking a mile in his or her moccasins," explains the purpose of these activities. Additional knowledge can also be gained from individual disability organizations and government agencies.

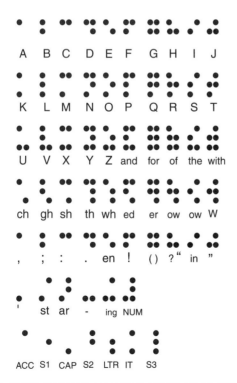

Braille consists of six dots arranged in different order with a number given for each position in a cell. Each cell has its own letter, capital sign, number sign, and punctuation mark. There are also contractions that are shorter forms of words, written with fewer cells.

Visual Needs

- Students can learn the Braille alphabet, feeling the textures of cells.
- Blindfold selected seated children in class while using the chalkboard.
- Use a six-tray muffin pan with tennis balls inserted as one kinesthetic way to copy the Braille alphabet, or use an egg carton cut in half.
- Write words to a poem in a tiny font, *such as this,* to distort the words.
- Ask students to close their eyes while seated at an assembly or in the lunchroom.
- Purchase magnification pages and games such as checkers or Monopoly from the American Foundation for the Blind for your classroom.
- Ask a speaker who is blind to talk to the class. As a thank you, give him or her flowers and send a taped recording of the class's appreciation.

Hearing Reflections

- Give students oral directions while playing loud background music.
- Ask students to listen to a quiet story, one that you "read" to them without talking, to see if they can follow the plot with pictures or lip reading.
- Play static on a radio to simulate sounds hearing aids might produce.
- Explain the difference between listening and hearing.
- Turn off the sound of a closed-captioned movie.
- Tell students to cover their ears for 3 minutes every 10 minutes for an hour.
- Teach students how to finger spell, or invite a sign language interpreter to explain gestures and teach the class to sign some sentences. Be certain that when the students ask questions, they speak slowly and face the presenter. Overemphasizing lip reading might also be insulting. Remember to tap the person who needs to lip read gently on the shoulder when addressing him or her, so that the person can focus attention before you begin speaking.
- Have the class research possible reasons for hearing loss at different ages and discuss the graph below, which indicates how high decibel levels affect hearing loss over time. Talk about how wearing ear plugs when people are involved in loud activities is *sound* advice to maintain hearing.

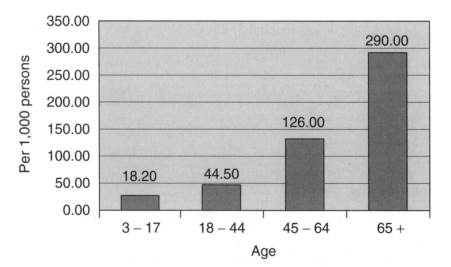

Prevalence of Hearing Loss

Decibel (dB) level	How this dB level can affect a person's hearing
110	Repeated over and over, everyday exposure for more than 1 minute risks permanent hearing loss.
100	Unprotected exposure—without ear plugs—for less than 15 minutes is recommended as the maximum.
85	Prolonged exposure to noise at or above this decibel level can cause gradual hearing loss over time.

Now here are the decibel levels of things you might use or be around every day:

Snowmobile—100dB

Firecracker—150 dB

Heavy traffic—85 dB

Motorcycle—95 dB

Loud stereo at highest volume—105 dB

Normal speaking—60 dB

Whisper—30 dB

Moral: *Use your ears soundly!*

Source consulted: National Institute on Deafness and Other Communication Disorders, http://www.nidcd .nih.gov/health/hearing/ruler.asp

Communication Thoughts

- Speech involves your brain, chest, nose, mouth, and muscles in your face. Speech disorders can be caused by a hearing loss or other factors.
- Speech therapy by skilled therapists with consistent home practice can help.
- If a child has an articulation problem, it will sound like talking with your tongue touching the roof of your mouth: "Thpeeking incowectly ith orful."
- If a child has a *dysfluency* such as stuttering, she will repeat sounds a lot, while stammering means the child is repeating words: "Ssspeaking in-in-in-c-c-correctly is aw-aw-aw-aw-ful." The child might cough periodically, which is another type of interruption of speech or thought.
- Voice disorders can mean that there is hoarseness, poor projection, or even breathiness. These disorders can sometimes be caused by neurological factors; trauma; or even voice abuse, like too much yelling.
- A child with a language problem knows what he wants to say, but can't put all of the words in the correct order: "Tough speaking not happy."
- Students who are nonverbal or some who have severe cognitive or multiple disabilities may need training on how to use communication boards such as this one to help let their needs be known.

Source: The Picture Communication Symbols, copyright ©1981–2004 Mayer-Johnson, Inc. Used with permission.

If a student has verbal or speech *apraxia* or *dyspraxia*, then he or she may display difficulties with motor and speech planning skills, e.g., tongue placements, phrasing, or sequencing. The next chart offers some insights to help teachers and students understand more about speech and language differences they may encounter in inclusive classrooms.

Speech & language terms	Descriptions	Classroom examples	*What to do*
speech	Involves voice, articulation, and fluency (smoothness of the speech)	Student may stutter, hesitate, mispronounce words, or avoid or minimize dialogue with others for fear of embarrassment.	Coordinate with speech-language pathologist (SLP) to visit and consult with teachers to offer practice exercises in the classroom and at home; be patient and do not finish student sentences.
language	Using sounds, symbols, and words to communicate with others	Student may have better receptive language (understanding) than expressive language.	Ask student to paraphrase what was said, or give student informal oral or written assessments to confirm understandings; offer more visuals.
pragmatics	Rules of language usage and social conversing	Student may have difficulties in cooperative learning activities or conversing at lunch or at recess, changing topics, or sharing thoughts.	Again coordinate with SLP, inviting him or her to observe, monitor, and intervene with the student in natural classroom environment and other social situations.
semantics	Rules involving the content of language with vocabulary and communication	Student may have difficulties with idioms and sarcasm.	Be specific in directions, and preteach new vocabulary in readings and subjects; play with words and sentences on index cards, sentence strips, and recordings.
syntax	Rules with grammar and ordering of words	Student may have difficulties in writing or logically conveying thoughts in sentences.	Use direct skill instruction with rules of grammar; teach student to diagram sentences, clearly labeling or color coding parts of sentences, e.g., subject/predicate, objects, nouns, verbs, and more.
morphology	Rules involving how words are formed, e.g., smaller parts/morphemes	Student may leave out word endings; may not understand about structural analysis, e.g., prefixes and suffixes.	Use guided practice with identification of word parts in isolation and text in all genres; compose a three-columned wall chart of different prefixes and suffixes that students continually add to as they discover words; teach and review meaning of commonly used prefixes and suffixes across the curriculum.
phonology	Rules of language and how sounds are organized	Student may mispronounce words and lose understandings across content areas.	Break up words into syllables and phonemes as needed; offer daily structured teaching, practice, and application of the sounds of letters with modeling of rules and exceptions; give pre- and posttest inventories to gauge progress.

Moving to Sounds Around

Directions: This activity shows that learning to communicate would be difficult if the appropriate words were missing and a new system needed to be learned. After being given brief instructions with these auditory prompts, can you *motorically* respond appropriately?

Finger snapping	——————➤	Touching your forehead
Clapping	——————➤	Running in place
Beeping	——————➤	Backward arm circles
Bell ringing	——————➤	Hopping on one foot
Playing maracas	——————➤	Circling hips

> What are some skills included in this activity?

Moving to Sounds Around involves the following:

1. Concentration

2. Memory

3. Listening

4. Auditory processing

5. Socialization

6. Kinesthetic movement to productively channel classroom energy (great to do after a long period of sitting)

7. Reminding students that learning about sounds can be fun!

Emotional Concerns

Often students with behavioral issues cannot express themselves vocally through acceptable means and will act out in negative ways that offend both teachers and classmates. Avoid this kind of isolation by allowing the child to have more space or an opportunity to remove himself or herself from tense situations.

This type of disability is often one of the most misunderstood, since it's usually a hidden one, not visible. It is a broad topic with many individual concerns, and it requires tremendous sensitivity and training.

Emotions can range from depression and withdrawal to mood swings and outbursts with little warning, like a volcano that suddenly explodes.

Safety issues are of the utmost importance for all children. If a child is being volatile, it is important to secure a safe environment for all students and to instruct other children as well on how to behave. A list of appropriate behavioral classroom rules can be posted or discussed ahead of time with the entire class. Role-playing hypothetical situations can prepare and alert students for possible scenarios. Peer mediation training and channeling anger with such activities as yoga or art are also effective. Understand that some days are better than others for kids who need more guidance with their behavior.

Emotional Scenario

Directions: Cooperatively choose at least 1 of the following 10 statements:

1. I'm going to count to 10.
2. I will take a deep breath and relax.
3. There's no need to get upset; I can handle this.
4. Violence never solved anything.
5. I better not blow this out of proportion.
6. I'm in control.
7. There must be something I can learn from this.
8. I know I can get mad, but it won't help.
9. There's definitely some humor in this.
10. I'd better figure out what to do.

Now think of a hypothetical classroom situation whose resolution could be the statement you've chosen. Act out the scenario.

Learning Differences

- Ask students to solve 30 difficult math problems in a 5-minute period, or require them to read a passage and answer questions containing vocabulary at least two reading levels above their independent level. Then ask them how they felt when they could not complete the assignment.
- Demonstrate how to make a pinwheel using origami, giving rushed directions with ineffective modeling.
- Play a song in a different language, and then ask your students to write about what they just heard.
- Require students to memorize 10 unfamiliar science or social studies words in an unreasonably short amount of time.
- Ask meth to eard entsences uchs sa hits to misutale a reabgin pisorber. (Translation: Ask them to read sentences such as this to simulate a reading disorder).

Physical Insights

- Have students write or catch a ball with their nondominant hand.
- Ask children to tie their shoes while wearing mittens.
- After having students take turns sitting in a wheelchair for about an hour, ask them to express how it felt to watch their nondisabled peers while being immobile.

- Arrange for a speaker with a physical disability to talk with the class.
- Give each student a small square paper to fold into quarters and ask them to hold it against their forehead. Then instruct them to write their name on the paper using their nondominant hand (pencils are recommended). This activity causes brain confusion and simulates fine-motor difficulties. The reversals and illegible handwriting simulate someone who has fine-motor difficulties or perceptual difficulties that are evidenced by poor handwriting.
- Remind students that these were only simulations, but to think about how frustrated they felt.

Negative Effects of Labeling: Edible Simulation— Background Information for Teachers

This edible simulation involves five groups: apple, chocolate, lemon, pretzel, and nut people. Collectively, each group describes its characteristics with guided questions below. Reflections include how stereotypes impact the learning environment. Teacher expectations of a child who is included, or how classmates view someone who is different, may very well be based upon preconceived thoughts of a group, and may not allow for individual differences within that group or label. The objective of the activity is to help students think about the negative effects of labeling people with specific categories or disabilities. For example, all students with AD/HD are not the same, nor do all people with learning, physical, or emotional needs have the exact same characteristics or require the same delivery of services or strategies. Labeling is sometimes used for budgeting purposes to allocate funding for specific disability groups. Hopefully, concrete, edible accompaniments will make these insightful analogies more pleasant to digest.

Directions for Students: You are a(n) _____ (apple, chocolate, lemon, pretzel, or nut) person. Describe yourself by listing your characteristics. What do other people think about you? If you could talk, what would you say? Describe how you can be combined with other edibles, but during this simulation, you may only eat from the category you have chosen, and only speak to your food group.

Characteristics of a _____ person:

What people think about a _____ person:

What a _____ person would say:

Who/what can a _____ person be combined with?

Food for thought: Labeling individuals into specific categories or disabilities can be harmful to all.

Thinking About Dis*abilities*

After participating in some of these activities, answer the following questions:

1. How did you feel when you couldn't _____?

2. What were you thinking as you watched or heard others?

3. Would you like to try the activity again?

4. What strategies helped you cope?

5. What have you learned?

6. Would you recommend this exercise to a friend? Why or why not?

7. What's the difference between this simulated activity and the experience of someone who has an actual disability?

8. What effect does labeling have on individuals?

Bibliotherapy: Literature Circles

Students cooperatively read children's literature about various disabilities; possible roles are listed below for groups of four:

Connector (tells how the book relates to other readings, writings, or his or her own life, what it reminds the person of)

Talker (thinks of questions prompted by the book and begins dialogue, promoting conversation)

Quoter (retells favorite, funny, sad, or interesting parts)

Artist (illustrates favorite scene or characters from the book)

> Even though these books are written on elementary levels, they deal with specific concepts such as sibling interactions, frustrations, and societal reactions to those with disabilities, which are complex issues. Fact sheets about individual disabilities are included in some books.

List of Children's Literature

- *Joey and Sam*, by Ilana Katz and Edward Ritvo (autism)
- *Apt. 3*, by Ezra Jack Keats (blindness)
- *Be Good to Eddie Lee*, by Virginia Fleming (Down syndrome)
- *Ian's Walk: A Book About Autism*, by Laurie Lears
- *The Don't-Give-Up Kid*, by Jeanee Gehret (dyslexia)

- *All Cats Have Asperger Syndrome*, by Kathy Hoopmann
- *All Dogs Have ADHD*, by Kathy Hoopmann
- *Sosu's Call*, by Meshack Asare (physical disabilities)
- *Views From Our Shoes: Growing Up With a Brother or Sister With Special Needs*, edited by Donald Meyer
- *Zipper, the Kid With ADHD*, by Caroline Janover
- *Silent Lotus*, by Jeanne M. Lee (deafness)
- *I Wish I Could Fly Like a Bird!* by Katherine Denison (learning differences)
- *The School Survival Guide for Kids With LD*, by Rhoda Cummings and Gary Fisher (step-by-step academic and social hints)
- *Our Brother Has Down's Syndrome*, by Shelley Cairo
- *Eagle Eyes*, by Jeanne Gehret (AD/HD)
- *Putting on the Brakes*, by Patricia O. Quinn and Judith Stern (AD/HD)
- *I Have a Sister, My Sister Is Deaf*, by Jeanne Whitehouse Peterson
- *Talk to Me*, by Sue Brearley (language disabilities)
- *Sneetches*, by Dr. Seuss (differences)
- *What's Wrong With Timmy?* by Maria Shriver (cognitive disability)
- *Knots on a Counting Rope*, by Bill Martin and John Archambault (blindness)
- *Leo the Late Bloomer*, by Robert Kraus (abilities that bloom)
- *Thank You, Mr. Falker*, by Patricia Polacco (reading differences)
- *Rolling Along With Goldilocks and the Three Bears*, by Cindy Meyers
- *Where's Chimpy?* by Berniece Rabe (Down syndrome)
- *Spinabilities: A Young Person's Guide to Spina Bifida*, edited by Marlene Lutkenhoff and Sonya Oppenheimer
- *I'm Tougher Than Diabetes!* by Alden Carter
- *Dyslexia*, by Alvin and Virginia Silverstein and Laura Dunn
- *Shelley, the Hyperactive Turtle*, by Deborah Moss
- *Chuck Close, Up Close*, by Jan and Jordan Greenberg (artist with learning disabilities)
- *Helen Keller*, by George Sullivan
- *How Smudge Came*, by Nan Gregory and Ron Lightburn (Down syndrome)
- *My Buddy*, by Audrey and Rand Osofsky (muscular dystrophy)
- *The Summer of the Swans*, by Betsy Byars (intellectual differences)
- *Crazy Lady!* by Jane Leslie Conly (alcoholism, peer pressure, intellectual differences)
- *Joey Pigza Swallowed the Key*, by Jack Gantos (AD/HD)
- *Of Sound Mind*, by Jean Ferris (deafness)
- *Small Steps: The Year I Got Polio*, by Peg Kehret
- *Freak the Mighty*, by Rodman Philbrick (learning and physical differences)
- *The Man Who Loved Clowns*, by June Rae Wood (Down syndrome)
- *Hank Zipzer: Niagara Falls or Does It?* by Henry Winkler and Lin Oliver (dyslexia)
- *The Silent Boy*, by Lois Lowry (1900s view of autism)
- *Mom Can't See Me*, by Sally Hobart Alexander and George Ancona
- *My Thirteenth Winter*, by Samantha Abeel (dyscalculia)
- *Stories of Disability in the Human Family: In Search of Better Angels*, by J. David Smith

From the Mouths of Babes

These two letters from fourth-grade students in response to Disability Awareness classroom presentations delineate how such programs can positively influence a child's perception of someone with a disability.

Dear Mrs. Karten,

I learned today what it is like if you can't read, see, or can't learn as fast. I also learned that you should not make fun of someone because of those things. They could be just as good as you. Can't wait to see you next time!

From,
L. M.

Dear Mrs. Karten,

You did a wonderful job today. You taught me a lot. I had felt sorry for people with a disability. But I never let it show because in the last visit you said, "people don't want to be treated any differently because they have a disability." Your lesson really paid off because a girl in my Hebrew class has a disability and now I know the perfect way to treat her (the same as anyone else).

Love,
F. L. (please come back soon)

DIFFERENT CHOICES

My Thoughts

Directions: Think about how you would act toward a student who . . .

- Needed more attention from the teacher.
- Wanted things repeated a lot.
- Required more time to do math problems.
- Could not see well.
- Had sloppy handwriting.
- Could not hear some sounds.
- Had trouble sitting quietly.
- Could not read the same level text as the rest of the class.
- Did not have enough time to complete a test.
- Tried his or her best, but kept failing tests.
- Did less homework than other students.
- Was unable to take notes.

How will you help that person? I will _____.

> Question for adults and older students to ponder: Does fair translate to equal?

Activities for Classroom Digestion

Act out these situations through role-play:

1. Pretend a child has a cut on his or her finger.
   Solution: Place a Band-Aid on the finger.

2. Pretend a student had a fight with his or her parents.

   Solution: Place a Band-Aid on a finger.

3. Pretend a child failed a test.

   Solution: Place a Band-Aid on a finger.

Moral/Fact: Band-Aids do not fix all problems. Differences exist, but handling this fact varies among students and teachers.

Shake It Up!

The next few activities try to concretely increase students' awareness that they should not judge people from superficial facts, appearances, or if they do not have the person's prior experiences.

In this first activity, the teacher places the following items in three separate, identical empty coffee cans: a dollar bill in can #1, 20 pennies in can # 2, and 1 quarter in can #3. The teacher then shakes each can and asks the class, which one do they think is worth more? The moral here is that the more valuable things are not always the easiest to identify and also may be the quietest. What you hear or see on the outside does not tell the whole story!

In the second activity, the teacher again places items in three separate, identical empty coffee cans. Now, #1 can has a dollar bill, # 2 can has 100 pennies, and #3 can has 4 quarters. The teacher then shakes each can and asks the class, which one do they think is worth more? The moral here is that you don't always know what's on the inside by what you see or hear on the outside. In this case, the cans are all equal, but in different ways. People are equal in different ways, too!

In the third activity, the teacher places equal amounts of rice grains in a coffee can, opaque orange juice container, and paper bag; use your best judgment here with quantity, no need to count! The teacher then asks the students, "What do you think is on the inside of these containers?" Elicit student responses and then have a class discussion. The moral here is that even though these things appear differently on the outside, the contents or insides of each are the same. Every person on this planet has the same worth, regardless of what they look like on the outside.

In the fourth activity, ask the students what they think is worth more, rice or money. Discuss how if a hungry person was left on a deserted island, the rice would be worth more than the money, if he or she were starving for food! The moral here is that each person has different needs. *Shake it up!* teaches about the value of money, and people, too. We're the same in some ways, and different as well! People *can be like cans:* Some are just *a little shaky.* Others are willing to *shake it up!*

Source: Karten, T. (2008). *Embracing disABILITIES in the classroom: Strategies to maximize students' assets.* Thousand Oaks, CA: Corwin.

Shake It Up! Student Worksheet

Activity #1: Circle the can that you think is the most valuable:

Can #1   Can #2   Can #3

Activity #2: Circle the can that you think is the most valuable:

Can #1   Can #2   Can #3

Activity #3: What do you think is on the inside of these containers?

Coffee can _____

Juice container _____

Paper bag _____

Activity #4: Circle which choice is worth more.

Rice   Money

Something to think about: What do you think it means when someone says, "You can't judge a book by its cover"?

I think it means _____

_____.

Dis*ability* Statements to Ponder

Directions: Write either true or false by the following statements:

_____ 1. A person with one arm can be a physical therapist.

_____ 2. A teenage girl with Down syndrome can have highlights put in her hair.

_____ 3. A person who is blind can *read* a visual dictionary.

_____ 4. Someone with dyslexia can go to college.

_____ 5. People with cerebral palsy can be public speakers.

_____ 6. A child with autism can be successfully employed.

_____ 7. An artist can have no hands.

_____ 8. Someone with cognitive impairments can have children of his or her own.

_____ 9. A person who is blind can *see* what you mean, or even climb Mt. Kilimanjaro.

_____ 10. People with disabilities need opportunities to show their abilities.

All of the above statements are true.

Keep in mind, when in doubt, apply sensitivity and common sense!

PREPARATION FOR SUCCESSFUL INCLUSION

"_____ **might need help with** _____" **is a preparatory statement** that can erase the shock or tendency to shy away from someone who is different. Teachers can alert, instruct, and guide students by modeling and informing a class on specific appropriate ways they can help classmates and others.

Dis*ability* Charts (Resource A)

Some of the barriers that prevent children from leading productive lives as members of the adult community are lack of exposure to the grade-level curriculum, untrained teachers, and negative societal attitudes. Teachers, students, administration, community, and families must be equipped with appropriate knowledge to circumvent unplanned inclusion that could lead to inevitable failure. Preparation, sensitivity, and more knowledge for all are crucial.

The dis*ability* charts in the resources at the back of the book (Resource A) list possible causes of certain common disabilities/syndromes, characteristics of people who have these syndromes, educational strategies to use with these students, and resources to help you. Please note that dis*abilities* are heterogeneous and that *each of these charts describes a syndrome, not a specific child.* In addition, some characteristics and strategies may be shared and overlap with others. Remember that clinicians are trained to make diagnoses. The purpose of the information in the charts is to broaden knowledge and does not make anyone informed enough to diagnose. Diagnoses and labels are serious things! Information for the charts in Resource A was obtained from field experts, individual disability organizations listed, NICHCY, the Council for Exceptional Children (CEC), professional journals, and diagnostic criteria from *DSM-IV-TR*. Contact these references for additional personal and professional perspectives and more resources about specific disabilities.

Sources: American Psychiatric Association. (2000). *Diagnostic and statistical manual of mental disorders (DSM-IV-TR),* 4th ed. Available online at http://www.dsmivtr.org. Washington, DC: Author.

National Dissemination Center for Children with Disabilities (NICHCY), 1825 Connecticut Ave NW, Suite 700, Washington, DC 20009, (800) 695–0285. Available online at http://www.nichcy.org.

Teachers who know individual disability characteristics can effectively apply appropriate strategies that match children's individualized education programs.

Wow! That sure was a loaded sentence, but not an impossible task. Instructional learning strategies help students of all abilities.

Directions: Complete the disability web and business card activities on the following pages.

Choose Your Learning Web

Directions: As a way to absorb, reflect, and apply the knowledge on the pages in the resource listing different syndromes' characteristics, possible causes, and educational strategies to cope with them, choose one of the disabilities that you would like to discover more about, and fill in the blank with its name. Use information previously given, your prior knowledge, cooperative help from peers, disability tables in the resources at the back of the book, and other available research to answer these questions.

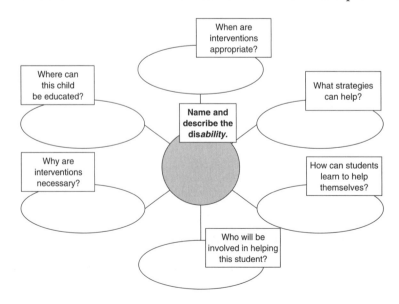

FOCUSING ON ABILITIES

Knowing different characteristics of various dis*abilities* helps teachers appropriately modify lessons. Most important, concentrating on students' strengths rather than weaknesses instills a greater self-confidence level, thereby encouraging learning. More progress can always be achieved through focusing on abilities, not *dis*abilities.

> Suppose someone with a certain dis*ability* was to open a business. What would it be?

Directions: After selecting a dis*ability,* cooperatively create a business card for possible employment that a child with _____ might be suited for when he or she reaches adulthood and enters the community. Place the specified characteristics on the corresponding locations of an index card or larger paper. The criteria described in the template below focus on positive traits, since *disability does not translate to inability.*

Business Card Activity

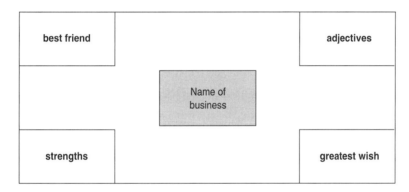

Sample Business Cards

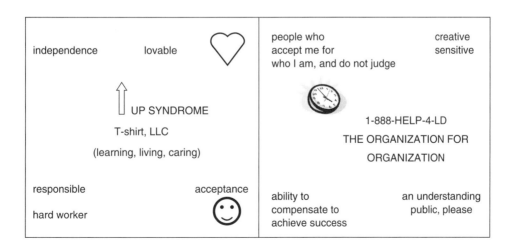

Some Biographical Readings and Research

Read biographies in texts or online about people with disabilities who have accomplished great things in their lives:

Louis Braille (created a way for people with blindness to read when he himself was blind)

Thomas Edison (inventor of the light bulb who had learning, attention, and hearing differences)

Ludwig van Beethoven (composer who was deaf)

Harriet Tubman (rescuer of slaves who had epilepsy and suffered seizures)

Juliette Gordon Low (founder of the Girl Scouts, had profound hearing loss)

Helen Keller (author and activist who was blind and deaf)

Franklin Delano Roosevelt (U.S. president who had polio and thought he needed to hide his disability due to less accepting attitudes in the 1940s)

Frida Kahlo (artist with polio and physical difficulties from an accident)

Roy Campanella (baseball player who was paralyzed due to spinal cord injury)

Bob Dole (politician with paralyzed arm from war wounds)

Stephen Hawking (physicist with amyotrophic lateral sclerosis—ALS— otherwise known as Lou Gehrig's disease, which affects walking and speaking)

Patty Duke Astin (actress with a psychiatric disorder, including manic-depressive symptoms, who went public to help others realize mental illness is a disease)

Stevie Wonder (musician who developed blindness from premature birth)

Tom Cruise (actor with dyslexia who is also an advocate of literacy programs)

Jim Abbott (baseball pitcher who was born without a right hand)

Jackie Joyner-Kersee (Olympic athlete with exercise-induced asthma [EIA])

Marlee Matlin (actress who is deaf due to childhood roseola)

Heather Whitestone (Miss America 1995, deaf from childhood antibiotics for influenza)

Chris Burke (actor, speaker, and writer from the TV program *Life Goes On* who has Down syndrome)

Wilma Rudolph (Olympic athlete who had polio early in her life and could not even walk—went on to win three Gold Medals in track)

Wilma Mankiller (political advocate for Cherokee Nation who has muscular dystrophy)

Itzhak Perlman (violinist who had polio and difficulties walking and standing)

Henry Winkler (actor and author who has dyslexia)

Marla Runyan (runner who is legally blind)

Geri Jewell (actress and comedienne with cerebral palsy)

Christopher Reeve (actor and author who became quadriplegic after being thrown from a horse, and later lobbied on behalf of those with spinal cord injuries)

Mark Wellman (mountain climber who is paraplegic)

Patricia Polacco (children's author with dyslexia, wrote *Thank You, Mr. Falker*)

Josh Blue (comedian with cerebral palsy)

Michael Phelps (Olympic swimmer with nine Gold Medals who has AD/HD)

Resource to check out: *Extraordinary People With Disabilities,* by Deborah Kent and Kathryn Quinlan

SEASAW ACTIVITY OF PEOPLE WITH ABILITIES

Directions: Collectively list famous scientists, entertainers, artists, sports figures, advocates, and writers with physical, learning, cognitive, and behavioral disabilities. Other categories could include political figures along with fictional characters in books and movies.

S (Scientists)

E (Entertainers)

A (Artists)

S (Sports figures)

A (Advocates, with or without disabilities)

W (Writers)

More Categories

Political Figures

Fictional Characters

FAMOUS PEOPLE WITH DISABILITIES
(A MERE PARTIAL LISTING)

Research sources to find out more about these and other inspiring people.

S (Scientists)

Thomas Edison (LD, hearing loss)
Albert Einstein (LD)
Alan Shepard (Meniere's syndrome)
Marie Curie (pernicious anemia)
Stephen Hawking (ALS)
Aristotle (communications disorder)
Alexander Graham Bell (LD)
Leonardo da Vinci (learning
    disability/dyslexia)
Louis Braille (blindness)

E (Entertainers)

Stevie Wonder (blindness)
Lou Ferigno (hearing loss)
Cher (LD)
Christopher Reeve (spinal injury)
José Feliciano (blindness)
Marlee Matlin (deafness)
Ray Charles (blindness)
Richard Pryor (multiple sclerosis)
Itzhak Perlman (polio)
Robin Williams (LD)
John Lennon (LD)
Michael J. Fox (Parkinson's disease)
Harry Belafonte (LD)
Tom Cruise (dyslexia)
Whoopi Goldberg (LD)
Henry Winkler (dyslexia)
Josh Blue (cerebral palsy)
Chris Burke (Down syndrome)
James Earl Jones (stuttering)

A (Artists)

Henri de Toulouse-Lautrec
    (short stature)
Vincent van Gogh (emotional- and
    self-imposed disabilities; cut
    off his ear)

Michelangelo (lost vision painting
    Sistine Chapel)
Walt Disney (LD)

S (Sports figures)

Wilma Rudolph (polio)
Bruce Jenner (LD)
Carl Lewis (LD)
Jim Abbott (pitcher who was born
    with one hand)
Casey Martin (golfer with birth
    defect in right leg)
Magic Johnson (AIDS)
Greg Louganis (AIDS, stuttering,
    asthma)
Florence Griffith Joyner
    (asthma)
Roy Campanella (paralyzed from
    spinal injury)
Michael Phelps (AD/HD)
Mark Wellman (paralyzed from
    climbing accident)

A (Advocates, with or without disabilities)

Helen Keller (deaf-blindness)
Anne Sullivan (Helen's teacher, had
    visual impairment from
    childhood disease)
Christopher Reeve (spinal injury)
Dana Reeve (wife of Christopher
    Reeve)
Doug Flutie (has a child with
    autism)
James Brady (physically disabled
    from gunshot wound)
Eunice Shriver (founder of Special
    Olympics)
Temple Grandin (autism)

Tom Cruise (dyslexia)
Jerry Lewis (telethon for muscular
    dystrophy)
Michael J. Fox (Parkinson's disease)
Clay Aiken (spokesperson for
    developmental disabilities)
Rose Kennedy (was parent of a
    child with cognitive needs)
Bob Love (stuttering)
Roy and Dale Evans
    (had daughter with Down
    syndrome; Dale wrote 1953 book,
    Angel Unaware)

W (Writers)

John Milton (blindness)
Homer (blindness)
Edgar Allan Poe (emotional—
    speculated to have had manic-
    depressive bipolar disorder)
Aldous Huxley
    (visually impaired)
Agatha Christie (LD)
John Callahan (quadriplegic)
Ernest Hemingway (mental
    illness—suicidal depression)
Christopher Reeve (spinal injury)

Henry Winkler (dyslexia)
Patricia Polacco (dyslexia, dysgraphia)

More Categories

Political Figures

Janet Reno (Parkinson's disease)
Woodrow Wilson (LD)
Winston Churchill (LD)
Alexander the Great (epilepsy)
Franklin D. Roosevelt (polio)
Nelson Rockefeller (dyslexia)
Abraham Lincoln (may have had
    Marfan syndrome—connective
    tissue disorder)
John F. Kennedy (back injury)

Fictional Characters

Huck Finn (LD)
Captain Ahab (wooden leg)
Hunchback of Notre Dame
    (physical deformity)
Elmer Fudd (articulation disorder)
The Beast from *Beauty and the Beast*
    (physical deformity)
Forrest Gump (cognitive disability)

Life offers different choices to accommodate different tastes. Even the Yellow Pages lists an assortment of businesses to match individual needs. The universe is not made up of clones, with robotic blueprints, but people with unique fingerprints. Simply put, different vehicles accommodate different people, transporting them to the places they need to go. As long as the destination is safely reached, who has the right to judge one's needs or choices in life? A child with differing abilities must be understood as just that: a child with diverse and unique needs who is then educated within school systems and hopefully, if appropriate, within inclusive classrooms.

Education needs to make adjustments for learning, sensory, emotional, behavioral, developmental, communication, and physical differences as individual levels are uncovered. Teachers who are unwilling to accommodate these varying student needs are only making their own jobs more difficult. Complaining takes more time than accommodating. Besides, once accommodations are successfully in effect, it's smoother sailing for all, as teachers proudly watch students reap the rewards when they are allowed different ways to show what they know. *Ableism*, which involves thinking that people with a disability are not as capable as those without disabilities, exists in schools and many more settings. Additional experiences with students with disabilities, increased knowledge from literature and research, and infusing more positive examples about disabilities in content areas with role models will alter those attitudes (Storey, 2007).

Just think, how many ways can you . . . ? read a book	research a topic	shop	multiply numbers	sing a song
do laundry	cook a meal	communicate with a friend	interpret educational legislation and research	hear a conversation
appreciate flowers	vary teaching objectives	exercise	talk	include students in classrooms

Establishing Successful Inclusive Classrooms

Knowing more about the legislation, research, and often complicated terminology naturally leads to this next topic of determining ways teachers can meet individual student needs in their classrooms. These pedagogical strategies benefit any student population by teaching students on their ability levels with expansive instructional techniques, using sound learning principles as well as different modalities to appeal to multiple intelligences, interests, and background knowledge. All classroom learners benefit with interventions that have initials such as UbD (understanding by design) and UDL (universal design for learning). Thinking ahead about outcomes and being prepared with differentiated lessons and resources involve proactively planning and valuing just how desired lesson goals will reach the unique characteristics of students. As delineated in this chapter, proper content and teaching processes yield more effective student results, making us all more abled! Blank or *universal* templates for teacher-friendly implementation are included.

STRATEGIES THAT WORK WITH ALL LEARNERS

Special education strategies are applicable for all classroom populations. Sometimes in their haste to thrust knowledge upon students and deliver the curriculum, teachers lose children. In today's classrooms, it is unfair for teachers to ask all students to achieve the same competencies if the means of instruction and assessment are not varied. Some students when included also need to learn how to follow routines and know what to do when the routines change as well, dealing with transitions from one subject to the next, from one school to the next, and then being prepared for meaningful post-secondary choices. Diverse strategies develop competencies and create lifelong learners who view school as a place for successes, not failures. These experiences are then translated into productive adult choices. With proper methodology, inclusive classrooms benefit all.

Imagine entering a classroom where supportive, structured, research-based education allowed learners to effectively demonstrate their knowledge. Ingredients include relevant and meaningful instruction with diverse learning strategies that capitalize upon students' strengths. Or, what if such a classroom did not exist?

The *Audubonimable** Classroom

All of the birds decided that they needed to improve their status in the world, so they organized a school. The principal, Ms. Audubon, drew pictures and classified each type of bird. From the school's beginning, many disputes developed among the administration, community, teachers, and students, thwarting any educational successes.

The peacocks thought that they were the smartest, since they had the brightest multitude of colors. The owls didn't attend because basically they didn't give a hoot about learning. The mockingbirds laughingly thought the whole thing was a joke, while the hummingbirds constantly made noises in class and would not listen to Ms. Audubon.

Parents of other animals heard about the birds' attempts to soar above their young and decided to fill out applications for their offspring, but the birds would not allow their admission. The bird administration refused to give the camel an inch and would not permit the giraffe to stick its neck where it didn't belong. They simply tweeted at the other animals and told them if they were admitted, they would be like fish out of water and never achieve flying colors. They even made the deer homeless since they broke ground for the new school on the deer's land.

Eventually, some of the birds graduated from the school but were never successful in life, since the only subject they had been taught was flying. Ms. Audubon had sadly chosen a curriculum that parroted the birds' needs, but ignored the rest of the universe.

Questions for Discussion

- What do you think about this *abominable* classroom?
- Is it possible for educators to successfully teach students of all abilities together in one classroom?
- How can educators help students achieve *flying colors*?

---

*John James Audubon, known for his study of birds in the early 1800s, was not a success in school because he spent too much time outside watching and painting birds. This parable *stretches* his name and describes an *abominable* time when schools did not value other strengths, ignoring different ways of being smart. Today, the National Audubon Society works hard for the preservation of wildlife, while classrooms also work hard to preserve and cultivate individual minds and interests.

Moral: Diverse classrooms can help prepare all learners for life. This classroom is for the birds, since a homogenous, one-size-fits-all approach is an abomination.

EFFECTIVE INGREDIENTS

Hopefully, this book will give teachers palatable skills to appetizingly serve to hungry students who deserve more of an entrée than an *abominable* classroom. Educational practices can be compared to baking a cake.

What's involved in baking a cake?

1.

2.

3.

4.

5.

What's involved in effective education?

1.

2.

3.

4.

5.

Special TIPS

The following acronym, TIPS, highlights four major school considerations:

Topic (concrete vs. abstract concepts, unfamiliar subjects vs. material review, amount of prior knowledge, complexity, number of lessons in a unit, interest)

Individuals (including teachers, students, administration, parents, guardians, and related staff—encompasses supportive attitudes; skills; experiences; teaching styles; family views; awareness of dis*ability* characteristics with sensitivity preparation for teachers, students, and all staff; ongoing legislative parties; community advocates; and academic and emotional support to go with learners' motivations and cognitive levels)

Planning (goes beyond choosing a topic to how you are going to teach it— cooperative learning; learning stations; varying objectives/strategies; repeated exposure to subject matter; multiple intelligences; UbD to think about outcomes at the onset; UDL to honor existing differences and brain networks; possible modifications required; and matching instruction with individual needs and assessment methods, including both formal and informal reviews before, during, and after lesson to determine mastery level and instructional plans)

Setting (physical classroom design either in general education classroom or setting for smaller groups or individual students, texts, curriculum materials, school/district policies, class size, distractions, and environments that are conducive to adaptations)

APPLYING DIVERSE STRATEGIES

> It is difficult to apply diverse strategies without reflecting upon these educationally action-packed words.

Verb-Driven Education

assessing   exploring   researching   discussing   documenting   evaluating   monitoring

analyzing   refining   revising   reflecting   practicing   learning   socializing   generalizing

applying   observing   anticipating   communicating   interacting   role-playing   instructing

rewarding   informing   modeling   encouraging   enhancing   fostering   embracing   developing

Questions to Consider

- Who are you teaching?
- What are you teaching?
- How will you teach it?
- Did it work?

Directions: Choose 10 of these verbs and use them to write an effective educational paragraph, including **TIPS** above!

**Valuable and Applicable Things to Do in
All Classrooms on a Daily Basis**

1. Establish prior knowledge.

2. Plan lessons with structured objectives, allowing inter/post planning that delineates goals and desired student outcomes.

3. Proceed from the simple to the complex by using discrete task analysis, which breaks up the learning into its parts.

4. Use a step-by-step approach, teaching in small bites, with much practice and repetition.

5. Reinforce abstract concepts with concrete examples, such as looking at a map while walking around a neighborhood or reading actual street signs.

6. Think about possible accommodations and modifications that might be needed such as using a digital recorder for notes, reading math word problems aloud, or if necessary reducing an assignment.

7. Incorporate sensory elements—visual, auditory, and kinesthetic-tactile ones—across the disciplines.

8. Teach to strengths to help students compensate for weaknesses, such as encouraging a child to hop to math facts, if the child loves to move about but hates numbers.

9. Concentrate on individual children, not syndromes.

10. Provide opportunities for success to build self-esteem.

11. Give positives before negatives.

12. Use modeling with both teachers and peers.

13. Vary types of instruction and assessment, with multiple intelligences, cooperative learning, and universal designs.

14. Relate learning to children's lives using interest inventories.

15. Remember the basics such as teaching students proper hygiene, respecting others, effectively listening, or reading directions on a worksheet, in addition to the 3R's: Reading, 'Riting, and 'Rithmetic.

16. Establish a pleasant classroom environment that encourages students to ask questions and become actively involved in their learning.

17. Increase students' self-awareness of levels and progress.

18. Effectively communicate and collaborate with families, students, and colleagues, while smiling; it's contagious!

STRATEGIC CURRICULUM APPLICATIONS

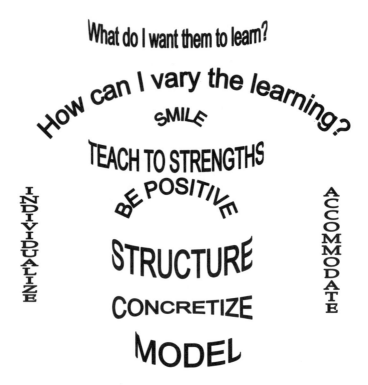

Knowing Students and What to Teach

Knowing what students already know can help the teacher gauge prescriptive instruction with clear-cut objectives. Basically, all students are learning, but on their individual levels within the same classroom. Teachers must be aware of levels of learning before instruction begins.

Levels of Learning

Independent Level

Student does not need instruction and can accomplish tasks independently, given direction and intermittent teacher reinforcement. Teacher first informally checks if prior knowledge is correct and periodically monitors.

Classroom examples: Student completed a unit about Native Americans and is asked to fill in a chart telling about the lives of different groups of Native Americans in the early colonies. Classroom text is used for information. Early learners might complete a study of patterns and then be asked to underscore the unit of each pattern constructed.

Instructional Level

Student needs teacher's guidance to understand concepts and cannot independently complete assignments without specific instruction.

Classroom examples: Student is reading a grade-level story with new vocabulary words. Story includes similes and metaphors, which the teacher needs to explain. Student then writes his or her own story, using figurative language. Another example could be one in which the student is sorting pictures of living and nonliving things. Teacher would need to clarify the critical attributes of living things.

Frustration Level

Learning is way too difficult for the student and can lead to shutdown, frustrations, and an unwillingness to complete academics assigned for fear of failure. In most cases, students are missing prerequisite knowledge.

Classroom examples: Student could not divide by two-digit divisors because he or she lacked the understanding of concepts of multiplication and division or did not know basic math facts. Student needs to work on independent or instructional levels, reviewing basic facts; proceed with clear-cut explanations, step-by-step instructions, and modeling.

Early learner may be unable to complete the construction of a number line; student needs to have multiple daily experiences counting aloud while pointing to each number.

> Teachers must continually assess prior, inter-, and post-knowledge levels!

ESTABLISHING PRIOR KNOWLEDGE

Pre-Assessment Guidelines for Teachers

Tell everything you know about _____ [TOPIC].

Sample Curriculum Questions

Who _____?

Where _____?

Why _____?

When _____?

How _____?

What _____?

Grades K–2

What is a community?

Where do earthworms live?

How do you spell

Grades 3–5

Why does it rain?

Where did the Pilgrims land? Show your answer on a map of the United States.

Which of the following dictionary guidewords will help you locate the word *learn*?

• FRIEND—FUNNY   • LIGHT—LOUD   • LAUGH—LIP

Grades 6–8

Identify and list the contributions of this civilization:

When was World War II?

How would you solve this problem? $2a + 6 = 16$

Grades 9–12

What are appropriate ways to behave in a job interview?

How can elements form compounds?

What plays were written by William Shakespeare?

Name an Asian country.

After the pre-assessment, which outlines varying levels of prior student knowledge, the teacher can address the different learning needs of the class. Students are divided into cooperative groups, working together to understand more about any given curriculum topic, learning on appropriate individual levels.

Some Cooperative Group Ideas

- A group of students could write from picture prompts on any topic, using a variety of genre and writing techniques, giving each picture a meaningful caption.
- Other students could use textbooks to create time lines of historical dates, define/review vocabulary, or answer content-related questions with research.
- Another group might design a product using auditory, visual, and tactile/kinesthetic learning styles, or complete assignments at classroom stations, maybe role-playing academic or social situations, or debating viewpoints.
- Students could answer or design curriculum-related WebQuests, given approved sites to work from.

Divided-Column Charts

Divided charts are quick classroom guides to levels. The first column asks for background knowledge about any subject, and at a quick glance helps the teacher assess varying classroom levels, while at the same time dispelling any myths or incorrect information. The second column, telling what students know, is vital because the students' questions, needs, and concerns are identified, thereby letting instruction fit students' levels. The final TBC (to be continued) column is left blank, since further study, research, and experiences later on add to this column. Cooperative roles such as these are then assigned:

Recorder (writes on chart paper for class gallery walk)

Reader (shares findings with other groups)

Focuser (assures that group members concentrate on the task)

Goodies person (gathers the chart paper, tape, markers, etc.)

Processor (helps others apply thoughts to the assigned task)

Encourager (compliments and acknowledges contributions of others)

To establish equal, simultaneous, and individual participation, each person records the answers on individual charts. The recorder transcribes the final copy on larger paper that will be posted in the classroom, allowing the entire class to see each group's response in a gallery walk. In this scenario, children are learning alongside each other, under the teacher's direction.

Curriculum connection is shown with a sample topic on dis*abilities*. The positive effects of prior knowledge are evident, from courses in biology (Ozuru, Dempsey, & McNamara, 2009) to teachers' perceptions about inclusion (Symeonidou & Phtiaka, 2009), or in reading with patterns in books such as repetition, alphabetical progression, and counting, since schema are more predictable within students' prior experiences and knowledge (Zipprich, Grace, & Grote-Garcia, 2009). Charts like these help establish students' independent, instructional, and frustration levels on any topic. The last column (TBC) is revisited after the unit of learning is completed and can also be an assessment tool. Using three-columned learning or pre-assessment questions establishes prior knowledge before learning misconceptions are evidenced by both teachers and students. The ultimate goal is to prevent incorrect prior knowledge from interfering with the learning process.

Prior Knowledge About *Special* Education

Directions: Write things you know about dis*abilities,* special education, and inclusion in the first column. In the second column, list all of your concerns and topics you would like to know more about. Leave the last column vacant; this is the one you will revisit later on to determine if needs and questions in the second column were addressed.

Special Education Inclusion Disabilities	? Tell me more about that	TBC (To Be Continued)
Independent Level	Instructional Level	Assessment Level

Pre-Assessment at a Glance

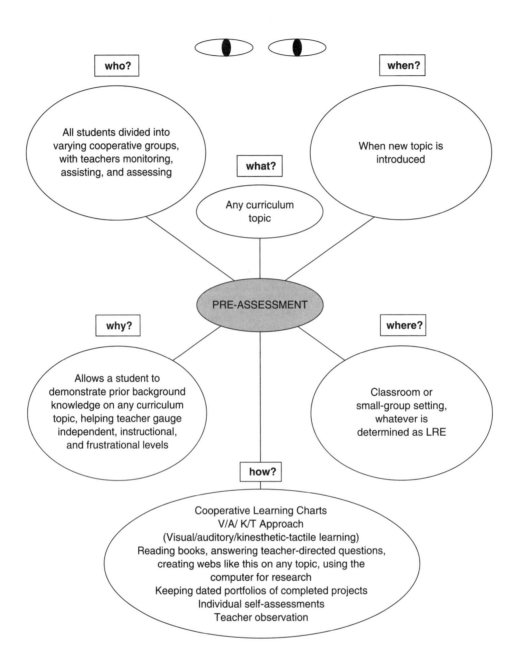

who?

All students divided into varying cooperative groups, with teachers monitoring, assisting, and assessing

what?

Any curriculum topic

when?

When new topic is introduced

PRE-ASSESSMENT

why?

Allows a student to demonstrate prior background knowledge on any curriculum topic, helping teacher gauge independent, instructional, and frustrational levels

where?

Classroom or small-group setting, whatever is determined as LRE

how?

Cooperative Learning Charts
V/A/ K/T Approach
(Visual/auditory/kinesthetic-tactile learning)
Reading books, answering teacher-directed questions, creating webs like this on any topic, using the computer for research
Keeping dated portfolios of completed projects
Individual self-assessments
Teacher observation

SCORING WITH METACOGNITION
(KNOWING WHAT YOU KNOW)

Where do you begin? *Awareness* is definitely the first step. A massive dose of *metacognition* for all involved parties is highly recommended. Without motivation and a good measure of perseverance, reaching any goal is a bit like running on a treadmill, since your destination remains the same. Basic education involves learning objectives but must also include effective anticipatory sets that motivate, entice, and encourage students to listen and learn. Without the right attitude, even the best research-proven strategies will fail. Questions to ponder include the following:

> Why are the students there?
> Why are the teachers there?

There's a difference in the learning outcomes if students perceive themselves as *school prisoners rather than eager participants* in the learning process. This attitude applies to the teaching staff as well. Again, metacognition is critical.

Students can keep track of their own grades and behavior in their portfolios and decide on future goals. They need to ask themselves, *How am I doing? Do my grades and behavior show improvement? What is my goal?* Learning success is the ultimate goal of all education.

Being goal-oriented is the reason hockey fans scream deliriously as the puck reaches the net and the team scores a goal, but what is the goal of special education or perhaps for all education? Those who enjoy math might love deciphering the following mathematical self-correcting exercise to discover the goal of *special* education.

THE GOAL OF *SPECIAL* EDUCATION

Directions: Solve each mathematical problem and place the correct letter above each blank. Numbered answers correspond to the order of the letters in the alphabet as shown in the code below. Try to think of different mathematical problems, without duplicating the ones on this page, to complete the rest of the sentence. The message reveals the goal of *special* education.

<u>T</u>   <u>O</u>   __   __   __   __   __   __   __

5×4   12+3   32÷2   6×3   60÷12   4×4   10÷10   9×2   30÷6

__   __   __   __   __   __   __   __   __   __   __   __   __

9÷3   16÷2   3×3   9+3   20−16   36÷2   40÷8   2×7   10×2   30÷2   3×4   5×1   18÷18   −5+9

__   __   __   __   __   __   __   __   __   __

8×2   12+6   3×5   −8+12   63÷3   27÷9   10×2   54÷6   11×2   3+2

__   __   __   __   __   __   __   __   __   __   __

63÷7   30−16   🕐   3+2   9×2−2   12÷2−1   7×2   100÷25   100÷20   9+5   1000÷50

L   I   V   E   S   A   S
__   __   __   __   __   __   __

M   E   M   B   E   R   S
__   __   __   __   __   __   __

O   F   T   H   E   A   D   U   L   T
__   __   __   __   __   __   __   __   __   __

C   O   M   M   U   N   I   T   Y.
__   __   __   __   __   __   __   __   __

A B C D E F G H I J K L M N O P Q R S T U V W X Y Z

1 2 3 4 5 6 7 8 9 10 11 12 13 14 15 16 17 18 19 20 21 22 23 24 25 26

Self-Checking Exercises

The preceding exercise assumed specific prior mathematical knowledge. Comfort levels, along with time taken to complete the exercise, may vary, as will individual motivation and frustration. The self-checking component allows students of all ages to gain their own feedback, before teachers correct their mistakes. Adding this type of self-correcting exercise is also interdisciplinary, connecting math skills with reading. Mathematical problems will vary, depending upon student levels of learning. It's an excellent avenue to reinforce computational skills, while reading about the main idea in the science, social studies, art, music, or language domains.

NUMBERS + LETTERS + WORDS = RETENTION OF MEANINGFUL IDEAS

Directions: As you solve each mathematical problem, place the correct letter on each blank, since the numbered answers correspond to the order of the letters in the alphabet. The first word has been done for you. Then you can think of mathematical problems to match the remaining letters at the end of the sentence. Try to think of different problems without duplicating the ones on this page. If you have done everything correctly, you will discover . . .

PICK A CURRICULUM TOPIC AND DESIGN YOUR OWN ALPHABETICAL MESSAGE

A B C D E F G H I J K L M N O P Q R S T U V W X Y Z

1 2 3 4 5 6 7 8 9 10 11 12 13 14 15 16 17 18 19 20 21 22 23 24 25 26

MOTIVATING AND PERSONALIZING LEARNING CHOICES

It's amazing how some children are so turned off to learning. Even though education is compulsory, physical attendance alone does not constitute attention. If a student does not possess the drive or desire to learn, frustrated teachers perform to empty audiences. When interests are heightened, meaningful learning connections are made with more understandings achieved. By asking children what they like, learning can be personalized, allowing students to become more involved in their learning. Not every lesson can be tailored to each child's likes, but perhaps making personal connections can awaken a present body, but dormant mind, letting motivation be a precursor to learning.

When a teacher is selecting a reading book, it is important to know what a student likes. For example, if a child loves dogs but dislikes reading, by picking a compelling story such as *Old Yeller, Sounder,* or *Where the Red Fern Grows,* odds are that this particular student will be more drawn into the reading process. Interest inventories can also help in the writing process. Teachers who always assign writing topics are not allowing students to pick topics *from within.* Topics from within are the ones students will more freely write about. Although some writing assignments are mandatory, always giving students prompts is not allowing for the *impromptu creativity* that personal topics yield. For example, introducing a unit on poetry has more merit if initially you allow students to share their favorite poem, and then ask them to mirror that style. Knowing what students like actively involves them in their own learning destiny and will lead to future retention.

Interest Inventories

Teachers can motivate learners to make necessary connections to their own lives to achieve lasting insights. Some curriculum connections in Grades K–12 follow.

K–3

- Draw or cut out pictures from magazines of their favorite things.
- Word banks, clip art, or picture/visual dictionaries are also great alternatives.
- If help is needed with handwriting, configuration strategies, stencils, computer programs, templates for words, digital recordings, or scribing to a peer can be used as scaffolding techniques to improve the appearance of the printed word or to let interests be shared without requiring the handwriting component.

4–6

- Use an interest inventory for selecting writing topics during the year (see page 80).
- If possible, try to acknowledge students' likes and dislikes in the lessons.
- Have students periodically review inventories that they fill out at the beginning of the year, which can be conveniently kept in their writing folder to see if interests changed.

- Students exchange thoughts with peers by sharing ideas.
- Inventories can be turned into a class graph.

7–8

- Students create their own categories.
- Design a cartoon, advertisement, or chart based on interests.
- Create a poem, short story, news article, word search, picture book, or slide show.

9–12

- Compare students' interests to family/school surveys.
- Form cooperative writing groups based on student interests.
- Match interests with a variety of genres in reading and writing across all subjects.
- Collaborate with teachers of other disciplines to create interdisciplinary lessons that acknowledge and honor students' interests to increase motivation and time on task.

Another great advantage of interest inventories is their ability to draw students closer together. Students discover things about their peers they might never find out with the *heads-forward learning approach.* Socially, students become more interpersonal by sharing introspections. Teachers who complete and share the same interest inventory are making a meaningful bond that connects them to their students. Even teachers and students can have things in common. Learning about each other is very *interesting.* Overall, there are many merits obtained for all by asking, "What do you like?"

"What Do You Like?"

A Few of My Favorite Things

FOOD	PERSON	PLACE
BOOK	MOVIE	TV SHOW
SEASON	PET	CAR
SONG	SUBJECT	TIME

Exploring Potentials With Many Ways of Being Smart

Howard Gardner and his colleagues, working on a research project at Harvard Graduate School of Education (www.pz.harvard.edu/index.cfm), expanded the idea of intelligences to multiple domains such as logical thinking, linguistics, music, movement, interpersonal activities, and self-knowledge. As Gardner notably pointed out, intelligence is not always as quantifiable as measuring someone's height. According to this school of thought, since measurement of intelligence is not always exact, classroom teachers can help students learn to tap into their stronger intelligence, maximizing what they are good at, rather than instructing or assessing through weaknesses. This theory helps teachers and students to achieve more successes.

What Is Intelligence? Solving Problems,
Creating Products—Information

- We each have capabilities in varying degrees that are influenced by exposure and specific training.
- Students with disabilities need to work through their strengths (stronger intelligences to improve weaker ones). For example, children with learning disabilities who are weaker in verbal-linguistic and logical-mathematical intelligences may be stronger in visual-spatial and bodily-kinesthetic ones. Instruction then addresses individual differences via assignments, delivery, and assessments.
- Teachers must also be aware of their own preferred (stronger) intelligences, as well as their weaker ones, since sometimes teachers will shy away from their more uncomfortable ones. For example, I rarely sing in front of a class, due to what I perceive as my weaker intelligence (musical-rhythmic), yet I would encourage my students to display their own competence in the musical area and be aware of classroom sounds.

MULTIPLE INTELLIGENCES OF STUDENTS

Depending upon the students' stronger or preferable intelligences, these are some of the classroom behaviors that teachers may see. Nothing is this clear-cut, since students may have two or three favorite intelligences, but usually weaker ones are most evident. Knowing students better helps teachers to plan more productive lessons, tapping into student strengths.

Verbal-Linguistic

- Adept at offering excuses, student can convince you that the dog ate the homework.
- Even though verbal skills are child's preference, he or she may be overly sensitive to criticism or sarcastic remarks.
- Student may use acronyms or mnemonics to memorize written information.

Logical-Mathematical

- Student prefers a high degree of organization in a structured classroom.
- Usually not comfortable in chaotic settings
- Likely to be computer literate

Visual-Spatial

- Student can be overwhelmed or frustrated by print-only material or long written assignments.
- Often visualizes learning concepts
- Prefers concrete, semi-concrete, or semi-abstract levels of presentations
- May be a doodler. Determine if doodling interferes with learning before modifying behavior, since doodlers very often multitask and are actually listening.

Musical-Rhythmic

- High sensitivity to classroom sounds (e.g., quiet noises), human voices, and rhythmic patterns
- May tap fingers, hum, or whisper during silent reading

Bodily-Kinesthetic

- Has difficulty sitting still for long periods of time
- May be distracted by movement of others
- Will remember what is done rather than what is said

Naturalistic

- Pays attention to minute details, relationships, and sensory information
- Learns best when knowledge is connected to prior topics
- Quite aware of his or her place in surroundings

Interpersonal

- Learns best when allowed to interact with others
- Enjoys cooperative learning, peer editing, and team-building activities

Intrapersonal

- Needs wait time to respond to questions and reflect on learning
- Responds well to empowerment activities with choices in assignments
- Likes journals or writing notebooks for personal thoughts

Existentialist

- Asks questions as a critical thinker and problem solver
- Likes to reflect upon reasons for learning and nature of tasks

- Responds well to open discussions, quotes, questionnaires, surveys
- Thinks beyond sensory data

Multiple Intelligences Resources to Check Out

Armstrong, T. (2000). *Multiple intelligences.* Alexandria, VA: Association for Supervision and Curriculum Development.

Armstrong, T. (2003a). *The multiple intelligences of reading and writing: Making the words come alive.* Alexandria, VA: Association for Supervision and Curriculum Development.

Armstrong, T. (2003b). *You're smarter than you think. A kid's guide to multiple intelligences.* Minneapolis, MN: Free Spirit Publishing. (Dr. Armstrong's Web site is http://www.ThomasArmstrong .com)

Campbell, B. L., & Dickinson, D. (2004). *Teaching and learning through multiple intelligences.* Boston: Pearson Education.

Chen, J.-Q., Moran, S., & Gardner, H. (Eds.). (2009). *Multiple intelligences around the world.* San Francisco: Wiley.

Gardner, H. (1991). *The unschooled mind. How children think and how schools should teach.* New York: Basic Books.

Gardner, H. (1993a). *Creating minds.* New York: Basic Books.

Gardner, H. (1993b). *Frames of mind: The theory of multiple intelligences.* New York: Basic Books.

Gardner, H. (1993c). *Multiple intelligences: The theory in practice.* New York: Basic Books.

Gardner, H. (2006a). *The development and education of the mind: The collected works of Howard Gardner.* London: Routledge.

Gardner, H. (2006b). *Multiple intelligences: New horizons.* New York: Basic Books.

Project Zero, Harvard Graduate School of Education, 124 Mount Auburn Street, Fifth Floor, Cambridge, MA 02138, (617) 496–7097, http://www.pzweb.harvard.edu.

Silver, H., Strong, R., & Perini, M. (2000). *So each may learn.* Alexandria, VA: Association for Supervision and Curriculum Development.

MULTIPLE INTELLIGENCES SURVEY

Directions: Place the numbers 1 to 9 in the following boxes to rank your preferable intelligences, with "1" as your favorite intelligence, while "9" would be your least favorite intelligence. This will help you think about how you learn best.

Verbal-Linguistic

Interpersonal

Bodily-Kinesthetic

Naturalistic

Intrapersonal

Musical-Rhythmic
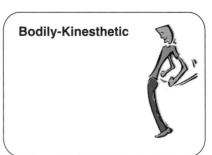

Visual-Spatial
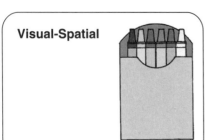

Logical-Mathematical
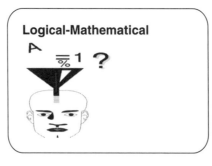

Existentialist

LEARNING ANALYSIS

Education requires preparation that analyzes each step of the learning process. The old adage "Rome was not built in a day" can most definitely be applied to many learning situations.

A Cupful of Learning

Illustrated below is a step-by-step drawing that transforms an oval into a cup. Draw the previous steps in the boxes at the right of each drawing. Repeating the prior steps each time yields further retention.

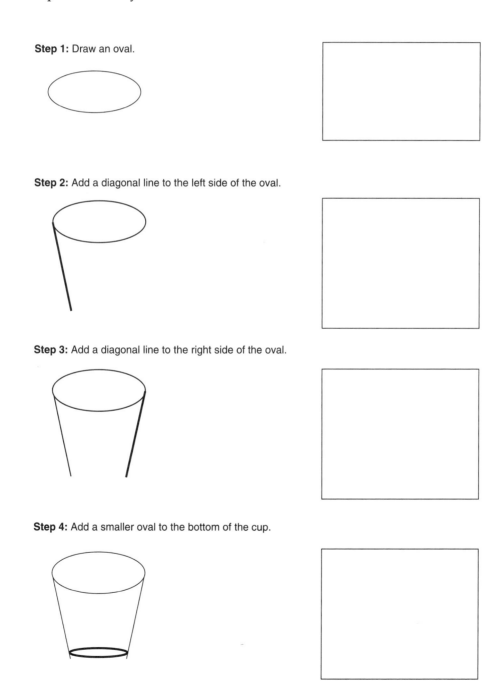

Step 1: Draw an oval.

Step 2: Add a diagonal line to the left side of the oval.

Step 3: Add a diagonal line to the right side of the oval.

Step 4: Add a smaller oval to the bottom of the cup.

Applying the Step-by-Step Process to Learning Situations

Suppose you were trying to teach a first grader how to write the letter "b."

Step 1: Draw a line.

Step 2: Place your pencil point about $\frac{2}{3}$ of the way down the line.

Step 3: Add a small circle from that point to the bottom of the line.

Sample Curriculum Connections

Reviewing each step along the way helps students to reach the end product. Whether a student is drawing a cup or writing the letter *b*, outlining individual skills involved can ensure mastery and further retention. Even though this is the old stick-and-ball method, the underlying principle is to help students with letter formation and directionality. To further assist learners, rules can be verbalized while using wide-lined paper at first, before paper with smaller, more confined lines is given. Again, breaking up the learning requires systematically outlining different components involved in lessons that some learners automatically grasp, while others need this type of instruction to master the same principles. For example, if a student's goal was to count objects 1–10, then at first that student may just practice counting and identifying sets of 1–4 objects, then add sets of 5–7, and ones with 8–10 objects, with review and repetition of all numbers from 1–10 to reinforce and periodically maintain the counting skills. Yes, it requires more time, but the results are worth it, because the former type of instruction, which does not match individual needs, is an unproductive use of student and teacher time and efforts. Better to master some steps than to be overwhelmed and frustrated by the entire lesson, and gain no skills at all. Specific grade-level examples of step-by-step applications follow.

K–2

Putting on a coat. Washing hands. Tying a shoe. Writing a heading on a paper. Drawing a picture of the student's neighborhood. Putting a group of words in alphabetical order. Counting how many syllables or phonemes are in a word. Classifying the shapes of objects. Identifying what sounds letters, digraphs, or diphthongs have. Ordering numbers. Copying patterns. Giving eye contact during conversations.

3–5

Dividing with two or more steps involved, with a one-digit divisor into a three-digit dividend. Identifying the subject of a sentence. Using guidewords. Estimating the product of 2 three-digit factors. Writing a paragraph about a favorite book. Telling what a plant needs to grow. Finding the greatest common factor of two numbers. Identifying the parts of words: prefixes, suffixes, and root words. Summarizing a book, chapter by chapter. Learning about weather or ecosystems. Working cooperatively with peers.

6–8

Using a microscope. Finding the mean, median, mode, and range of a set of numbers. Editing work on a computer word-processing program, such as Word. Diagramming a sentence into its subject and predicate. Identifying the direct and indirect objects of sentences. Describing the layers of the earth. Writing a five-paragraph essay. Finding the latitude and longitude of a city, or applying other map skills such as a scale of miles. Demonstrating appropriate daily hygiene. Creating a time frame for completing a long-range assignment.

9–12

Graphing a linear algebraic equation. Balancing chemical equations. Setting up a research paper. Writing a haiku. Identifying types of analogies. Describing how the stock market works. Telling how a bill becomes a law. Determining the correct change to be received in a store. Filling out a bank deposit slip. Traveling with public transportation. Writing a résumé. Transitioning to post-secondary settings.

Applying a Step-by-Step Approach to Learning

Directions: Think of particular content or functional areas and how tasks can be broken up into their learning components. Possibilities are endless, while results can be fruitful for all.

Topic: _____

Description of academic/functional objective:

_____

_____

_____

_____

Step 1: _____

Step 2: _____

Step 3: _____

Step 4: _____

Step 5: _____

Sample Activity: Adding Mixed Numbers

Learning Analysis Worksheet

Teachers review each step or skill and determine its components, deciding what accommodation/modification might be needed. Simply put, it's step-by-step teaching and learning. This grid is more than just task analysis, since teachers and students identify and strengthen exact areas of need within lessons. When teachers concretely keep track of steps, students are noticed and rewarded for incremental accomplishments.

Sample Activity: Adding Mixed Numbers

Steps	Yes/Not Yet	What Happened?	Accommodation/ Modification
1. Copy problem in notebook.	Y	Checked for accuracy	
2. Decide if fractions need common denominators.	Y	Identified fractions with different denominators	
3. Find common denominators.	Y	Able to find lowest common multiples	
4. Add fractions.	NY	Added denominators as well and combined whole numbers as part of the numerators	Separate whole numbers and fractions.
5. Reduce fractions or change to improper fractions.	NY	Cannot change improper to mixed numbers or vice versa	Review mixed-number conversions.
6. Add whole numbers.	Y	Accurately performed task at familiar level	
7. Combine whole numbers and fractions.	NY	Inverted fractions	Fraction circle manipulatives, semi-abstract presentation level, more guided and then independent practice

Learning Analysis Worksheet

Objective/Activity: _____

Steps	Yes/Not Yet	What Happened?	Accommodation/ Modification

Inclusive Student(s) _____

_____

_____

_____

Additional comments on how inclusive learner(s) performed:

_____

_____

_____

_____

CONCRETIZING LEARNING

> After you have established the student's prior knowledge and interests and have analyzed the learning steps and frequency, it is time for concretization.

Levels of Presentation

Concrete: Using a real object to demonstrate a concept (e.g., using a sneaker to teach how to tie a shoe or a meter stick to teach metrics, having students follow along on a computer while learning keyboarding skills, seeing a rock imprinted with a fossil or a cut tree to show the age rings inside, using coins to count change)

Semi-Concrete: Using a representation of an object to demonstrate a concept (e.g., using Cuisenaire rods, algebra tiles, and other manipulatives in math; cutting up an apple to represent fractions; or using a model of a heart in a biology class)

Semi-Abstract: Using a picture of an object to illustrate a word or concept (e.g., magazine pictures or clip art of words with initial or final consonants, artwork depicting events in American history, a diagram showing labels of microscope parts, U.S. Civil War time line, reproduction of a historical diary entry, or a cut-up map of the world to teach about plate tectonics)

Abstract: Teaching a concept from the textbook, without any visual or concrete accompaniment (e.g., using math worksheets or simply lecturing to students)

Cutting Up and Tossing the World

Concept to Be Demonstrated: Approximately ¾ of the world is water, and ¼ is land. To reinforce or concretize this concept, the teacher presents it on a semi-concrete level.

Examples: The teacher brings an apple to school and cuts it into four parts, sets aside three of those parts, and compares them to the water or blue part of the world. Later on, an assessment on this topic can include a circle, which students are asked to divide and label to represent the earth's water and land. These edible fractions now solidify the *global* learning. An inflatable globe is then tossed and caught for 50 trials while students record and chart the results of where their right index finger landed (water or land). Think of your own lesson to concretize.

Sources: Cassidy, J. (1994). *A kid's geography museum in a book.* Palo Alto, CA: Klutz Press. The tossing activity is a component of a Special Science Teams program developed at Rutgers, The State University of New Jersey, funded by the National Science Foundation and Research for Better Schools.

Teacher's Concrete Planner

Concept to Be Demonstrated: _____

Level of Presentation: (concrete, semi-concrete, semi-abstract, abstract)

Step-by-Step Procedure

_____

_____

_____

_____

_____

_____

Evaluation/Assessment

_____

_____

_____

_____

_____

_____

Follow-up

_____

_____

_____

_____

_____

_____

LEARNING DESIGNS

Universal Design for Learning (UDL)

UDL refers to universal design for learning, which advocates having learning options and accommodations already in place instead of waiting until needs arise. It initially entered society as an acronym that referred to architectural accessibility—for example, curb cuts on sidewalks or an inclined ramp for those in wheelchairs also helps parents with baby carriages and strollers or even a child navigating the city on a skateboard or roller skates. Another example is closed captioning—although initially intended to help those with hearing impairments, it universally appeals to people who speak another language with written transcriptions, as well as people with dyslexia who are learning to read. Classrooms with UDL practices vary presentations, expressions, and engagements with built-in flexibility for students' differing strengths. There is a wide array of resources, strategies, deliveries, sensory approaches, and advocacy for differentiation available right away, rather than waiting and then frantically scrounging for ideas, resources, and approaches when the needs arise.

Examples of UDL can include, but are not limited to, the following list:

- Setting up sections in the inclusive classroom as quieter study areas
- Establishing sponge activities and ongoing projects for students who master assignments before their peers, e.g., ongoing classroom newspaper or poetry corner or even writing, reading, math, art, or music stations with delineated activities prepared
- Understanding that some students need to move about to release excessive energy; setting up approved spaces and activities for students to productively channel what may otherwise be deemed as inappropriate behavior, e.g., word walls, sensory and motoric opportunities, brain breaks
- Transcribing novels and worksheets into Braille or larger font prior to the placement of a student with visual impairments or blindness
- Teaching sign language to the whole class
- Valuing multiple intelligences for instruction and assessment
- Having talking Web sites and digital texts, e.g., Talking Books, Digital Accessible Information System (Daisy)
- Setting up a strategy table with items such as pencil grips, page blockers, highlighters, counters, kneaded erasers, Koosh balls, transitional word lists, headphones, magnification pages, calculators, clips, index cards, and more

Classroom Application of Universal Design Principles With Access to All	
Descriptions	**Objectives**
Content-related visual dictionaries and thematic clip art	To help students better understand vocabulary by offering semi-abstract connections for written works and sometimes abstract texts, helping students to visualize the concepts
Textbooks and literature on tape, e.g., Daisy Talking Books, LeapFrog, or ones with same content, with perhaps larger font, different vocabulary, or fewer words on each page	Easier to follow comprehension of stories and information that honors the ages, integrity, and independence of all learners, even if hearing, visual, or reading levels may vary due to physical, sensory, perceptual, or learning differences
Cut-up tennis balls on the bottoms of chairs	Lowers extra noises and distractions and assists students with attention issues
Increased technology, e.g., Smart Boards, word prediction programs, sound field amplification systems, swivel chairs	Helps with note taking and focusing, especially beneficial for students with fine motor, attention, and hearing concerns such as dysgraphia, AD/HD, limited hearing, and auditory processing disorders
Lesson plans that consider individual students' needs, likes, and dislikes, e.g., more strategies built into lessons to help students with learning, such as outlines, graphic organizers, color coding, or infusing interest inventory responses into lessons	Motivates and connects students to learning on their instructional level rather than their frustrational level. Allows students with perceptual or processing issues to understand concepts and gives better organizational skills to all students. Assists with guided notes that later serve as study guides, which students independently review
Treating all students with dignity	Higher student self-esteem, which translates to taking ownership of learning and attempting even more difficult tasks, whether the student is nonverbal, has learning challenges, or is gifted
Computer technology UDL (www.cast.org) Picture Exchange Communication System (PECS), curriculum-related software sites, e.g., www.funbrain.com	Helps all students gain access to information, allowing for individual communication, sensory, physical, and cognitive levels, e.g., talking Web sites, math and reading software, worksheets and graphic organizers, curriculum-connected visuals, animated graphics, along with PowerPoint slide presentations
Portable, handheld, speaking electronic dictionaries, e.g., Franklin Speller	Allows all learners to hear the information to reinforce the written word. In addition to helping those students who are blind or have dyslexia, increases understandings of vocabulary in literature and curriculum without having the words, or encoding, decoding, or reading levels interfere with conceptual understandings
Modeling lessons with increased praise	Reinforces academic, social, emotional, and behavioral levels of students to increase motivation, self-esteem, self-efficacy, and academic focus

Adapted from Karten, T. (2008). *Embracing disabilities in the classroom: Strategies to maximize students' access.* Thousand Oaks, CA: Corwin.

Understanding by Design (UbD)

This approach of thinking about the curriculum offers a framework set up into stages, focused on several core concepts that are correlated with what students are expected to know for specific disciplines or skills. UbD involves thinking about the overall learning outcomes at the outset, rather than proceeding with a lesson and then setting up assessments that might focus upon trivial or irrelevant information. Stages are delineated as follows:

Stage 1: Desired results of what students will ultimately understand—the BIG picture

Stage 2: Indicators of real-world learning applications or assessment evidence

Stage 3: The instructional learning plan steps

In addition, UbD advocates continual reflection on the design of learning by fine-tuning assessments, the examination of results, quality and quantity of work, and appropriate student engagement with curriculum standards and desired skills. It involves designing diagnostic and formative assessments to yield effective, meaningful student accomplishments that encourage eventual independent transfer of learning based upon essential evidence and thoughtfully designed activities.

Source to review: Wiggins, G., & McTighe, J. (2005). *Understanding by design* (2nd ed.). Alexandria, VA: Association for Supervision and Curriculum Development.

The next model serves as an example of a UbD lesson on inclusion for preservice educators.

Stage 1: Preservice students will understand the complexities involved in designing an inclusive lesson for heterogeneous classes, answering the following questions:

- What will I do if I am teaching a lesson to students with a range of reading levels?
- How will I document students' progress?
- How will I honor students' academic and functional objectives?

Stage 2: Evidence and indicators of the learning will be 80% mastery of curriculum lesson objectives with students in inclusive fieldwork settings, thereby demonstrating knowledge and skills through research, discussion, planning, teamwork, curriculum-based oral and written assessments, student work samples, pre- and post-assessments, data review, and observation.

Stage 3: This stage will include instruction and demonstration of how to implement and honor multiple intelligences, cooperative learning activities, peer mentoring, and establishment of prior knowledge, with learning objectives in three levels of mastery under the qualifiers of baseline, more advanced, and challenging academic and functional objectives with differently leveled reading texts and appropriate vocabulary pretaught. Models related to the curriculum will be offered with student portfolios, work samples, data, and research monitored and reviewed to gauge progress and instructional pacing across subjects.

KINESTHETIC CONNECTIONS

Kinesthetic and tactile learning simply means moving, feeling, experiencing, touching, or manipulating learning objects to reinforce abstract concepts. *Kinesthetic* refers to body movements, while *tactile* pertains to the sense of touch. Examples include clay models of elements' electrons, neutrons, and protons; skywriting the shapes of letters with their fingers in the air; writing spelling words in salt; using raised glue to write words; using Cuisenaire rods, algebra tiles, yarn, or magnetic numbers; writing syllables on index cards; doing scientific experiments; and so on. Researchers have shown that exercise and physical activity meaningfully affect reading, spelling, math achievement, and memory, reducing stress and depression and increasing overall learning performance (Jensen, 2000; Mitchell, 2009; Ratey, 2008). Disassociated information will be better remembered if it has been repeatedly demonstrated in a concrete, meaningful way with movements that facilitate cognition, interpersonal connections, and class cohesiveness. Sometimes breaking away from the learning with meaningful activities actually improves comprehension, with opportunities for more attention after completing a physical activity. Perhaps that's why television programs have commercials every 15 minutes or so and then return to the scheduled programming!

Do remember that safety is paramount with appropriate levels of class management and student engagement that match students' individual IEP goals, interest levels, and recommended physical activity, e.g., adapted physical education (PE) or occupational therapy (OT) for students' fine or gross motor skills. Overall, the brain attends to *moving* physical activities!

The next concrete activity uses "meetballs." Materials needed are people arranged in small circles of 8–10 and a soft foam ball.

Meeting With Meetballs

Yes, that is spelled correctly. It's a way to remember names rather than wearing those stickers that say, "Hello, My Name Is _____." It beats walking into a store or restaurant and being personally greeted by total strangers since you have forgotten to remove the adhesive label. "Meetballs" help you to meet others!

Meetball Recipe

Directions: Form circles of 8 to 10 people and have them randomly toss a soft round object (e.g., a Koosh ball or Nerf ball) to each other. When someone receives the ball, the person says his or her name. The tossing continues until everyone feels confident about remembering each other's names. The next step is to try to remember a person's name and toss the ball to that person as you say the name. Adding more soft objects to simultaneously toss, and repeating or reversing the order, varies the game. If everyone already knows each other's names, personal information or answers to content/curriculum-related questions can be shared when the ball is caught. Sample curriculum connections follow.

Kinesthetic Curriculum Connections

Toss a ball around a classroom and ask students of varying ages and grade levels the following:

"What do you think about inclusion?"

"How did imperialism change the world?"

"What words begin with the consonant blend *tr?*"

"How can math help you be successful in life?"

"Who is your favorite character from literature?"

"When do earthquakes occur?"

"Why were Native Americans displaced by colonists?"

"What are the factors of the number 54?"

"How should you dress for a job interview?"

"Use the word *advantageous* in a meaningful sentence."

"Name some careers that incorporate geometry."

People Finders are another way to mobilize and think about learning concepts while interacting with one another. The *special* People Finder that follows is a perfect example of kinesthetic learning that leads to discussions on any given topic. Students rotate around the classroom, finding a peer who can sign a given descriptor (see below). People Finders can be designed by teachers or students on just about any curriculum topic.

A Special People Finder

Directions: Have participants circulate about the room and find someone who would sign his or her name by the appropriate descriptor. Continue until all lines are filled.

_____ Can read a newspaper while listening to the radio

_____ Believes IEPs are useful tools

_____ Thinks special education is heading in the right direction

_____ Likes frequent vacations

_____ Thinks a person who is blind can go bowling

_____ Sometimes needs things repeated several times

_____ Doesn't have a junk drawer at home

_____ Likes to use landmarks to find his or her way

_____ Has experienced a physical disability

_____ Thinks inclusive classrooms can be successful ones

_____ Has experienced frustrations with children

_____ Would like more planning time to implement ideas

_____ Makes lists to remember things

_____ Is very grateful for the computer spell checker

_____ Cannot assemble a swing set

_____ Hates to mow the lawn

_____ Thinks education needs more accountability

_____ Believes in the same standards for all children

_____ Does not read directions

_____ Has better receptive than expressive language

_____ Dislikes this *People Finder*

Eclectic People Finder Curriculum Connections

Find someone who would sign his or her name by the following descriptor:

_____ Knows why the American Civil War began

_____ Can name the steps in photosynthesis

_____ Knows the percent for the fraction 2/5

_____ Can identify the protagonist in *Macbeth*

_____ Can name the final consonant of this picture

_____ Knows the name of the planet closest to the sun

_____ Can describe an isthmus

_____ Knows the number of U.S. presidents

_____ Can tell what a mathematical product is

_____ Knows who painted the *Mona Lisa*

_____ Can say where the Olympic Games began

_____ Can identify three countries in Africa

_____ Can list the 13 original colonies

_____ Can name two adverbs

_____ Has read a historical novel

_____ Can hum "The Star-Spangled Banner"

_____ Can hop on one foot for 30 seconds

_____ Knows what the commutative property is

_____ Can spell two homonyms for *there*

_____ Can graph an inequality

_____ Can _____

Learning Strides

Kinesthetic cards are used to introduce a unit or topic or as a review of previously taught information. Learning material this way helps fidgety learners who need acceptable ways to channel excess motor energy. Socially, students are interacting with each other, instead of the *all heads facing forward while learning* mentality. Relinquishing control of the learning, the teacher then becomes more the facilitator of the knowledge than the disseminator. Classrooms might be noisier, but they are filled with the sounds of learning as students move about at the same time.

Sample Curriculum Connections for Matching Kinesthetic Cards

Directions: Teachers or students place questions and answers on two differently colored index cards. Cards are then shuffled and distributed to each student in the classroom, some receiving answers and the others receiving question cards. Students then walk around, finding an answer for their social studies or science question, synonyms for vocabulary words, or maybe a solution to an equation.

synonym for happy	content
How do you say, "My house is your house" in Spanish?	Mi casa es su casa.
A novel by Toni Morrison	*Beloved*
Name of this shape ⬡	hexagon

Playing charades with vocabulary words on index cards also works across subject areas.

More Kinesthetic Examples to Help Learning Jump Off the Page

Kinesthetically Teaching the Circumference of Circles

Form a circle while sitting on the floor, with one person in the middle, identified as the *center*. Then toss a foam ball from the center person to someone sitting on the outer circle or the *arc.* Each time the ball is passed to the person in the center, a *radius* is created. To illustrate the kinesthetic definition of *diameter,* pass the ball over the head of the person in the middle to someone else. Draw circles with radii and diameters for further concretization of these concepts. Teacher then models how multiplying the diameter by Pi, or π (3.14), will yield the *circumference,* or distance around the circle. Students check this out by taking a piece of yarn to measure around the circle and comparing that measurement to the product received when the diameter is multiplied by π. More-advanced students verify that for any circle, when you divide the circumference by the diameter, it will equal Pi. Students can use other circular objects such as paper plates or coins. Some students will need more guidance, while others will independently complete more intricate problems, such as figuring out the radius based on the circumference.

Kinesthetically Teaching New Vocabulary Words, Learning

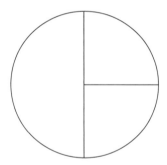

About Characters in a Fictional Book or Historical Figures

Cooperatively create dramatic skits. While preparing demonstrations, notice how much extra learning is involved. Suddenly students ask, "Can we use the textbook or story for more information?" Eureka! Try pantomiming vocabulary words, settings from novels, and so on.

Kinesthetically Teaching How to Follow Directions

Place a compass rose on the chalkboard and point to specific directions such as north, south, east, and west. On a simpler level, just call the arrows, up, down, left, or right. For more complexity, southwest, southeast, northeast, and northwest can be added. Ask everyone to stand up and point their arms in the direction that a leader indicates or says. As students progress, the teacher can then instruct them to point or say the opposite direction. It's a quick way to release energy while listening and following directions. When the students sit down, notice how much more attentive they are.

Kinesthetically Helping Students to Spell and Decode Words

Writing letters in the air or in a bowl of salt, or with Ziploc bags filled with paint or shaving cream, clapping hands, or tapping fingers or feet to letters and syllables are other ways to learn letters and word parts.

Kinesthetically Teaching Left to Right Progression in Reading

A student creates a sentence by writing one word on each index card. Then cards can be rearranged or different ones inserted in the original sentence, changing and expanding the meaning or creating questions. Here are some examples: "I like ice cream." "Do you like ice cream?" "I do like ice cream." Verbs, nouns, adjectives, and adverbs can be placed on different-colored index cards, along with punctuation marks.

Kinesthetically Teaching the Song "B-I-N-G-O"

Students sometimes have a difficult time learning when to clap without singing. Select five students and give them each one letter card. Students hold up their letter card each time that letter is sung. When it is time to delete that letter and clap, that student sits down (in place). The class then claps each time they come to a seated student.

Kinesthetically Teaching Angles

Students in groups of three are each given a card with a point on it, labeled A, B, or C. They are then asked to collectively form an angle by two students stretching out their arms as rays in opposite directions, while the third student is the vertex, naming either angle A, B, or C. Each time the vertex is changed, the angle is renamed. Other variations can include more students as arrows to represent rays, line segments with students' fists as endpoints or outstretched arms to indicate that the line continues in one or both directions, while squares and rectangles will have four vertices, and other polygons such as hexagons will be two groups of three with differently labeled points. The *point* is that the kinesthetic possibilities here are *endless*!

Kinesthetically Surveying Class Responses to Find Out What Students Know

When teachers want to simultaneously ascertain the understandings of the whole class, they can ask students to respond to written or oral multiple-choice questions by holding up an appropriate number of fingers that correspond to their answer choice—e.g., pointer finger for choice *a*, pointer and middle finger held up together for choice *b*, three fingers for choice *c*, four fingers for choice *d*, or holding up a fist to indicate *I don't know*. Teachers can use this approach or clear communication boards holding marked worksheets when delivering interactive quizzes online, e.g., www.brainpop.com, using a *Who Wants to Be a Millionaire?* format, or self-created curriculum-based verbal queries to establish prior or post knowledge. This quick assessment then assists teachers in gauging what instruction or skills to repeat or how to divide students in the class into review, maintenance, or accelerated learning teams and groups. If there are two teachers or an instructional assistant in the room, he or she could quickly check off kinesthetic student choices.

Can I Kinesthetically Teach This?

(Remember that kinesthetic teaching means students will be moving, feeling, experiencing, touching, or manipulating learning objects or representations of concepts.)

Think of a Curriculum Topic: _____

Kinesthetic Plan (A Walk-Through Lesson):

Objective: _____

_____

Materials: _____

_____

Procedure: _____

_____

Follow-up: _____

_____

SENSORY APPROACHES AND LEARNING MODALITIES

> Modalities refer to the way that sensory information is used to learn. People usually process information through the modalities of visual, auditory, and kinesthetic cues. Generally, individuals learn by seeing, hearing, touching, doing, and moving. Sometimes one sense of learning is stronger than another. Modalities affect how you interpret reality and communicate with others. Senses are the main tools you use to learn about your environment.

Teachers can incorporate sensory elements into lessons to *reinforce learning and the retention of concepts.* If a student is weak or deficient in one modality, teachers can reinforce the learning by presenting facts through a different one. For example, provide more visuals to someone with hearing impairments and more auditory stimuli to students with visual needs. I once arranged for a speaker who is blind to talk to a fifth-grade class about her disability. She was well received by the class who gave her flowers and a taped thank-you message as their appreciation!

Some still remember the lunchroom smell of their elementary school's cafeteria. What about the smell of those old mimeograph sheets? Quite pungent! My son's friend claimed that when he studied, he wore certain cologne, and then when he took the test, he wore it again to trigger his memory. There are also studies about the healthy effects of aromatherapy, e.g., reducing stress, anxiety, and depression (http://health.top54u.com/post/Positive-Effects-of-Aromatherapy.aspx). Think about all those thriving candle shops!

Children can be helped to learn through many modalities. Tracing letters in the air or in a bowl of salt can tactilely reinforce handwriting skills more effectively than just using paper and pencil. Seeing a documentary about World War II can make more of an impression on students than just reading textbook pages. High school science without laboratory experiments, studying art without experiencing different media, talking about music instead of listening to it, or reading about exercise without sweating has less learning merit. A learning theorist, Helen Irlen (www.latitudes.org/articles/irlen_tips_research.htm), talks about the power of different colors to help students remember information better, such as when different-colored highlighters are used. Colored overlays placed over reading material block out distractions and help some students read better. Even having them write their work on yellow lined paper or copying and distributing worksheets and tests on colored paper assists students. Removing students from window glare beneficially removes distractions. Auditory factors also come into play under the topic of sensory influences. Even *quiet sounds* in the environment will sometimes distract learners who are never bothered by their own extra noises. Sensory awareness is an important learning component. "Touchable" learning material can be as meaningful as those wooden blocks we eagerly manipulated in childhood.

For more information about sensory integration for children with and without disabilities, investigate www.fhsensory.com, *The Out-of-Sync Child*, by C. Kranowitz, and *Parenting a Child With Sensory Processing Disorder*, by C. Auer and S. Blumberg.

Concretizing Conceptual Relationships

Relationships of objects are reinforced by using sensory modalities. Manipulating three different-sized objects easily concretizes the concepts of small, smaller, smallest or large, larger, largest, allowing degrees of differences to be seen in similar objects. For example, apples, oranges, and balls all have spherical shapes, although not everything round can be eaten. Understanding the difference between two words such as *hard* and *harder* can be demonstrated with a bar of soap and a rock, by tactilely concluding that one can dig one's fingernail into the soap, but not into the rock. Gathering their own classroom items, students can classify them according to different sensory similarities or differences to develop higher-level thinking skills. Students simply fold lined paper into three columns, listing items, similarities, and differences under appropriate headings. Higher-level relationships can be investigated, while complexities across grades and levels of learners can vary.

Self-Discovery Chart

Items	Similar	Different
Pencil, chalk, marker	All used for writing	Materials, texture, width, color, malleability

Sensational Party: What Do I See, Hear, Smell, Taste, and Touch?

Directions: Design a *sensational* party. Pick a setting and list what you see, hear, smell, taste, or might touch. Senses help us to visualize learning, understand relationships, and thereby concretize many otherwise abstract (or *senseless*) concepts.

Possible Settings

Beach	Carnival	Laboratory	
Park	North Pole	Museum	Battlefield
Baseball Field	Football/Hockey Game	12th Century	Video Arcade
Rainforest	Library	Safari	Parthenon
	Other?		

Sights	Sounds	Smells	Tastes	Touch

Visualization: Abstract Thinking

Visualizing concepts is a way to internalize and concretize otherwise abstractly presented facts, rather than just being recipients of boring lectures or dry textbook facts. Imagining encourages role-play, with learning protagonists. Close your eyes and imagine!

Imaginable Curriculum Connections

Social Studies: Imagine that you are a slave, living in the colony of Virginia in the year 1740, being put up for auction. Look around and describe your thoughts.

Science: You are a plant with roots too small for your pot. How do you feel? What are your needs? Describe your greatest wish.

Math: You are a number that is a multiple of 7, but less than 100. Who are your friends? Place yourself in several computational word problems and solve them.

Reading: You are the best friend of a story's main character. What activities do you do together? Where would you vacation? Tell how you would change the plot.

Think of your own learning visualizations:

Imagine . . .

Next, Writing and Applying the IEP (Individualized Education Program)

This chapter offers more information on what to include in IEPs, as well as ways to effectively implement and document them in individual classrooms. Guidelines for using and writing effective IEPs that align with the curriculum will benefit all students. The children of today are tomorrow's workforce and need the right skills to make productive contributions. The delivery of the IEP, as shown in this chapter, need not be frustrating or complicated. It is a plan for teachers, parents, guardians, students, and all staff who must act as allies toward the achievement of written, agreed-upon, realistic school goals.

After the reauthorization of IDEA in 2004, goals written in IEPs, although still individualized, are more aligned with the general education curriculum with evidence-based practices and instruction. This requires a planning process that advocates higher expectations for students with IEPs. It involves the general education curriculum and all that then follows in life, with an educational program that prepares students to be part of society with both academic and functional skills. Legislation for students with disabilities has evolved throughout the decades, beginning with PL 94-142 in 1975 and progressing to IDEA 1990, then to amendments in 1997, with more improvements and reauthorizations in 2004. IEPs before the 2004 reauthorization are compared to present practices in the chart that follows.

Prior IEP mind-sets, before 2004 reauthorization	Present IEP mind-sets now based upon legislative impacts
Less inclusion of students with disabilities with GE curriculum standards and classroom objectives	GE curriculum standards aligned with the needs of students in inclusive classrooms
Deficit-driven instruction based on what students cannot do, often inadvertently highlighting students' weaknesses	Growth paradigm for what students can and will achieve, based upon strengths and research-based strategies to achieve desired outcomes
Students with disabilities were more often omitted from district and statewide testing.	Students with disabilities are part of the accountability picture with district and statewide assessments, unless students have severe cognitive disabilities and must take alternate assessments.
Separate GE & SE programs and facilities for students, with less collaboration between staff	Increased collaboration between GE and SE programs and staff within inclusive environments; consultative services with common threads intertwined and woven across disciplines, facilities, and programs
Modifications automatically offered, sometimes assuming that students *can't get it*, before saying, *"How will they get it?"*	Exploration of accommodations vs. modifications without the automatic dilution of outcomes, saying, *"We'll figure out a way that the students will get it!"*
More time for other activities, involving daily living and functional skills	Fun activities often sacrificed in favor of academic skills, test preparation, and data collection
Lack of research-based criteria before the recommendation of IEP services and programs; increased referrals for special education	More use of research-based interventions in classrooms even before IEPs are written, taking proactive RTI steps instead of waiting for students to fail, or automatic testing and labeling students with classifications

PRACTICAL GUIDELINES FOR USING AND WRITING THE IEP

What Exactly Is an IEP?

- Written plan for a child who is eligible for special education services
- Based upon student's individual needs
- Developed specialized instruction and services with reviews and revisions
- Present level of academic achievement and functional performance (PLAAFP) is stated; e.g., current reading, math, spelling, language, perceptual, social skills are delineated
- Psychoeducational evaluations, including observation and discussion with the students, teachers, staff, parents, and guardians
- Input from parents and guardians concerning developmental history

- Integration of all home and school reports
- Decisions about placement based upon current levels of performance, which are determined by multidisciplinary instructional support groups and teams, not the availability of services
- Environmental and ecological circumstances that consider how and where skills will be both learned and applied within school and outside community settings
- Determination of extent to which the student can participate in general educational programs
- Necessary aids, supports, and related services
- Accommodations and modifications listed, including frequency, location, and duration of services
- Parent and guardian participation and communication are incorporated in both planning stages and reporting child's progress.
- General and special education teachers are included.
- Any teachers or staff considered by the school district or families to be beneficial to the student's success in school are included in IEP planning with faculty members such as speech therapists, occupational therapists, physical therapists, mobility trainers, guidance counselors, instructional assistants, and paraprofessionals.
- All parties who work with student must read the IEP to effectively apply appropriate strategies, unless parents or guardians prohibit certain people from accessing the document, as allowed in some states.
- IDEA does not use the term *inclusion*; however, it does require school districts to place the students in the least restrictive environment (LRE) to the maximum extent appropriate, alongside their nondisabled peers, unless the nature or severity of the disability is such that success in the general education classroom cannot be achieved, even with the use of supplementary aids or services.
- If the IEP cannot be implemented in the regular or general education classroom of the school the child would attend if not disabled, then that classroom is not the LRE placement for that child. It would render the general education classroom as inappropriate.
- Student needs are the basis for the child's placement.
- Supplementary aids and services such as a note taker, instructional assistant, computer, communication boards, and Braille are specifically described in the IEP.
- A child can receive related medical services, unless it would require the direct supervision of a physician and cause an undue burden upon the district. Examples of appropriate services are catheterizations or feeding tubes administered by a trained school nurse.
- Both educational and nonacademic benefits to the student with a disability must be considered in placement decisions.
- Students are exempt from a standardized assessment if it is stated in the IEP; e.g., alternate means of assessment with modified achievement standards are permitted for a small percentage of those students with IEPs, who even with accommodations cannot participate in the standardized testing. States must then ascertain these students' proficiencies on alternate assessment tests to demonstrate that learning has taken place. These alternate evaluations are

based upon modified achievement standards with assessments then developed by individual states.

- IDEIA (Individuals with Disabilities Education Improvement Act) states that when a student reaches the age of 16, the IEP must include a statement of transitional service needs. This statement can also be included at a younger age, if it is appropriate to that child's individual needs. The statement focuses on post-school goals, but most important, it stipulates what educational experiences or vocational training will best suit a particular child's program. The Division of Vocational Rehabilitation Services (DVRS) for each state and the Division on Career Development and Transition (www.dcdt.org), a division of the CEC (www.cec.sped.org), offer technical consultation and assistance for vocational training and guidance with employment issues. Transition services are detailed in students' IEPs, with specific statements about adult plans. Community involvement, related services, employment, functional living skills, and the establishment of connections with outside agencies are included. Skills need to be included in the IEP to prepare the student toward this goal. For instance, self-help skills, personal hygiene, other independent-living skills, plans for community integration, or vocational training are some objectives that may be applicable. Teenagers can also be helped with transition to life after high school, whether that decision involves continued education or entrance into the workforce, such as offering life skills classes in school settings.

- The IEP provides an appropriate educational experience for each student, with effective communication between home and school. It includes continuity of services based upon students' present levels of performance with consideration toward the future. There is a zero-reject clause, meaning that no child with a disability can be excluded from education. The evaluation must also consider the student's culture, language, and background.

- Noncompliance with the law means that states and school districts will face consequences for ignoring the mandates outlined in IDEA.

Check with local curriculum guidelines and state assessment requirements. The federal law mandates what information must be included in the IEP, but each state or individual school system decides what the IEP paperwork will look like. There is no standard IEP form, as evidenced by its varying appearance in different states and districts. IDEA revisions aimed at reducing paperwork by clarifying that no additional information is necessary in the IEP, beyond what federal regulations require.

The individualized document is collaboratively planned with input from the following stakeholders:

- Special education teachers
- General education teachers
- Parents or guardians
- Administration

- Team members known in some states with initials such as CST (Child Study Team), SST (Student Study Team), IST (Instructional Support Team), MET (Multidisciplinary Evaluation Team), or MDT (Multidisciplinary Team). Members of these teams usually include a social worker, learning disabilities teacher consultant, and a school psychologist.
- Case manager, who may be a member of the team
- Speech/language therapist
- Other related staff members
- Student (if age and input are appropriate)

Inclusive IEP Elements

- Present levels of academic achievement and functional performance (PLAAFP)
- Individualized goals and benchmarks as major components of what you want the child to achieve. The Individuals with Disabilities Improvement Education Act of 2004 eliminated benchmarks and short-term objectives, which are now only required for those students with severe cognitive disabilities. States can include them but are not required to do so.
- Emphasis on student outcomes rather than compliance
- Modifications and supplementary aids or services needed in the general or special classroom along with supports for extracurricular/nonacademic activities
- Method and schedule for reporting student's progress, e.g., quarterly reports, such as report cards
- Related services that can include but are not limited to speech, occupational therapy, physical therapy, or appropriate technology
- Behavioral plan and interventions
- Extended school year (ESY) if appropriate to maintain skills
- Statement of transitional services mandated at age 16, or older. Can develop appropriate future goals if student is younger
- Extent of participation in district and state assessment programs and graduation requirements
- Signed parental/guardian consent and signatures of all who planned the IEP

APPROPRIATE GOALS AND SKILLS
TO CONSIDER WHEN WRITING AN IEP

Phonics/Word Identification—Clapping to syllables, identifying consonant clusters, decoding grade-level word lists or street signs, isolating prefixes and suffixes

Reading Comprehension—Locating the main idea; knowing the elements of a story (setting, characters, plot, resolution); inferential reading skills (cause and effect, sequencing events, prediction of outcomes); ordering from a menu; reading a newspaper or periodical, e.g., to understand current events, finding out the weather, reading classifieds, selecting a time and location for a movie, and more

Mathematics—Counting objects, ordering numbers, finding patterns, computations with all operations, fractions, measurements, understanding and unraveling word problems, identifying geometric shapes, solving algebraic expressions, telling time, getting change in a store, figuring out the answers to vertex-edge problems

Science—Seasons; plants; senses; nutrition; scientific methods such as hypothesis or observation; reading a periodic table; balancing formulas; relating scientific principles to concrete daily activities in physics, chemistry, health, and more

Social Studies—Community, map skills, world history, civil rights, economics, cultural awareness, character education, global connections

Language—Listening, speaking, capitalization, punctuation, grammar, categorizing words, writing paragraphs, letter writing, essays, research reports, poems, figurative language, responding to prompts with speculative essays

Computers—Identifying computer parts, keyboarding, bolding text, preparing a résumé, writing a research report, finding clip art, paraphrasing online sources

Study Skills—Attending to the teacher, taking notes, bringing home appropriate books, preparing for tests and long-range assignments, organizing work area, maintaining a daily list of completed assignments, communicating needs

Motor Skills

Gross Motor—Sitting or standing balance, sitting upright in a wheelchair, activities with multiple motor movements, appropriate touching, throwing a ball, laterality

Fine Motor—Manuscript or cursive handwriting or lettering, holding a pencil or crayon, cutting, folding paper, writing within given parameters, using utensils

Communication Skills

Vocalizations, articulations, gestures, receptive (understanding) and expressive (speaking) language, following directions, using proper volume when speaking, exhibiting conversation skills, expressing ideas verbally and nonverbally

Cognitive

Auditory—Remembering and processing information, discriminating between sounds of letters, understanding cues from environmental sounds such as a fire drill, retelling a story using the correct sequence, filtering out background noises from essentials

Visual—Matching colors and shapes, seeing likeness and differences of similar letters (b, d, p), classifying pictures or written words into categories, understanding figure–ground relationship, following a written line of print, lining up math problems, forming images to improve visual memory, recognizing patterns

Preparation for Adult Living

- Knowing home address and number
- Reading circulars
- Shopping in a store
- Writing a letter
- Talking on a phone
- Holding utensils
- Proper hygiene
- Reading road signs
- Using a telephone directory
- Reading a map
- Developing interpersonal skills
- Sequencing daily events
- Maintaining a calendar
- Signing name on a check
- Balancing a checkbook
- Using a calculator
- Counting change
- Being punctual
- Reading bus or train schedules
- Identifying emergency signs
- Using conversational skills
- Establishing eye contact
- Interacting appropriately with peers and strangers
- Being goal-oriented
- Walking around a shopping mall
- Ordering food in a restaurant
- Understanding safety issues such as with household appliances, toaster, stove, iron
- Applying first-aid skills
- Texting, emailing, safely communicating online

Social Goals

Better Interpersonal Skills. Saying thank you, respecting the rule that one person speaks at a time, smiling, increasing positive interactions with peers, working effectively in cooperative groups, engaging in conversation, peer tutoring

More Self-Control and Self-Awareness of Behavior. Keeping a journal, exhibiting appropriate behavior in stressful situations, using a problem log, thinking before reacting, substituting an acceptable response, charting or graphing daily moods, giving more positive peer and self-references

Appropriate Classroom and School Behavior. Staying in seat, raising hand in class, using appropriate voice volume, following classroom routine, walking quietly in the hallway, sitting properly on the bus, being prepared and motivated to learn

Behavioral Considerations

- Using proactive strategies that reinforce appropriate behavior and teach problem solving
- Determining if misbehavior is related to the disability (e.g., a child with epilepsy would not be expelled from class for having seizures)
- Adapting curriculum and instruction to meet individual needs
- Teaching thinking skills and giving specific direction on how students can cope with emotions, stress, and peers
- Remembering that the educational/social skills need to be consistently delivered over a long period of time and continually reinforced since learning is evolutionary
- Including a home-school component where empowerment is given to parents and families to coordinate with school efforts with family education and supports
- Supervision and encouragement to participate in recreational and extracurricular activities at school and in communities that promote social competencies
- Continued instruction on how to resist peer pressure
- Interim alternative educational setting (IAES) for students with chronic behavioral problems (e.g., carrying a gun to school, using illegal drugs, engaging in behavior that is harmful to self and others) permits the school personnel to place the student in another setting for up to 45 school days. Interventions should begin in the IAES while following the student's IEP. Services then need to be continued to the next placement with appropriate coordination between the settings.
- Interventions to address behaviors and factors that led to disciplinary action
- Ongoing staff development with all school personnel involved
- Emphasizing positive interventions over punitive ones

HOW TO TRACK AND DOCUMENT IEPs

The IEP is a procedural safeguard that is meant to benefit all learners. Just like a recipe that might need more salt or less sugar, the IEP is a living document that can be amended. Teachers, parents, families, guardians, administrators, support staff, and students act as a team and a cohesive group, rather than sparring partners engaged in seeking alternate goals and objectives. Everyone benefits when the IEP is vigilantly planned, followed, supported, shared, and translated to the classroom. Goals and skills attained can be reviewed at interim periods during the school year such as quarterly marking periods, with parents and guardians being informed of their children's progress as outlined in the IEP. When teachers have made a dedicated effort to support the advancement of a student's individual needs, they cannot be held accountable for a student's lack of progress or regression when they have diligently applied the educational interventions. Teachers can document students' partial progress in their lessons, with varying student accommodations. Deliberately ignoring or refusing to address a child's needs as outlined in an IEP means that the school district is not being compliant with agreed-upon IEP decisions. When progress does not occur, then many variables must be reviewed; hence, the educator is a contributing, but not sole, factor in a student's advancement. If changes need to be made, staff, team members, families, and—if appropriate—students reconvene and adjust programs, services, frequency of services, accommodations, and more. If parents or family support systems are still dissatisfied with placement, progress, or enforcement, then all parties can continually meet to plan for more effective changes, or ask for mediation, bringing in an objective third party not involved in the disagreement. If another school meeting or mediation still does not solve the matter, then parents or guardians can ask for a due process hearing where both families and school personnel present their sides of the matter and views on issues in contention. If parents or guardians believe that the IEP is still being violated, a complaint can be filed with the state education agency (SEA), which must try to resolve the complaint within 60 days, unless extreme circumstances exist. IDEA improvements now allow local or state education agencies to be awarded attorneys' fees if a parent's complaint is deemed frivolous, unreasonable, or without foundation. A *frivolous* case is determined by legal precedent. This differs from past practices of only allowing parents who win cases to recoup attorneys' fees.

Implementing Modifications by Charting Lessons

Both GE and SE teachers can use notes from IEPs they've read and monitor how their lessons align with accommodations, modifications, and goals listed in the IEP. If modifications or strategies are not working, then it should be reported to the IEP team so that changes can be made. In today's legislative thrust based upon more accountability, the curriculum standards are expected to be mastered, but first some scaffolding or accommodations must be given to students who need this interim type of support. Students with more severe cognitive impairments are also expected to achieve progress, but on levels that offer alternate assessments and, sometimes, modified expectations toward mastery of the curriculum standards. This chart offers a glimpse of the types of classroom adaptations that can be documented.

Modifications/Accommodations

How can we make this work?

Modifications/Accommodations
G—Grading modified
S—Seating
HW—Homework modified/reduced
P—Preteaching
R—Reteaching/Repetition
A—Assessment varied/simplified
SG—Study Guide
V—Visuals
T—Extra time, or wait time for tasks
BP—Behavior Plan
C/T—Computer/Technology
M—Alternate Materials
OW—Oral/Written presentations
MS—Multisensory techniques
TGS—Team & Group Support
HFI—Home/Family Involvement
B—Buddy system
NT—Note-Taking system
LOV—Learning Objective Varied
O+—Other modifications
MBHE—Modified, But High Expectations

Subject: _____

Teachers: _____

Students	Accommodations/ Modifications	Assessments/Dates Mastery Level	Comments

Related Services: _____

Teachers observe and review children's progress during class lessons and chart individual modifications. For effective class management, this table can document progress for 10 students or record progress of 1 child over a period of time.

Content Area: _____

Objectives: _____

_____

Student(s) (name/ initials) and/or Dates	Able to fully participate in the same lesson as peers	Needs modified expectations or extra materials to accomplish lesson's objective	Can independently participate in a different, but related, assignment in the room	Requires supervision/ assistance to complete or attend to assignments	Cannot proficiently complete task in classroom even with support	Brief comments, observations, needs, modifications, notes, V/A/K/T concerns, future plans

MOCK IEP (IT'S EDUCATIONALLY PRUDENT!)

WHAT? + HOW? = PLAN

Directions: Act out an IEP (Individualized Education Program) meeting. The IEP may be for an actual or hypothetical student. If it is a real student, the name must be changed to respect confidentiality. Include current academic and functional levels, an LRE (Least Restrictive Environment) statement, academic and social goals, strategies, accommodations, modifications, levels of mastery hoped to achieve, behavioral plans, transitional services, assistive technology needed, along with location, frequency, and duration of placement. Consideration needs to be given to the curriculum and the delivery process, including what you want to teach and how it will be accomplished and assessed. Remember to include only academic goals that disability impacts upon. For example, if student demonstrates attention and study-skill difficulties that impact upon reading, but has excellent reading comprehension, then it would not be appropriate to include reading comprehension objectives since it is not an area of deficit. In this case, study-skill strategies and attending to task are more appropriate goals. View sample IEP goals given, along with listed components, understanding how the student's present level of academic achievement and functional performance leads to goals that are aligned with curriculum standards, which then lead to appropriate services with necessary accommodations. The IEP also lists related services and explains the extent to which the student will and will not participate with nondisabled children in the regular, or what I prefer to say, general education classroom (since SE is not an *irregular* classroom, if that is what a student needs) and other school activities. Include the child's strengths, results of evaluations, and a plan for reporting progress to parents and guardians. Also include type of professional training and support needed for all staff members to effectively implement the IEP. Remember that each person acts as a member of a team, collectively deciding how to individualize instruction for each child's unique needs, with the possession of high expectations for all students. Collecting baseline data is crucial to determine the effectiveness of educational interventions. This can include but is not limited to teacher observation; informal written or oral quizzes and tests; CBAs (curriculum-based assessments); student work samples; and family, parent, or guardian input. Keeping track of learning then requires a comparison of students' work and levels of proficiency.

Overall domains to consider include the following:

- Cognitive/Academic
- Speech/Language/Communication
- Social, Emotional, Behavioral
- Fine/Gross Motor Skills/Adaptive Behavior

Other student variables to consider include the following:

- Limited language proficiencies—English language learners (ELLs) require more visuals and academic support with modified or supplemental curriculum materials that have the same content, but different reading levels that appropriately honor interests and ages.

- Communication needs—Students with autism may need augmentative communication and PECS (picture exchange communication system), or a student with deafness may need a sign language interpreter or more visuals to accompany abstract concepts. Teachers need to regularly consult and collaborate with the speech and language pathologist for classroom connections.

- Visual impairments—Students may need Braille; magnification of text or worksheets; additional tactile curriculum connections, e.g., standing in a circle with yarn used to demonstrate the concepts of *diameter* and *radii.*

- Physical or mobility differences—Students may need a scribe for dysgraphia, a word prediction program or portable keyboard and word processor to ease fine motor requirements, modified goals for physical education, or alternate access to classroom and school facilities.

- Emotional/behavioral differences—Students may require BIPs (behavioral intervention plans) to address areas such as impulsivity, defiance, compulsivity, depression, aggression, increasing self-awareness, ways to improve peer interactions, and more. BIPs state behavior desired, and plans or steps to achieve that behavior as an outcome.

- Attention difficulties—Students may need a seating change to thrive, along with lessons that match interests, closer proximity to the instruction, rewards and praise for time on task, reinforcing attending behavior, allowing more kinesthetic classroom movements, assistive listening devices.

- Autism (with more cognitive impairments)—Students may need additional adult or structured peer support with daily routines; simplified commands with visual cues; sensory motor breaks; adapted physical education, art, and music programs; behavior modification plan; coordination with speech/language pathologist to improve receptive and expressive language, e.g., verbal requests, dialogue, social reciprocity, pragmatic language, increased modeling with more concrete presentations to explain abstract ideas, additional time, pacing lessons.

- Learning differences—Students may require interventions with structured reading programs, e.g., *Jolly Phonics, Fast Forward, Wilson Language,* for decoding and encoding needs; direct skill instruction with comprehension skills; direct teaching of social skills; praise for approximations toward standards; guidance with information processing and organizational and study skills; and more guided instruction before independent assignments are given. Ask student to paraphrase understandings.

The following people's input should be considered in your *educationally prudent* IEP meeting:

- Parents/guardians
- Students
- General education teachers
- Special education teachers
- School psychologists
- Social workers
- Speech/language therapists
- Learning disabilities teacher consultants
- School guidance counselors

- Physical therapists
- Occupational therapists
- Assistive technology staff
- Administration

- Instructional assistants/ paraprofessionals
- All other support staff for related services

The following reviews important IEP considerations, or what I call *EE*s for *IEP*s (Translation: Essential Elements to consider in Individualized Education Programs). The first chart has the duos, trios, quartets, and pentatonic initials, while the second one has the translations for the initialized SE terms.

PLAAFP	RTI	CBA	AT	ELL
BIP	LRE	FBA	LD	FAPE
EIS	ESY	FERPA	CI	OHI
TS	GE	SE	STOs	TGIF

Translation of initials that often enter IEPs:

Present level of academic achievement and functional performance	Response to interventions	Curriculum-based assessments	Assistive technology	English language learners
Behavioral intervention plan	Least restrictive environment	Functional behavioral assessment	Learning differences	Free and appropriate public education
Early intervening services	Extended school year	Family Education and Right to Privacy Act	Communication impaired	Other health impairments
Transitional services	General education	Special education	Short-term objectives as per state requirements	Thank goodness inclusion's feasible!

Recommended Resources to Stay Current on IEP Requirements

U.S. Department of Education—www.ed.gov/index.jhtml

Wrightslaw—www.wrightslaw.com

Council for Exceptional Children—www.cec.sped.org

IEP4U—www.iep4u.com

Introducing Social, Emotional, and Behavioral Issues Into the Curriculum

Physical inclusion in the general education classroom, which may be outlined as part of a child's IEP, does not guarantee social acceptance. This chapter provides teacher tips and practical strategies regarding how to address complex and diverse social, emotional, and behavioral issues to build more successful classrooms. As delineated in this chapter, with proper guidance, teachers can help students connect to themselves, others, the curriculum, and—most important—life!

CONNECTING COGNITIVE AND AFFECTIVE SKILLS

Balancing both cognitive and affective skills is essential, since academics and socialization are two vital classroom ingredients. Teachers need to know how emotional factors often influence student performance. Sometimes how much students learn is dependent upon how they feel while they are learning. Teachers and staff within inclusive environments set the learning stage for assisting students with academics as well as managing internal thoughts to heighten confidence levels and help them get along with others.

Understanding the Whole Child

Students with special needs are at times confused by the many rules. The hidden curriculum of how to act sometimes escapes them. Questionable self-esteem and lack of security or safe havens in their lives impact academic performance. Socially, students with disabilities struggle to be accepted by their peers, who will often tolerate students with differences in their academic classroom setting, but exclude them in their social circles. Other students' and teachers' perceptions, attitudes, and knowledge affect how successful the inclusion experience will be (Burke & Sutherland, 2004; Kniveton, 2004; Siperstein, Parker, Bardon, & Widaman, 2007).

Very often, students with special needs still have separate sports teams, cluster together at their own table in the school cafeteria, or hear about other kids' sleepovers or birthday parties but are uninvited. In our haste to provide the best possible education, we sometimes overlook some of the detrimental social, emotional, and behavioral implications when children face rejection and isolation. When children's self-esteem is sacrificed, they are not free to be themselves, without the judgmental attitudes of peers who are seeking their own niche in the classroom hierarchy. Physical inclusion alone does not translate into successful social or academic outcomes.

Unfortunately, you cannot control unfair factors that children are exposed to at an early age. There is sometimes no equity in the distribution of safe, protective, and nurturing environments. Poor attendance, behavioral issues, and generally apathetic attitudes compound the resulting low academic performance. If nobody cares about these students, why should they care about themselves? Although students rarely vocalize this sentiment, it is engrained in their every movement and the choices they make in their lives concerning school, family, friends, everyday decisions, and future goals. How do you stop this cycle of failure? Other children have behavioral issues that interfere with the learning of their classmates, and need set disciplinary actions and workable plans within an inclusion setting. Sometimes students just need gentle reminders or private signals to increase their awareness to focus on more positive behavior, without facing embarrassment in front of peers. Because academics and socialization are often interrelated, instruction and practice are necessary for both areas.

Social issues that educators can help students improve upon include the following:

1. Setting Goals
2. Self-Control
3. Managing Stress & Frustrations
4. Self-acceptance
5. Honesty
6. Motivation
7. Sense of Responsibility
8. Feeling Capable
9. Willingness to Accept/Help Others
10. Having Conversations: Eye Contact, Tone of Voice
11. Social Greetings & Appropriately Approaching Others
12. Knowing About Personal Space
13. Cooperating With Adults/Students/Parents
14. Thinking About Consequences
15. Dealing With Anger
16. Effective Work Habits
17. Positive Peer Relationships
18. Understanding Nonverbal Communication
19. Making Generalizations
20. Monitoring Progress

Sources: IEP Planner: Vision Management Consulting, LLC. (n.d.). *A compendium of educational and behavior goals and objectives.* Available at http://www.visionplanet.com; http://www.behavioradvisor.com/SocialSkills.html.

Check out these sources for some excellent social and behavioral tips for teachers in schools and for educators to share with families:

Baker, J. (2001). *The social skills picture book: Teaching play, emotion, and communication to children with autism.* Arlington: TX: Future Horizons.

Baker, J. (2005). *Preparing for life: The complete guide to transitioning to adulthood for those with autism and Asperger's syndrome.* Arlington, TX: Future Horizons.

Dr. Mac's Behavior Management Site: http://www.behavioradvisor.com

LD online: Behavior & Social Skills: http://www.ldonline.org/indepth/behavior

Online Autism Support Group: http://www.mdjunction.com/autism

Teen Autism: Social Groups: http://teenautism.com/social-groups

ADDRESSING EMOTIONAL INTELLIGENCES

Howard Gardner's theory of multiple intelligences speaks about two emotional intelligences, *intra*personal and *inter*personal. Intrapersonal is being self-smart, while interpersonal describes how people relate to others. Some children and adults feel more comfortable working alone to self-check and reflect upon their progress, while others prefer to be part of a group, with peers collaborating together.

Intrapersonal Activities

- Keeping a journal
- Self-kept graphs of progress
- Writer's notebook
- Self-checking activities
- Independent study under teacher's auspices
- Setting goals
- Personalizing learning
- Interest inventories
- Individual projects
- Portfolios
- Poetry
- Keeping a To Do list
- Teaching and encouraging relaxation techniques (yoga, deep breathing, counting slowly)

Interpersonal Activities

- Cooperative learning
- Study buddies
- Tutoring or mentoring a classmate
- Teams
- Board games
- Group projects & classroom centers
- Collaborative reports
- Plays
- Planning class/school function
- Debates and discussions
- Helping others with conflicts
- Empowering students as consultants (give them an official clipboard)

Cooperative learning offers an alternative to lecturing and seatwork, while effectively promoting social skills. Some ideas and models can be viewed at these sites by researchers D. W. Johnson, R. T. Johnson, and M. B. Stanne, and by S. Kagan:

http://www.co-operation.org/pages/cl-methods.html

http://www.teach-nology.com/currenttrends/cooperative_learning/kagan

In cooperative learning situations, students interact with peers in a positive way to achieve a cooperative academic outcome. This is different from group learning, which just has children physically working together, since with cooperative learning, each student is more responsible and accountable. Cooperative learning is not just grouping kids together, but offers more learning structure, while encouraging interpersonal skills, such as collaborative planning and reports.

Positive Interdependence—

Everyone is actively involved to complete the assignment.

Individual Accountability—

Each person documents his or her own work.

Equal Participation—

All children are given responsible voices.

Simultaneous Interaction—

During a given time period, all students are learning.

Note: Spencer Kagan at www.KaganOnline.com has many resources on cooperative learning.

BEHAVIORAL APPROACHES FOR EDUCATORS

Self-Advocacy Skills

Students with self-advocacy skills are able to express their interests and take an active role in decisions regarding current and future placements. Self-advocacy involves an awareness of levels of learning, being actively assertive in getting help, and being part of the team that plans objectives. A student who attends an IEP meeting and gives input is practicing self-advocacy by communicating his or her opinions. A child who can look at both the positives and negatives of a situation; the child who records his or her own grades; one who plots behavior, decides on transition plans, or records assignments on weekly and monthly calendars; or a child with Asperger's syndrome who understands the causes and effects of his or her behavior in daily interactions with peers is exhibiting self-advocacy skills. The following is a checklist you can use with students to help them develop self-advocacy.

Name _____ Date _____

My checklist of ways to help me learn more about _____.

Place a check next to each idea you think will help you in school:

___ Listening more with intent to remember

___ Knowing what topic is coming next

___ Reading over my notes

___ Asking parents/other adults to help, such as when reviewing work at home

___ Moving-around activities instead of sitting at a desk

___ Teacher repeating directions

___ Someone to read more difficult words

___ Dividing a large test into smaller parts

___ Being familiar with test format

___ Seeing a written sample of an assignment

___ Knowing expectations

___ Having an outline

___ Study groups

___ Working with a partner

___ Making a chart or graph

___ Knowing why the lesson is important

___ Using a graphic organizer

___ Knowing key points or main idea

___ Rewriting notes

___ Calculator and manipulatives

___ Study guide

___ Highlighter

___ Extra time in class to complete work

___ Mnemonics (a word or sentence made up to help me remember a lot of information)

___ Using a computer

___ Seating change

___ Knowing lesson vocabulary beforehand

___ Activities/games that help me understand and play with the info

___ More visuals like pictures and graphs

___ Keeping myself more organized

___ Using other reading materials

___ Reviewing a behavior chart

___ Other help or support I need: _____

Please note: If students are non-readers or struggling readers, then as an alternative, students can fill out the checklist with an adult, e.g., teacher, assistant, or parent, with fewer options accompanied by pictures and more explanations. As another option, to invite more metacognition and collaboration, allow students to collaboratively fill out or self-create checklists in study skill groups with peers. The following student pledges, to be duplicated and recited daily, ask students to take an oath to be integral players in their learning outcomes, valuing individual identity and interactions with others under social studies standards.

Student Pledge (to be recited with enthusiasm!)

I know it's the morning (afternoon)

And we're still yawning (leaving soon)

But this is my promise for today (now)

When I will say (vow)

That I will do my best

And it's not said in jest

To really care

And be sincere

To listen and learn

And respect each in turn

We all have many a need

But we all can succeed

If we use our mind

And to each other be kind

So here I am in school

Where not only teachers rule

But it's each student

That needs to be prudent

If I have a positive attitude

I could master math, reading, and even latitude

The implications are great

I decide my own fate

So I'll give it my best try

And that's no lie

It's my promise, no fingers crossed

I'll ask questions when I'm lost

I'll care about this stuff

Even when the going gets tough

And I think I'll even smile

May as well, I'll be here awhile

Source: Karten, T. (2007). *More inclusion strategies that work! Aligning student strengths with standards.* Thousand Oaks, CA: Corwin.

Younger learners or students with lower vocabulary or reading levels can view digital movies or candid snapshots of themselves during classroom learning and then write behavioral captions or numerically rate their level of attention. Students can also increase social, emotional, and behavioral metacognitive levels by reading or repeating a simpler pledge such as this one:

I can

Plan

And say

Each day

Will be fine

I won't whine

I will always try

And that's no lie

There are a lot of facts I need	Because being smart
That will feed	Is an art
My budding brain	So I promise to grow
And I won't complain	To be a kid who'll know!

Source: Karten, T. (2007). *More inclusion strategies that work! Aligning student strengths with standards.* Thousand Oaks, CA: Corwin.

FUNCTIONAL BEHAVIORAL ASSESSMENT (FBA)

Educators are faced with the difficult task of teaching diverse students within the same classroom. When this diversity is complicated or accompanied by behavioral issues, then teaching can often become a harrowing experience. FBAs offer a concrete alternative that asks teachers and students to look at inappropriate behaviors and discover the reasons for their occurrences.

A student who is refusing to do work may be frustrated by work that is too difficult, or perhaps may just be uninterested in the assignment. Teachers who identify the underlying reasons for certain behaviors can then develop and implement appropriate classroom interventions.

The following FBA questions must be answered:

1. Is the behavior related to a skill deficit?

2. Is the student acting out for more attention?

3. Is the student trying to avoid or escape an assignment or task?

4. Is the task too demanding or boring?

5. Does the student consider rules, routine, or expectations irrelevant?

Source: Center for Effective Collaboration and Practice (CECP)/American Institutes for Research (AIR). (n.d.). *Addressing student problem behavior.* Funded under a cooperative agreement with the Office of Special Education Programs (OSEP), U.S. Department of Education, http://cecp.air.org/fba/problembehavior/text.htm.

After the problem is identified and documented through observation and recording behavior in a variety of settings, educators and students think of a solution that addresses changing the behavior—*not just controlling it!* Punishments such as homework slips or detention may only control the symptom, not the cause. By getting to the root of a problem, teachers can even hypothesize instances when the behavior is likely to occur and determine how classrooms can be modified to manipulate antecedents. These types of pupil-specific interventions increase motivation for more appropriate behaviors and offer students opportunities for intrinsic as well as extrinsic rewards. The psychologist B. F. Skinner was a proponent of *operant conditioning,* which rewards children for steps taken toward their goals with positive reinforcers that offered immediate feedback (see http://tip.psychology.org/skinner.html). Functional behavioral assessments lead to the development and implementation of strategies to improve behavior. Teachers and students then keep anecdotal records, or chart appropriate behaviors in order to evaluate effectiveness of plans.

Charting Daily Behavior

The following questions, charts, and tables help students and teachers to both analyze and evaluate behavior. Before charts are filled in, the teacher and student together must decide which behavioral goals need improvement, such as the following:

- Paying attention to the teacher with body language and eye contact
- Using appropriate language
- Getting along with other classmates
- Following written/oral directions
- Staying on task, doing what needs to be done
- Treating other students with respect
- Completing homework
- Taking turns in conversations

The student consistently needs to be aware of his or her individual goal, which is always stated in *positive language.* Remember, although undesired behaviors exist, always write exactly what you wish the student to achieve, not the behavior you wish the student to extinguish. For example, rather than saying, "Stop sleeping in class," you can restate it as "Concentrate or focus on classroom lessons." Charts such as this one help teachers, students, and parents see patterns of behavior as well as what might trigger events.

Charting Behaviors

How I Was Today

Time/ Day	WOW 5 points	Good 4 points	Better 3 points	OK 2 points	????? 1 point	
Totals	_____ +	_____ +	_____ +	_____ +	_____ =	_____ Total Points
Name _____						

????? means that the behavior is questionable and needs to be both improved and discussed. It allows the teacher to ask the student questions—for example, "Why did you _____?" or "When you _____, what were you thinking?" The student can also fill out a What's Going On? form if it's appropriate (see later in this chapter). Younger children may need shorter time increments tracked.

A Visual Tool for Early or Concrete Learners

TIME/DAY	WOW!	GOOD CHOICE	Needs Reminders	Poor Choices

> Daily behavioral charts such as these can be duplicated and used to make students more aware of their behavior. It is deliberately small, so other classmates won't notice. Daily copies are held by the student or teacher or kept on index cards. A teacher can check off or initial appropriate ratings for each time slot, period, or day, and then help the student total daily points. Even though this might be difficult to implement in busy, full-sized classrooms, the time spent is well worth it. Some children need this type of concrete structure to improve behavior, making them more aware of their own patterns and choices. The extra positive attention may well extinguish prior inappropriate behaviors.

Next Step: Daily/Weekly Graphing

?????, OK, Better, Good, and WOW are given points from 1–5, respectively, which are then totaled for the week or day, charted onto graph paper, and held in a separate student folder as a running record. For example, if a child has 5 WOW days in a row for 6 daily time slots, it is conceivable that the weekly score could be plotted as high as 150, since a daily score of (5 x 6) multiplied by 5 days would equal 150 (for 6 different time slots). The lowest score for the week would be 30, since ????? ratings are worth 1 point each. Younger learners can also be assigned points such as 4 for the WOW column and decreasing to 3, 2, and 1. Together, the teacher and student total the weekly or daily behavioral points and plot them onto the graph paper. By creating a visual that strings several days together, children will not be upset if they have an off day, since they are able to look at the whole picture with one glance and see that those days are just part of the bigger picture. Once a desired behavior improves, the goals can be enhanced, added, or changed as agreed upon with student, teacher, and/or family/parent conferencing and collaboration.

Graphing concretizes the acceptable behavior; creates more metacognition; and establishes a trusting, positive relationship between a student and teacher that consistently *values, recognizes, and rewards students' achievements in a structured manner.* If necessary, children can also graph daily points. Younger students can count check marks in each happy-face time slot or use simpler, larger graphs.

Points   **Weekly Graphing**

Points																																	
150																																		
145																																		
140																																		
135																																		
130																																		
125																																		
120																																		
115																																		
110																																		
105																																		
100																																		
95																																		
90																																		
85																																		
80																																		
75																																		
70																																		
60																																		
50																																		
40																																		
30																																		

Dates: _____

Name: _____

TRANSITIONAL SERVICES

What do I want to be when I grow up? is a question children continually ask themselves. Some students may also need help to even realize that not every day of their lives will be monitored. Transitional planning involves helping students make decisions that will lead to successful lives as productive members of their community—a plan for the future. Transitional plans honor students' choices, goals, and dreams, yet also outline and delineate possible barriers and strategies. Transitional plans focus on capitalizing upon students' strengths and abilities to circumvent possible challenges along the adult road ahead, whether it is a paved or bumpy one. They center on post-school outcomes, post-secondary education decisions, vocational training, and overall school-to-community-to-life connections with appropriate academic, social, emotional, and behavioral skills.

Transitional Elements for Students to Consider

1. Current academics and appropriate preparatory classes

2. Vocational training/employment internships

3. Related agencies/services (e.g., guidance counselor, Social Security benefits or aid for qualifying college students, voting, employment opportunities) and places to go for more help

4. Community integration/social skills

5. How to develop self-advocacy skills; being assertive, not aggressive or passive

6. Likes, dislikes, stronger and weaker intelligences

7. How to secure outside living arrangements

8. Extent of family involvement, e.g., support in navigating systems and services

9. Future educational planning/post-secondary schools

10. Available technology services

11. Transportation options

12. Money management ideas and planning

13. Health care: dentists, doctors (internists, audiologists, ophthalmologists), physical therapists, psychologists

14. Independent living skills

15. Work ethic with colleagues and employers/organizational skills, such as updating a résumé or being punctual

16. Appearance/hygiene

17. How to develop better interpersonal and intrapersonal skills

18. Transferring classroom learning to the outside world. Overall, transition plans for students' future aspirations!

Transitional Resources and Tools

- PACER—www.pacer.org/tatra/resources/postSecondary.asp
- College Options for People with Intellectual Disabilities—wwwthinkcollege.net
- The HEATH Resource Center, Online Clearinghouse for Postsecondary Education for Individuals with Disabilities—www.heath.gwu.edu
- AHEAD, Association on Higher Education and Disability—http://www.ahead.org
- Division on Career Development & Transition. A division of Council for Exceptional Children—www.dcdt.org
- LD Online College Prep for Students with Learning Disabilities and ADHD—www.ldonline.org/indepth/college
- Just One Break (JOB), Inc., a nonprofit organization for employment placement for people with disabilities—www.justonebreak.com
- National Clearinghouse on Disability and Exchange, a project of Mobility International USA—Provides information to people with disabilities who want to study, do research, and volunteer, along with international exchange opportunities—www.miusa.org
- State Vocational and Rehabilitation (VR) Agencies—Provide and coordinate many services for persons with disabilities, including counseling, evaluation, training, and job placement. Individual offices are located throughout the United States—www.workworld.org/wwwebhelp/state_vocational_rehabilitation_vr_agencies.htm
- National Rehabilitation Information Center—www.naric.com
- MAPS, Making Action Plans—www.ric.edu/sherlockcenter/publications/MAPS.pdf
- PATH, Planning Alternative Tomorrow of Hope—www.inclusion.com/path.html, www.pisp.ca/strategies/strategies61.pdf

WAYS TO TEACH SOCIAL SKILLS

In order for educators to provide appropriate interventions, they must understand how students perceive their place in the world and why students might misbehave. *All behavior has meaning*, whether it is evident to teachers or not. Sometimes it's a way for children to achieve a sense of belonging or control. Other times it's for the attention, whether positive or negative, just so they are noticed. Social skills can be taught and organized.

Teachers can . . .

- Establish trust by consistently listening to concerns without judging.
- Outline class rules and consequences with the students, working within a structured, well-organized classroom.
- Separate the behavior from the child, letting the student know that they value him or her, but do not approve of given behavior.
- Understand how a student might perceive a given situation by exploring his or her perspective and listen to the student for more insights.
- Engage in structured role-playing; have student fill in dialogue for hypothetical social situations or blank comic strips.

- Model appropriate behavior and language.
- Remain calm, despite immediate reaction, avoiding power struggles.
- Try to talk to the student privately about negative behavior.
- Allow for constructive movement times as a release.
- Have high expectations for all children.
- Establish an ongoing method of communication with other teachers.
- Include parents/home in child's school progress and try to map out effective behavioral plans that can be used in both home and school environments.
- Have a sense of humor!
- Use student worksheets such as What's Going On? and specific behavioral charts to help students be more aware of their own behaviors.
- Reward and individualize appropriate desired behaviors with stickers, notes, positive talks, looks, or just more smiles.

☺ ☺ ☺ ☺ ☺ ☺ ☺ ☺ ☺ ☺ ☺ ☺

The *Friendship Corner,* where one child holds a card with the word *mouth* and may speak while the other children listen (holding the cards with ears), is a concrete way to resolve conflicts and develop listening skills in the primary grades.

One Person Speaks at a Time

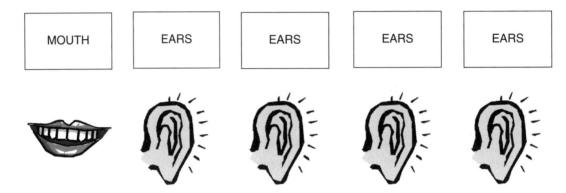

Peer mediation/conflict resolution programs are effective strategies to help students in higher grades gain these same valuable insights.

What's Going On? is a tool that models how teachers can structure a writing exercise to build organized communication. Younger learners could verbally complete the following phrases with an older student or scribe. Students are empowered since they are not required to answer every question, but are given choices for their responses in order to have them reflect upon their behavior and perhaps diffuse their anger, and to be more aware of their emotions.

What's Going On?

Directions: Read all of the words on the next two pages, and then fill in at least five blanks you would like to tell more about.

Name _____

Well, this is what happened:

First, _____

_____

Then, _____

_____

My friends _____

_____

My family _____

_____

The world seems _____

_____

Keep Going!

I love it when _____

_____

I hate it when _____

_____

Sometimes I am confused when _____

_____

One day I want to _____

_____

Keep Going!

Next time, _____

_____

I need _____

_____

I wish _____

_____

_____

OK, Here's My Plan

First, I will _____

_____

_____

I'll try to _____

_____

_____

I'll try not to _____

_____

_____

I'll get help from _____

_____

_____

I'll help myself _____

_____

_____

I won't get upset when _____

_____

_____

My plans include _____

_____

_____

Other things I need to say: _____

_____

_____

Social Circles

Continually reexamining personal contacts helps students reflect upon relationships in their lives.

Directions: The students place names of people fitting descriptors in concentric circles. Names of people nearest to them are in the closest circles, while further circles contain people who should be kept at a distance. Circles like these concretize abstract emotions for students with poor social judgments and for some with cognitive difficulties, while increasing personal reflections for all. For classroom instruction, teachers can model their own social circle, showing students how there are many people around us, each having a different place in our lives. By including more personal information about their own lives, teachers are also telling students that they are willing to share information, which may serve as a catalyst for children to follow, establishing a trusting and communicating relationship. At the same time, it helps students concretely understand a variety of social interactions they encounter, and how there are appropriate distances for different people.

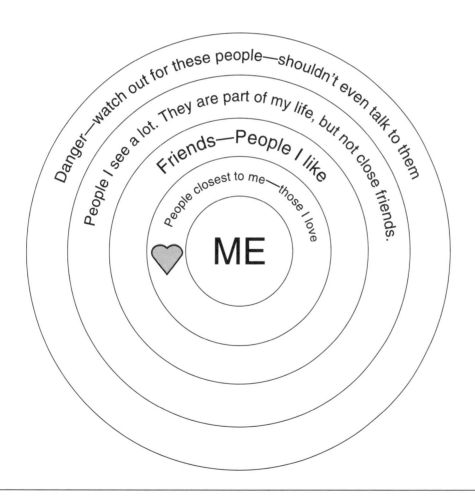

Source: Adapted from O'Brien, J., & Forest, M. (1989). *Action for inclusion: How to improve schools by welcoming children with special needs into regular classrooms.* Toronto, Ont., Canada: Inclusion Press.

CLASSROOM CLIMATE

Just as critics write reviews that make or break restaurants, Broadway shows, movies, and books, opinions also influence children and teachers. Teachers want complimentary evaluations by administrators, while children seek good grades, praise, and recognition from peers and adults in their lives. Students who are constantly criticized or put down by a teacher, peer, or family member may form negative self-images that thwart future successes. The obverse, positive recognition can enhance a person's self-worth. One way to accomplish this is to use a *Put-Up* envelope, which can house positive statements. It allows students to recognize one another's good deeds by writing positive comments. These comments can be read daily or weekly, depending upon the amount. A pad and pencil, kept nearby, allow for these *uplifting* comments to be recorded.

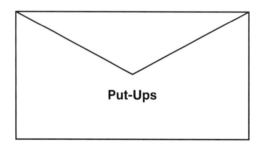

Put-Ups

Moral: Put-ups can be used in individual classrooms to establish an environment that is conducive to learning, by recognizing the *good* things about one another. It is suggested that the teacher always be the reader of the comments, since he or she has the option to delete anything negative and add more positive remarks to boost the self-esteem of a child who thought nobody noticed or cared. Everyone beams when given a compliment! Even academics can improve in a classroom that focuses on *positiveness*. It changes the adage, "If you have nothing nice to say, say nothing," to . . .

"Say nice things!"

A Touch of Lucky Charms

I often think of one student of mine who would leave school not knowing if his family would be evicted from their home that day, or which father would be present. The one thing I could offer him was a bowl of Lucky Charms* each morning, because that was his favorite cereal, while the custodian provided the milk. It was not much, but in his eyes it was a sign that someone cared.

> There is no giant eraser that makes the ugliness disappear, but teachers can make the school hours as nonthreatening and productive as possible.

Five Helpful Factors

1. Develop a personal rapport with students.

2. Sharpen academic skills while involving students in positive school experiences.

3. Increase self-awareness of students' goals and strides.

4. Create and implement a plan that includes appropriate interventions while defining specific support that will be available.

5. Be ready with a bowl of Lucky Charms!

---

*Actual cereal was Froot Loops, but it was his "lucky charm."

Reaching and Coteaching Your Students

Many inclusion classrooms today value coteaching to meet the needs of children who are identified with learning differences. Servicing students through this model, rather than pull-out programs, stops classified students from feeling so different from the general school population. Special and general education teachers, along with administrators, support staff, students, and families, are all stakeholders who collaborate to achieve successful student outcomes. As shown in this chapter, classroom lessons can be structured to offer direct skill instruction, allowing students to spend more time with their peers, while working to achieve attainable academic and social results within inclusive classrooms.

EDUCATIONAL COLLABORATION

The days of a closed door and the philosophy of "doing my own thing" have been replaced by a revolving classroom door that brings new meaning to the revised phrase, *No teacher is an island*. General and special education teachers need to share ownership in all phases of the learning objectives for their students: planning, instructional delivery, offering extra help, accommodations or modifications, and assessments. A full commitment to inclusion includes administrative support and scaffolding that allow coteachers and instructional assistants sufficient planning time and opportunities for frequent communication to evaluate and assess the effectiveness of programs. All staff must be informed of children's needs as outlined in their IEPs, since they exist not only in the classroom but also at lunch; in gym, art, and music classes; and on the bus to and from school. *Communication and coordination ensure consistency of academic and behavioral programs.*

Effective inclusion sometimes means two or more teachers working together in a classroom, sharing responsibilities for both general and special education students. Coteaching has often been compared to a marriage, with two personalities spending a considerable amount of time together. In today's society, you often spend more time with your coworker than your spouse. For premium effectiveness, the professional coteaching assignment should be a compatible one that matches teachers who have similar or complementary approaches. Harmonious pedagogical relationships yield beneficial student outcomes. What follows are "prenuptials" of what to consider.

BUILDING PRODUCTIVE RELATIONSHIPS

Educational Prenuptials

Focusing on common issues and pedagogical concerns predetermines whether some collaborative relationships will be successful educational marriages. It is intended to lead to good discussions between coteachers and prepare educators for realistic situations that they may find themselves in one day. Professional compatibility helps!

What's Important in My Classroom?

Directions: Circle only five descriptors that you think are the most important for learning.

1. Listening skills

2. Following written directions

3. Communication skills

4. Reading comprehension

5. Vocabulary development

6. Following classroom routines and rules

7. Math computation

8. Study skills

9. Written expression

10. Self-confidence

11. Organizational skills

12. Concentration

13. Logical thinking

14. Performing assignments carefully

15. Remembering information

16. Completing work on time

17. Positively interacting with peers

18. Behaving appropriately in classroom groups

19. Working independently

20. Knowing how to get help

Something to ponder: These 20 items can be weaknesses of children with learning disabilities (difficulties with language, word decoding, reading comprehension, abstract concepts, social skills, organization, and so on).

It would be wonderful to say that every coteaching and instructional assistant relationship will be tremendously beneficial for the general education and special education staff and all classroom students involved. Yes, it would be a wonderful statement, but one that totally lacked veracity. As we well know, it's a big world filled with many people who have varying personalities, ages, years on the job, background experiences, mind-sets, educational foundations, attitudes about teaching, desires to instruct students with and without differences, degrees of flexibility and amenability, support systems, with additional differences and of course many commonalities as well. That's probably why it is a diverse country and world with partnerships that work between and within spouses and families, communities, states, countries, business corporations, global affiliations, and lifelong friends versus acquaintances.

Now with that stated, let's turn to our options and see how coteaching and working with staff and colleagues can be realistically implemented in an ideal inclusive school, and what to do if that classroom situation turns out to be one that you would not choose to be part of, but might very well be one where your only option will be to learn how to make *inclusive lemonade*. The next table lists situations that are ideally inclusive, some that are not so ideal, and some simple ideas for what to do to make it all work better. When coteaching and staff relationships are harmonious, it's like an educational marriage or family made in heaven with both students and pedagogy benefiting from the experience. Perhaps some of these listings and scenarios you will find familiar and can affirm, while others that you have not experienced will help guide you on the path to more productive coteaching and healthier relationships that work for all collegial partners and students.

Inclusive Partnerships

Ideal situation: From the first day that the general education and special education teacher meet, they feel like they have known each other their whole lives. After the second week, they are finishing each other's sentences, and even dressing alike in the same colors and styles, regardless of the fact that their gender differs. It does not matter who leads the lesson or who follows with the lesson, each supporting the other teacher. There is no one person who appears or needs to be in charge. The class and paraprofessional are inspired and guided by the two teachers who are waltzing through the lessons to deliver the curriculum standards. Students with and without IEPs are thriving and passing all assessments given. Sometimes there is whole-group instruction, while other times there are small groups, individualized instruction, and combinations of all types of learning. There are stations and centers set up, allowing students to circulate about and cooperatively perform tasks and other sponge activities. No one knows who has IEPs and who does not. Planning, delivery, grading, and all classroom tasks are equally shared. When there are disagreements or differing opinions, they are privately discussed and ironed out, with sound compromises made. The paraprofessional is given information about the students' levels beforehand, with knowledge about the abilities of the students, classroom management ideas, and ways to best deliver the inclusive strategies.

By the way, everyone is smiling 90% of the time—both students and adults, with the administration offering praise and accolades, thinking about duplicating the successes next year. All families are delighted with the inclusive occurrences and progress of the students. Other teachers applaud what's happening in this classroom, while students exhibit high levels of comfortability with their peers, with no one thinking that he or she is better than the next person, either students or teachers.

Not-so-ideal situation: The classroom tension can be cut with a machete. When anyone walks into the room, he or she wants to turn around and leave. If one teacher says *yes*, the other one says *no*. The students with special needs are clustered together and will only work with each other, not their peers without IEPs. The special education teacher is handed the lesson plans each week and never asked for his input on the content, process, delivery, or assessments for the lessons. Most times, the general education teacher leads the lesson and is annoyed when the special education teacher opens his mouth to try to get the students to reflect or to discuss what was taught. There are visuals offered on PowerPoints, but the pacing is way too rapid for the students to grasp, with vocabulary and depth of content that exceeds students' reading levels and prior knowledge about the topic. There are no connections with functional academics or meaningful and concrete ways for students to connect to the learning. Overall, most students with IEPs are so frustrated that they prefer instruction outside the classroom, since they are experiencing high levels of anxiety and humiliation in not being able to keep on par with their peers. A few have even expressed that they cannot learn because they are *special*. The paraprofessional tries to help ease the situation but is not sure of what to do, where to stand, or who to help. The administration is aware of the situation and tells both teachers to work it out.

By the way, no one is smiling and few are learning; most students are in the skill-and-drill mode, wanting to succeed on tests rather than gain intrinsic knowledge. Fun is a rare commodity for all parties.

What to do to make it better: First off, when feasible, administrators need to honor teachers' requests to work together. Would you choose to marry someone you had little respect for, or could you hope that oil and water mix nicely together? When faced with a situation you have not chosen, try to remember the bottom line, which is to help students succeed and work backward from there, figuring out the elements that are necessary to make that happen. Remove the personal frontal attacks and concentrate on how to increase communication with more planning time. Share students' successes, and try to find something to respect in the other person. Make it about the students, not about you. Share knowledge and strategies with all staff, both teachers and paraprofessionals. Be allies and try to create common ground with each other, students, families, and administration. Create a united front in the classroom and teacher's lunchroom. Practice yoga and count to 10, 20, 30 . . . 100, and more! Smile as well, with your head held high. It might be contagious! Read on for more ideas.

A few coteaching options follow:

1. Whole-Class Instruction

All students are taught together with teachers bouncing ideas off each other, both creating and modeling academic dialogue.

Classroom Examples:

SE teacher: "Wow! I cannot believe that people were treated that way as slaves during the triangular trade in the early 17th century. Would you like to have lived then?"

GE teacher: "No way! I am so happy that things are different today. Now class, why don't we create a list comparing and contrasting what things were like then, hundreds of years ago, to how they are now in terms of democracy and personal freedoms."

One teacher leads the discussion while the other teacher creates a table in a Word document that records students' responses as they appear on a Smart Board. The instructional assistant circulates about the room, encouraging students to look through their textbooks for details. Roles can vary, as will length of the discussion or which teacher assists or leads. No one monopolizes the lesson, and each adult's input is valued. Notes from the interactive boards are then printed out as a Word document and distributed to students with attention issues, dysgraphia, or visual impairments, and other students who would like to check the accuracy of their note taking.

2. Class Division

Two groups are created, each instructed by a different teacher—one SE, one GE teacher—while one student receives individualized instruction from an instructional assistant or a peer mentor.

Classroom Examples:

Students walk in and complete the *Do Now,* which asks them to find the slope of a line using the formula

$$m = \frac{y^2 - y^1}{x^2 - x^1}$$

that was in the previous class lesson. The students hold up their worksheet answers to the teachers, which they have placed in clear communicators. The teachers quickly discover that out of 28 students, approximately 65% of the class has the correct answer, while 35% of the class needs further instruction. The GE teacher helps those students who require more instruction and explains about vertical and horizontal rises, while the SE teacher gives a few enrichment problems to the 18 students who understand what to do with additional graphing of distance and slope problems. The paraprofessional or peer mentor is working with a student who has more intellectual challenges, creating a visual dictionary of slopes, e.g., ski slopes, driveways, playground slide, ramp by the school for a person in a wheelchair or a mom wheeling a baby carriage. Student also draws and measures his own slopes with trained peer mentors from either group assisting with the measurements, by plotting up and down points to represent the vertical (y) and horizontal (x) coordinates. The visual is then shared with the whole class at a later time. After the two groups have had time to master given assignments, the class gathers together as a whole, discusses the learning outcomes, and then moves on to the next lesson. Scenarios will vary, as will group sizes, assignments, and which teachers work with which groups. The atmosphere is an accepting collegial one in which students' levels are continually assessed, potentials are honored, and differences in learning paces and teachers' personalities are respected. Exit cards are given before students leave with a question related to the lesson just taught, to reassess if some students need additional instruction before proceeding to the next lesson.

3. Learning Activity Centers

This option can be offered to introduce a thematic unit, motivate students to delve into the learning after instruction, as an authentic cooperative assignment, or to assess students' application of concepts. While students are completing assigned lessons, the teacher(s) circulate about the classroom, offering social, academic, emotional, and behavioral assistance to both gauge and clarify understandings.

Classroom Examples:

After learning about what plants need in order to grow, students are offered opportunities to demonstrate what they know in stations and tasks such as the following:

- Performance Station: skit, song, dance, commercial
- Picture This Station: bubble dialogue, captioned illustrated picture
- Research Station: info on approved Web sites, texts, magazines
- Teacher Station: Students design a test on material studied.
- Word Station: crossword puzzles, word searches, charades

More delineation of these stations is shown in the reading section on pages 191–205. Results could include songs about chlorophyll; cartoons with the sun or water as protagonists; open-ended, multiple-choice, or essay tests; along with crossword puzzles and additional research. The best part is that students are constructively discovering more concepts as teachers and students *plant* the ideas with collaborative classroom *roots*!

Survey of Teaching Styles to Promote Productive Relationships (to Circumvent Possible Oil-and-Water Relationships Between Teachers)

Directions: Write some brief thoughts about the following topics:

Classroom Modifications and Accommodations

(Varying learning objectives, requirements, instructional materials)

Curriculum Concerns

Varying Classroom Rules/Organization Preferred

Instructional Style

Assessment Methods/Grading

COLLABORATING AS A TEAM

Teaching for Two

- Think ahead, *planning* and organizing the content, considering materials, environment, and individual needs of students.
- Use *multiple approaches* to teaching, based upon the needs of the students, curriculum difficulty, and comfort levels of teachers. Abandon the *all heads face forward and listen* approach; try more cooperative learning, research projects, and awareness of multiple intelligences.
- Be kind to each other and students. Remember that all changes and relationships take time to develop. Learning is *evolutionary.* Although teachers may have different expertise in the subject matter, different favorite movies, or be from Generation X or Y, they usually possess the same professionalism to help all children succeed. Give it time to work, and stay focused on achieving class objectives and IEP goals for all students.
- General education and special education teachers are helping *all students* in the classroom through different types of classroom grouping. Examples can include both teachers teaching the lesson together, or dividing the class into smaller groups while the same or alternate content is taught. That means that sometimes the GE teacher may be teaching the group who needs extra help while the SE teacher may be instructing the more advanced group, or vice versa. In an ideal coteaching classroom, the roles would be interchangeable ones, meaning that each teacher is responsible for all students. Other options can have students involved in cooperative learning, classroom learning stations, and independent work while both teachers assist, supervise, and instruct both general and classified groups of students.

C ooperation	**C** urriculum addressed
O ngoing	**O** pen to ideas
P re/Inter/Post	**T** eam working together
L essons	**E** veryone involved
A ssessments	**A** ccommodations given
N eeds	**C** ohesive
	H ierarchy of modifications

A Review of Thoughtful Inclusion by Working Together

- Both teachers are in the classroom, with one teaching (GE or SE)* and the other one assisting by verbally or physically supporting instruction.
- Teachers can also be teaching separate groups within the same classroom, or simultaneously rotating about to support learners while providing clarification to students completing individual assignments.
- Both teachers are responsible for the planning, instruction, and assessment for all students.
- Students work independently and cooperatively under teachers' auspices and modeling, at their learning level.
- Centers with ongoing projects are available to students.
- Teachers keep anecdotal records and document modifications and accommodations. Nothing elaborate is necessary; even a dated composition book works.
- Classroom reflection exists for students, teachers, and administration.
- Communicate with next year's teachers to bridge learning and behavioral objectives.

Unfortunately, this is not always the scenario in all school districts, where high caseloads force the SE teacher to write the IEP, while the GE is left to plan, instruct, and assess with minimally trained instructional assistants. If the worst scenario exists, then teachers must ask for more qualified support from administrators and case managers, specifically naming what personnel or materials will be needed. When a dedicated GE teacher holds the child's best interest in his or her heart, but is not given the proper supports to make the plan work, then the lesson in inclusion becomes one of exclusion and frustration. Working together means everyone is on the same team.

Collaborative Tips to Remember

1. Involve all staff.

2. Share information and ideas.

3. Remember that everyone benefits!

---

* GE = General Education and SE = Special Education, which will, when combined in collaborative classrooms, equal EE (Excellent Education) for all!

Teaching for Results

Educational diets include a variety of concepts, using different presentations. Yes, repetition is crucial to maintain facts, but learning must proceed before boredom occurs. What would happen if the only computational skills students learned about were the addition and subtraction of whole numbers? Suppose they never tasted multiplication or division. If fractions, decimals, and percents were permanently deleted from their diet, wouldn't they develop educational malnutrition? For example, I always thought Roman numerals were too difficult for weaker math students, so I would skip them and move on to what I deemed more beneficial. One day I introduced them, and the students were thrilled. They had always seen these odd letters/numbers in books, on clocks, dates, and movies, but never understood them. Once I started teaching them, I saw how much was involved. XXXIV as 34 is really teaching $10 + 10 + 10 + (5 - 1)$. Now students are adding and subtracting and learning how to expand numbers. Within a diverse classroom, learners of all abilities must be *tastefully* challenged.

> *Simple Point:* Do not teach to mastery or saturation if students are frustrated by the concepts. Expose students to learning material in varying degrees, with tweaked objectives. Sometimes you will need to move on, and then repeat the concepts at a later time, within a spiraling curriculum. Keep track of which students require more instruction for mastery or must gain additional skills to move on, and then offer support, extra examples, and assistance as needed, but never assume that education cannot be tasteful for all!

CLASSROOM DYNAMICS

The next activity explores classroom dynamics from a child's point of view. It typifies how classrooms are faced with the dilemma of educating many different levels within the same room. Within 10 minutes of instruction, everyone will try to use the chart below to solve the algebra story problem.

> During the classroom simulation, one person tries to teach the lesson, remaining calm, supportive, and focused despite unusual comments and actions taken on by assigned roles of *circles, squares, rectangles,* and *ovals.* Later on, all can reflect upon this experience.

Classroom Simulation

Shapely Descriptors

- Circles love to raise their hands to answer questions, but their responses are completely unrelated to the questions.
- Squares are highly intelligent, but quite arrogant and intolerant of others' errors.
- Ovals need things repeated several times to gain understanding of oral directions.
- Rectangles smile a lot, but are totally clueless unless a visual accompanies spoken words.

Story Problem: In a boy's bank, there is a collection of nickels, dimes, and quarters that amounts to $3.20. There are 3 times as many quarters as nickels, and 5 more dimes than nickels. How many coins of each kind are there?

	Amount x	Value*		
Let n = amount of nickels	n	.05	5	$5n$
Let $3n$ = amount of quarters	$3n$	.25	75	$75n$
Let $n + 5$ = amount of dimes	$n + 5$	.10	10	$10(n + 5)$

*Multiply by 100 to make computations easier; then set up the equation:

$$5n + 75n + 10(n + 5) = \$320$$

$$80n + 10n + 50 = 320$$

$$90n + 50 = 320$$

$$-50 \quad -50$$

$$\frac{90n}{90} = \frac{270}{90}$$

$$n = 3$$

(Answer: 3 nickels, 9 quarters, 8 dimes)

$.15 + $2.25 + .80 = $3.20

Reflection

How can a teacher strategically plan to meet the needs of this diverse group?

The teacher can . . .

Measuring Learning Ingredients With Right Angles

Obviously, teachers cannot present all students with the same breadth of material if prior knowledge and academic levels differ within the classroom. The *right angle* approach reaches and teaches all learners on their appropriate instructional levels, with a plan for successful outcomes. Some students achieve all objectives, while others obtain partial mastery, working on their individual instructional levels.

The basis for calling this concept *right angles on learning* is the fact that not only is it the "right" approach, but there are also 90 degrees in a right angle. So how does this relate to inclusive classes? Shouldn't we think of 100% of learners achieving the objectives, not the figure 90? What happens to the other 10% of learners? Well, those students are the ones who are achieving mastery toward each tiered objective in the lessons. Using specified objectives, teachers can plan lessons based upon prior knowledge and levels of the students. The total of 90% of learners mastering objectives allows for 10% uncertainty for borderline or varying levels, since there are different degrees of learning levels. Percentages for objectives will vary, but stagnation is never an option. Remember that not everyone will begin on the same level, yet learning improvements in increments are gains and building blocks for more learning. All students are learning when teachers are using the *right angles*!

Curriculum Connections—Samples of Ways to Apply Right Angles

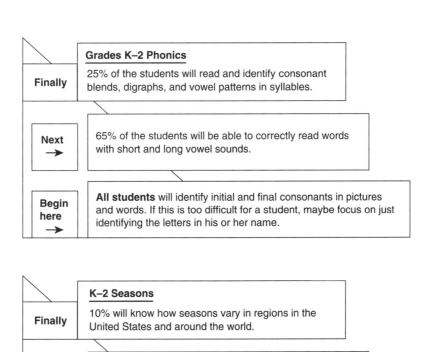

Finally

Grades 3–5 Word Analysis

15% of the students will read and identify words from lists two grade levels above, achieving at least 80% mastery.

Next →

75% of the students will demonstrate structural analysis by identifying suffixes, prefixes, and base words of grade-level lists of words.

Begin here →

All students will identify parts of compound words, read grade-level word lists, and clap to identify the number of syllables in words. Objective for some is to just repeat clapping pattern.

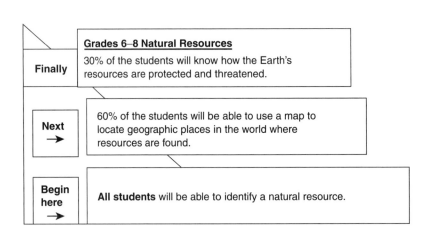

Finally

Grades 6–8 Natural Resources

30% of the students will know how the Earth's resources are protected and threatened.

Next →

60% of the students will be able to use a map to locate geographic places in the world where resources are found.

Begin here →

All students will be able to identify a natural resource.

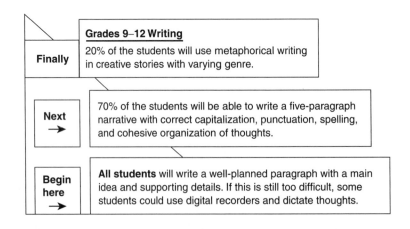

Finally

Grades 9–12 Writing

20% of the students will use metaphorical writing in creative stories with varying genre.

Next →

70% of the students will be able to write a five-paragraph narrative with correct capitalization, punctuation, spelling, and cohesive organization of thoughts.

Begin here →

All students will write a well-planned paragraph with a main idea and supporting details. If this is still too difficult, some students could use digital recorders and dictate thoughts.

Applying Right Angles

Now think of any curriculum topic and make divisions for learning objectives, using the triangular template below. Fill in approximate percentage levels in the boxes below.

Topic _____:

Finally*

Next →

Begin here →

---

*Please note that there really is no "finally," because the learning will be revisited at another time, in another way, shape, or form. Even right angles need remeasuring!

Applying Right Angles in Your Classroom

Questions You Might Ponder

1. How can classes be learning-related concepts, with different complexities?

2. What about classroom management?

3. Can one teacher divide the class into focused groups?

4. Do I need a large protractor to do this right angle stuff?

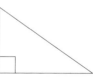

It's simple, if you think about your classroom in the following ways:

1. Everyone is learning together in one room.

2. Different thought processes and levels (independent, instructional, frustrational) exist within the same room.

3. Teaching everyone does not mean that everyone is learning the same breadth of material at the same time.

4. The ultimate goal is progress for all, based upon individual needs.

5. Always keep mastery in mind for all, with appropriate pacing and scaffolding as strategic tools, never expecting too little from your students or yourselves!

How? Some Suggestions

Think of how your lessons can be composed of these three different stages:

1. Whole

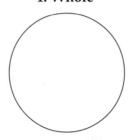

2. Part

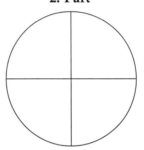

3. Whole

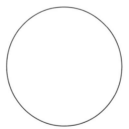

Classroom Structure

First:

Whole

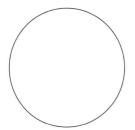

Everyone in the class could

- Listen to the same story, poem, or mathematical word problem.
- Look at the same picture prompt related to the content.
- Chorally read or write a story together on chart paper.
- Have a group discussion about . . .
- Be introduced to science and social studies vocabulary.
- Preview and discuss what skill(s) the lesson will focus on (e.g., digraphs and diphthongs, scientific method, time lines, decimals, finding the main idea, determining cause/effect, how to improve writing by substituting words).
- Be involved in a teacher demonstration or experiment, handling concrete objects or lesson-related manipulatives.

Next:

Part

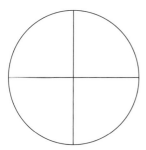

Students can work with smaller groups, partners, or individually,

- Completing an assigned reading or writing task.
- Creating a product based upon what was learned (e.g., poem, story, short skit, illustrating captioned pictures, crossword puzzle, word search, solving given problems, reenacting an experiment, researching on the computer, reading and learning more about . . .).
- Completing various activities from text, dividing assignments on matching colored paper (e.g., green, blue, yellow, white) for better classroom management, having students complete one of each color on their own or in groups.
- Learning under teacher's auspices, which now exists for all students.

During this time, the teacher walks around supervising or instructing smaller groups or individual students while recording observations and individual needs evidenced.

Then:

Whole Again

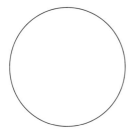

Together the class becomes a whole unit again, while individual students, teachers, partners, and groups share

- What else they learned or discovered about the topic from a book, computer, other student, teacher, or by themselves.
- A finished product created.
- What they now know, giving specific details.
- What they still wonder about.
- Questions about the material presented.

It's basically a time for all learners to celebrate their discoveries and progress with each other, while validating and reflecting upon their own learning.

Finally

Again, remember that *finally* is a term used just for now, because _____.*

*Answer: Learning always needs to be revisited at another time, or in another way, shape, or form. Just because something was taught 3 months or 3 weeks ago does not mean that it is remembered by all students. Reviewing increases retention of prior concepts. Students may need that 100% mastery on some concepts to move on in that topic or subject. Afford them the opportunity to revisit the concepts, since they now have increased prior knowledge to capitalize upon.

Three-Question Lesson Design: Objectives, Not Objections!

Lesson design requires asking these three simple questions:

1. What are you going to teach?	⟶	OBJECTIVE
2. How are you going to teach it?	⟶	PROCEDURE
3. Did it work?	⟶	ASSESSMENT

Special education can be special for all, if teachers considered the following factors. Remember that not every lesson requires all of these ingredients, but perhaps being cognizant of their importance will allow these objectives to evolutionarily diffuse into the repertoires of all teachers. Think how these points fit into a lesson.

Special Lesson Outline

Topic:

Desired goals (Social/Academic/Emotional/Physical/Cognitive):

Baseline knowledge:

Motivating activity:

Visual/Auditory/Kinesthetic-tactile sensory elements:

Critical/Creative thinking skills:

Interpersonal activity/Cooperative roles:

Curriculum connections:

UDL considerations:

Possible accommodations:

Parallel activity:

Anticipated roles of General Educator/Special Educator/Instructional Assistant/Student/Peers/Family/Specialists/Related services/Administration:

Adult/Peer/Self-assessments:

Closure:

Revisitation dates:

INCLUSION DILEMMAS

Directions: Read over descriptions of these students, telling how diverse learning strategies and educational plans will meet academic, emotional, social, and behavioral needs. Include things such as sensory components, concretization, accommodations, inclusion tips, right-angled objectives, elements in the special lesson design, and other related appropriate services.

Students

Friendship is a second-grade student who has auditory and visual-perceptual difficulties that interfere with her learning. Friendship can be quite personable, but can also create disturbances in the classroom when confronted with difficult assignments. She can scream loudly and have temper tantrums that disrupt the other children. What strategies can her teachers use to address her problems and the needs of the other students in the classroom?

Sweet Sara is a fourth-grade student with Down syndrome. She has excellent home support and is well liked by her classmates, who eagerly include her in their school activities. Sara loves playing baseball during gym and is delighted when she is part of a team. At times, abstract assignments present difficulties for Sara; she is currently unable to keep pace with the rest of the class as they are learning two-digit multiplication. She is also experiencing difficulties on the bus and in the cafeteria with other children teasing her. What would be your plan for addressing academic and social concerns?

Taylor Mills will be in Ned Nice's sixth-grade social studies class. Taylor can read fluently and independently answer questions on a third-grade level. Heidi Helpful is a special education teacher who will be working with Ned Nice. How do you think Taylor will be able to handle the class, especially the textbook? What type of appropriate adaptations can be made for Taylor during class? How can Ms. Helpful and Mr. Nice work together to help Taylor?

Arthur, a 12-year-old boy, has autism. He is in a sixth-grade class, with an instructional assistant who helps him. At times, Arthur is inattentive and distracted by his own thoughts, missing the facts and concepts presented in lessons. His poor study skills affect his test performance, since he is disorganized. He works well with peers in cooperative groups, often modeling what other children do, but rarely carries on conversations, unless he chooses the topic (he loves talking about animals). Home support is inconsistent, with his mom stating that he is difficult to handle. Long-range projects are rarely completed. What behavioral and academic strategies will improve Arthur's school and home performance?

Kind Calvin is an eighth-grade boy who has learning disabilities. His tested intelligence level is low, but he is performing on grade level in math computations, language, and reading, with in-class support. He is able to memorize social studies and science facts, but cannot grasp higher-level concepts that require creative or critical thought; most of his learning requires a concrete level of presentation. He was introduced to beginning algebra, but needs more remediation in this area. Calvin has a strong desire to learn and has excellent parental support at home. Calvin loves sports and will effortlessly devote a great deal of his time to being a participant in or observer of athletic events. What recommendations would you make for Calvin's high school program?

Tammy Talker is a seventh-grade student with average intelligence. She has a mild hearing loss and often reads lips. Tammy's word decoding skills are excellent. She can accurately pronounce and spell most seventh-grade words, but has a poor grasp of word meanings. Tammy has difficulty understanding critical thinking questions; her inferential reading skills are on a fourth-grade level. Tammy loves to draw and is learning to creatively express herself in written form. Socially, Tammy Talker is well liked by peers and will focus excessive attention on friends and classroom dynamics, often missing the crucial elements of classroom instruction. Her mom thinks that Tammy's younger sister is smarter, more trustworthy, and a nicer child than Tammy, who is well aware of her mom's sentiments. What academic and social recommendations could be offered by the general education teacher and instructional support team to help Tammy be successful?

Rollercoaster Ryan is a 15-year-old, tenth-grade boy who is athletically inclined. He has a strong desire to succeed in his sports teams, wrestling and football. He wants to do well in the classroom, but both his learning and emotional difficulties interfere with his progress. He gets frustrated very easily with schoolwork and tends to slack off, usually playing an incessant amount of video games. He craves attention, whether it is negative or positive. One minute he's having a good day, and the next minute, he's having a bad day, and is therefore set off easily. What type of program and classroom strategies would you recommend for Ryan?

How to Meet Student Needs

Friendship: Most important is to find out Friendship's reason for her misbehavior. Are the temper tantrums related to frustrations from difficult classroom assignments? Determine the extent of perceptual difficulties and use kinesthetic ways of instruction. Try setting up a behavioral intervention plan that rewards Friendship's appropriate strides. Teach social skills in small groups, gradually increasing the number of students in the group. Enlist the help of the guidance counselor, if available. Instruct peers about appropriate ways that they can help Friendship with social and academic issues.

Sweet Sara: Children on the bus and in the cafeteria who are bothering Sara need to be identified and given direct sensitivity instruction through guided character education awareness. Activities are needed to help them gain more insights on how and why they can and should help rather than tease Sara. Enlist a bus buddy and train and empower chosen peers to offer help and support at lunch, recess, and in other social situations to include Sara. Social relationships need to be taught to Sara as well, letting her know whom she can turn to for more support. A step-by-step learning approach is needed with delineated objectives in all academics, presented at a concrete level of instruction. Perhaps as others in math are learning two-digit multiplication, Sara can sort, classify, and count manipulatives in groups or again work with a trained peer mentor.

Taylor Mills: The textbook needs to be used as a reference, supplementing it with reading materials on Taylor's level containing the same subject matter. Perhaps the text can also be made available on audio, through organizations and resources such as Recording for the Blind and Dyslexic, Daisy Talking Books (www.rfbd.org, www.daisy.org). Heidi Helpful and Ned Nice can preteach vocabulary and concepts so Taylor can follow along better in class. Homework assignments also need to be modified and simplified. Both teachers need to assess Taylor's progress through benchmark assessments, varying types of grading criteria with multiple intelligence approaches, giving Taylor ample diversified opportunities to demonstrate what she knows, and not penalizing her for reading difficulties.

Arthur: Arthur needs organizational support, breaking long-term projects into smaller increments. The instructional assistant can help him refocus attention with a private, agreed-upon signal to increase eye contact and to watch gestures of the teacher to pick up on cues. Teacher's and assistant's proximity need to vary to improve Arthur's concentration and to promote independence. Cooperative grouping needs to be structured, holding Arthur consistently accountable. Use his interest in animals for independent reading and writing assignments, and to reward completed academics. Connect his mom with support groups to help manage her wide range of emotions and gain helpful insights from others. Coordinate with his mom and multidisciplinary teams as well, establishing a behavioral support plan for home and school. Offer much praise for Arthur's improvements.

Kind Calvin: Capitalize on Calvin's strong motivation and excellent parental support by giving him extra practice to improve inferential reading skills. Use manipulatives such as algebra tiles (http://mathbits.com/MathBits/AlgebraTiles/AlgebraTiles.htm) or hands-on equations (www.borenson.com) to concretize abstract concepts. Conduct a learning analysis to determine Calvin's prior knowledge of topics. Use sports as a motivator, trying to relate it to lessons when appropriate. Have Calvin develop self-advocacy skills and a transitional plan that includes future goals. Recommend a high school program that includes athletics, extra help, and peer tutoring if available.

Tammy Talker: Foremost, Tammy's social issues call for increasing her self-esteem and praising strides, since family dynamics are complicated. The instructional support team needs to help the GE teacher present learning to Tammy on a semi-abstract level, letting pictures concretize concepts. Provide more outlines, visuals, and handouts. Allow Tammy opportunities to illustrate answers, capitalizing upon her strong visual-spatial intelligence. Use a visual dictionary and teach on her instructional, not frustrational, level. Here are a few sources for accompanying curriculum-related visuals: http://visual.merriam-webster.com, www.infovisual.info, and www.clipart4schools.com. Usborne Publishers has visual dictionaries in many languages on topics, from physics to ancient civilizations, at www.usborne.com/default.asp. Since Tammy likes her peers, include more cooperative learning assignments. The GE teacher will need to vary Tammy's objectives due to her fourth-grade reading level. If Tammy is lip reading, the teacher should try to face her when giving directions, speaking slowly and clearly in a conversational voice. Have a few swivel chairs in the classroom for Tammy to easily view peers (without being singled out as different), or try to seat class in group configurations that allow her maximum access to face students. Check with school nurse, home, and team members to be certain that she is receiving the maximum technology available for her hearing difficulties, e.g., sound-field amplification system.

Rollercoaster Ryan: Determine reason for misbehavior, having Ryan increase his metacognition while plotting progress to decrease frustrations. Use sports as an outlet and reward, perhaps incorporating Premack's principle, e.g., *eat your veggies and then you can have dessert.* Incorporate more kinesthetic learning approaches in classroom instruction. Coordinate with home to decrease video games, and replace them with appropriate technology with Web sites and computer programs that augment the curriculum, e.g., www.funbrain.com, www.studyisland.com, http://mathforum.org, www.homeworkspot.com/high/english. Allow Ryan the option to attend his IEP meeting and self-advocate. Include transitional skills and behavioral interventions in his IEP as well.

MORE LESSON CONCERNS

Preschool Students

Increased exposure to socialized learning experiences at an early age is critical for future school successes. Part of IDEA includes *Child Find,* where states must actively seek out and plan for the education of young children with special needs (e.g., advertising on local television, newsletters, etc.) who may not have entered the school system yet. Such programs try to afford preschoolers with special needs equal beginnings through early individualized interventions that target cognitive, language, communication, behavior, social, emotional, and physical developments.

When early educators actively involve students in a variety of learning activities, the children become more curious to explore the world. Using appropriate curricula, materials, and procedures is a position that is supported further by the National Association for the Education of Young Children (www.naeyc.org) and the Council for Exceptional Children's Division for Early Childhood (www.dec-sped.org). Their joint position advocates that inclusion is for every infant and young child along with his or her family, giving them the right to participate in a broad range of activities within many environments and contexts, regardless of abilities. Family involvement and guidance are essential ingredients, as is a play-based arena of assessment, with teachers observing and recording needs. Play activities must allow enough space to promote active engagement and opportunity for more learning at home and in school settings. This includes social and early academic skills that promote full involvement with high expectations for functional, cognitive, social, behavioral, perceptual, emotional, and physical opportunities to achieve higher standards alongside peers. Early educators have the important task of effectively instructing young students who are entrusted to their care. It is not a task that can be taken lightly, since teaching smaller children is a large undertaking.

Gifted Education

The list below offers some heterogeneous characteristics and strategies to recognize the *gifts* all learners offer. Some students are also considered twice exceptional, exhibiting unusual strengths, yet some weaknesses that directly impact their learning.

- Learners may excel or show interest in some topics or skills, but be weaker in or dislike others. For example, some may be better in science compared to writing, or have better math skills than physical coordination, or be excellent in verbal skills but poor writers. Interdisciplinary approaches and those that reflect multiple intelligences take this into consideration by appealing to stronger areas to improve weaker ones.
- Cognitive skills do not always match social maturity. Be cognizant of the whole child, thinking of a child's hobbies and interests, and letting academics mesh with appropriate social development.
- Classrooms with instruction that values varying background knowledge, differing motivations, curiosity, and thinking skills give students a greater opportunity to learn. Ongoing stations or learning centers offer a vast variety of directed activities across the curriculum in math, music, science, art, reading, writing, and social studies. Set up stations that allow for differing learning rates while fostering independent cognitive skills and individual creativities, such as chess centers, artist studios, composers' land, time zones, and authors' world.

- Share realistic expectations with students while they keep dated portfolios as evidence of their academic achievements.
- Remember to continually offer organizational support and always encourage further critical thinking skills.
- Include positive parental communication and home support.
- Understand that some students may also be twice exceptional, having areas that they excel in with weaker ones as well, e.g., excellent readers, but with poor social or organizational skills.
- Know that sometimes educators need to accelerate, accommodate, and of course appropriately individualize lessons to differentiate curriculum, instruction, and assessments.

Recommended Resources

National Association for Gifted Children (NAGC): http://www.nagc.org
The Association for the Gifted (TAG), Division of the Council for Exceptional Children: http://www.cectag.org
Twice-Exceptional Online Newsletter: http://www.2enewsletter.com

Cultural Concerns for Special Learners

> There are a large number of minority students in special education, due to language difficulties, unfair assessments, poverty, different cultural values, experiences, and family backgrounds. These diverse groups of students then enter an even greater special education diversity and sometimes suffer from prejudices that yield inappropriate educational services.

Unfortunately, there is no legislation that can outlaw the negative connotations of being different from others. Self-awareness is the first step. The survey below allows teachers an opportunity to reflect upon their own self-awareness before they address the needs of diverse learners within their classrooms.

Cultural Self-Assessment

Directions: Beside each of the following 10 statements, indicate whether you believe it is **A**lways, **S**ometimes, or **N**ever true.

1. ___ I have an awareness of my own cultural heritage.
2. ___ I am willing to learn about others.
3. ___ I am willing to learn from others.
4. ___ I believe that being different is okay.
5. ___ Cooperative activities encourage the acceptance of differences.
6. ___ All people are the same.
7. ___ Planned classroom lessons in various content areas can address different cultures.

8. ___ Cycles of oppression continue throughout generations.

9. ___ Textbooks are generally written from a Eurocentric point of view.

10. ___ Evaluation techniques should be the same for all students.

Special Needs of Cultures

Some disability groups consider themselves as a separate *culture,* with a different way of life, and prefer not to fit in with the *mainstream* culture. Interviewing parents, guardians, children, disability support groups, and community members validates that student's culture and says that differences are okay. In addition, schools must evaluate students in their native language to see if a disability exists, without letting a student's language proficiency interfere with the testing. Interpreters also must be provided for parents and families during all phases of the special education process, from notification to evaluation, allowing parents and guardians comfortable levels of planning input during all school contacts.

Taking it a step further, we can learn *about* other cultures, but *from* them as well. Prejudice involves looking at others who are different from the mainstream in negative ways, or prejudging them. *Both children and adults need to increase their own sensitivity and awareness to learn from others.*

> Increase self-awareness activities, since those who have a high self-esteem will have less need to put others down in order to feel good about themselves. Incorporate programs that value character education, and include prejudice-reduction activities, which help students develop positive attitudes toward cultures and diversities.

Use your senses to think about prejudice.

Looks like	Sounds like	Tastes like	Smells like	Feels like

Resources to Explore

- Teaching Tolerance, Southern Poverty Law Center: http://www.tolerance.org
- Anti-Defamation League: http://www.adl.org

- Dave's ESL Café: http://www.eslcafe.com
- Multicultural Resources: http://www.teachersfirst.com/multicult.htm

TEEN CULTURE

Teens have a distinct culture as well. Many children, including teenagers, think that the sun rises and sets just for them. As the mother of an adolescent, I was faced with the dilemma of giving my son his personal space with room to grow, and at the same time demanding his daily itinerary. It is a turbulent time for a teenager, and for a teenager with a disability, it is a doubly difficult time. Adolescents generally strive to be the same as their peers, but an adolescent with a disability feels that much more pressure to belong. Trusting and letting go is a difficult task for any parent. Handling tough issues, such as independence, relationships, dating, and sexuality, is compounded by this ever-complicated world we live in. Judgments and social decisions are influenced by hormones, cyberspace, the media, tweeting, and differing societal views on *fitting in.* In this complex world, all children are not afforded the same financial or emotional opportunities. Sometimes societal and peer pressures can further complicate the process of leaving childhood to enter the almost-adult world. Dr. Stanley Greenspan's book *The Child With Special Needs* (1998) delineates the importance of not overloading an adolescent's experiences. He explains that if things become complex too quickly with too much to process and comprehend, a child may become disorganized rather than able to handle abstract situations.

Even though students may be older, the same basic learning strategies apply. Teachers need to use higher interest level, age-appropriate curriculum materials, along with step-by-step multisensory approaches that include kinesthetic-tactile, visual, and auditory elements. Establishing prior knowledge with lessons appealing to multiple intelligences, and ones including cooperative learning principles, honors the diverse academic and social levels and needs of teens. Universal design for learning (UDL) and understanding by design (UbD) need to enter the inclusive adolescent classroom to connect with future goals and the needs of diverse students.

Unfortunately, not all children get to pick their experiences. That's where involved adults can help students handle whatever cards are dealt. Making choices that will affect the rest of their lives is not an easy task. Suddenly, adolescents are asked to seriously think about what they plan on doing *when they grow up.* Erik Erikson's (1968) theory on psychosocial development identified adolescents going through a stage labeled as *identity vs. role confusion* in middle school and high school, while Piaget's (1952) stages of cognitive development identified difficulties that adolescents encounter with formal operations dealing with abstract thoughts and reasoning to solve problems. Even though these psychological icons did not live in the 21st century, their schools of thought are still applicable to teenagers today who are continually trying to find their place in the world and within their own bodies as learning concepts become more abstract. This is a time when the grownup world places more demands on adolescents' performance in school, at home, and in their community as they prepare for life beyond educational walls. If adolescents have good role models, decision making is then an easier task due to situational osmosis. Drugs, depression, suicide, and violence are unfortunately all adolescent issues of concern. Depression is the most common emotional issue during adolescence, with students feeling worthless, moody, and isolated (Snowman, McCown, & Biehler, 2009). Educators, guidance counselors, and positive community involvement can direct adolescents during these turbulent times.

Teachers can model problem-solving techniques, with systematic questioning for academic and social areas, offering teens successful options for appropriate discussions, reflections, and applications. This means teaching social skills to students with Asperger syndrome as well as understanding the adolescent needs of a student with intellectual differences. Adolescents in inclusive classrooms with and without disabilities require honed information-processing skills, learning how to attend better to organize, synthesize, and generalize abstract concepts. Educators must also help students to *know what they know.* Assist them with ways to better access and retain information by increasing self-advocacy skills through guided experiences that help them to realize just how they learn best, e.g., by recopying notes, talking into a digital recorder, reviewing online Web sites, using peer mentors, having study sessions, using more visuals, and more.

Students need to be reminded that good values along with solid academics will open many doors, and when maturation kicks in, decision making will be an easier task. Setting up positive channeling activities helps avoid the negative choices some teenagers face as a result of peer pressure. This may require strategies that range from social journals to social scripts. Giving adolescents pats on the shoulder also goes a long way! Teach, but listen, respect, and encourage each adolescent to value himself or herself as well!

Resources for Adults and Teens

Canfield, J., Hansen, M., & Kirberger, K. (1997). *Chicken soup for the teenage soul.* Deerfield Beach, FL: Health Communications.

Crawford, G. (2004). *Managing the adolescent classroom: Lessons from outstanding teachers.* Thousand Oaks, CA: Corwin.

Cummings, R., & Fisher, G. (1993). *The survival guide for teenagers with LD.* Minneapolis, MN: Free Spirit Publishing.

Gill, V. (2007). *The ten students you'll meet in your classroom: Classroom management tips for middle and high school teachers.* Thousand Oaks, CA: Corwin.

Gore, M. (2003). *Successful inclusion strategies for secondary and middle school teachers: Keys to help struggling learners access the curriculum.* Thousand Oaks, CA: Corwin.

Karten, T. (2009). *Inclusion strategies that work for adolescent learners!* Thousand Oaks, CA: Corwin.

Mooney, J., & Cole, D. (2000). *Learning outside the lines: Two Ivy League students with learning disabilities and ADHD give you the tools.* New York: Fireside.

Using the Three R's to Guide Instruction and Assessment

When I was a newlywed (a few decades ago), my poor husband was regularly greeted by the new casserole of the week. Well, I remember thinking, if I threw in a little of this and that, with an extra can of something in the pantry, sprinkled it with parmesan cheese, and then baked it in a preheated 375-degree oven, wouldn't it be delicious? Now, in this age of information explosion and drives for assessing students, classrooms have become a little bit like that dreaded casserole. The purpose of this chapter is to help teachers stick to, and complement, the educational basics: reading, writing, and math. Included are student templates to reinforce concepts across the curriculum, while at the same time giving merit to the three R's, thereby yielding higher student performance. Increasing vital literacy and numeracy skills requires direct skill instruction within inclusive classrooms.

FIRST R: READING

Reading is a complex process for some students whose brains are not automatically wired to read. An eclectic approach to reading values both word identification and comprehension. *Phonological awareness*, the awareness of the sound structure of the spoken word, includes the ability to distinguish among the smallest units of speech, such as the syllables in a word and their individual phonemes. Phonological awareness is taught using controlled texts and grade-appropriate literature. Although reading novels teaches the joy of delving into a story, some students require direct skill instruction with structured reading activities for the application of skills. Literacy rises if reading material is related to a child's life, increasing both retention and motivation. It is recommended that a developmental reading assessment (DRA) first be administered, since it offers teachers insights into the reading accuracy, fluency, and comprehension levels of students at set times during the year, e.g., at set marking periods. As students read, the responses are looked at to determine the types of errors (e.g., insertions, substitutions, omissions, repetitions), time taken to read, and general comprehension of nonfiction and fiction passages to ascertain independent and instructional reading levels.

Word Identification

Word decoding and identification involves several components such as understanding vowel patterns, syllabication rules, context clues to identify unfamiliar vocabulary words, structural analysis, and dictionary skills, along with computer language tools such as how to use a spell checker or thesaurus.

Five Reading Strategies to Help Identify Unfamiliar Words

1. Vowel and consonant patterns identified

2. Syllabication rules applied

3. Context clues discovered

4. Structural analysis understood

5. Defining words

An example of these five reading ingredients is delineated in the boxed sentence below.

Figuring Out Words

> The aromatic smell coming from the kitchen was a culinary dream to the patrons as they eagerly awaited their ecstatic meal.

Vowel Rules and Consonant Patterns

Short *e*: smell, ecstatic. Long *e* using *ea:* dream, eagerly
Consonant blends: ec**st**atic has *st* blend, and pa**tr**ons has *tr* blend

Syllabication Rules

kit-chen   ec-stat-ic   cu-li-nar-y

Context Clues

An aromatic smell and a culinary dream must mean that something good is being created in the kitchen since people are eagerly awaiting what is described as an *ecstatic* meal.

Structural Analysis

Aromatic has the base word *aroma*, with a suffix, *tic*, added. *Eager* has the suffix *ly* added, which makes it into an adverb, *eagerly*. *A-wait-ed* can be broken up into three parts, with a prefix, base word, and suffix.

Defining Words

I'm still not certain of what *ecstatic* means, so I think I'll use my dictionary, computer thesaurus, or electronic speller. More examination and application of these rules continues below.

Remember that all learning needs to be repetitive for further retention.

"Examining Words Closely" Worksheet

Primary and reading teachers can consistently model this strategy, selecting one reading rule at a time. As students gain understanding of each rule, select more word(s) so they can practice applying it.

Explanation of Strategic Reading Rules

1. Sound out the word by looking at vowel and consonant patterns. (For vowels, this means a, e, i, o, u, or any combination of these letters at the beginning, middle, or end of words.) Vowels may be short, long, *r* controlled, or combined with another vowel. Consonants also blend (*fl*ag) or have *digraphs*—two letters with one sound (such as *wh, sh, th, ch*). Digraphs can also combine with other consonants (lu*nch*).

2. Try to say one syllable at a time; each syllable needs at least one vowel.

3. Find the parts of words by looking for the root words, prefixes, and suffixes.

4. Use context clues by reading surrounding words in the sentence to guess the meaning. Understand the sentence in relation to the passage.

5. Find the word meaning and pronunciation in the dictionary or on the computer.

Using the above five strategies, choose 10 words that appear in a book and examine them closely. Explain which strategy you would apply to help read each word.

Word	Strategy Used
1.	
2.	
3.	
4.	
5.	
6.	
7.	
8.	
9.	
10.	

Guided Questions to Help Students Increase Phonemic Awareness

> Words are made up of basic units of sound called phonemes. These sound units are formed by letters that are combined in different ways. The following guided questions can help students of all ages learn about phonics and how to pronounce unfamiliar words.

Isolation of a Sound

What is the beginning sound in *success*?
What is the ending sound in *planning*?

Discriminating Among Sounds

Which of the following words has a different beginning sound from the others?

assessment   accommodations   outcomes

Blending Sounds

What word would you have if you put the following sounds together?

s / c / a / n

Matching Sounds to Words

Is there a *p* sound in *cooperate?*

Matching Words to Words

Do *curriculum* and *connections* begin with the same sound?
Find two words that have the same *er* sound as in *learning.*

Dissecting or Identifying Sounds as You Stretch Words

What sounds do you hear in the word *study*?

Rhyming Sounds

Think of two words that rhyme with *study.* Make rhyming charts such as the following:

at	putty
mat	study
rat	buddy
flat	muddy

Deleting a Phoneme

What word would be left if the *s* were taken out of *self*?

Adding a Phoneme

What would be the resulting word if a *p* were added to *art*?

> Moral: Phonemic knowledge is essential!

Troublesome Words That Are Close But Not Close Enough

> During the course of several years, I recorded students' misread words in the context of reading literature. Compare the pronunciation differences between the two lists on the following pages. Misread phonemes can definitely thwart reading comprehension! After all, *peppercorn* and *popcorn* have similar letters, but there's quite a difference in taste.

sweet butter	sweat bitter
barter goods	butter goods
calm down	clam down
interpret this	interrupt this
watch out	witch out
imagine that	manage that
change it	charge it
applause	applesauce
immediate family	intermediate family
selling lemonade	spelling lemonade
it's the beginning	it's the being
hot meal	hot metal
delay	daily
Idaho	Iowa
bought	brought
aviator flies planes	aviator flies plants
it's a threat	it's a treat
in the groove	in the grove
steep valley	step valley
invitation	invasion invention
buckskin	duckskin
angels in the sky	angles in the sky
grandmother's sixtieth birthday	grandmother's sixteenth birthday
commanded orders	committed orders
sturdy table	study table

what a price	what a prize
inch through the mob	itch through the mob
read a fairytale	read a fair tailor
shouts of people	shots of people
stitch of clothing	switch of clothing
Denise	Dennis
started	stared
assign work	assassin work
flowers smelled	flowers smiled
yoga class	yogurt class
hundreds place	hundredths place
context clues	contact clues
skills developed	skulls developed

Classroom Reading Identification Suggestion

Students need more awareness of the mistakes they make in their reading, so word errors are not repeated. Misreading words directly impacts a student's comprehension when substituted words are not close in meaning. Daily time should be set aside for individual oral reading. Teachers can rotate about to individually read with some students, while others are silently reading or involved in classroom assignments. Within a half-hour period, a teacher can comfortably meet with five students for 5-minute periods to record individual reading sheets. If this is done with five different students each day, the whole class can read with the teacher each week. Other options include utilizing digital recorders for students to record their passages, allowing teachers to make corrections to be shared with students at a later date. The worksheet on the next page can then be shared with the students and parents as part of their *readacognition* (awareness of their reading program). Students regularly read the words on these sheets to ascertain types of errors, reinforcing corrections.

Readacognition: Words I Now Know

Name _____

Date	Word I Said	Correct Word

How Students Learn by Manipulating Letters

Instead of repeatedly writing misspelled words or rereading word errors, students learn more about words and their phonemes by actually manipulating letters. Students cut out the letters below and then use these letter cards to tactilely reinforce letter sounds. As a teacher calls out various words, students who each have their own set of laminated cards form the words and make corrections, without erasers. Students can also write letters on index cards. Teachers can increase difficulties, depending upon students' levels. For example, *fat, fate, late, inflate, deflate, inflated* might be one sequence read, or *in, win, tine, wind, twin, twine*. Possibilities for words to use are endless.

a	a	a	a
b	b	b	b
c	c	c	c
d	d	d	d
e	e	e	e
f	f	f	f
g	g	g	g
h	h	h	h
i	i	i	i
j	j	j	j

k	k	k	k
l	l	l	l
m	m	m	m
n	n	n	n
o	o	o	o
p	p	p	p
q	q	r	r
r	r	s	s
s	s	t	t
t	t	u	u
u	u	v	v
w	w	x	x
y	y	z	z

Teachers can laminate these cards for students to cut out and store in their own letter envelopes. Since students are physically manipulating the letters, the sensory impression will lead to further retention. Repeated practice works!

Try manipulating the cutout letters to make the words in the list below.

Spelling Rules	ad
	red
1. Teach spelling patterns.	read
2. Teach in small units.	**reading**
3. Provide sufficient practice and feedback.	or
4. Select appropriate words.	row
5. Maintain previously learned words.	word
6. Teach for transfer of learning.	**words**
7. Motivate students to spell correctly.	he
8. Include dictionary training.	**helps**
9. Use visuals.	we
10. PRAISE strides!	hen

Spelling Rules

1. Teach spelling patterns.
2. Teach in small units.
3. Provide sufficient practice and feedback.
4. Select appropriate words.
5. Maintain previously learned words.
6. Teach for transfer of learning.
7. Motivate students to spell correctly.
8. Include dictionary training.
9. Use visuals.
10. PRAISE strides!

ad
red
read
reading
or
row
word
words
he
helps
we
hen
when
you
to
ouch
touch
he
the
let
letters

Check out these Web sites:

Orton-Gillingham approaches—www.ortonacademy.org

International Reading Association—www.reading.org

Reading Online—www.readingonline.org

International Dyslexia Association—www.interdys.org

Wilson Language Training—www.wilsonlanguage.com

Jolly Phonics—www.jollylearning.co.uk/jp.htm

Note: See *Making Big Words,* by Patricia Cunningham and Dorothy Hall (1994), for more ideas on how to move the letters about to form words.

Stop to Manipulate Letters

How many words can you make out of this sign?

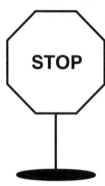

1.
2.
3.
4.
5.
6.
7.
8.
9.
10.
11.
12.

Students can manipulate letters in games such as Scrabble, Boggle, crossword puzzles (www.puzzlemaker.com), jumbles, word searches, and other fun word games.

Possible	Answers
1.	spot
2.	so
3.	top
4.	tops
5.	to
6.	pot
7.	pots
8.	post
9.	opt
10.	opts
11.	sop

Word Analysis Chart

Words can be dissected into their *affixes,* or word parts. The columned table below zeroes in on prefixes, suffixes, base words, and the two parts of a compound word. Increasing student awareness of how words are formed allows learners to transfer decoding skills to their reading. The chart below lists examples of words, with specific page numbers listed from the novel *The House on Mango Street,* by Sandra Cisneros. Primary-grade teachers need to focus on one affix/part of speech at a time, modeling extensively before requiring students to do this type of activity. Creating a classroom wall chart is also recommended.

Prefixes	Base Words	Suffixes	Compound Words	Page Number
			down stairs	3
	care	ful		3
			butter flies	33
			lunch room	54
			lunch time	54
	burn	ing		59
	luck	y		62
re	build	ing		67
			lip stick	67
			repair man	71
	damp	ness		70
	danger	ous		82
dis	appear	ing		95
	bare	ly		103
			for ever	110

My Word Analysis Chart

Directions: As you finish reading for the day, fill in words in the columns below.

Name: _____

Title of Book: _____

Prefixes	Base Words	Suffixes	Compound Words	Page Number

Reading Comprehension

Some children have a rapid oral reading pace, but poor comprehension. Read the following educational passage and fill in reading skills below.

> The days of the teacher sitting in front of the classroom with all student eyes facing forward have long passed. Teachers are currently encouraged to de-emphasize lecturing and concentrate more on active approaches in their classrooms. Less time is now spent on reading from textbooks and having students regurgitate isolated facts. Strict memorization without developing analytical skills will only serve students useless information that is unrelated to real-world problems. In contrast, developing critical thinking skills can be carried across all curriculum areas. Hopefully, all teachers will adapt this win–win approach to their individual educational environments.

Directions: Match each statement with the correct reading skill listed in the box below.

1. Students need active learning.

   _____

2. Memorizing isolated facts is ineffective learning.

   _____

3. Teachers will become facilitators, rather than disseminators, of knowledge.

   _____

4. The writer has read extensive educational research.

   _____

5. Teachers must help students to become critical thinkers.

   _____

Main Idea	Cause and Effect	Predictions
Inference	Sequencing	Summarizing

In the next activity, after being given short reading passages, students are asked to work backward, thinking of their own questions, rather than answering teacher-created ones. It is recommended that the teacher first model an example with the entire class, and have students use the Think of a Question template. Primary students could use a graphic organizer with fewer words, with clouds or bubbles to separate different types of questions and achieve the same goal of increasing reading understandings.

Think of a Question

Name: _____

> *Directions:* **After you have read the pages your teacher assigned, think of questions that relate to these reading skills. Exchange your questions with a classmate.**

Main Idea

This is the *most important idea of the story.* Asking about the main idea might involve using words such as *who, what, when, where, why,* or *how.* The main idea may be found anywhere in a paragraph, from the first to the last sentence. Sometimes it is not specifically stated with exact words, so you must figure it out. Discover the main idea and reword it into a question.

> *Main Idea Question:*

Details

These are *facts that tell more about the main idea.* Suppose you just read a paragraph whose main idea was *Dogs are great pets.* The paragraph also states that Labrador retrievers are a lovable breed that can be trained to bring in a newspaper. The sentence about Labradors is a supporting detail for the main idea. Such details may be specific names, dates, locations, directions, or perhaps descriptive words.

> *Details Question:*

Predictions

You've been asked to stop reading and write a prediction question such as the following (with the blanks filled in). What will happen next if _____? When will _____? How will _____? Where will _____? Predictions deal with the future. If you have finished reading a book or passage, what might a sequel be about? What might happen to the characters?

> *Prediction Question:*

Inferences

These are tough kinds of questions. You are being asked to take a step beyond the written words you have read, and write about *what the author implied or hinted at, but did not actually state in so many words.* Your inference needs to be supported by what you just read, by noting an example, comparison, mood, or maybe a relationship between events and details presented.

> *Inference Question:*

Sequencing

Order in the reading! Words such as *first, next, later, after,* and *finally,* along with other story clues, help to indicate the sequence. Questions might involve asking, What happened before _____? after _____? during _____?

> *Last, But Not Least, a Sequencing Question:*

Classifying Words

As you read a novel, notice how nouns, verbs, adjectives, and adverbs *add spice* to otherwise bland sentences. List different kinds of words in appropriate columns, with the page number next to each one. Try to imitate the writing style of authors you read, and use different kinds of words in your own writing. Remember that reading and writing are "relatives," with words as the common blood they share. Words can jump off pages and be stored in a word-mind bank!

Nouns	Verbs	Adjectives	Adverbs
• Naming word: a____, an____, the____ • Some may end in *er*, or *tion, sion,* or *ness.* • Nouns indicate a person, place, thing, or idea.	• Can indicate an action, expression, or occurrence Examine your verbs: • Many verbs end with *s, es,* or *ing.* • Verbs also have a past tense.	• Used with a noun or pronoun to describe it • Can be found between an article and a noun—the *friendly* girl, *another* table, *delicious* apple, *five brown* horses • Adjectives answer the questions, What kind? Which one? How many?	• Tell about verbs, adjectives, and other adverbs • Sometimes end in *ly.* Adverbs express cause and manner, and to what degree: "He ran well. She is extremely capable." • Adverbs answer the questions, How? (degree, manner) When? (time) Where? (place)
learner p. 5	learning p. 8	creative p. 12	skillfully p. 17
class p. 23	instruct p. 30	pleasing p. 38	constantly p. 38
imagination p. 55	shared p. 62	several p. 75	now p. 105

Reading Cloze Exercises

Cloze exercises delete important words, asking students to substitute their own. As a modification, a word box can be included. If inappropriate words are given by students, the level of reading or subject matter may be too difficult. If students do not use a word box, more than one answer is acceptable. As a further accommodation, some students may need the sentences and words read orally to them, so the teacher can ascertain comprehension rather than word identification level.

The following passages are examples of cloze exercises. Word boxes are included, but appropriate free responses are also welcomed.

Learning Disabilities

1. _____the processes and strategies.

2. Allow students to demonstrate learning in _____ways.

3. Teach _____-regulation and give positive feedback.

4. Provide opportunities for extended _____ and _____.

5. Adjust _____loads and _____ requirements.

Word Box (1–5)

accommodations	self	practice	multiple
work	time	model	application

Attention-Deficit/Hyperactivity Disorder

1. Can display _____ and/or _____.

2. _____ with poor delay of _____

3. Increased _____ of task performance

4. Diminished _____ behavior

5. Give students _____support.

6. Maintain a _____.

7. Arrange the _____to facilitate attention.

Word Box (6–12)

impulsivity	inattention	gratification
schedule	variability	hyperactivity
environment	rule-governed	organizational

Design a Cloze Exercise

Directions: Cooperatively design a cloze passage on any topic. First pick vocabulary words, and write them in the boxes at the bottom of the page. Then, write sentences in the large blank box below, substituting blanks where the words would be filled in. Sentences must tell more about topic.

Word Box

Compartmentalizing Reading

Works of fiction have these story ingredients: characters, setting, problem/plot, and resolution. The graphic organizer "Story Stuffing," which appears a little further on, helps students visually separate these story elements and ensures ongoing comprehension as plots develop. The graphic organizer "Vocabulary Review" concretely helps learners compartmentalize their thoughts by having them write a word's definition, the sentence with the vocabulary word from the story's context, and their own sentence using the same vocabulary word. Students can also draw pictures of key vocabulary words in the sentence, and identify synonyms, antonyms, and analogies.

Classroom book clubs are another way to improve reading comprehension, vocabulary development, and word identification. Adding a social dimension through cooperative grouping draws even the most reluctant reader into a book. Specific reading requirements are given to a group of at least five children who together review the same novel, showing their understanding in different ways. By working with peers under the teacher's direction, students become actively involved in their own course of learning as they eagerly share their knowledge, learning from each other under the teacher's auspices. Collectively they achieve a grade, while individually they are each accountable for a packet of materials. At first, it is recommended that everyone in the class reads the same novel, so the teacher can extensively model the skills that will be required in cooperative reading assignments. Simply put, students need to crawl before they can successfully walk or run, or in this case, before they can branch off from the teacher to read cooperatively. When I was the inclusion teacher in a fifth-grade classroom, everyone in the class read *The Lion, the Witch, and the Wardrobe,* by C. S. Lewis. While the class read the same book together, each child was responsible for completing his or her own reading packet. After that, children in the class were given a choice of 1 of 5 novels: *I Got a D in Salami; Dog Song; 1,001 Balloons; Jimmy Spoon;* and *In the Year of the Boar and Jackie Robinson.* After students made their book choice (based upon interest and reading levels), book clubs were cooperatively required to read their chosen book and complete collated assignments that consisted of the following duplicated pages. The general education teacher and I rotated among the groups to monitor understanding and fill out *readacognition* sheets. Books on tape were also available as an option for the class to listen to as they read independently or in groups.

Classroom Templates

Teacher Directions for Novel Book Club Reading Packets

Appropriate variations can be given for grade levels and students' individual academic or social needs. Workload and time requirements can also be modified. Read on for more directions and reading templates that combine literature with direct skill instruction.

1. *Chapter Summary Pages*—Students list the main idea of each chapter in well-constructed, detailed sentences. (Number of pages depends on how many chapters are in the book. For example, 7 sheets with 3 summaries per page would be enough to summarize 21 chapters.)

2. *Vocabulary Review Pages*—Definitions of chosen vocabulary, sentences from the story using the words, and students' own sentences showing word meaning. (Ten sheets with 2 vocabulary words on each page are enough for 20 vocabulary words.)

3. *Reading Graph*—Students are asked to date, grade, and plot what they think about a book, giving it a grade such as WOW (85–100), GOOD, OK, ???? (not sure what's going on), or ———— (so bad that there's no comment for the book).

   Quite often, students might not want to give a book a chance, but by plotting their reading reactions on a daily basis, they can visually identify which parts interest them most before dismissing a book.

4. *Story Stuffing Page*—Graphic organizer is used to increase students' knowledge that every story has these essential ingredients: characters, setting (where and when), plot, climax (turning point or zenith), and ending or resolution. Students can continue to fill out this template as more details, events, and characters unfold.

5. *Word Analysis Page*—This page asks students to identify affixes with specific prefixes and suffixes, base words, and compound words. Students then become less fearful of those long words, since they can now identify the meaning and pronunciation of longer words by breaking them apart.

6. *Columned Nouns, Verbs, Adjectives, Adverbs*—Students find words in their chosen novels and place them in appropriate categories, depending on how they are used in specific sentences. This page becomes much easier to do after the teacher has guided them through it in the novel they have read together. Book club members can work together to cooperatively identify the parts of speech at any time while reading the novel.

7. *Readacognition*—Students periodically read with teacher and review vocabulary words their group has chosen.

Story Stuffing

Characters

(Who?)

```
┌────────────────────────────────────────────┐
│                                            │
│                                            │
│                                            │
│                                            │
└────────────────────────────────────────────┘
```

Setting

(Where? When?)

```
┌────────────────────────────────────────────┐
│                                            │
│                                            │
│                                            │
│                                            │
└────────────────────────────────────────────┘
```

Plot/Climax

(How did it happen? What's the problem? What's the exciting part?)

```
┌────────────────────────────────────────────┐
│                                            │
│                                            │
│                                            │
│                                            │
└────────────────────────────────────────────┘
```

Resolution

(Tell about the ending.)

```
┌────────────────────────────────────────────┐
│                                            │
│                                            │
│                                            │
│                                            │
└────────────────────────────────────────────┘
```

Vocabulary Review

Words/Definitions From the Story/Text That I Now Know:

- Word: _____

Definition: _____

_____

- Word: _____

Definition: _____

_____

Sentences From the Story That Use Vocabulary Words:

_____

_____

_____

_____

_____

_____

_____

_____

_____

_____

_____

_____

My Own Sentences Using Vocabulary Words:

_____

_____

_____

_____

_____

_____

_____

_____

_____

_____

_____

_____

Chapter Summaries

Story Title: _____

Author: _____

_____

_____

_____

_____

_____

_____

_____

_____

_____

_____

_____

_____

_____

Student Critique: Grade Your Book Chapter by Chapter

Directions: Place date of your reading under each vertical line and grade your book, scoring it from 5 to 100 according to the descriptions in the key below.

_____ 's Reading Graph

Book: _____ Author: _____

W	100																									
O	95																									
W	90																									
	85																									
G	80																									
O	75																									
O	70																									
D	65																									
O	60																									
K	55																									
?	50																									
?	45																									
?	40																									
?	35																									
?	30																									
—	25																									
—	20																									
—	15																									
—	10																									
—	5																									

DATES :

WOW: I love it!   GOOD: I like it!   OK: Not bad!   ????: No idea what is going on.   ----:Yuck!

SOARING INTO READING

Scan

Outline

Analyze

Read

Understanding Nonfiction

Reading *nonfiction material* requires different skills from those needed for reading fiction. Children need specific tools to help them extract pertinent details from textbooks, newspaper articles, periodicals, online sources, and other nonfiction literature. Reading nonfiction can be as difficult a task as trying to identify ingredients of a meal that you have not personally prepared. You might know what it tastes like, but how was it made? Nonfiction books can be as layered as that delectable chocolate cake. Specific strategies such as *scanning, outlining,* and *analyzing* help students comprehend their reading. Cooperatively working in groups based on common interests fosters further understanding. This *SOARing* technique is helpful for teachers of subjects such as social studies and science while *uncovering* textbook chapters. *The more ways they read, the better their comprehension becomes.*

How SOARing Works With Stations

By scanning the material, students familiarize themselves with the layout of the textbook, noticing pictures, graphs, highlighted words, chapter divisions, table of contents, glossary, index, length, and other dimensions of the nonfiction reading material. Afterward, students form their own outlines with the main idea, details, and personal reflections (M/D/Y Station), which are used as templates to help them organize and analyze notes. After outlining the main idea, students soar into the material with stations. Learners choose stations for assigned textbook pages, specific articles, or other nonfiction material. Station choices include the following:

- Picture This Station (drawing more about main ideas)
- Word Station (creating a word search, pantomiming words, word acrostics)
- Teacher Station (designing a test based on textbook readings)
- Performance Station (creating a skit, poem, song, commercial, video game, or dance about the readings)
- Research Station (finding out more about specific topics; using other resources such as texts, computers, encyclopedias, and the library)

Note for Teachers

SOARing Into Reading is designed to help all students become actively involved in their learning under the teacher's auspices. Specific classroom stations allow learners to choose their own way of understanding nonfiction. SOARing Into Reading pragmatically translates effective educational research about good teaching practices while motivating learners through differentiated instruction. Any of these stations can be modified according to students' needs and levels. Each group consists of four to six students who independently rotate around the classroom to cooperatively complete tasks outlined in written, distributed station directions. Even though students work together, all students are responsible for the finished product. Some students may find the assignments too difficult, while others may need more challenges. For example, the Word Station could be modified by requiring fewer words for the word search, or just assigning the acrostic to students who need greater challenges. Teacher discretion is then required for modifying the grading rubric. Teachers can encourage students to work with different classmates or may even randomly assign children to stations. The objective is to soar into reading, changing children's perspectives of reading textual material; some may even say, "More, please!"

Soaring Directions for Students

Scan

Look at all of the titles, pictures, bold letters, highlighted words, charts, graphs, and other cool things in print that you see in your textbook.

Outline

Read only the title headings of each section or chapter to determine what the main ideas are. Place the main idea inside the *M* section of your M/D/Y chart.

Analyze

You are not ready to read quite yet. *Think* about what you wrote as the main idea and how the pictures, charts, vocabulary, and other things you saw on the pages relate to that main idea. Get a general *understanding* of your topic.

Read

Now you are finally ready to *read* because you have previewed your topic. After you finish reading, fill in the *D* (Details) and *Y* (You) sections on your M/D/Y chart. The readings will now make a lot more sense.

After you have filled out the M/D/Y Station sheet, you will further explore the textbook pages by stopping at one or two of the following stations:

- Research Station
- Performance Station
- Word Station
- Picture This Station
- Teacher Station

Cooperatively work together to complete assigned tasks, following each station's directions. Plan your train ride carefully as you read more about your itinerary. Try to continually work with different classmates.

All Aboard for More Station Directions

The *Main Idea/M* and *Details/D* sections can be completed cooperatively. The *Y (You)* section on your M/D/Y chart is all about your reaction to the reading. It is to be completed individually. Tell if you have ever heard of words or ideas in this text material before. Did you like what you read? Do you want to learn more about this topic? Again, *Y* means *you*. At the bottom, there's a spot for vocabulary words and their definitions.

After you have cooperatively completed and shared the M/D/Y Station, just like trains, everyone will *continue making more station stops.* Each student must pick another station. If this is your second time doing this activity, pick a different train stop from the last time. *Follow all directions for individual stations and work cooperatively with other passengers.* Prepare your *oral presentation,* using note cards, following *presentation page directions.* Using the *peer-rating page,* let peers rate your helpfulness. *Study the rubric* to make sure all work is completed. Your teacher will then check all of your work. After your teacher reviews your completed oral and written assignments, a grade will be recorded on a *Soaring Reading Report.*

Most important, have fun on your textbook journey. Remember the book *The Little Engine That Could!*

Sound the whistle. All aboard!

M/D/Y Station

for pages _____

in my _____ textbook

Name: _____

Directions: Use the bolded titles or section headings in the textbook to help outline the main ideas. Read the words under these headings to discover and list important details. The last section, You, is completed individually. It is a chance to tell your thoughts about the reading. Write neatly in small but readable handwriting.

Main Idea	Details	You
Look at the headings and titles of each chapter and section. Scan the pictures, charts, vocabulary, and other elements on the pages to understand the main idea of assigned pages.	Read the selection to discover details about the main idea. Concentrate on particulars that answer the questions who, what, when, where, why, and how.	Did you like the reading? Can you connect it to anything you have learned before? Did it remind you of a TV show, movie, book, or magazine or newspaper article you read on the same topic? Do you think this information will be helpful?

Vocabulary	Write new words and their definitions.

Picture This Station

Directions: Illustrate concepts from your reading that show more related details about the main ideas in the given boxes below. Refer to your M/D/Y sheet for the main ideas and include a caption for each picture. The group should cooperatively divide the textbook pages so each person illustrates different details about the main idea. Then, the illustrators share pictures with each other by cutting them out and pasting them onto larger construction paper to create a group scrapbook. Students sign individual pictures.

Illustrator: _____

Brief sentence explaining the picture: _____

_____

Illustrator: _____

Brief sentence explaining the picture: _____

_____

Word Station

Directions: Choose *10 vocabulary words* from the reading selection. Using graph paper, create a *word search* for another classmate. Write your words in the box below. Then try to *pantomime one of the words* to see if members of your cooperative group can guess which vocabulary word you are demonstrating through your gestures and actions. Create *two-word acrostics* that further explain the vocabulary words.

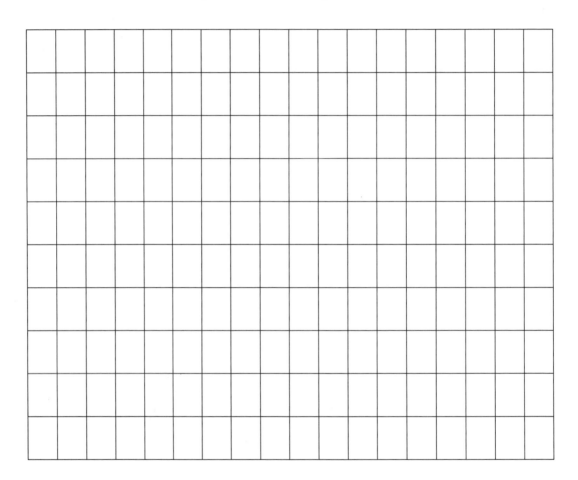

Look for these vocabulary words:

1. _____ 2. _____

3. _____ 4. _____

5. _____ 6. _____

7. _____ 8. _____

9. _____ 10. _____

Word Search Creators: _____

(Word Station, cont'd.)

Directions: Students work together in pairs, trios, and quartets.

Word Acrostic sentence examples:

<table>
<tr>
<td>

Seeing data is what a scientist does.

Comparing information is important.

Inquiry can lead to discoveries.

Experiments help us learn about the world around us.

Now I understand more about the procedures involved.

Collecting data for research aids the process.

Evaluating the hypothesis is part of the scientific method.

</td>
<td>

People are part of the community.

Existing together is not an easy task.

Organizing governments requires a political process.

Planning together to reach agreements is necessary.

Living with diverse cultures will help this nation grow.

Environmental differences affect how people live.

</td>
</tr>
</table>

Choose two vocabulary words from the word search to create your sentence acrostics.

<table>
<tr>
<td></td>
<td></td>
</tr>
</table>

Acrostic created by _____

Teacher Station

Directions: It's your chance to be the teacher. Your group will design a test based upon the textbook readings. You can use the following question starters to help you begin. Remember to *vary the types of questions* and *use both big and little thought questions.* A little question can be answered with one word, while a big question requires more thought and details. All questions need an answer, either next to the question or on a separate answer key. The group must also decide the value (points given for correct answers) for each question, with the total possible test grade of 100%.

Sample Questions

Little thought question example: What is your name?
Big thought question example: Why do you attend school?

Sample Question Starters:

What is _____ ?

A: _____

Where is _____ ?

A: _____

How is _____ ?

A: _____

Why did _____ ?

A: _____

Which one of the following describes a _____ ?

A: _____

When did _____ ?

A: _____

Which is *not* an example of _____ ?

A: _____

Tell the difference between _____ and _____ .

A: _____

Vary your questions by including the following question types:

True/False	Multiple choice	Fill-in
Essay	Matching	Short answers
Open ended		

Examiners: _____

Performance Station

Directions: The group chooses one of the following cooperatively, and works to bring to life concepts or stories they have read.

1. Write a *short skit* or *television commercial* to demonstrate what you read. Remember that your characters must relate to the reading. It's your chance to make words come alive! Be creative!

2. Create a *poem, song, video game, advertisement,* or *dance* about the reading. Again, concentrate on stories or textbook concepts that you read.

Available classroom resources can be used (e.g., digital cameras, recorders, dictionaries, computers, thesauruses, rhyming lists, and CDs).

Performers: _____

_____

_____

Research Station

Directions: Using classroom and library resources such as computers, encyclopedias, and other available references, the group will find out more facts and details about the textbook material or story you have read. If you are using a computer, print out related information and highlight important facts that you will orally share with the class.

Researchers learned the following: _____

_____

_____

_____

_____

_____

_____

_____

_____

_____

Materials used: _____

Sources must be correctly cited using the format shown in the bibliography guidelines following.

Research conducted by _____

Bibliography Guidelines for Citing Sources From Research Station

Book—One Author

Author's last name, initial of first name. (year of book's publication). *Title of the book.* Place of publication: Name of Publisher.

Example:

Hoopmann, K. (2009). *All dogs have ADHD.* London, England: Jessica Kingsley Publishers.

Book—Multiple Authors

First author's last name, initial of first name, next author's last name, initial of first name. (year of book's publication). *Title of the book.* Place of publication: Name of Publisher.

Example:

Winkler, H., & Oliver, L. (2003). *Niagara falls or does it?* New York: Grosset & Dunlap.

Book—Editor Instead of Author

Name or names of editors—last name first, then first initial. (Ed.). (year of publication). *Title of book.* Place of publication: Name of Publisher.

Example:

Evans, J. (Ed.). (2006). *Ultimate visual dictionary.* New York: DK Publishing.

Magazine Article

Author's last name, first initial. (year, month, and day of publication). Title of article. *Title of magazine,* page range.

Example:

Fischer, D. (2001, November 12). Feel good sports stories. *Sports Illustrated for Kids,* 47.

Online Information

Author's last name, first initial (if known). (Year, or n.d. if no date is listed). *Title of work.* Retrieved (retrieval date), from (Web address)

Example:

Kalish, N. (2009). *Summer homework should be banned!* Retrieved October 20, 2009, from http://www.timeforkids.com/TFK/kids

Peer Rating Form

Directions: Place your name above the line where it says *your name,* and ask two peers (classmates) to evaluate your helpfulness at different stations. Your peer must indicate at which station you cooperatively worked and how you were helpful, and sign the statement. The peer can give you a rating from 1–5, with 5 being the most helpful and highest rating, 3 describing someone who was of average help, and 1 being for someone who offered little assistance. Add the two scores for your total.

First Peer Rating

_____ helped me _____

(your name)

_____

_____ at the _____

Station by _____

_____ .

Number Rating (1–5): _____ Peer's Signature _____

Second Peer Rating

_____ helped me_____

(your name)

_____

_____ at the _____

Station by _____

_____ .

Number Rating (1–5): _____ Peer's Signature _____

First Peer Rating Score: _____

Second Peer Rating Score: _____

Total Peer Score: _____

Oral Presentations

Presentation Page Directions

Speaking Hints

1. Look at the audience.

2. Glance at your notes, but do not read from them.

3. Use appropriate hand gestures to help your presentation.

4. Share relevant information with teachers and classmates.

5. Be prepared for your speech by using the following note card guidelines.

Note Card for Speech Explaining Station Chosen

Name of station: _____

People you worked with: _____

_____

What Did You Learn?

Main idea: _____

Supporting details: _____

_____

_____

Procedure Followed in Correct Sequence

First _____

Next _____

After _____

Finally _____

Briefly Summarize What You Learned at the Station

_____

_____

_____

_____

Teacher's SOARing Reading Record for Station Grades

Student	M/D/Y	Picture This	Word	Performance	Research	Teacher

Textbook: _____ Pages: _____

Rubric for SOARing Stations

	Beginning 1	Developing 2	Accomplished 3	Exemplary 4	Score
All verbal and written station directions were completed.	Missing more than three station requirements. Unorganized. Illegible writing.	Legible but disorganized. Missing two station requirements.	Presentable work. Evidence of organization. Missing one station requirement.	Finished product is well organized and neat with all station requirements met. Completed and followed all written directions.	
Worked effectively with cooperative group at stations.	Few positive statements from peers, with a peer rating total of 1 or less. No teacher observation of social interaction.	Some positive statements from peers, with a peer rating total of 2–4. Some teacher observation of working well with peers.	More positive statements from peers. Peer rating total of 5–7. Frequent teacher observation of positive social interaction.	Positive statements from both peers, with rating total of 8–10. Constant teacher observation of cooperatively working well with peers.	
Oral Presentation	Incoherent speech. Little acknowledgment of audience. Did not stick to topic. Could not explain station work.	Difficulty retrieving information. Read from written work with little audience contact. Able to speak about work, but lacked continuity. Concentrated more on details than the main idea.	Could answer most oral questions given by peers and teacher. Good eye contact and gestures. Evidence of recall and good sequencing of station work in speech. Acknowledgment of audience. Focused on main idea and supporting details.	Able to explain work performed at each station, by sharing relevant information with teachers and classmates in speech. Excellent eye contact and gestures. Logical order of main idea with supporting details. Maintained audience interest.	

Source: Created using rubistar.4teachers.org. Copyright © 2000–2004 ALTEC at the University of Kansas, which is supported in part by the U.S. Department of Education awards to ALTEC (Advanced Learning Technology in Education Consortia). These include Regional Technology in Education Consortium 1995–2005, awards #R302A50008 and #R302A000015. Resources used do not necessarily reflect the policies of the U.S. Department of Education.

SECOND R: 'RITING

Basic Writing Rules

1. Think about what you are going to write.

2. Use an outline, list, web, or template to help organize your thoughts.

3. Begin writing your rough draft—it doesn't need to be smooth! Always skip lines; it leaves space for revisions.

4. Writing means rewriting, which means you need to repeatedly look at what you have written to make it better. Learn about Ed's Car! (how to revise writing)

5. Remember, writing is like talking on paper, since you can tell others what you are thinking through a short story, play, poem, newspaper article, tall tale, and more. Writing is a written connection and gateway to all subjects!

 =

Translation: Writing = speaking on paper.

Ways to Think Before Writing

Suppose your topic is successful classrooms. Think of relevant words and list them by the appropriate letter. Using the alphabet as your guide helps to organize thoughts across the curriculum. Writing can be as easy as the ABCs!

Successful Classrooms

A	accommodations, assessments
B	
C	
D	
E	
F	
G	
H	
I	
J	
K	
L	
M	
N	
O	
P	
Q	
R	
S	
T	
U	
V	
W	
X	
Y	
Z	zero-reject

A–Z lists are used to introduce or review vocabulary across various curricula.

A–Z Listing for Social Studies

A	
B	
C	
D	
E	
F	
G	
H	
I	
J	
K	
L	
M	
N	
O	
P	
Q	
R	
S	
T	
U	
V	
W	
X	
Y	
Z	

A–Z Listing for Science

A	
B	
C	
D	
E	
F	
G	
H	
I	
J	
K	
L	
M	
N	
O	
P	
Q	
R	
S	
T	
U	
V	
W	
X	
Y	
Z	

Revising Writing

What's Ed's Car?

Expand, Delete, Substitute, Combine, and Rearrange

E xpand—Write a simple sentence, then make it longer by asking the *who, what, when, where, why,* or *how* questions.

For example,

The dog ran.

What kind of dog?
The cute dog ran.

Where did the dog run?
The cute dog ran around the block.

Why did the dog run around the block?
The cute dog ran around the block because the cat was chasing it.

When did the dog run?
The cute dog ran around the block yesterday because the cat was chasing it.

How did the dog run?
The cute dog quickly ran around the block yesterday because the cat was chasing it.

D elete—Take away unnecessary words that repeat the same thought. *The big canine dog ran* can be changed to *The dog ran.* Writing less is better if the same thought is conveyed. Adding the word *canine* is unnecessary since it means the same as dog.

S ubstitute—Change words if another word can be more exact, or put in substitutes for overused words. *It was a good dog because it did good things.* That's quite a vague sentence. Here's the new one: *The loyal dog obeyed commands.* By substituting more descriptive words for *good* and *things,* the sentence's meaning becomes clearer.

C ombine—

And

R earrange—Combine similar thoughts expressed by subjects and verbs, and change placement of words.

The playful dog ran today. The playful dog listened today.

New sentence: *Today, the playful dog ran and listened.*

If these strategies are too difficult, then some students in Grades K–1 or beginning writers could just focus on the expansion.

The following sign can be posted as a reminder to write with *Ed's Car* strategies.

Source: Mnemonic designed by Adam J. Karten.

Ed's   Car

E XPAND

D' ELETE

S UBSTITUTE

C OMBINE

A nd

R EARRANGE

Application of Ed's Car (Revising Writing)

> Inclusion can help students. Inclusion is a way of teaching students. It can benefit students a lot. They can prepare for their future. Inclusion meets social, academic, and cognitive needs.

Revision Questions

- What word is often repeated?
- What phrase needs to be deleted?

Revised Writing

> Helping diverse students to achieve positive outcomes can be accomplished through inclusion. Using a variety of accommodations and planning strategies addresses social, academic, and cognitive needs. Inclusion, a way of approaching teaching, prepares students for future successes.

Writing Tips Explaining Revisions

1. The first sentence says that inclusion helps students, but the revised version expands the sentence by telling what *kind* of student (diverse). It also varies the sentence beginning by starting with a verb (helping), instead of repeating the same word (inclusion).

2. The second sentence expands the original thought by telling *how* those needs are met. It also substitutes the word *met* with a more exact word, *addressed*. The original sentence was deleted because the writer had already stated that students are helped by inclusion. Even though the word *help* was changed to *benefit,* the thought was the same. There is no need to say it twice.

3. The last sentence combines and rearranges two separate sentences by using an *apposition*—telling more about the noun by using a qualifying phrase: *Inclusion* (a noun), *a way of approaching teaching* (telling more about the noun), *prepares students for future successes* (verb phrase).

4. Proofread and then read it again. That's when you'll catch that repeated word or perhaps decide that you want to write the paragraph differently. Also, walking away from your writing helps, since you'll return with a fresh eye.

Collecting Writing Thoughts

Quite often, students need help to get started with their writing. Writing templates, easily accessible in writing folders, circumvent that "Where do I begin?" dilemma by neatly organizing thoughts. As students develop more confidence and familiarity with the writing process, they are weaned off the templates. It's comparable to using a special holiday cake tin for the batter. The ingredients make the taste, not the container. It's the students' writing, but it is organized by the template.

Writing Planner (K–2)

Cars are important. First of all, _____

_____

_____

_____

_____

In addition, _____

_____

_____

_____

_____

_____

_____

Finally, _____

_____

_____

_____

_____

_____

_____

After the words are filled in, the entire passage must be rewritten so that students gain a coherent writing experience.

Our Earth

Directions: Use the word box and outline below to help write a persuasive essay. Then, rewrite all sentences on another piece of paper.

pollution	water
ecology	air
environment	help
recycle	world
planet	future

First Paragraph: Introduction

Here are some reasons we should care about the Earth.

First, _____

_____. In addition, _____

_____. Also, _____

_____

Second Paragraph (expand upon the first reason) _____

_____

_____

_____. _____

_____. _____

Third Paragraph (expand upon the second reason) _____

_____. _____

_____. _____

_____

Fourth Paragraph (expand upon the third reason) _____

_____. _____

_____

_____. _____

_____

Fifth Paragraph (sum up all three reasons) In summary, _____

_____. _____

_____

_____

Sensory Writing Planner

This planner helps add sensory elements to setting stories. First, think of a place, and then put sensory words in columns to describe that place. The planner is then turned into a three-paragraph story about somewhere the student visited or read about. As an adaptation, some students might begin by choosing sentences that describe only one sense and location (e.g., hearing—a parade; sight—a museum). Later on, the paragraph is expanded to include other senses.

When I am at the _____, I can _____ .

Hear	See	Smell	Touch	Taste

First Paragraph (Introduction) The _____ is a place where _____ _____ .People _____ _____ and _____ there. The most interesting thing about _____ is that _____ _____ .

Second Paragraph (sensory details from chart) There are many different sights, sounds, smells, tastes, and things to touch at the _____ . Some include _____ and _____ . It sounds like _____ and looks like _____ . My favorite things there are _____and_____ .

Third Paragraph (conclusion) Overall, _____ is a place that _____ .It can best be described as _____ , and _____and _____are the most exciting things there. To sum up, I think _____ about _____ .

Personal Narrative: Writing Planner for Grades 4 to 12

Directions: Collect your thoughts, and place them in the corresponding boxes as a planner for your narrative (the story about yourself). List words, not sentences.

Past—Yesterday, what already happened

What did you do when you were younger? Where were you born? What is your favorite memory? Remember past events.

```
┌─────────────────────────────────────────────────────────┐
│                                                         │
│                                                         │
│                                                         │
│                                                         │
│                                                         │
└─────────────────────────────────────────────────────────┘
```

Present—Today, what's happening now

What is your life like? Tell about your favorite things. Include information about family and friends. Concentrate on now.

```
┌─────────────────────────────────────────────────────────┐
│                                                         │
│                                                         │
│                                                         │
│                                                         │
│                                                         │
└─────────────────────────────────────────────────────────┘
```

Future—Tomorrow, what will happen in the time ahead

What are your plans? Have you picked a career?

What are your goals? Focus on thinking ahead.

```
┌─────────────────────────────────────────────────────────┐
│                                                         │
│                                                         │
│                                                         │
│                                                         │
│                                                         │
└─────────────────────────────────────────────────────────┘
```

Directions: After you have filled in the past, present, and future boxes on your planner, follow these steps for writing your personal narrative:

Paragraph 1: Tell about your present life in 1 to 2 sentences. Include 1 to 2 sentences that refer to the past, and 1 to 2 sentences about the future. Do not include any details, only main ideas.

I am presently a _____ who _____,
_____, and _____. In the past, I did
some fun things like _____, _____, and
_____. In the future, I hope to
_____.

Paragraph 2: Tell about past events only. Use minimum of 3 to 5 sentences.

When I was younger, I _____. I once
_____. I remember _____
_____. I also_____.

Paragraph 3: Tell about present events only. What are you currently doing?

Today, I _____
_____. I like _____. My
friends   and   I   _____.   Sometimes,   I
_____.   My   family   members   include
_____.   We   like   to   _____
together. One of my favorite hobbies is _____.

Paragraph 4: Tell about the future only. Where do you see yourself 5 or 10 years from now?

In the future, I want to _____. Some of my
dreams include _____
_____. One day I will _____
_____. Ultimately, _____
_____.

Paragraph 5: This is your conclusion.

To sum it up, my life has been _____ so far. I
presently think my life is _____. Eventually, I hope to
_____. In conclusion, _____
_____.

Well-Planned Writing: A Balanced Meal

First Paragraph

Introduce your topic or story. Tell what it is about, without giving specific details. This paragraph should briefly explain to the reader what you will be writing more about, and should answer questions such as the following:

Who? _____   Where? _____

What? _____   Why? _____

When? _____   How? _____

A p p e t i z e r

You can use sentences like

It all began when _____.

In the beginning, _____.

First, _____.

Early on, _____.

Second Paragraph

Tell the reader what happened next. Think about the main idea of the paragraph, and then add more details about that main idea with additional sentences.

Main Idea: _____

_____

Details:

1. _____

2. _____

3. _____

S o u p

You can use sentences like these in your following paragraphs:

Next, _____.

Immediately following, _____.

Shortly after, _____.

Then, _____.

3rd Paragraph:	**SALAD**	**4th Paragraph:**	**ENTREE**	**5th Paragraph:**	**DESSERT**
Main Idea: _____		Main Idea: _____			
_____		_____		**CONCLUSION**	
Details:		**Details:**		**Words like**	
1._____		1._____		All in all, _____.	
2._____		2._____		Finally, _____.	
3._____		3._____		Ultimately, _____.	
Words like		**Words like**		On the whole, _____.	
Afterward, _____.		After a while, _____.		To summarize, _____.	
Suddenly, _____.		Some time later,_____.		Looking back, _____.	
Later, _____.		Eventually, _____.			

Developing My Writing With a Rough Draft

Use this planner to start the rough draft.

First Paragraph: Introduction (Appetizer)

Questions to answer: Who, What, When, Where, Why, How?

- First,

Second Paragraph (Soup)

Main Idea:

- Next,

Third Paragraph (Salad)

Main Idea:

- Then,

Fourth Paragraph (Entree)

Main Idea:

- After that,

Fifth Paragraph (Dessert)

Conclusion:

- Finally,

How to Expand Writing With Figurative Language

Language Locater

Find similes or metaphors in the story or textbook, or create your own, based upon what you read.

Examples:

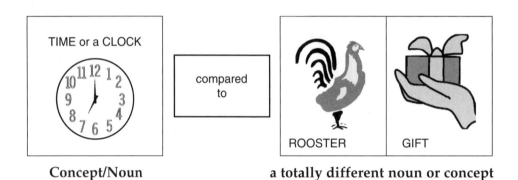

Concept/Noun   a totally different noun or concept

Simile: A clock is like a rooster that jolts us from our sleep.

Metaphor: A clock is a rooster, jolting us from our sleep.

Simile: Time is as precious as a birthday gift, given with love each year.

Metaphor: Time is each year's cherished birthday gift.

Now find or create your own similes or metaphors:

word/picture   word/picture

compared to

Concept/Noun   A Totally Different Noun or Concept

Simile: _____

_____

Metaphor: _____

_____

Writing Reflections

Cooperative Writing Idea

All of these suggestions add a social component to writing, making it less of an isolated activity.

Students can pool thoughts together to cooperatively write stories. Even though children's ideas are shared and brainstormed, each child must physically write the same story. Of course, remind them to skip lines for revisions, while implementing the strategies offered in Ed's Car. Some cooperative ideas include the following:

- Selecting a class topic, groups can cooperatively write different stories; fill in A–Z lists; and think about the who, what, where, when, why, and how questions. For example, everyone can write about Halloween, early colonies, endangered species, football, dancing, or a favorite book with several versions, twists, or in a different genre.

- Two students can interview each other and record differences in a planner, such as a Venn diagram, which can later become a four-paragraph story:

  1st Paragraph: Introduction (telling about both students)
  2nd Paragraph: Similarities
  3rd Paragraph: Differences
  4th Paragraph: Conclusion

- Teacher can read a picture book to the class and then model how to retell that story using a different genre such as a tall tale, poem, or news report. Students will then choose their own picture book and retell the story with their chosen genre in groups of three or four.

- Using any curriculum topic, students can first answer the questions below as their planner, and then organize those thoughts into paragraphs, with a separate main idea and appropriate details for each one.

  o Who?
  o What?
  o When?
  o Where?
  o Why?
  o How?

- Shown a picture prompt, students will cooperatively and creatively write a story, giving their picture a past, present, and future.

  What already happened?
  What's happening now?
  What might happen later?

Writing Sources to Explore

Berninger, V., & Wolf, B. (2009). *Helping students with dyslexia and dysgraphia make connections: Differentiated instruction lesson plans in reading and writing.* Baltimore: Paul H. Brookes.
Gess, D., & Livingston, J. (2006). *Teaching writing: Strategies for improving literacy across the curriculum.* New York: Write Track.
The Write Track: (800) 845–8402, http://www.thewritetrack.com

Students can also create their own books. Check out these sources:

CAST Universal Design for Learning (UDL) Bookbuilder—http://bookbuilder.cast.org
Treetop Publishers—http://www.barebooks.com

Genre Menu: Keeping Track of What I've Read and Written

Name: _____

Genre	Date	Title
Poem		
Biography or Autobiography		
Historical Fiction		
Mystery		
Comic Strip		
Graphic Novel		
Letter		
News Article		
Play		
Advertisement		
Fairy Tale or Fable		
Fantasy		
Realistic Fiction		
Myth		
Nonfiction		
Science Fiction		
Tall Tale/Legend		
Other		

Remember, the idea is to try different types of reading and writing!

Writer's Notebook Ideas

Decorate your notebook with wallpaper, construction paper, pictures from magazines, comic strips, something you drew, or whatever you like best. This notebook could be a place for a favorite poem, an honor roll certificate, a shopping list, or a picture of your pet. Maybe one day you will choose to write about one of these things. It is your unique collection of thoughts and a home for your ideas.

Include items such as the following:

- Observations in the classroom

- Lists

- Pictures

- Drawings

- Recipes

- Birthday card

- Something special

- A flower you found

- Thoughts about . . . anything else you desire!

Using Guided Questions to Assess and Reflect Upon Writing

Date	a. Self b. Peers c. Teacher	Title of Work	Comments/Suggestions/ Reflections (Write number of each question used)

Questions to Ponder:

1. Were thoughts clearly stated?

2. Is the writing well organized?

3. Were words repeated? Should another word be substituted? Was the same thought or concept repeated, using different words?

4. Did the writing flow with transitional words such as *first, in addition, later, to sum up,* helping the reader know that a new thought is coming?

5. Did each paragraph have a separate thought with its own main idea and supporting details? Were sentences choppy? Could some sentences be combined?

6. Were there spelling errors?

7. Were the capitalization and punctuation reviewed?

8. Did you like reading/writing the piece? Why?

9. Do you understand what you just read/wrote?

THIRD R: 'RITHMETIC

Why Math?

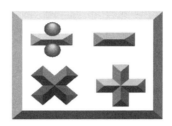

Math was never one of my favorite subjects, until I began to teach it. I hated those ridiculous word problems that only gave you a headache. Basically, who cares if so and so only had 4 boxes that fit 5 cookies each and had 25 friends who needed to eat those cookies? Does your head hurt yet? Math can be so much more than that!

It's about classifying, organizing, estimating, and understanding the world around you. Yes, you sometimes must add, subtract, multiply, and divide, but it need not be boring. Students need to know that different approaches can solve the same math problem. Math is a way of logically thinking and reasoning that carries over into all subject areas as a cognitive process. Verbalizing steps along the way helps, as does visualizing numbers in problems. Teachers need to assess whether students understand the problem itself, or if the reading vocabulary in a word problem is the handicap. Students can learn more about numbers in a fun way, practicing basic skills and applying thought.

Math is a complex subject requiring a variety of computational skills involving pictures, shapes, whole numbers, fractions, decimals, and words. Mathematical concepts and computational skills can be taught by applying sound educational strategies, such as establishing prior knowledge, proceeding from the simple to the complex, breaking the learning into its parts, using concrete examples, modeling the procedures, and varying instruction. Repeated practice, along with much praise for successes, *multiplies the learning*. Most important, math can be fun! No more headaches, please!

A Cornucopia of Skills

Ways to Approach Math, From the Simple to the Complex

Computational and conceptual skills such as these can be taught. These problems can be paired with explanations by students of why they chose that answer/solution.

Readiness Skills: Never Assume

How many apples and books are shown?

_____ apples

_____ books

Can you write and solve a word problem that tells about this picture?

If I had 3 apples and 4 oranges and someone took 1 of the apples, what amount of fruit would be left? Circle the number sentence that would help solve this problem.

$$3 + 3 = 6 \quad 4 - 3 = 1 \quad 7 - 1 = 6 \quad 3 + 1 = 4$$

Draw as many happy faces as should be in the third box below.

What numbers come just before and after the one below?

_____ 15 _____

How many more things does the largest group of objects have than the smallest one below?

What time is shown on this clock?

Draw a 6-inch line.

Explain why 500 is the larger number by writing each number with words.

    55.3   500

Round these numbers to the places named:

56 _____ tens place

156 _____ tens place

156 _____ hundreds place

2,156 _____ hundreds place

2,156 _____ thousands place

21.45 _____ tenths place

21.456 _____ hundredths place

How many parts are in the circle below? _____

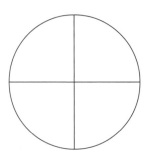

Which number sentence below would best describe this circle?

$$\frac{1}{4} + \frac{1}{4} = \frac{2}{8}$$
$$2 + 2 = 4$$
$$\frac{4}{4} = 1$$

What shape would fit into this space?

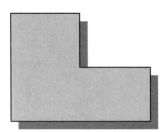

Can you name these shapes?

 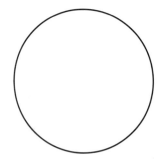 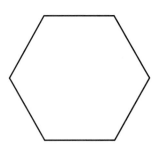

_____ _____ _____

What's the value of this number?

$$4^2 = \underline{\hspace{1.5cm}}$$

Equations and More

Can you solve this equation?

$$5 + (2 + 3)^2 - 6 \div 2 - 7 \times 2 - 1 = \underline{\hspace{1cm}}$$

Solve using the mnemonic **P**lease **e**xcuse **m**y **d**ear **A**unt **S**ally. Even though mnemonics and rules do not offer conceptual insights, they help students plunge into correct processes. Model a solution step-by-step:

Do what's inside the **p**arentheses first: $(2 + 3) = 5$

Next, solve the **e**xponents if they are in the equation: $5^2 = 25$

Then, **m**ultiply or **d**ivide, whichever one comes next. In this case, it's

division.

Division: $6 \div 2 = 3$, which is subtracted from 30.

Multiplication follows: $7 \times 2 = 14$

Adding is next, but there is none to do.

Last comes **s**ubtraction, which means that you must subtract 1.

Whew! The solution is $5 + 25 = 30$; then subtract $6 \div 2$, which is 3; next is $30 - 3 = 27$; then, multiply $7 \times 2 = 14$; and then subtract 14 from 27 for an answer of 13; and finally, subtract 1. The final answer is 12; yes, that's my final answer!

Write 25% as a decimal: _____

as a fraction: _____

Can you identify what these signs mean?

$$\cong \qquad \neq \qquad \approx \qquad \geq \qquad \Pi$$

_____ \qquad _____ \qquad _____ \qquad _____ \qquad _____

Solve this equation: $2x + 7 = 19$

Solution: First, subtract 7 from both sides, leaving $2x = 12$. Next, divide each side by 2, with a solution of $12 \div 2 = 6$.

Answer: $x = 6$

Remember always to check by substituting your answer for the variable.

Algebra hints: Students need to know that when solving equations, they must perform the same operations or procedures on both sides of the = sign. This can be compared to balancing weight on a seesaw. Manipulatives such as algebra tiles or hands-on equations offer concrete balancing representations.

Making Math Easier

Step by step, math becomes a lot easier.

Picture operations:

A

D

D

+

I

N

G

———

ADDING

SUBTRACTING-ING = SUBTRACT

DIVID-
———
ING

MULTIPLYING   MULTIPLYING   MULTIPLYING
                       MULTIPLYING

> Mathematics helps to develop thinking skills across the curriculum. Math is part of life!

Math Resources to Explore

Everyday Mathematics—http://everydaymath.uchicago.edu
Interactive math activities—www.aplusmath.com
Key Math Diagnostic Inventory of Essential Mathematics—www.keymath.com
The Math Forum at Drexel Math Library—An Internet mathematics library from Drexel University—www.mathforum.org/library
National Council for the Teachers of Mathematics (NCTM)—www.nctm.org
Singapore Math—www.singaporemath.com
Touchmath—www.touchmath.com

Math Tools That Help

Reinforcing Computational Skills: Using a Wheel

Practice of basic computational skills is important. Color coding the related spokes might be a way to revisit the facts once they have been written.

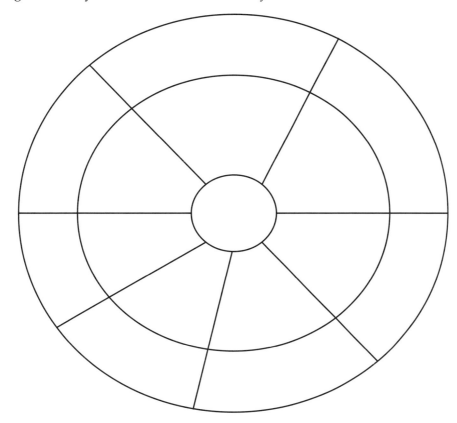

Directions: Place one of the operational signs in the middle circle with a given number, as in the following examples:

$$+6, -3, \times 9, \div 4$$

Then, fill in the inner circle with other numbers. The outer circle is where the answer is placed. Repeated computational practice can be used with circles such as these, store-bought flashcards, or even index cards.

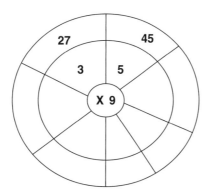

Many Web sites in the technology chapter of this book (Chapter 11) also reinforce computational skills in a fun way for students in Grades K–12.

Addition Chart

+	0	1	2	3	4	5	6	7	8	9
0										
1										
2										
3										
4										
5										
6										
7										
8										
9										

Choose the correct words from the box below to fill in the blanks.

1. Addition makes things _____.

2. The answer in an addition problem is called a _____.

3. Subtraction makes things _____.

4. The answer in a subtraction problem is called a _____.

bigger	smaller
sum	difference

Multiplication Chart

Notice that shaded areas of multiples can also be used to teach equivalent fractions.

×	0	1	2	3	4	5	6	7	8	9	
0											
1	0	1	2	3	4	5	6	7	8	9	
2	0	2	4	6	8	10	12	14	16	18	
3	0	3	6	9	12	15	18	21	24	27	
4	0	4	8	12	16	20	24	28	32	36	
5											
6											
7											
8											
9											

Choose the correct words from the box below to fill in the blanks.

1. Multiplication makes things _____.

2. The answer in a multiplication problem is called a _____.

3. Division makes things _____.

4. The answer in a division problem is called a _____.

bigger	smaller
product	quotient

Hundreds Chart

Use this chart to skip count by 2's, 3's, 4's, 5's, 6's, 7's, 8's, 9's, or 10's by moving your fingers across the boxes and rows or by highlighting numbers in boxes to follow given patterns. Multiples of each number can be colored with different selections as multiples are found. Notice patterns going across (horizontally) and down (vertically). Circle only the odd or even numbers. Go backward to subtract; color multiples to multiply or divide. Have fun with the numbers!

1	2	3	4	5	6	7	8	9	10
11	12	13	14	15	16	17	18	19	20
21	22	23	24	25	26	27	28	29	30
31	32	33	34	35	36	37	38	39	40
41	42	43	44	45	46	47	48	49	50
51	52	53	54	55	56	57	58	59	60
61	62	63	64	65	66	67	68	69	70
71	72	73	74	75	76	77	78	79	80
81	82	83	84	85	86	87	88	89	90
91	92	93	94	95	96	97	98	99	100

Meaningful Connections

Math relates to life, but if children and teachers do not view it that way, then everyone is shortchanged. Students will only study for the test and not learn any lessons connected to life, while teachers record a meaningless grade. Concepts taught in lessons that actively involve students in real-life situations are better remembered. Below are examples of real-life applications that enhance math lessons much more than complete reliance on textbook instruction.

Teacher Questions	*Real-Life Applications*
How can I teach about averages?	Weather Reports: weekly, monthly temperature readings compared to prior years, locations, average precipitation
	Batting Averages
	Report Card Grades
How can I teach geometry?	Looking at objects around, noticing different shapes
	Studying architecture of past civilizations
	Students can analyze famous paintings, noting the shapes, lines, and perspectives artists used.
How can I teach about graphs?	Children cooperatively conduct a classroom or schoolwide survey on any topic, such as favorite food, subject, sport, book, movie, or television show. Then they construct a graph that visually records data. Vary graphs: picture, pie, bar, line

How can I teach about _____?

Real-life applications are infinite . . . .!

Meaningful Connections: How Do You Spend Your Day?

Name: _____

Day chosen: _____

	Fraction	Decimal	Percent
School			
Eating			
Sleeping			
TV			
Video Games			
Computer			
Music			
Telephone			
Reading			
Sports			
Studying/HW			
Friends			
Family			
Exercise/Weights			
Working/Chores			
Other Activities			
Totals:			
	No more than 24 hours	No more than 1.00	No more than 100%

Thinking Skills

Word Problem Strategies: A Penny for Your Thoughts

1. Read the word problem once.

2. Now read the word problem again for more understanding.

3. Write down necessary information in the data box.

4. Write the question you need to answer in the question box.

5. Place a penny or an X in the strategy box you have chosen.

6. Using a step-by-step approach, figure out the answer to the question.

7. Go back to the question box. Does your answer make sense?

Data Box	Question
	Answer

Choose a Strategy

Estimate It's about _____. (28 is almost 30)	**Guess and Check** 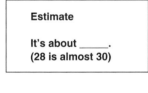	**Draw a Picture** 
Make a List 1. 2. 3.	**Break It Into Parts** 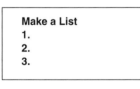	**Create a Chart or Table** 
Look for a Pattern 2, 4, 6, 8, 10 ...	**Work Backward** 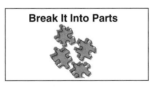	**Act It Out** 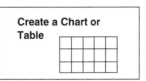
Use Logical  **Reasoning**	**Solve a Simpler Problem** How can I make this easier? 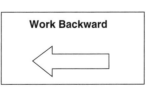	**Set up an Equation** A + B = C C − B = A 

Using Estimation

What is a reasonable answer? Do students know how to estimate addition, subtraction, multiplication, or division problems to help them see if their answers make sense? Quite often, math becomes a rote process, and students fail to acquire clearly developed thinking skills. Sometimes, it's a race to see who can finish the worksheet or test first. However, in that race to the finish line, logical thinking is not used. Using estimation leads to more conceptualizations.

Estimations are simple to implement. Ask students to fold their papers into two columns, with one side for the estimated answer, and the other side for the actual or exact answer. Holding horizontally lined paper vertically helps students who have fine-motor or eye–hand coordination difficulties to keep columns straight.

	(E) ESTIMATE					(A) ACTUAL ANSWER				

			9	0	0			9	4	5	
x				3	0	x			2	8	
2	7,	0	0	0	2	6,	4	6	0	

Then ask students to compare the sums, differences, products, and quotients in the E and A columns. Final questions include the following:

- Does my answer make sense?
- Are the estimated and actual answers close?

Obviously, the estimated answer of 27,000 is fairly close to 26,460. This kind of exercise helps students to think more about the numbers rather than performing operations by rote, without internalizing number sense.

Step-by-Step Rounding Tips

1. Ask students to circle the place they are rounding (hundreds).

$$5,(7)\ 5\ 2$$

2. Then, tell them to underline the next place to the immediate right.

$$5,(7)\ \underline{5}\ 2$$

3. If the number to the right is *5 or more,* change the circled number to one number higher.

$$(7) \text{ becomes an } 8$$

4. Everything to the right of the 8 becomes zeros. **5, 8 0 0**

5. Students can round numbers to the nearest place values (e.g., tens, hundreds, thousands) as long as they are consistent with their rounding choices within the same problem. Teachers should use their discretion and accept reasonable ranges of estimations.

ESTIMATE		ACTUAL ANSWER
200 + 40 = 240	220 + 40 = 260	217 + 38 = 255
25,000 + 68,000 = 93,000		24,581 + 68,356 = 92,937
900 × 80 = 72,000		895 × 84 = 3580 + 71600 = 75,180
42,000 ÷ 60 = 700		42,846 ÷ 56 = 765 R.6

Division estimates require finding the nearest basic division fact. In this example, it is 42 ÷ 6 = 7. Before doing division problems, some students may need to write the multiples of the divisor. For example, in this problem, 6, 12, 18, 24, 30, 36, 42, 48, 54, and 60 are the multiples of 6; students can count that 42 is the seventh multiple of 6. Multiples can also be highlighted on hundreds charts. When doing longer division, students then refer to the multiples each time they bring down a number.

When initially teaching this concept, using differently colored pencils helps.

An Edible Estimation

How many jellybeans, M&M's, or Cheerios would fit inside these different-sized circles?

Directions: Write your *guesstimate* on the chart below; then, write the actual answer and calculate the difference.

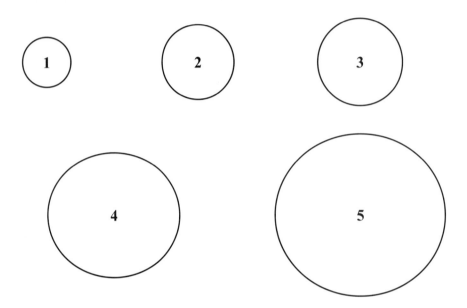

	Guesstimate	Actual Answer	Difference Between G and A
Circle 1			
Circle 2			
Circle 3			
Circle 4			
Circle 5			

Jellybeans, M&M's, and fruity Cheerios can also be sorted by colors and then graphed. As a precaution, always check individual children's records with the school nurse to be certain food allergies or diet restrictions do not interfere with children ingesting edible manipulatives. As a healthier option, estimate carrot slices instead!

Toothpicks and More

> Developing thinking skills can be accomplished through various mediums. Math manipulatives include toothpick designs, tangram shapes, fraction pizzas, abacuses, flashcards, Cuisenaire rods, algebra tiles, and more. The objective of the following lessons is to have students think about what they are doing, using logical sequencing while kinesthetically imprinting learning. Skills like these are then transferred to inferential reading comprehension and all kinds of cognitive thought across the curriculum. Aside from that, using toothpicks and more makes learning more appetizing!

Toothpick* Exercises

Follow directions to meet written toothpick requirements, always returning to this original position, using 12 toothpicks.

Note: There's a difference between the words *move* and *remove*.

Starting Position

1. Move 2 toothpicks to make 7 squares.

2. Move 4 toothpicks to make 10 squares.

3. Remove 2 toothpicks to make 2 squares.

4. Move 3 toothpicks to make 3 squares.

---

*Flat toothpicks can be purchased in local supermarkets.

Toothpick Answers

1. Move 2 toothpicks to make 7 squares.

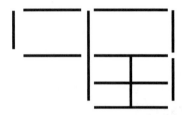

2. Move 4 toothpicks to make 10 squares.

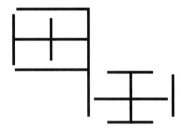

3. Remove 2 toothpicks to make 2 squares.

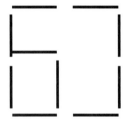

4. Move 3 toothpicks to make 3 squares.

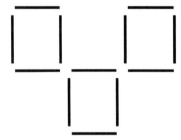

Check out this site for more ideas: http://www.madras.fife.sch.uk/maths/toothpickworld/

Tangrams

Directions: Form a perfect square using all of these seven geometric shapes: 5 triangles (2 big, 1 medium, 2 small), 1 parallelogram, 1 square.

Try to make these shapes, too!

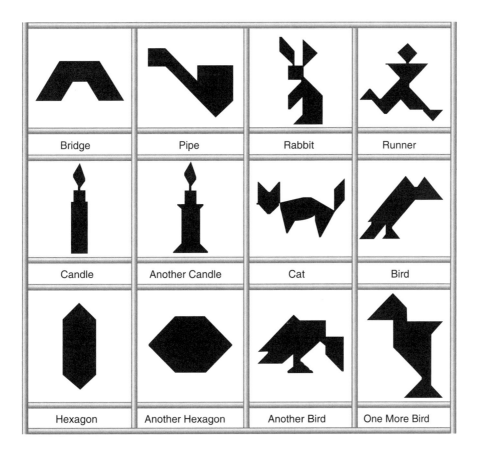

Bridge	Pipe	Rabbit	Runner
Candle	Another Candle	Cat	Bird
Hexagon	Another Hexagon	Another Bird	One More Bird

Source: Images courtesy of Lee Stemkowski.

> The Web site www.curiouser.co.uk/tangram/template.htm gives you a printable tangram to cut out and manipulate.

Tangram Answer

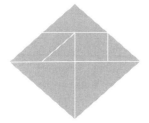

Logic Boxes

Directions: Solve a word problem together using a logic box, filling in yes or no answers.

	_____	_____	_____	_____
_____				
_____				
_____				
_____				
_____				

Math Problem

Just before an All Star baseball game, the luggage got mixed up for players Albert Pujols, David Wright, Evan Longoria, and Mark Teixeira. One suitcase contains a pair of size 11½ shoes. Another has a pair of size 12. One has a pair of size 13, and the last suitcase has size 15 shoes.*

Clues

Albert's size is not an integer.

David's size is a multiple of 4.

Mark's size is a prime number.

Who wears size 11½? _____

Who wears size 12? _____

Who wears size 13? _____

Who wears size 15? _____

*Shoe sizes for players are fictitious.

Learning needs to hold students' interest; for example, this word problem was about baseball. Even students who do not like math might be encouraged to attend to the task at hand since the subject matter, baseball, may have relevance and be of interest to them.

COMPLEMENTING THE BASICS

Investigative Learning

Reading, writing, and arithmetic are essential curriculum areas that are the basics of all education, but they do not exist in a vacuum. Teaching number sense, vocabulary, and how to express thoughts on paper can be accomplished while students are doing science experiments, researching historical events, listening to music, and being artistic. Lifelong learners emerge when thinking skills are developed across the curriculum.

In this age of information explosion, it is sometimes difficult to shop at all stores, yet exposure to the world opens up avenues of learning that can yield worthwhile returns. Emphasize the basics in conjunction with life!

BASICS + KNOWLEDGE + DELIVERY = EFFECTIVE
LEARNING ON LIFE'S MANY ROADS

Biographies Across Subject Areas

Directions: Tell more about one of the people listed below. There are four required documents and other document choices from which you must pick two. Originality, accuracy of information, and proper language mechanics are required. Tell how this person was (is) a contributing citizen to our society and world.

Required Research Documents

1. Birth certificate

2. Résumé

3. Journal entry

4. Advertisement of contributions

Other Document Choices (Pick 2)

- Biographical song
- Visual of setting where the person lived
- Dance portraying a life event
- Newspaper article
- Commemorative poem
- Cartoon/Portrait/Caricature/ Bubble Dialogue

- Diagram/Model of work
- Obituary from the newspaper
- Letter of reference written by a contemporary
- PowerPoint presentation
- Time line of important events

Choices Across the Curriculum

Math: Pythagoras, Euclid, Escher, Pascal, Archimedes, Nash

Science: Hippocrates, Copernicus, Galileo, Fahrenheit, Marie Curie, Isaac Newton, Charles Darwin, Thomas Edison, Albert Einstein, Jane Goodall, Bill Gates, Carl Sagan, Jacques Cousteau, Louis Pasteur, Jonas Salk, Anton van Leeuwenhoek, Stephen Hawking, Elizabeth Blackwell, B. F. Skinner

Art: Pablo Picasso, Rembrandt, Claude Monet, Leonardo da Vinci, M. C. Escher, Jackson Pollack, Michelangelo, Mary Cassatt, Jacob Lawrence, Frida Kahlo

Literature: Shakespeare, Chaucer, Ernest Hemingway, Maya Angelou, Toni Morrison, Theodore Geisel (Dr. Seuss), Edgar Allan Poe, Shel Silverstein, J. K. Rowling

Music: Richie Havens, Beethoven, Barbra Streisand, the Beatles, Bruce Springsteen, Itzhak Perlman, Diana Ross, Eminem, Billy Joel, Mozart, Louis Armstrong, Michele Branch, George Gershwin, Jonas Brothers, Britney Spears, Rihanna, Beyoncé, Frank Sinatra, Liberace, Bach, José Feliciano, Stevie Wonder, Michael Jackson

Sports: Jim Thorpe, Babe Ruth, Willie Mays, Michael Jordan, Joe DiMaggio, Wilma Rudolph, Mickey Mantle, Nancy Lopez, LeBron James, Venus Williams, Billie Jean King, Jackie Robinson, Michael Phelps, Pelé, Lance Armstrong

Social Studies: George Washington Carver, Abraham Lincoln, Indira Gandhi, Winston Churchill, King Hussein, Julius Caesar, Simón Bolivar, Benjamin Franklin, Montezuma, Barack Obama

Children Around the World: Penpals

Growing up, I distinctly remember my elementary school principal returning from a trip to a faraway place called Europe, with a bag filled with letters from a school in a country called Greece. My fourth-grade teacher distributed these letters to the class, and that was the beginning of my correspondence with Georgia Dermati, who lived in a town right outside of Athens. We exchanged music (I gave her a recording from Peter, Paul, and Mary); sandals; and many letters about politics, food, and fun things for about 5 years, making our two worlds seem a lot closer. Another time, our class wrote letters to a different neighborhood school in the same city, but about an hour away. Since I grew up in Brooklyn, New York, such a school was like a totally different country. Again, the world became a smaller but less narrow place.

Introducing students to other children their own age is a wonderful way for students to learn how peers in another neighborhood, city, state, or country live. Learning about different cultures exposes children to a broader view of the world instead of the same sights and familiar perspectives. The best part is that they explore these avenues by sharpening their writing skills through purposeful writing.

Online Ways to Find Class Penpals (With Adult Supervision Only)

http://www.surfnetkids.com/penpals.htm
http://www.friendshiptrougheducation.org

Including Content Areas

Music to My Ears

Music has powerful effects that can help you to drift, relax, uplift your spirits, or focus better. Optimum learning occurs when there is an unthreatening atmosphere of relaxation. Music can motivate you to be more creative as well as awaken thinking skills in a brain more primed for learning. Music and rhythms are one of the intelligences recognized by Howard Gardner in his work on multiple intelligences. Some children with exceptionalities can better express themselves through music. Varied activities are not limited to these, but can include the following:

- Rhythmic movement
- Transitioning to auditory cues
- Singing
- Playing an instrument
- Discriminating among sounds
- Sensing moods in music
- Attending to sounds
- Learning how music is a form of communication, with its own written language
- Developing music appreciation
- Improving self-concept through musical creativity
- Relating music to curriculum areas with jingles, raps, and more!

Curriculum Connections

Math: Rhythmic patterns with subdivisions of time into fractions

Physical Education: Coordinating fingers, hands, arms, lips, cheeks, facial movement, throat, lungs, stomach, and chest muscles with sounds sent through the ears, and then interpreted by the brain; marching bands

Social Studies: Teaching about other cultures around the world, telling about their ethnicity, history, and environment

Science: Acoustics and the science of hearing sounds, charting frequencies, intensities, adjusting volumes, pitches, melodies, and harmonies; learning how instruments are made

Languages: Universal language with global symbols that have no borders

Psychology: It's an individual choice that makes you feel good!

Resources to Explore

Adamek, M., & Darrow, A. (2005). *Music in special education.* Silver Spring, MD: American Music Therapy Association.

Anderson, O., Marsh, M., & Harvey, A. (1999). *Learn with the classics.* San Francisco: Lind Institute.

Vogt, J. (2006). *The amazing music activities book: Ideas and exercises for exploring: Music basics, ear training, music styles, and famous composers.* Dayton, OH: Heritage Music Press.

American Music Therapy Association—www.musictherapy.org

MusicFriends—www.musicfriends.org

National Association for Music Education—www.menc.org

Songs for Teaching, Using Music to Promote Learning—www.songsforteaching.com

ARTFUL EDUCATION

> Art is a nonverbal form of expression that uses both sides of the brain. Creativity is channeled through the right side, while the mechanics of writing itself stem from the left-brain language centers. Art, like music and many other disciplines, is more than the finished product; it is the process itself. It can also be used as a way for children to express themselves while learning many classroom concepts. Most important, art is about seeing.

Seeing the world around you, while paying attention to details, is not an easy task. Betty Edwards, in her book *Drawing on the Right Side of the Brain* (1989), tells how art is not a talent, but is more about learning how to see, processing visual information in a different way. Being aware of just how the brain handles that visual information helps us to draw our perceptions.

After almost a decade as an avid amateur artist, I have finally realized that I need not frame everything I create but can just enjoy the process of creation. The therapeutic advantages of art have helped many children with emotional issues deal with the sometimes unfair world around them. Art therapy allows many children of all ages a cathartic form of expression, with a healthy output (www.arttherapy.org).

Cognitive, physical, emotional, social, behavioral, and sensory elements must be considered in art programs that disseminate the knowledge at different levels that honor high expectations for all students. Art programs that allow everyone to have access to information accomplish this through a variety of sensory modes that incorporate not only visual modalities but auditory and kinesthetic-tactile ones as well. This may involve verbal descriptions, talking books, other accompanying writings, or opportunities to touch the art through raised experiences (www.artbeyondsight.org/sidebar/yellowpages.shtml).

Museums such as the Museum of Modern Art (MoMA) in New York (www.moma.org/learn/programs/access) allow students access to the art and also have programs that foster higher thinking skills. MoMA advocates teacher training that looks to build students' self-confidence. The goal is to offer all students with varying abilities the opportunity to both learn about the art and grow from their experiences. This includes resources for students who are blind, visually impaired, hard of hearing, deaf, or have autism, or Down syndrome, and many more students with a range of physical and cognitive potentials. The idea is to capitalize upon students' strengths and interests. Participation in educational art programs is an option open to people of all abilities. This includes both art appreciation and art creation with school, family, and community collaborations, which can be set up in local museums whether students are visiting interactive programs online (http://icom.museum/vlmp) or in person on a class field trip. Just as in all other disciplines, art educators plan lessons that reflect upon students' differing needs to build strengths within art and across the disciplines. Multiage stations can relate to the curriculum with themes from water or dinosaurs to Ancient Egypt or Escher's tessellations (www.mcescher.com). When GE and SE teachers share their lessons with art teachers, then the student benefits are truly masterpieces!

Art Relates to Curriculum

Social Studies: Learning how other cultures, regions, and people creatively express themselves; thoughts about their environment, politics, and history through art

Science: Seeing how different mediums react and combine with each other, mixing and separating colors, learning how pigments and dyes come from nature

Math: Being aware of the perspectives and geometric shapes that are artistic elements; using proportions to reduce and enlarge pictures or create rotations, transformation, and reflections.

Reading: Learning about the aesthetic value of different art, and how the artists themselves developed. Read on about the perceptual connection.

Perceptual Skills: Practicing and slowing down helps students concentrate better and improve their visual motor integration and laterality, which then aids reading.

> Some artistic mediums include pencils, charcoal, watercolor, oil paint, clay, string, beads, felt, crayons, photography, and so on. Forms of expression can be displayed across curriculum areas with the creation of charts, posters, graphs, dioramas, picture books, models, scrapbooks, greeting cards, collages, and more!

Perceptual Fun With Configuration

> Students can learn more about letters by placing them in the appropriate boxes and isolating them from the whole word. Concentrating on individual letters helps those with handwriting difficulties realize that letters have different sizes and shapes. These boxes stop those *dancing letters*. Students then transfer this skill to lined paper, now knowing that there's a reason for those lines!

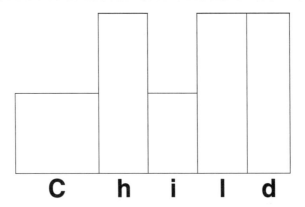

Write your own words in the box below; then, try to configure their makeup by drawing correctly sized boxes that match the direction and size of each letter's lines.

Graphing a Picture

This graphing activity encourages students to create a drawing by enlarging a picture, box by box, on graph paper. The objective is to demonstrate a way that students with perceptual difficulties can be taught to pay attention to details by concentrating on individual elements. Using graph paper, a simple picture, scissors, tape, and rulers, students can cut, tape, and then alphabetically and numerically grid and copy a chosen picture, by properly scaling proportions to enlarge the original picture. Perceptual proportions involved in this activity require a great deal of concentration, yet the exercise helps alleviate the fears of some that they can't draw. Step-by-step is quite easy when you are just concentrating on lines, instead of the whole picture. Graph paper and some pictures follow.

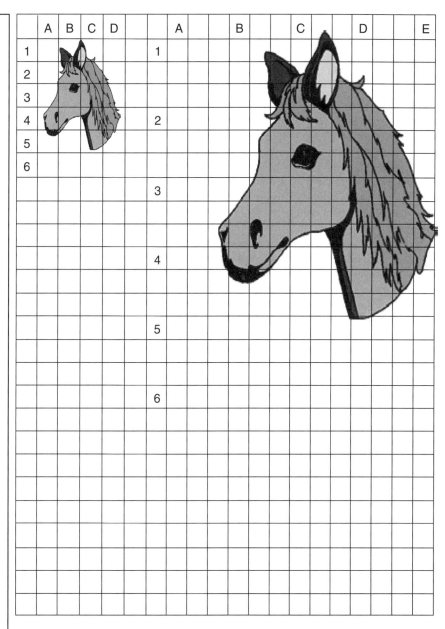

Students with learning difficulties need to slow down and pay closer attention to details. Sometimes they want to complete projects or assignments without accurately following each step. They might have neurological/perceptual needs that can cause letter reversals and therefore must be taught to look carefully at details such as lines and shapes. The goal is not to draw the picture, but to examine the intricacies it is composed of, box-by-box. (A-1, B-2 . . .) In the picture above, the ratio of smaller picture to larger one is 1:3, since one box in the smaller horse is equivalent to three boxes in the larger one.

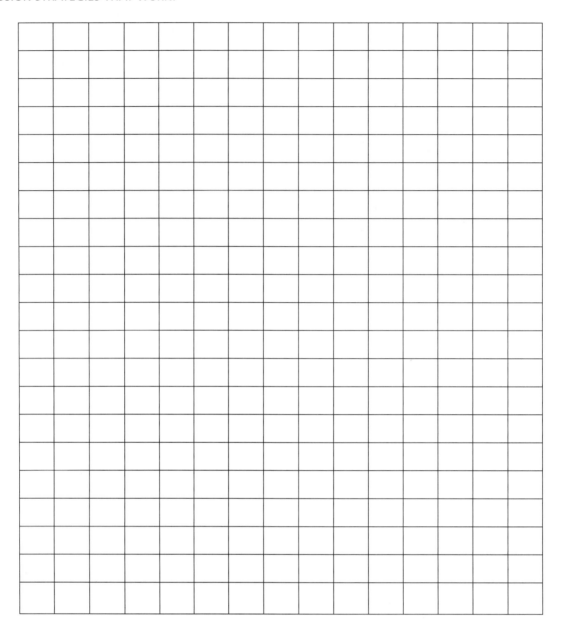

Directions: Choose, cut, paste, grid (with a ruler), and then enlarge one of these pictures or a choice of your own on graph paper.

Focusing on Shapes

Directions: Look around your school, house, or community. Notice how everything is made up of shapes.

A circle ⬤ can become a 🏀

A triangle △ can become a ⊿

A square ☐ can become a ⬛

Create your own picture, using as many shapes as possible.

[blank box]

Artists to Investigate

Paul Cezanne, Pablo Picasso, Piet Mondrian, Paul Gauguin, Frida Kahlo

Source: Yenawine, P. (2006). *Shapes* (2nd ed.). New York: Delacorte Press.

The following resource with raised, textured images helps people who are blind to *see* pictures of masters. The book *Art & the Alphabet* was produced with TechnoPrint and TechnoBraille with assistance from Rebecca McGinnis from Access Programs for the Blind at the Metropolitan Museum of Art and Ileana Sanchez, along with a grant from Sappi, Ideas That Matter, (www.sappi.com/ideasthatmatterNA/index.asp). Its raised medium helps all students and art lovers understand more about the essential elements and shapes in pictures, giving *insightful* perspectives to all!

Sanchez, I., & McGinnis, R. (2003). *Art & the alphabet: A tactile experience.* Humacao, Puerto Rico: Creative Creativo.

SCIENCE BY OBSERVING, DOING, AND THINKING

Students need to understand

Science is about their life.
Scientists study our world.
Science has changed the way we live.
Science will change the way we live.
Science explains everyday occurrences from seeds to space shuttles, and everything in between.

Inquiry-based learning strategies and critical thinking skills in science can be presented, from the simple to the complex. Only having students list or define scientific terminology is okay to increase their knowledge, but it does nothing to develop higher-level thinking skills or the possibly *dormant scientist* within. Teachers can incorporate Bloom's taxonomy—across the curriculum—in their lessons to develop *inquiring minds.*

Hierarchy of Bloom's Taxonomy for Scientific Classrooms

This resource transcends all time; however, the former descriptive nouns from Bloom's taxonomy are now verbs! The original levels as nouns included the following in order:

Knowledge, Comprehension, Application, Analysis, Synthesis, Evaluation

Bloom's Taxonomy is now revised to the following verbs:

Remembering: Memorizing or repeating general information such as vocabulary definitions, along with basic recall

Understanding: Explaining and/or relating information to other examples, paraphrasing information, describing data, drawing a diagram, or researching

Applying: Role-playing, constructing, demonstrating, distinguishing, experimenting, discovering, interviewing, collecting and organizing data

Analyzing: Comparing and contrasting, differentiating, deducing, determining, inferring, choosing, outlining, surveying, discovering, drawing conclusions

Evaluating: Summarizing in a position paper, evaluating data, judging, ranking, pretending, developing logical arguments, supporting choices

Creating: Constructing or designing products (written or concrete), inventing, writing an imaginary story, combining different facts

The next curriculum example offers what I call a *G.A.M.E. plan* where students G=gather, A=apply, M=manipulate, and E=evaluate the learning in *astronomical* ways!

Topic: About the Earth in the Solar System

G = Students identify the eight planets in order from the sun, making clay models and gathering factual information. Students realize that the Earth's movements affect our daily lives. They physically role-play how the Earth spins, or rotates, on its axis.

A = This group understands the specific effects of the Earth's movements—e.g., a revolution is the amount of time it takes for each planet to revolve around the sun; the Earth revolves around the sun in 365 days, or one year; and how a rotation translates to days and nights around the world.

M = Students explore the research and decide whether or not it is possible for plants, animals, and people to live on other planets.

E = These students learn how space exploration has affected life here on Earth, e.g., medical advances, environmental concerns, everyday products.

This type of GAME plan allows teachers to differentiate objectives and assignments in a content area, with all students investigating more on their independent or instructional levels.

Source: Adapted from Karten, T. (2008a). *Embracing disABILITIES in the classroom: Strategies to maximize students' assets.* Thousand Oaks, CA: Corwin.

Science Resources

Bloom, B. S. (Ed.). (1956). *Taxonomy of educational objectives. Cognitive domain.* New York: David McKay.

Forte, I., & Schurr, S. (1995). *Science mind stretchers* (Rev. ed.). Nashville, TN: Incentive Publications. (Original work published 1987)

Havasy, R. (2001, November 7). Getting a clue. We need a revolution in the way we teach science. *Education Week,* p. 49.

Karten, T. (2007). *More inclusion strategies that work!* Thousand Oaks, CA: Corwin.

Science DayBooks, Developed in collaboration with NSTA-National Science Teachers Association, Great Source Education Group at http://www.greatsource.com/

Sciencesaurus: A Handbook, Grades 4–5. (2004). Great Source Education Group. Available at http://www.greatsource.com/grants/sciencesaurus.html.

Special Science Teams program, developed at Rutgers, The State University of New Jersey, funded by the National Science Foundation and Research for Better Schools, advocating science that is inclusive for all students. See http://www.rci.rutgers.edu/~cfis

Tachell, P. (2003). *Science encyclopedia: Usborne Internet-linked discovery program.* London: Usborne Books.

How to Do an Experiment

The following outlines more about Bloom's Taxonomy, giving classroom applications to develop better critical thinking skills. It supports prior chapters on learning the analysis of a process and also includes an interpersonal follow-up.

Remembering

1. Identify your topic.
2. List materials in your experiment.
3. Define vocabulary.

Understanding

1. What are you doing?
2. List the steps:
   First, _____
   Next, _____
   Later, _____
   After, _____
   Finally, _____

Applying

1. Conduct the experiment.
2. Record data:
   What was done?
   What was seen?

Analyzing

1. Think about what your results mean.
2. What are your conclusions?

Evaluating

1. Were you satisfied with the results?
2. What did you learn?
3. Criticize or defend the experiment.

Creating

1. Create a picture, graph, model, chart, diagram, poem, song, dance, news article, or PowerPoint presentation about the topic.
2. List some predictions about what would happen if you changed the procedure or any of the variables.

Interpersonal Follow-Up

Pastabilities: Mining Experiment
Place four types of pasta on the floor, such as bow ties, elbows, rigatoni, and shells. Divide class into cooperative groups of four and assign each group a pasta type. Then allow one person from each group some time (approximately 2 mins.) to excavate or grab his or her group's pasta. As each member excavates the pasta, the amount mined is counted and recorded. Individual group results are then graphed and shared. Each member should be taking less and less pasta as the natural resources are depleted with each excavation. The knowledge, comprehension, application, analysis, synthesis, and evaluation are then addressed. Perhaps as a follow-up, pasta primavera can be served!

Source: Used with permission. Activity is adapted from the Special Science Teams program developed at Rutgers, The State University of New Jersey, funded by the National Science Foundation and Research for Better Schools.

SOCIAL STUDIES: CONNECTING STUDENTS TO THEIR WORLD

Social studies is more than a subject; it teaches students about life and how to better connect with each other to become global learners. Acquiring wisdom from past generations does not mean that students memorize facts in the texts. It's more important that the students learn to link those facts to themselves within their communities and world. Topics such as history, economics, civics, government, and geography come alive when teachers infuse the social studies curriculum into students' everyday lives.

Time Lines in Social Studies and Life, From Then to Now

Question: How old is the United States?

Frightening Student Answer: 1,000 years old

Directions: Using time lines can help everyone learn more about sequencing. Start with a time line related to your life, listing specific years and details about the events below under the *Me* column. Then think of events related to our country, and list the specific years and brief details under the *Country* column.

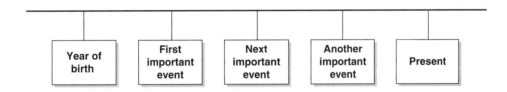

Illustrate sequential events on another paper.

Dates		Details	
Me	Country	Me	Country

Where in the World Is . . . ?

Can you identify countries at these locations? Use an atlas if you need extra help.

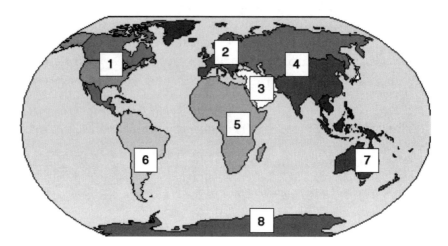

Label oceans in proper locations.

1. North America

2. Europe

3. Middle East

4. Asia

5. Africa

6. South America

7. Australia

8. Antarctica

> Further investigation: Compare and contrast the
> governments and cultures of two countries.

Can You Identify These U.S. States?

Directions: Place numbers inside locations of states you can identify, and name them in columns below.

Numbers	States	Numbers	States

Note: AK and HI are not in their proper locations. Find a world map to locate these two states.

Possible Accommodations

Some students can refer to a map of the United States to identify the abbreviations. Other students may need a map of the United States cut up as a jigsaw puzzle with a color-coded template to follow along with, to properly place only the states in certain regions, e.g., Northeast, Southwest, rather than writing abbreviations, since knowing the locations of regions would be a more meaningful task. Having a raised relief map would be an excellent tactile way for students to differentiate and locate landforms. Other students may require an even more advanced task, since this one may be too easy and result in bored and disinterested learners; e.g., have them research how the geography affects how people make a living there.

VALUING PHYSICAL EDUCATION

Just as children have differing cognitive levels, they also have various physical levels. A well-designed physical education program promotes each student's individual growth. Some children might hate to think while stationary in a classroom chair but be delighted to make decisions while actively moving about. Why not consider a physical education program that age-appropriately values each child's needs, strengths, and abilities?

Physical education teachers assess current levels, use basic learning principles, and build upon prior skills. It's no different from teaching fractions or conversational Spanish. Three simple questions are asked:

1. What are you going to teach?

2. How are you going to do it?

3. Are the students learning?

Preschool–Grade 3 Skills

- Locomotor activities such as jumping, running, hopping, skipping
- Manipulating by bouncing, kicking, catching, throwing, and more
- Movement to increase body awareness, rhythm, and balance
- Simple games to promote interaction and following basic rules
- Exhibiting safety and respect for others

Grades 4–12

- Gymnastics, dance, physical fitness, team sports
- Muscular strength
- Reaching goals and solutions with increased endurance and flexibility
- Attaching cognitive, emotional, behavioral, and social skills to physical activities, creativity, and healthy mind-sets

Modifying Physical Education

- Vary time requirements by slowing down an activity or number of repetitions.
- Use different equipment—for example, a ball with a bell for someone who is blind, or one with flashing lights for someone with auditory needs. Use lighter bats, or maybe lower basketball or volleyball nets.
- Provide structure, but eliminate distracters. Use signals with children.
- Increase rest time.
- Vary limits and expectations with outlined directions modeled.
- Remember that fair does not always mean equal.
- Concentrate on safety by specifically teaching rules.
- Communicate with special/general education teachers and case manager.
- Challenge children. Don't make more skilled students do easy activities, since the flavor of a game or exercise can be preserved without being diluted for all.

Ultimate Goal

Children feel good about themselves while being included with peers. Very often, when you ask children to name their favorite subject, the response is gym! Try integrating more movement activities into the classroom. Brain research confirms the fact that movement facilitates cognition.

> Exercise strengthens brain power!

Resources/Contacts

American Association for Health, Physical Education, Recreation, and Dance (AAHPERD)—(800) 213–7193, http://www.aahperd.org

Jensen, E. (2005). *Teaching with the brain in mind* (2nd ed.). Alexandria, VA: Association for Supervision and Curriculum Development.

Kasser, S. (1995). *Inclusive games.* Champaign, IL: Human Kinetics.

The Leonard Gordon Institute for Human Development Through Play of Temple University—http://www.pecentral.org/websites/playsites.html

Lieberman, L., & Houston-Wilson, C. (2002). *Strategies for inclusion: A handbook for physical education.* Champaign, IL: Human Kinetics.

Positive Living for Active Youth—http://www.playfoundation.net/

Rouse, P. (2010). *Inclusion in Physical Education: Fitness, Motor and Social Skills for Students of All Abilities.* Champaign, IL: Human Kinetics.

Sports and Recreational Activities for Children with Physical Disabilities—http://www.cureourchildren.org/sports.htm

Sylwester, R. (2000). *A biological brain in a cultural classroom.* Thousand Oaks, CA: Corwin.

Torbert, M., & Schneider, L. (1993). *Follow me too: A handbook* for *movement activities for three- to five-year-olds.* Boston: Addison-Wesley.

INTERDISCIPLINARY APPROACH: EDUCATIONAL SALADS

Thematic Teaching

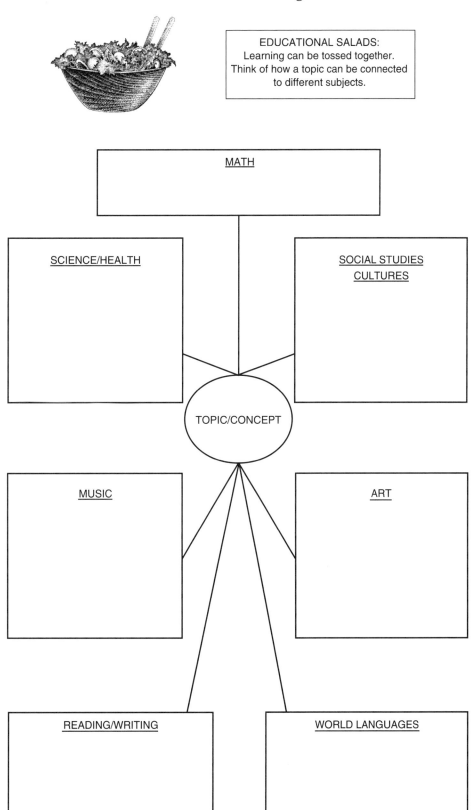

EDUCATIONAL SALADS:
Learning can be tossed together.
Think of how a topic can be connected
to different subjects.

MATH

SCIENCE/HEALTH

SOCIAL STUDIES
CULTURES

TOPIC/CONCEPT

MUSIC

ART

READING/WRITING

WORLD LANGUAGES

The following unit takes the famous painting *Starry Night*, by Vincent van Gogh, and offers some interdisciplinary connections across the curriculum.

- Science/Technology: Examine the sky, analyze the cloud depictions, explain what causes nighttime, tell what a star is composed of, investigate epilepsy, create a PowerPoint that dissects and elaborates on the individual elements of the painting.
- Math: Isolate and replicate the geometric shapes you see; figure out the circumference and area of the circles depicted; calculate how much money Van Gogh would have today, if he was still alive, from the sale of five selected paintings.
- Music: Listen to Don McLean's song, "Vincent" (a.k.a. "Starry, Starry Night"); then, change it into a rap or a strictly instrumental version.
- Language Arts/Writing: Create a biography of Van Gogh's life; choose 10 adjectives that best describe the painting, write a haiku about the art; send a friendly letter from Van Gogh to Gauguin, Monet, or Pissarro; read a biography about Van Gogh; write a persuasive essay telling him why he should not have committed suicide.
- Social Studies: Investigate the setting of the painting, e.g., Netherlands, mid-nineteenth century; describe what the culture in Europe was like then; locate the village of Saint-Remy-de-Provence, telling its latitude and longitude.
- Art: Obviously, there are innumerable connections!

The next interdisciplinary example depicts a thematic, *nutritious,* inclusive primary lesson plan across many disciplines, ranging from language to social skills and many others *sandwiched* in between. The two codes, AA and FP, honor the PLAAFP (present level of academic achievement and functional performance) requirement of IEPs:

AA: Academic Achievements

FP: Functional Performances

The next three codes honor the basic ingredients of lesson plans, telling what you plan to teach—*content*, how you will do it—*process*, and if it worked—*assessments.*

OMG: Objectives, materials, goals

PS: Procedures/strategies

CBA: Curriculum-based assessments

The CBAs can include but are not limited to work samples, portfolios, quizzes, tests, observations, cooperative group work, written essays, discussions, and center/station work.

Please note that the lesson plan includes interdisciplinary themes, and it is also differentiating in that it has baseline, more advanced, and knowing beyond objectives that proactively prepare for a classroom of diverse learners.

The sentence BE WISE translates to the following:

By the end of the week, inclusion strategies will educate learners to

---

BE WISE Primary Lesson Plan Theme: Nutrition* Week beginning: <u>9/20/10</u> Revisitation date: <u>11/22/10</u>**

AA: Outline nutrition knowledge and healthy exercise habits through mathematics, readings, writings, social studies, and science.

FP: Acknowledge and apply sound nutrition and exercise choices to daily lives and the curriculum.

More Advanced: Students will calculate how different ingredients are grown, prepared in recipes, and distributed to other locations.

Reading

OMG: Establish prior knowledge with discussion and vocabulary about food origins, diet, and exercise while improving fluency, sight word recognition, knowledge of initial and final consonants, written and oral reading comprehension with sequencing, context clues, main idea, details, and inferential skills.

Books to be read as a class and in small groups:

Fiction: *Cloudy With a Chance of Meatballs* by J. Barrett

Nonfiction: *Food, Nutrition, and the Young Child* by J. Endres

---

PS: Have whole-group discussion about nutrition and orally read books. Then, actual concrete food items with labels and ingredients listed on index cards are sorted according to phonetic and dietary guidelines, e.g., initial/final consonants, consonant blends, milk and dairy products, bread, vegetables. Sequencing cards are given to each group to put story details in order. Students can work with digital books and talking Web sites using headphones.

CBA: Cooperative groups respond to questions distributed on index cards, looking for the answers in their books. Teacher circulates about, listening to and recording fluency and responses. Some students will circle or draw pictures as answers, while others will write sentences or paragraphs.

Language Arts & Writing

OMG: Identifying parts of speech and writing poems. Students will use rhyming and electronic dictionaries. The goal is to share poems with peers in class-created book that includes use of vocabulary words: grains, vegetables, fruits, milk, meat/beans, fats, oils, and sweets, as well as goods, services, calories, balanced diets, and exercise.

PS: Students will sort words into their parts of speech, e.g., *meatball*—noun, *healthy*—adjective, *exercise*—noun and verb, *smartly*—adverb. Students will create diamantes about favorite foods, exercise, or sound nutritional ideas with pictures that are either hand drawn or from clip art.

CBA: Individual work samples and presentations of illustrated poems.

Mathematics

OMG: Understanding concepts of ordering, fractions, capacities, and applying computations. Materials include measuring cups, spoons, calculators, math texts, and recipe book.

PS: Students double and halve favorite recipes and cooperatively create, share, and solve word problems with diet, nutrition, and exercise facts learned

---

CBA: Quiz given with student- and teacher-created word problems.

Science & Technology

OMG: Identification and classification of foods along with accessing knowledge online.

(Continued)

(Continued)

PS: Students sort foods according to their ingredients, classifying different food types. Visual with the food pyramid will be shared and discussed (www.mypyramid.gov/downloads/MiniPoster.pdf). This site will be used to read more online books: www.enchantedlearning.com/books/food.
CBA: Finding clip art, sorting the pictures into categories, and writing captions, which students will hand in to teacher in individually signed envelopes or created collages and food charts.
Social Studies/Global Studies **OMG:** To explore map skills, e.g., directions, latitude and longitude. Identify climates and landforms in countries in different hemispheres, and understand how similarities and differences affect economies, occupations, food choices, and daily living.
PS: Cooperative groups will outline where different products are found, and countries at given coordinates and hemispheres.
CBA: Map test on latitude, longitude, cardinal and intermediate directions, and continents.
Perceptual/Sensory/Physical **OMG:** To increase auditory and visual perceptual skills, fine-motor skills, and laterality.
PS: Students follow teacher-given directions to cut out and trace shapes of continents and place them on world maps in response to where foods are found. Visual tracking exercise asks students to circle nutrition and exercise vocabulary words broken up into syllables in alphabetical order from left to right, e.g., bal-ance, con-trol, di-et, ex-er-cise, nu-tri-tion, por-tion. Coordination with physical education teacher, PT, and OT.
CBA: Student worksheet mirrors classroom instruction to follow oral and written tracking directions. PE teachers offer classroom movements that students safely imitate and expand upon. Exercise logs are kept.
Communication/World Languages **OMG:** Learn names of common foods in the language each student is studying. Goal is for each student to give a brief presentation in front of the class.
PS: Illustrated student-created dictionaries with visuals and language translations of food terms are cooperatively completed.
CBA: Observation and student-completed work samples.
Study Skills **OMG:** Keeping track of weekly work to increase self-monitoring with food and exercise diaries.
PS: Students will fill in dated learning journals/diaries and check off tasks as completed.
CBA: Teacher–student conferencing about nutrition and exercise learning logs.
Social Skills **OMG:** Goal is to improve social reciprocity and to review food etiquette.
PS: Daily pictures of students' table manners during lunch and snack time will be taken and shared. Proper etiquette is modeled and reinforced.
CBA: Teacher observation, digital photos, and self-rating scale, e.g., *I was great! Need to improve.*
*This is a LOL: Lifelong ongoing lesson! **Talking about nutrition before Thanksgiving is truly capitalizing upon an opportune time!

Source: Karten, T. (2010). *The inclusion lesson plan book for the 21st century.* Port Chester, NY: Dude Publishing. Used with permission.

Emphasizing Comprehension and Study Skills

In order to succeed and navigate in this world, critical thinking skills and being aware of ways to increase understandings are essential. Rote memorization short-changes many students with disabilities from developing higher levels of cognitive thought, which then translates to lower post-secondary options. Yes, they might score a decent grade on Tuesday's test, but then the following week that knowledge is lost, or shall we say, never really gained. Without effective study skills, even the basics are hard. This chapter provides ways that teachers can help students develop these lifelong skills, emphasizing comprehension of content, rather than rote memorization. Teacher/student templates are included.

LEARNING MORE ABOUT LEARNING

Inventory of Skills

Study Skills—Learning Vowels/Vows

A E I O Us

Attitude	• Am I primed (ready) to learn? • Do I care about what's going on in the classroom? • Why am I here?
Effort	• Am I trying my best? • Who can I ask for extra help? • Will I review this after class?
Involvement	• Will I ask questions if I don't understand something? • Am I just watching the others, or am I really listening to the teacher?
Organization	• Am I *consistently* prepared for class with a pen/pencil, binder, or notebook with daily dated neat notes, books, homework, and anything else that is required for class?
Understanding	• Do I understand that improvements will not happen overnight? • Am I patient and kind to others—parents, teachers, classmates, siblings, bus drivers, lunchroom aides, classroom assistants, and most of all myself?

This chart could be posted on a classroom wall to be periodically reviewed with students. Older students could self-monitor and cultivate these life skills.

How Well Do You Study?

Name: _____

Check all appropriate answers:

1. When do you look at/read your textbook or class notes?

    ___ at night before a test

    ___ in class only

    ___ daily at home and in class

    ___ occasionally

    ___ never

2. Where do you do your homework?

    ___ in a quiet place

    ___ in the kitchen

    ___ at a desk or table

    ___ on the bus ride home from school

    ___ other _____

3. Why do you study?

    ___ to get good grades

    ___ because parents give rewards or prizes for good grades

    ___ it makes me feel good about myself to do well in school

    ___ my parents force me to

    ___ I don't think I have to study

    ___ other reason _____

4. How do you study for a test?

    ___ juggle books

    ___ study while watching television

    ___ review notes

    ___ reread textbook

    ___ rewrite notes

    ___ use a study guide

    ___ another way _____

5. What do you think about school?

    ___ it can help me later on in life

    ___ it's a waste of time

    ___ it's boring

    ___ I love learning

    ___ other thoughts _____

Timed Exercise: What Do You Know?

Directions: Read all questions before you begin. This is a 5-minute, timed exercise on different school topics.

1. Write your first and last name in the upper right-hand corner.

2. Underline the word *directions.*

3. Write the odd numbers from 1 to 50.

4. List the continents in alphabetical order.

5. Write the lowercase alphabet in cursive or manuscript.

6. Draw a picture of something that is recyclable.

7. Whistle a patriotic tune.

8. List five words that rhyme with *school.*

9. Stand up and shout, "I love school!"

10. Now that you have read everything, do numbers 1 and 2 *only,* and patiently wait and watch classmates complete the worksheet.

Moral: Always read all directions carefully!

Mnemonics, Acronyms, and Massive Initializations

MI Theory—Not Multiple Intelligences, but Massive Initializations

Acronyms are a wonderful way to remember information and use abbreviations or monograms to represent specific titles. Since the beginning of special education (BOSE), there has been a colossal tendency to abbreviate, shorten, or rename jargonish terms in the special education (SPED) field as the following indicates.

ED	Emotionally Disturbed
SED	Seriously Emotionally Disturbed
SLD	Specific Learning Disability
OHI	Other Health Impairment
CP	Cerebral Palsy
MS	Multiple Sclerosis, or Master of Science
MD	Muscular Dystrophy, or Medical Doctor
AT	Academically Talented or Assistive Technology
RR	Road Rage
FOED*	False Optimism Elevator Disorder (continually punching a lit elevator button to reach one's floor faster)
ISD*	Intentional Shameful Disorder (using the supermarket express lanes, even though you have more than 15 items)
PDD*	*not* Pervasive Developmental Disorder, but Posterior Distress Disorder, which is a result of sitting too long in meetings
Dyslyrica	Singing the wrong lyrics to songs
Dysnomia	Inability to remember names
I R & S	Interventions, Referrals, and Strategies, *not* Internal Revenue Service
RTI	Response to interventions, but more importantly remembering to include!
CSI	Common sense inclusion

*Source: Zirkel, P., & Richards, D. (1998, May/June). The new disorder maze. *Teaching Exceptional Children, 30*(5).

Compile your own list of missed abbreviations:

1.

2.

3.

4.

5.

6.

7.

8.

9.

10.

Sound Familiar?

Using words or short phrases to recall unrelated facts, rules, concepts, or information is a valuable study tool. Do any of these ring *memory bells*?

1. My very educated mother just showed us nine planets—now needs to be revised since Pluto is considered to be a dwarf planet. Perhaps this one would work instead: My very educated mother just served us noodles!

2. FOIL

3. Every good boy does fine.

4. HOMES

5. Please excuse my dear Aunt Sally.

6. Daddy, mommy, sister, cousin, brother

7. All very determined students deserve many more opportunities than school has ever offered.

8. TGIF

9. BFF

10. LOL

Answers:

1. Order of 8 planets from the sun: Mercury, Venus, Earth, Mars, Jupiter, Saturn, Uranus, Neptune

2. Order of factoring to create a trinomial expression (first, outer, inner, last)—for example, $(2x + 7)(x - 2) = (2x)(x) + (2x)(-2) + (7)(x) + (+7)(-2)$, which when like terms are combined $= 2x^2 + 3x - 14$.

3. Notes on a treble musical staff: E, G, B, D, F

4. Five Great Lakes: Huron, Ontario, Michigan, Erie, Superior

5. Order of operations for solving mathematical expressions: Parentheses, exponents, multiplication, division, addition, subtraction, depending upon which of these is present. For example, $3 \times 8^2 + 6 \div (2 + 1) = 194$.

6. Steps in long division: divide, multiply, subtract, compare, bring down next number. Can also be remembered as *Does McDonald's serve cheeseburgers?*

7. Types of disabilities serviced by IDEA: autism, visual impairment, deafness, speech/language, deafness/blindness, mental retardation,* multiple disabilities, other health impaired, traumatic brain injury, specific learning disability, hearing impaired, emotional disturbance, orthopedic impairment

8. Thank God it's Friday, or inclusion's feasible.

9. Best friend forever

10. Laughing out loud!

   *Please note that as of this revision, *mental retardation* is still the term used, although many states prefer to call this classification by other names, e.g., *cognitive impairment* or *intellectual/developmental disability*.

List some of your favorite acronyms or mnemonics:

1.

2.

3.

4.

5.

DEVELOPING BETTER PRACTICES

These suggestions are helpful for both teachers and students.

1. Following Directions

a. *Written instructions* on reading worksheets, tests, texts, how-to kits, science experiments, math word problems, and so forth, *must be read and reread.*

b. *Spoken words* need to be carefully *listened to and understood* before doing anything, with undivided attention given to *the person talking.*

2. Highlighting Important Information

a. Study sticky notes with different colors, shapes, and sizes can be used to flag important facts and details, formulate questions about what was just read, or jot down any information to revisit.

b. Certain notations, such as the ones in the box below, can be given to key information on worksheets, books, or duplicated text pages.

Interesting fact—will probably be on the test.	H U H ?	What was the cause and effect of this event?

? CONFUSING	**♥** EMOTIONAL	**↑** POSITIVE
! SURPRISING	***** IMPORTANT	**↓** NEGATIVE

c. *Different-colored pencils, pens, or highlighters* help facts and details stand out from the words on the rest of the page.

d. *Columned or boxed learnings* are graphically friendly presentations that help learning become more digestible.

Study Guides With Matching Q & As

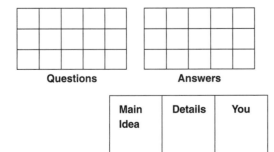

Word	Category	Details

Main Idea	Details	You

Memorization vs. Understanding

Parents and students often think that memorized facts prove that learning is taking place. Learning is more than rote memorization. Here are some memory factors to consider:

- Memory is a process that can be strengthened.
- Different memory spots in the brain are responsible for learning retrieval.
- Students can be great at remembering selective things, but weaker at remembering others, such as having good recall of television shows or names of dinosaurs, but only fair recall of multiplication facts.
- Sometimes what we remember is influenced by the following factors:
  - Importance
  - Our age
  - Time lapse (long-/short-term memory)
  - Attention
  - Association
  - Sensory elements
  - Concrete experiences (remembering what we do)
  - Traumatic experiences (either very happy or sad)

Everyone tends to forget things!

Memory Test

1. What did you have for dinner 2 nights ago?
2. On what day of the week were you born?
3. What did you have for lunch yesterday?
4. Name your second-grade teacher.
5. Who was your first childhood best friend?
6. Can you remember his or her phone number or address?
7. What is the zip code of the place you were born?
8. What was the first movie you saw in a theater?
9. Pick one of these three events and tell your age and location at the time of the event:
   a. John F. Kennedy's assassination
   b. Space shuttle *Challenger* accident
   c. 9/11
   (If you weren't born at the event chosen, use negative numbers for your age.)
10. What time did you go to sleep last Saturday night?
11. Name the 19th president of the United States
12. Who shot J. R.?

Quite often, students can do well on tests, but do not have a true grasp of the learning material. Some students are excellent memorizers, but when asked the same questions 5 days later, their responses do not match prior assessments. Students will understand more about any given subject area if there is repeated exposure to what they deem to be relevant or enjoyable learning. When they rotely memorize unrelated facts, there is a low understanding level. Learning is more than memorizing! In addition, research supports that students learn best when material is repeated and practiced to lock it into their long-term memory (Willingham, 2004).

(*Answers:* 9. Pres. Kennedy was assassinated in 1963; *Challenger* accident was in 1986; 9/11 happened in 2001. 11. Rutherford B. Hayes; 12. Sue Ellen's sister)

Conceptual Organization

Directions: Concept maps such as these can outline and connect facts, giving the learner a chance to view and study information at a quick glance.

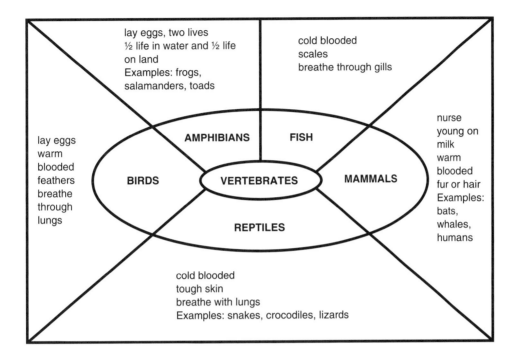

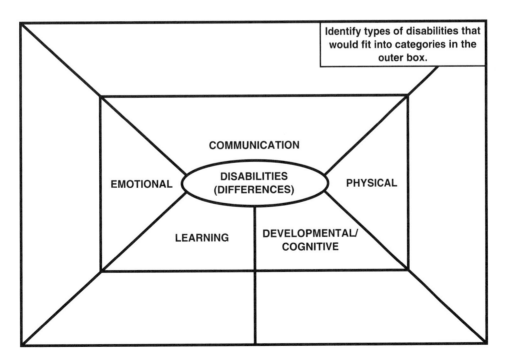

Calligram

Words can form pictures to help students organize and retain information. Visual learning accompanied by kinesthetic-tactile methods is an effective way to imprint information for learners whose strengths might be this type of learning presentation. Think of your own word to *draw*. Check out this Web site for primary learners to see words come alive: http://pbskids.org/wordworld.

Graphically Speaking: Tracking Progress

Study Tip: Have students place a progress chart like the one below in an individual folder, for periodic review. It circumvents conveniently forgetting that last test grade. Different dated sheets can be used for each subject and marking period. By graphing their test grades, they can see the *ups and downs* of their own learning. Students can notice patterns and try to improve their next test score. This type of graphic visual concretizes the meaning of metacognition. Even if a student does not do well on a particular test, that does not mean he or she is a failure. It's just a *learning dip.*

My Spelling Grades

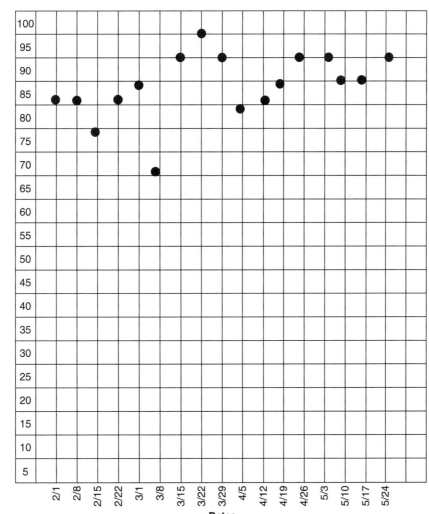

My Progress: Learning Graph

Setting Goals: Grades for Yesterday, Today, and Tomorrow

When? Now

How? Plot scores

Where? In class

Why? Important to see progress

Who? Me

What? Grades

Subject: _____

100																
95																
90																
85																
80																
75																
70																
65																
60																
55																
50																
45																
40																
35																
30																
25																
20																
15																
10																
5																

TEST SCORES (y-axis label)

Dates

My Personal Goal Statement (about grades):

I plan to _____

TEACHING FOR MORE UNDERSTANDING

Compartmentalization

Learning needs its own compartments to store and fit *bits or bites* of information. *Neatly packaged learning is a better sell to students.* Teachers' presentations often matter a great deal in aiding students' retention. Just as filing cabinets externally help organize paperwork, *compartmentalization helps students organize learning material for better absorption.* Individual worksheets that make use of *boxing thoughts* help students realize how facts are related to each other within the bigger learning picture.

Even though a bakery might sell muffins, donuts, rolls, cakes, and cookies, before you leave the store, these items are placed in different-sized boxes or bags. You would probably not be pleased if the cheesecake was placed in a paper bag, or too many rolls were squashed into a Ziploc bag. Just as a tie isn't really the right size for a shoebox, learning also has its own distinctive placement. Teachers need to separate the facts and help students to develop their own system of organization.

> Compartmentalizing thoughts helps students when they take notes or review for tests. Without this external organization, content is not processed. Eventually, these *learning boxes* become internalized, as the brain no longer needs to see these concrete separations.

Curriculum Connection for World History

Learning Boxes—A Way to Pair Visuals With Written Words

1. Lived near Mediterranean Sea, Carthage was a great city of theirs

2. Were traders with other civilizations in the region

3. Greatest contribution was the alphabet

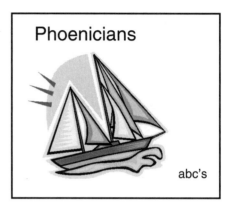

1. Cyrus the Great founded the Persian Empire around the 5th century B.C.

2. Darius I divided the Persian Empire into 20 provinces.

3. Royal road improved communication

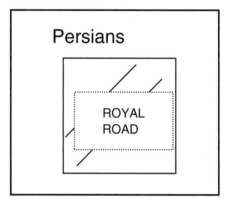

1. Iron weapons were used.

2. Cavalry on mounted horses

3. Strong military power

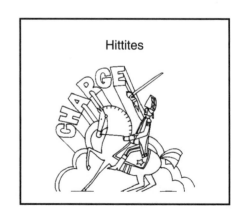

Fill in your own Learning Boxes below:

1. _____
_____
_____

2. _____
_____
_____

3. _____
_____
_____

1. _____
_____
_____

2. _____
_____
_____

3. _____
_____
_____

1. _____
_____
_____

2. _____
_____
_____

3. _____
_____
_____

This chart delineates the difference between just memorizing and understanding definitions of science vocabulary. Words are defined in the chart, yet at the same time relationships between words are seen at a quick glance, using the chart as a visual tool. Vocabulary words can be related to the same general topic, yet differ in meaning. In addition, students can create their own models of atoms by using Legos or clay as concrete examples, act out the terms through short science skits, or teach and review with a partner for more retention. This allows kinesthetic and visual learners a chance to form better memory connections, with active learning taking place. Just divide some lined paper into three sections for columned note taking.

Curriculum Connection for Science

My Notes: Telling More About Atoms and Molecules

Remember, all things in the universe are made of atoms, which are tiny particles. When two or more atoms are joined together, they make up a molecule: atom + atom = molecule. An electric charge means that atoms carry electricity with a positive or negative charge.

electrons	subatomic particle	(−) negatively charged whiz around nucleus # of electrons = # of protons
protons	subatomic particle	(+) positively charged found in nucleus
neutrons	subatomic particle	no electric charge found in nucleus
Remember, *matter is any physical thing that takes up space.* Matter is made up of atoms and molecules. Everything you see around you is either solid, liquid, gas, or plasma. **solids**	state of matter	always keep their shape with molecules packed closely together
liquids	state of matter	do not keep the same shape; molecules are loosely packed and take the shape of whatever container they occupy
gases	state of matter	molecules are the furthest apart, have no shape; most are invisible
plasma	state of matter	gaseous material electrons: stars, comets

Tell About . . . Planner

The following charts help learners to visually understand concepts. Just fold a paper into three columns such as these to delineate relationships.

levers	simple machine	fulcrum, load arm, force arm (seesaw)
inclined plane	simple machine	slope
friction	force	resistance when things rub together in air or water
gravity	force	the pulling force of the Earth
heat	form of energy	measured in joules, vibrate, kinetic energy
sound	form of energy	molecules in air vibrate frequencies resonance

These charts allow learners to understand information in a simply presented, compartmentalized visual. More concrete learners would require more pictures and fewer words to solidify concepts.

Tell About . . .

Better Study Guides

The next template is used to help students study. With the following format, students can focus on individual questions, rather than being overwhelmed by too much information. Guides like these visually separate questions into individual boxes, making them more manageable for students.

Students or teachers can write up to 25 questions on one grid sheet, while the corresponding 25 answers are placed on another matching grid. By using these grids, students quite often can study independently, testing themselves. Grids can be cooperatively completed in class, if students divide each row of questions and then share and record responses. Class groups can then collectively review answers.

Although students may use textbooks and class notes to locate information, they are not inundated with many pages of materials. This technique of reviewing and studying information allows them to transfer their knowledge to two user-friendly sheets. Different-colored sheets can be used to further distinguish question grids from answer grids.

Packaging makes a big difference in marketing, since people tend to gravitate toward more eye-appealing items. Students also need visually appealing items to whet their appetites for learning. The simple conclusion is that items of learning need improved methods of ingestion!

Boxed Musical Curriculum Connections

Directions: Test your musical knowledge by trying to answer these questions before glancing at the answers on the grid that follows.

Which German composer who lived in the late 18th and early 19th century was best known for his famous symphonies?	Which 20th-century American songwriter wrote "God Bless America"?	Name an American patriotic hymn from the 19th century that begins, "My Country, 'Tis of Thee."	Who composed the music to the opera *Porgy and Bess*?	What lawyer and poet wrote "The Star-Spangled Banner"?
What stringed musical instrument is widely used in folk music?	Name a percussion instrument that is a large, round, metal plate.	Name all four instrument families.	What music piece is an introduction to a longer work?	What is a musical drama that is totally or mostly sung?
Name a high-pitched woodwind instrument, held horizontally, which is played by blowing across a hole.	What name is sometimes given to the violin when it is used in folk music or bluegrass?	What musical group do the French horn, trumpet, trombone, and tuba belong to?	What is a song of thanksgiving or praise called?	What's a quintet?
Name three musical elements.	What's a melody?	What term describes the simultaneous sounding of two pleasing musical notes?	Define jazz.	What word describes an extended musical composition for an orchestra that has several movements?
What name is given to a group of related sequenced musical movements?	Name a musical group that includes two violins, a viola, and a cello.	What's the highest range of the female voice called?	Define a chord.	Name your favorite musician.

Musical Answers

Ludwig van Beethoven	Irving Berlin	"America"	George Gershwin	Francis Scott Key
guitar	cymbal	• brass • percussion • strings • woodwind	overture	opera
flute	fiddle	brass	hymn	A group of five musicians or a piece of music for five instruments or voices
• harmony • melody • rhythm	songlike sequence of tones	harmony	Musical art form and expression with African American cultural roots	symphony
suite	string quartet	soprano	Sound of three or more notes in the same musical key, played together	Answers will vary.

Template

Concentration

"I Ate Cereal for Breakfast"

Once during small-group instruction, while I was explaining how to divide decimals by a divisor with a decimal, a student proceeded to tell me about a funny thing his dog did over the weekend. Okay, it's nice to share, but . . . I inexplicably turned to him and said, "I ate cereal for breakfast." He looked puzzled, started to ask a question, and then stopped. The message was received loudly and clearly. For the rest of the year, when someone else went off on an unrelated tangent, he would say, "I ate cereal for breakfast." Listening is an art. Sometimes the teacher really did say something, but it was probably never heard by some students due to internal or external distractions. Share the suggestions below with students.

How Students Can Be Better Listeners

1. Concentrate on words being said in the classroom, without predicting or connecting everything to your own life, otherwise you might miss the lesson.

2. Listen to the actual words, but think about the meaning at the same time. Try to silently paraphrase what is said.

3. Focus, looking at the teacher or person speaking. Don't get involved in the extra stuff, such as desk playing or silly faces someone might be making, which distracts your attention.

4. You can write notes about important facts, or maybe things said that you are not sure about, but wait to ask questions, since they may be answered by the person speaking.

5. Be interested in what you are learning, even if you think it is boring!

Listening and Moving

Cruise or Dock

Two signs (see above) are placed on opposite sides of the room. Decide on ports of call for a cruise. Perhaps the boat is headed to the Caribbean, Mediterranean, or South Seas (great catharsis!). Directions below are given with one instruction and demonstration at a time, repeating the prior steps before adding a new one (similar to *I'm Going on a Picnic*). The objective of this activity is to reinforce listening skills. Classroom benefits include the merits of releasing excess motor energy after a tedious reading assignment. It's a mind-body connection and an excellent refueler. It's bodily-kinesthetic, interpersonal, intrapersonal, musical-rhythmic, and verbal-linguistic (listening and reading). It's also great for concentration, memory, spatial awareness, and following directions. Besides all of that, it's fun! Students respond to prompts that are written on signs.

Prompt	*Response*
Large Waves	Students join hands and bob up and down
Shark	Frenzied, quick movement
Party Time	Students mingle
Land Sighted	Hands are placed over forehead while looking toward the dock
Dinghy	Pretend to be rowing
Bridge Open	Everyone freezes to allow ships to pass
Food Served	Rub belly in circular motion with your hand

Check out these sources:

Inclusive Games, by S. Kasser (1995)

Silly Sports & Goofy Games, by Dr. Spencer Kagan (2000)

Adapted Physical Education and Sport, by J. Winnick (2000)

Adapted Games and Activities: From Tag to Team Building, by P. Rouse (2004)

JumpBunch Sports & Fitness for Kids—www.jumpbunch.com/kidsfitness games.html

Creative Dance & Movement—www.ataccess.org/resources/wcp/enhtml/en07Dance.html

ORGANIZED ENVIRONMENTS

Student-Friendly Signs

Teachers post these signs on the chalkboard or classroom bulletin board to highlight homework in different subjects. Each day, the work next to the sign changes, but students know where to consistently look for assignments. Signs can be laminated and magnetized. Activity/study centers in the classroom can be labeled as well, for a visually structured environment.

Tracking My Assignments

Subject	Date Due	Books/Materials	Check When Done

Organization With Calendars

Filling in dates and events for each month on calendars like this one helps students follow classroom routines. For example, students can make notations of assemblies, holidays, tests scheduled, when reports are due, birthdays, parent nights, spirit days, and much more. These monthly planners can be kept on students' desks. Small numbers in the right-hand corner of each box allow room for monthly activities. Keeping a calendar is particularly helpful for non-readers, emergent readers, and English language learners. Pictorial calendar concepts can be used with a large classroom calendar, with magnet-backed icons to designate various school events, or even daily routines. In addition, many schools distribute or encourage the use of daily student planners to record homework assignments, long-range projects, and upcoming events.

Month: _____						
Sunday	**Monday**	**Tuesday**	**Wednesday**	**Thursday**	**Friday**	**Saturday**

It is often quite helpful if student planners, along with homework assignment books, are signed and reviewed by both teachers and staff in school and parents or adults at home, or assigned study buddies who can check peers' planners and calendars for preparation and accuracy.

Assessing, Testing, and Grading Your Students

Now that students have studied, how do teachers assess just what they know? Grading is the hardest thing for both teachers and students. Students with disabilities are no longer out of the accountability loop, but expected to achieve the same curriculum standards as their peers without disabilities. The vast majority of students with IEPs are slated to take the same standardized tests as their classmates, unless it can be shown that even with accommodations and modifications, the test is not appropriate. Tests need to be both reliable (giving consistent results when repeated) and valid (meaningfully assessing what they claim to measure). Tests are also just one type of assessment, yielding valuable instructional knowledge. Included in this chapter is a discussion of assessment dilemmas, along with creative options teachers can explore to help students gain "expected" grades.

PURPOSEFUL ASSESSMENTS

Appropriate assessment can be used to guide instruction, particularly for students who have disabilities. When teachers study error patterns, this information can be used for future lesson planning. It's more than just the grade; it's knowing what a student needs help with! Purposeful testing involves looking at error patterns, since these act as indicators for teachers, helping them better teach students on their appropriate level. Grades students receive are not gifts, but should be earned by students. Recently I gave some math students a test, only I didn't call it by that name. I instructed students to head their papers with the following question: *What Do I Know?* It's critical for students to be aware of their levels, and exactly what they need more help with. Both teachers and students need to evaluate just what learning has taken place.

In addition, when teachers develop tests, they need to think about the big picture. Understanding by design invites teachers to think about the outcomes desired at the outset and then plan the learning activities to match those objectives. This approach differs from proceeding ahead with a lesson and then picking facts out of the text to be tested that were not emphasized or explored in class lessons. Test construction is just as important as the lessons themselves, with parallel concepts delivered and assessed. If GE and SE teachers are coteachers, then both can share input in the test design, type of questions offered, and formats for the class. Maybe some students will need tests orally read so as not to let reading difficulties interfere with content knowledge. Overall, accommodations and modifications need to match students' IEP requirements. Tests help gauge what students know and what educators may still have to teach to help students learn more. RTI, as discussed in prior chapters, values assessments as ways of determining where to proceed next in the learning. The following offers an analogy that shows how to *sandwich in* assessments.

RTI Sandwich:

- The "crust" of the matter includes assessment of student's needs, sandwiching in the next two layers.
- *Lettuce* means let us figure out, identify, and problem solve which interventions will best suit this student's current needs.
- The meaty parts of the RTI sandwich are the implementation of scientific research-based strategies, appropriate instructional approaches, and plans.
- Now, there are more assessments—back to the crust of the matter—determining if the interventions have produced acceptable results, and seeing if the interventions were appropriate ones.

Otherwise, change concerning intervention methods is warranted. New sandwich meat is required!

Source: Karten, T. (2009). *Inclusion strategies that work for adolescent learners!* Thousand Oaks, CA: Corwin.

Grading Options

The following are EPAs that need to be considered when grading students:

Effort	Working at optimum level
Progress	Growth over time
Achievement*	Mastery of standards and lesson's objectives
Self-awareness	Being cognizant of strengths and weaknesses, with a plan for improvement of skills

*Be cognizant of goals, accommodations, and types of testing procedures listed in IEPs.

Types of Grading

1. *Norm-Referenced:* Students' grades are compared to those of peers, with same standards for all students.

2. *Criterion-Referenced:* Evaluation is based upon mastery of standards, without comparison to others.

3. *Self-Referenced:* Grading is based upon noted improvement of skills, with individual needs, abilities, and efforts shown taken into consideration.

Don't forget about ABOWA (Assessment By Observation and Walking Around). Primary teachers are very skilled at ABOWA because they give fewer percentage grades. Teachers who watch students will informally learn to assess their understanding quite accurately. Error analysis often reveals areas that require remediation before marching onward. It is through assessments that more instructional knowledge is gained.

Accountability Issues

What Do Tests Measure?

Sometimes, tests can be a measure of students' *dis*abilities, not their competencies. In that case, the test is disabled, not the student. In the past, some school districts even omitted the scores of classified students from their databases. That scenario deleted the special education student from accountability. Assessments can be vital tools that determine if all students are learning, but a child with a disability often faces the difficult task of being given the same assessment as a student who does not have a disability. Accommodating those differences does not necessarily devalue the entire assessment. Students are asked to meet standards of learning, and all students are expected to attain a given knowledge set. The intention of education is for students to show academic improvement. If improvement is not evidenced over a period of time under the reauthorized ESEA/NCLB, schools can face penalties that include transferring students to more successful schools, providing tutoring, or even tougher sanctions such as a change in school management and restructuring. Since many schools do not want to be labeled as needing improvement, the law is being challenged in different ways. States have concerns over standardized tests for children of varying abilities, some even proposing to exclude certain students if there's a small population of special education or non–English-speaking children in the school, with schools claiming the results are not valid. Other states propose classifying some students with learning disabilities, such as those of low socioeconomic status, into another category such as children of poverty, to circumvent accountability again, since having a majority of students with low incomes influences a school's scores. The question being asked here is whether the students who have not had similar learning experiences are misidentified as having a learning disability, since their lack of educational exposures impacts their performance. It is then claimed that these students may unjustly influence and penalize that school's performance. Students with and without learning disabilities who are more affluent usually perform better on standardized tests. If that's the case, how can schools level the playing fields to account for the fact that many schools have students from families with lower socioeconomic status? These types of situational state allowances are currently being debated and tested by parents, educators, and the federal government.

Source: "States' End Run Dilutes Burden for Special Ed," by Diane Jean Schemo, June 7, 2004, http://www.nytimes.com/2004/06/07/education/07CHIL.html.

Students with disabilities must participate in districts' assessments. A small percentage of students with disabilities who have severe cognitive disabilities may take an alternate assessment based upon alternate academic achievement standards, known as AA-AAS. That occurs when the grade level test would be much too difficult for the students and not provide helpful information. Other students with disabilities may also take an alternate assessment based upon modified academic achievement standards, known as AA-MAS. In this case the test is aligned with grade level standards. This may be a test that has simplified language or perhaps a reduced number of questions, but it is still challenging and offers a result that is referenced to the same grade level in which the student is enrolled. IEP teams make these testing decisions. School staff members would do well to collectively discuss these challenging questions:

- Does fair mean equal?
- Should students be compared to one another?
- How can a written test accurately measure a child's knowledge if he or she has learning and language difficulties?
- When does effort count?
- Should teachers or schools be held accountable for a child's lack of progress?

Serving Knowledge

Food critics can enhance or demote a restaurant's status by the mighty pen that either raves about or deplores the meal served. As the review reaches vast audiences, restaurants may experience an increase in business or a devastating shutdown. However, consider how the following questions can affect the accuracy and value of a food critic's review.

1. Did the critic catch the chef on his or her best day?

2. How was the food prepared?

3. Did the critic ever eat that kind of food before?

4. Did the reviewer like the waiter or waitress who served the food?

5. What type of rating scale did the reviewer use?

Now consider the following educational concerns:

1. Did the teacher catch the child on his or her best day?

2. How were the students prepared for the test?

3. Had the student learned about that subject before?

4. Does the student like the teacher or have an interest in the subject matter?

5. What type of assessment format was used?

CLASSROOM SCENARIOS

1. can't/won't

> There's a fine line between can't and won't. Teachers must help, not enable.

2. filewild

If the word *wildlife* appears to the student as *filewild*, imagine how difficult written language is for such a student.

> Written testing accompanied by orally read questions would definitely be appropriate, since a test needs to measure a child's understanding of a concept, not his or her reading disability.

3. bed

A student with a hearing impairment responded that *bed* was the past tense for *be*. The student was applying his best effort but lacked an understanding of the spoken language.

> Tests should not penalize students if they truly do not understand concepts. Teachers are here to help, not punish students who are differently abled.

4. A.M.W.

A worksheet asks for the abbreviation for *a married woman*. The student responds with A.M.W., instead of Mrs.

> Some students are concrete learners who need direct skill instruction to compensate for varying background knowledge.

5. half credit

Given a multiple-choice question with three choices, a student circles two of the lettered choices. It turns out that one of the choices is correct, and the student argues for partial credit. No way!

> Rules need to be enforced. The assessment is a valuable learning tool and teaches the meaning of accountability, not how to beat the system.

Learning Choices: Alternate Methods of Assessment

Educational Contract Options

To prove that I understand about _____[Topic], I will

_____ create a play

_____ compose a song

_____ make a cartoon

_____ write jokes on the topic

_____ paraphrase a Podcast

_____ create a PowerPoint presentation

_____ perform a dance

_____ keep a learning log

_____ complete a take-home test

_____ work on a group project

_____ teach it to another student

_____ do a written report

_____ give a speech

_____ research Web sites with more information

_____ teach a class lesson

_____ interview people about the topic

_____ write a newspaper article

_____ compose a graph or chart

_____ compile a scrapbook with computer clip art or my own artwork

_____ create a sculpture

_____ design a game

_____ invent a product

_____ create a time line of important events or details

_____ other idea

Mutually agreed upon on _____ (Date) by _____
(Student's Name) and _____ (Teacher's Name). Will be
completed by _____ (Date).

Student's initials _____ Teacher's initials _____

Home/Parent signature _____

Paper is to be placed in student's portfolio as evidence of intended performance.

Portfolios offer an organized and concrete time line of children's growth that can be reviewed by teachers, families, and students themselves as a reflection of progress achieved throughout the year.

USER-FRIENDLY TESTING FORMATS

> Sometimes it's not a student's disability that causes poor performance, but the test itself that disables. Assessment should be visually appealing, with clear and precise directions.

Colonial Knowledge

Directions: Read the 12 statements below and place the correct numbers in the labeled colonial squares.

Roanoke	Both colonies	Jamestown

Colonial Statements

1. First settlement in American colonies

2. Second settlement in American colonies

3. Colonists traded with Native Americans

4. Located off the coast of Virginia

5. Located off the coast of North Carolina

6. Leader was John Smith

7. Leader was John White

8. Settled by the English

9. Colony failed with colonists disappearing

10. Colonists faced hardships before they were successful

11. Africans worked on tobacco farms

12. Located on the East Coast of the United States

> **Rationale:** Varying testing formats helps students to demonstrate their knowledge in a non-intimidating, jargon-free manner, with clear directions. This information was originally in multiple-choice format, but now the same knowledge is being tested using an approach that neatly boxes and numbers the information, helping students who have perceptual and writing difficulties.

Logical Matching

Directions: Draw a line from the definition in the left column to the correct word in the right columned box.

bottom number of a fraction	multiplication X
top number of a fraction	denominator $\frac{4}{5}$
mathematical operation that is repeated addition	numerator $\frac{3}{4}$
expressing a number out of 100	quadrilateral
a polygon with four sides	percent %

Rationale: An uncluttered format such as this one deviates from the usual matching design, by switching the definition to the left column and the word choice to the right one. It may seem inconsequential to most students, but those with reading difficulties appreciate this type of matching layout, since they are not required to laboriously read every definition before choosing the right answer. This way they can focus on one definition at a time, minimizing frustrations. Accompanying visuals further explain the written words.

Dramatic Assessment

Drama can be an alternative assessment to written tests as a way for students to demonstrate their knowledge, such as setting up a *Performance Center.* For example, when studying about the Roman Empire, students can role-play actions of the emperor, patricians, plebeians, artisans, and slaves as they include appropriate historical facts through dialogue and actions.

Directions: Think of some topics students can dramatize:

ASSESSMENT TRENDS

Unfortunately, many students visualize themselves failing the test before it is even given. The tension is usually self-induced and leads to many disappointing assessments, since this type of negative thinking is a self-fulfilling prophecy. If possible, try not to schedule tests on a day that you know you will be absent. Often, students stare at a teacher during the test because they are reenacting the learning situation, perhaps a lecture or a review. Seeing the teacher (and not a substitute) may help trigger the learning.

TEACHER TIPS

Teachers can help ease testing tensions:

1. Familiarize students with the testing layout, such as the type of questions that will be asked. (Will there be essays, short answers, multiple choice, fill-ins, open-ended, true or false, matching, word boxes, etc.?)

2. Tell students the material to be tested ahead of time. Some children need at least a week to prepare for larger unit exams. Give exact textbook page numbers, study guides, or outlines; copies of PowerPoints, Smart Board notes, outlines from programs such as *Inspiration* or *Kidspiration* software, podcasts.

3. Test frequently to alleviate the pressure of one test being the whole grade.

4. Use your discretion on when to give extra-credit assignments if a child wants to improve a grade.

5. Give students various ways to demonstrate their knowledge through other multiple intelligences besides verbal-linguistic and logical-mathematical ones.

6. Have students consistently keep track of their grades, charting progress.

7. Encourage good note-taking and organizational skills by consistently checking notebooks, loose-leaf folders, binders, desk, and work areas.

8. Communicate frequently with parents and families, making them aware of their child's needs and progress, so learning can be supported and bridged in both school and home environments.

9. Teach the philosophy *Big Deal, So What!* to a student who thinks the world is over because he or she did poorly on one test. Encourage that child to use it as a learning experience by examining the problem: Was the material too difficult? Or was it a lack of effort?

10. Reexamine the test: Was it a fair assessment of material taught?

Examples of testing accommodations for students with disabilities may vary in terms of the following:

- Presentation (how the lesson is delivered, e.g., large print, directions read aloud, Braille, signed, technology, amount of questions on a page)
- Response (avenues to answer, e.g., written, dictated to a scribe, calculator, computer, pointing to correct answers)
- Scheduling (time issues; e.g., frequent breaks, more time, mornings or afternoons, spread out over sessions or days)
- Location (where test is given, e.g., small group, general education classroom, separate or quieter setting, take-home test)

Consult these sources for additional research-based recommendations:

National Center on Educational Outcomes (NCEO): www.cehd.umn .edu/nceo/topicareas/UnivDesign/UnivDesignResources.htm

U.S. Office of Special Education Programs (OSEP) Ideas that Work:

www.nceo.info/OnlinePubs/AAMASParewntGuide.pdf

www.osepideasthatwork.org/ParentKit/index.asp

TESTING CHANGES

Let's talk about how accountability has impacted testing requirements and raised the expectations for students with disabilities. In June of 2002, the SAT, the most widely used standardized test for college admission, was modified to align it with curriculum and state standards. The College Board trustees voted to add an essay exam with students writing a reasoned argument, along with multiple-choice questions on grammar and usage; toughen its math section to include advanced algebra; and eliminate the analogy questions. An increased number of short, prose, critical reading passages with a mandatory writing section are now included to further test reading and writing abilities in and across academic and popular disciplines. In addition, the College Board now gives feedback to test takers on just what skills need improvement (www.collegeboard.com/parents/tests/meet-tests/21296.html).

What does this mean?

- Elementary, middle, and secondary schools vary their teaching strategies and testing formats.
- More reading and writing appears in all grades, across the disciplines, using a variety of formal and informal materials. Stronger algebra math skills are emphasized.
- Accountability is constantly being reexamined to determine successful outcomes by answering these simple questions:

"Are they really learning?"

"How can we find out?"

Schools assign an SSD (Services for Students with Disabilities) coordinator who contacts the College Board. The school coordinator then arranges testing accommodations for College Board tests, after appropriate eligibility forms are submitted and approved. Appropriate SAT accommodations may include but are not limited to the following: extended time, a Braille version, a computer for writing, large-type test formats, sign language interpreter, scribe, or other accommodations based upon individual needs.

Resources/Contacts

College Board Services for Students with Disabilities

P.O. Box 6226, Princeton, NJ 08541–6226

(609) 771–7137; (609) 882–4118 (TTY)

http://www.collegeboard.com/html/communications000.html

http://www.collegeboard.com/ssd/student/index.html

Rubrics

To eliminate vague, subjective assessments, teachers can design an authentic assessment tool for grading in reading, writing, math, speech, and more.

Sample Writing Rubric

Category	4—Excellent	3—Good	2—Fair	1—Needs Improvement
Introduction	The introduction is inviting, states the main topic, and previews the structure of the paper.	The introduction clearly states the main topic and previews the structure of the paper, but is not particularly inviting to the reader.	The introduction states the main topic, but does not adequately preview the structure of the paper, nor is it particularly inviting to the reader.	There is no clear introduction of the main topic or structure of the paper.
Transitions (Organization)	A variety of thoughtful transitions is used. They clearly show how ideas are connected.	Transitions clearly show how ideas are connected, but there is little variety.	Some transitions work well, but connections between other ideas are fuzzy.	The transitions between ideas are unclear or nonexistent.
Support for Topic (Content)	Relevant, telling, quality details give the reader important information that goes beyond the obvious or predictable.	Supporting details and information are relevant, but one key issue or portion of the storyline is unsupported.	Supporting details and information are relevant, but several key issues or portions of the storyline are unsupported.	Supporting details and information are typically unclear or not related to the topic.
Focus on Topic (Content)	There is one clear, well-focused topic. Main idea stands out and is supported by detailed information.	Main idea is clear but the supporting information is general.	Main idea is somewhat clear, but there is a need for more supporting information.	The main idea is not clear. There is a seemingly random collection of information.
Sentence Length (Sentence Fluency)	Every paragraph has sentences that vary in length.	Almost all paragraphs have sentences that vary in length.	Some sentences vary in length.	Sentences rarely vary in length.
Grammar, Punctuation, & Spelling (Conventions)	Writer makes no errors in grammar, punctuation, or spelling that distract the reader from the content.	Writer makes 1–2 errors in grammar, punctuation, or spelling that distract the reader from the content.	Writer makes 3–4 errors in grammar, punctuation, or spelling that distract the reader from the content.	Writer makes more than 4 errors in grammar, punctuation, or spelling that distract the reader from the content.
Word Choice	Writer uses vivid words and phrases that linger or draw pictures in the reader's mind, and the choice and placement of the words seem accurate, natural, and unforced.	Writer uses vivid words and phrases that linger or draw pictures in the reader's mind, but occasionally the words are used inaccurately or seem overdone.	Writer uses words that communicate clearly, but the writing lacks variety, punch, or flair.	Writer uses a limited vocabulary that does not communicate strongly or capture the reader's interest. Jargon or clichés may be present and detract from the meaning.
Conclusion (Organization)	The conclusion is strong and leaves the reader with a feeling that he or she understands what the writer is "getting at."	The conclusion is recognizable and ties up almost all the loose ends.	The conclusion is recognizable but does not tie up several loose ends.	There is no clear conclusion; the paper just ends.

Source: Created by T. Karten using http://rubistar.4teachers.org/index.php.

Working With Parents and Families of Students With Disabilities

Teachers must recognize the important role parents and families play in the learning process. Acting as allies, the parents, families, and teachers can work together to help children succeed. Coordination between home and school environments benefits learners. This chapter stresses that teachers cannot understand the student with special needs without effectively including parents and caregivers, understanding their struggles and perspectives as well.

VALUING PARENTS AND FAMILIES

Understanding Parental Emotions

After parent conferences, teachers have often been heard to say, "*So and so* is exactly like her parent whom I just met. The apple doesn't fall far from the tree." Unless you have experienced what it is like to have a *special* child of your own, you cannot begin to understand the intricate dynamics involved. The complexities involve more than apples.

The various emotive behaviors parents experience when raising a *special* child can be comparable to the grief or mourning process. Parental emotions can include the following:

Shock	(plans, dreams, expectations, and lives are changed)
Denial	(feeling of frustration, can't be happening, not true!)
Guilt	(whatever went wrong was my fault, helplessness)
Shopping Behavior	(looking toward experts for different diagnosis and strategies)
Depression	(sadness and withdrawal: I don't want to face the world!)
Hostility and finally	(state of anger, despair, overwhelm, exhaustion, pain, fear)
Acceptance	(courageous, stronger, optimistic)

Parental and Familial Understandings and Reflections

In addition to experiencing these emotions, parents and guardians must often deal with experts who complicate the process. Educators, doctors, friends, family, and well-intentioned others express a range of emotions as well. It is difficult enough for parents to trust or even know their own instincts at this time, let alone deal with how others feel. This adjustment process encompasses a broad spectrum, with parents and family members often being the recipient of contrasting emotions, ranging from pity to support.

Sometimes parents and guardians are not the ones in denial; it is the interventions of educators or experts that *deny parents* as being the experts, the ones who are the most knowledgeable about their own child's strengths and needs. Parents and guardians are quite often experts on their own children and need accepting ears and advice on how to best meet their children's challenging needs. Other parents, guardians, or teachers sometimes let prior unsuccessful school experiences interfere with impartiality and objectivity in the planning process. Even though parents may know that their child is not on par with his or her peers in academic, perceptual, sensory, communication, physical, behavioral, emotional, or social areas, it becomes even more traumatic when vast differences are concretely shown and sometimes magnified with harsh-sounding written evaluations. Overall, caution needs to be exercised, since labeling people in any type of holding pattern actually cuts off possibilities for future collaborative planning. Most important is to listen to each other's views.

Parents rarely forget that first disability diagnosis, whether it is at birth or in the school years. The toll on families is enormous. Marriages are strained as expectations for children become altered, while siblings are also impacted as attention is drawn away from them. Stress levels of parents have an effect on students' overall performance (Lessenberry & Rehdfeldt, 2004). Which stage parents and families are in when the teacher meets them will influence the relationship.

Teachers also need to reflect upon their own reactions, even with things that are not said, since actions or body language can sometimes speak louder than words. The children need to be the common ground for educators, parents, families, and support systems. Understandings and reflections for all are imperative.

PARENTS, FAMILIES, AND TEACHERS AS ALLIES

School–Home Communication

Parenting a child with special needs requires inner strength and much support from family and friends. Many support groups out there can help parents deal with difficulties that arise. Just knowing that others have gone through similar experiences helps parents and guardians a great deal. Other understanding parents and supportive family members can offer each other assistance, guidance, and comfort.

Mutual respect is first and foremost. It is understandable that the whole special education process, along with its associated jargon, can be overwhelming. Parents are often outnumbered by professionals at IEP meetings and can feel both threatened and anxious at the same time, trying to get the best program for their child. Families should be well-informed on changing special education laws, looking at the safeguards and knowing how to best use them to help their children. Educators should also be well-informed about the disabilities of the students within their classroom, understanding the difficulties families face.

Parental voices need empowerment to collaborate with teachers to make educational decisions based upon jointly decided appropriate services for children. Teachers, parents, and families are integral parts of this planning process, offering input to address the unique educational needs of each child with a disability. Even offering suggestions to parents and guardians such as which books to read with their children or describing some home activities to increase literacy or mathematical skills values the parents' and families' role as well. Always remember to also validate families' concerns and to point out the *good stuff,* too, e.g., through positive phone calls or showing improved student work samples.

Empowerment and Communication for All

Teachers	Parents/Families
Children	Guardians
Community	Siblings
Administration	

Frequent Parent–Home Communication

- Averts problematic situations.
- Sends a message of worth to the parents and guardians.
- Tells students that there's a connection between the school and home environments.
- Occurs not only at parent–teacher conferences or scheduled IEP meetings but throughout the school year if necessary.
- Can be verbal or written such as informal notes or letters, report cards, emails, phone contacts, interim grade reports, checklists, behavioral charts, or signatures on tests and homework assignments.

How Parents and Families Can Understand More

- Ask questions.
- Explain how you feel.
- Seek information.
- Maintain realistic expectations.
- Be patient with yourself, your child, and others.
- Learn to express emotions.
- Take care of yourself.
- Keep daily routines.
- Recognize that you are not alone.
- Be involved with your child's day.
- Maintain positive attitudes.

Parental/Family Input

Child's Name: _____

Parent's/Guardian's Name: _____

1. What does my child think about school?

2. What do I visualize my daughter or son doing in 10 or 15 years?

3. What are my child's needs?

4. Some words I would use to describe my child are _____, _____, and _____.

5. What are my child's favorite things to do?

6. What are my pet peeves about my child's school?

7. What do I like about my child's class?

8. My areas of expertise are _____ _____, and I am available to talk to my child's class on _____.

9. I'd like to volunteer to help _____ _____.

10. Contact me at

Email: _____

Telephone: Home _____ Work _____ Cell phone _____

Home Address: _____

_____

WE'RE ALL ON THE SAME SIDE

Parents and Families

+

Teachers

+

Administrators

+

Students

+

Community

=

Learning

Resources and Organizations for Parents, Guardians, and Families

The Council for Exceptional
  Children (CEC)
1110 North Glebe Road, Suite 300
Arlington, VA 22201
(703) 620–3660; TTY: (703) 264–9446
http://www.cec.sped.org

Exceptional Parent
65 East Route 4
River Edge, NJ 07661 (201) 489–4111
http://www.eparent.com

Parent Resource section of government Web site:
http://www.disability.gov/education/parent_resources

All Kids Count: http://www.osepideasthatwork.org/ParentKit/allkidscount1.asp

National Dissemination Center for Children with Disabilities
Basics for Parents: Your Child's Evaluation, a publication of NICHCY
1825 Connecticut Ave NW, Suite 700
Washington, DC 20009
(800) 695–0285 (Voice/TTY)
http://www.nichcy.org

Parent Training and Information (PTI) Centers

Contact information may be obtained from NICHCY's individual State Resource Sheets. Each state has a department with a division for Special Education, giving information and help. http://www.yellowpagesforkids.com/help/ptis.htm

National Parent Teacher Association
330 N. Wabash Avenue, Suite 2100
Chicago, IL 60611
(800) 307–4PTA (4782)
www.pta.org

National Center for Family Literacy
325 West Main Street
Louisville, KY 40202
(877) FAMLIT–1
http://www.famlit.org

Klein, S., & Schive, K. (2001). *You will dream new dreams.* New York: Kensington Books. (Excellent inspirational parental resource)

Parent Advocacy Coalition for Educational Rights (PACER)
8161 Normandale Boulevard
Minneapolis, MN 55437
(952) 838–9000; TTY (952) 838–0190
http://www.pacer.org

Shore, K. (2009). *A teacher's guide to working with parents.* Port Chester, NY: Dude Publishing.

Considering Technology in the Inclusive Classroom

This is an important topic, given the society in which we live and the increase in available tools to help our population of students with disabilities. Schools have undergone incredible changes throughout the years. Scientific discoveries have yielded benefits that have trickled down to educational forums to address student needs. The one-room schoolhouse certainly did not offer today's classroom's range of technological options available to help all learners with varying abilities succeed. Technology today offers ways to increase cognitive, physical, behavioral, social, and perceptual levels for students with varying dis*abilities* who in the past were not able to access the curriculum, nor the same opportunities to advance. Technology is an invaluable tool to differentiate classrooms with presentations, engagements, and assessments. However, never think that technology such as a Smart Board is smarter than the teacher! The technological possibilities for students with and without disabilities are enormous, but the computers or the technology offered by *techno tools* and devices cannot replace the interactions of human beings, nor can the technology itself be the lesson. Technology may accompany and enhance lessons, with students responding to the animations, deliveries, and access they offer, but it is the teachers and school media and computer specialists themselves who operate, choose, and decide upon which systems to use, how often, and to what degree who are the technology navigators. Included in this chapter are technological activities and resources that teachers can implement in their lessons. Technology, when used effectively, complements good teaching strategies.

BENEFITS AND PROMISING FUTURES

The Technology-Related Assistance for Individuals with Disabilities Act of 1988 and the Individuals with Disabilities Education Act (IDEA) Amendments of 1997 are two federal laws that mandate that schools provide students with disabilities with instructional and assistive technology services. When IDEA was reauthorized in 2004, the National Instructional Materials Access Center (NIMAC), a repository connected with the National Instructional Materials Accessibility Standard (NIMAS), was set up to provide instructional materials in a timely manner to students who require them. This involves the educational textbook industry, other publishers, state educational agencies, and local educational agencies following NIMAS's mandates to provide textbooks and other curricular materials in accessible media, free of charge, to students in elementary and secondary schools who are blind or may have print disabilities. This includes specialized formats such as Braille, audio versions, digital text, and large print.

The intent of these laws is for technology to maximize accessibility and increase relevance for children with disabilities. The Technology-Related Assistance Act of 1988 defines *assistive technology* as any item or product, whether acquired commercially, off the shelf, modified, or customized, that is used to increase, maintain, or improve the functional capabilities of individuals with disabilities.

Many technological advances have been achieved because of the personal dedication and commitment of caring individuals. Necessity is the parent of many inventions. For example, Louis Braille, who was blind, invented the raised tactile system of dots for writing and reading. His vision enabled others to see. An engineer, John W. Holter, who was also the father of a boy with hydrocephalus, invented the shunt, which is used to drain extra fluid from the brain. Alexander Graham Bell invented the telephone by accident while he was seeking to create an amplification system for those with hearing impairments, like his mother. In Christopher Reeve's book, *Nothing Is Impossible: Reflections on a New Life* (2002), he documented his progress as he tried to find a way for himself and others with spinal cord injuries to walk. He poignantly reiterated how the heart, mind, and spirit are not diminished by a body's limitations. Mr. Reeve didn't have the word *limitations* in his vocabulary. Technology and increased medical knowledge are also limitless.

Future technological advances offer endless possibilities for those with physical disabilities.

- The breaking of the genetic code offers hope in detecting predisposed conditions such as Alzheimer's and Down syndrome.
- Students with dyslexia, dysgraphia, and those who are blind use digitized texts, spelling tools that talk, word prediction programs, and speech-to-text applications. Students without disabilities often prefer this technology as well, e.g., Kindle, audio books, macro tools.
- Podcasts offer options for replay of lectures and better understandings of concepts in other environments, e.g., quieter setting, home review.
- PET scanning enables doctors to see inside the human body.
- Technologies such as the MRI and CAT scans have been developed that evaluate differences in our brains, making it possible to identify some emotional illnesses such as schizophrenia, and increasing the likelihood of better treatments for such conditions.
- Scientists are building smart wheelchairs, robotic limbs, and other devices that will help people manipulate objects and walk again. For example, Honda is working on Robolegs to help people walk, while Japan has a battery-powered suit that can assist people with disabilities to climb stairs. The innate UDL design also helps

people lift heavy workloads. Toyota has plans for a wheelchair that is controlled by a computerized cap that analyzes a person's brainwaves with the goal of helping people who are paralyzed walk by controlling impulses with their minds (www.disabilityscoop.com/2009/06/30/wheelchair-thought/3908).

- Screen readers help people who are blind to navigate sites online.
- Screen magnifiers assist those with visual impairments.
- Digital pens read written text.
- People who are deaf or have hearing impairments are helped with tools and technology such as computers, TTYs (telephone text), cochlear implants, hair cell regeneration, assistive listening devices, VOIP (Voices Over the Internet Protocol); changing analog phone signals into digital signals, which are then transmitted over the Internet), closed captioning, phone texting, and instant messaging (www.disabilityresources.org/AT-DEAF.html).

CLASSROOM/COMMUNITY IMPLICATIONS AND RESOURCES

Technology can be as simple as using larger writing implements and pencil grips, or taping paper to a desk to help those with fine motor difficulties. It might mean one child uses an eyedropper, while another uses a turkey baster. Technology augments the curriculum in a range of topics from the Brothers Grimm to Malcolm X. Students can be involved in an Iditarod virtual fieldtrip (www.field-guides.com/trips.htm) or even watch the virtual dissection of a frog (http://froggy.lbl.gov/virtual). eBooks with digital texts, email, instant messaging, voice-operated computers, video conferencing, and multimedia presentations are all examples of how technology enhances communications and learning. Technology can help students with disabilities increase their mobility and independence despite sensory or physical issues.

Students can gain academic information through both commercial and homemade products to achieve greater independence in schools and the community. Teachers can use technology to motivate and instruct students while increasing their own classroom productivity. Most important, teachers in inclusive classrooms use technology to augment the curriculum, guiding and monitoring student usage for effective instructional gains. Written work improves as students gain more information and understanding of topics under the teacher's guidance.

Everyone benefits when technological advances help those with disabilities become active participants in society. The level of disability acceptance a person with a disability has affects whether he or she might embrace or reject many of the technological changes, but just the mere existence of the technology offers increasing possibilities for the future.

Communication	Hearing	Physical	Visual	Academic
Communication boards for students with limited speech let them make their daily needs known by pointing to given pictures.	Closed captioning on television programs and videos	Alternative keyboards with switch access help physically challenged students. www .intellitools.com	Tape recorders play audiotaped versions of literature. National Library Service for the Blind and Physically Handicapped (NLS) www.loc .gov/nls	Software that augments content areas, e.g., www.brainpop.com, www.brainpopjr.com (movies) funbrain.com, www.inspiration.com, www.kidspiration.com
Text from Web sites can be read aloud with special software that also hooks up to dictionary definitions of more difficult vocabulary words.	TDD/TTY/ TT, telecommunication devices for the deaf, which transpose the spoken word into written text to allow telephone conversations	Hand splints, trackballs, or touch screens with body controls such as the blinking of eyes, raising eyebrows, or tapping of fingers or feet for students with limited mobility who cannot use a traditional mouse on the computer	Recording for the Blind and Dyslexic, www.rfbd.org, which assists students with print disabilities	Writing programs that predict the next word a child might type, or correct grammar and punctuation, e.g., www.mindplay .com, www.donjohns ton.com
Text-to-speech technology, for students to hear what they have written. Write Outloud, www.donjohnston .com	Assistive listening devices (FM systems) with teachers using a wireless microphone and students using receivers in hearing aids that amplify sounds	Wheelchairs range from those that allow people to stand up to ones made of PVC material that can be rolled onto a beach.	To learn more about Braille, www.afb.org/ braillebug	Hand-held electronic spellers to find correct spelling or vocabulary, e.g., www.franklin.com

Communication	Hearing	Physical	Visual	Academic
Talking picture and word-processing programs for students to write stories with pictures rather than typing words. Writing with Symbols, Mayer Johnson, www.mayer johnson.com. Communication tools can be as simple as accessible key rings that hold individual pictures or sticky notes that students and teachers can write on, point to, or read. Mirrors Clip art More visuals	Cochlear implants, Cochlear Implant Association, Inc. (CIAI), www.hearinglos sweb.com/res/ hlorg/ciai/ciai .htm Successful Adaptations for Learning to Use Touch Effectively, www .projectsalute.net Outlines Graphic organizers Sticky notes Communication boards www.agbell.org	Voice activation can bypass a keyboard; www.nanopac .com Sensors placed in legs help those with physical impairments. Talking word-prediction programs to help students with fine motor difficulties; Co-Writer, www.donjohnston .com. Velcro mat on desk. Beanbags for more comfortable classroom seating and gym activities	ATMs that talk Products such as checkers with different-shaped pieces, calculators with large print or ones that talk, copy machines that enlarge, books on tape, talking compasses, art books with pictures you can touch to see, or a ball with a bell inside; www .projectsalute .net	Multimedia instruction with videos, digital text, cameras, graphics, and sound, with auditory and visual instructions, and feedback Graphics program: www.inspiration .com Highlighters, portable keyboards, www.alpha smart.com Smart Boards Interactive whiteboards www.smarter kids.org

SAMPLE HIGH SCHOOL IN-CLASS LESSON—COMBINING LITERATURE AND TECHNOLOGY

Requirements for Literature Assignment: Students first read one of the four books, then complete assignment as follows:

1. Students conduct research with given Web sites or ones of their own to provide more detailed information about the characters (at least three), setting, plot, resolution, themes, concepts, and symbolism. Web sources and paraphrased notes are then submitted with final project.

2. An eight-paragraph essay as detailed below is then written:

   Par. 1   Introduction—Reason you chose this book, brief overview of what will follow

   Par. 2   Analysis of characters

   Par. 3   Setting—Where and when the story takes place

   Par. 4   Synopsis of plot, sequence of events

   Par. 5   Climax and ending, how story was resolved

   Par. 6   Themes/Concepts/Symbolism presented in book

   Par. 7   Compare book with online research about characters, settings, themes, authors

   Par. 8   Conclusion—State your opinion and overall impression of book and what further insights you gained from research.

	Book Choices			
	To Kill a Mockingbird, by Harper Lee	*The Crucible*, by Arthur Miller	*Of Mice and Men*, by John Steinbeck	*The Catcher in the Rye*, by J. D. Salinger
Characters	Scout, Jem, Dill, Tom Robinson, Atticus Finch, Arthur (Boo) Radley	Reverend Parris, Abigail Williams, Tituba, Betty Parris, Reverend Hale, John Proctor, Elizabeth, Sarah Good, Mrs. Putnam	George Milton, Lennie Small, Curly, Slim, Lulu, Candy, migrant workers	Holden Caulfield, Phoebe, Stradlater, Ackley, Sally Hayes, Mr. Antolini
Setting	Alabama, Great Depression, 1930s	Salem, Massachusetts, 17th century	California ranch, Salinas Valley, 1940s	New York City, Central Park, Penn Station, Rockefeller Center, 1950s
Plot/Resolution	Lawyer's conflicts with court, community, and family while defending a falsely accused black man in the poor South	Paranoia about witchcraft in Puritan society	Relationship between a man and his friend, as he tries to help him with his cognitive disabilities	Monologue told by 16-year-old boy, Holden Caulfield, who left a private school and went through some difficult times
Themes/ Concepts/ Symbolism	Race relations in the South Criminal justice Prejudice	Adversity Justice Compare to 20th-century Red Scare (communism), McCarthy era	Migrant workers Friendship Innocence Cognitive/ physical disabilities	Childhood vs. adulthood Teenage depression
Sites for Research	www.novelguide .com/to killamoc kingbird www.adl.org	www.novelguide .com/thecrucible www.questia.com	www.novelguide .com/ofmice andmen www.thearc.org/	www.novelguide .com/thecatcherin therye www.nmha.org

Using Computers as Reference Tools

Disability Curriculum Web Search

Answer these questions by using the sites below.

Focus Questions	Web Sites
1. What's the difference between the diagnosis of autism and that of Asperger syndrome? 2. What are the best strategies families and teachers can use to help students with a. Autism? b. Asperger syndrome?	www.autism-society.org www.asperger.org www.autismspeaks.org http://teenautism.com/social-groups
3. What types of modifications can be made in a classroom for children with hearing loss? 4. How do cochlear implants work?	www.agbell.org www.nidcd.nih.gov/health/hearing/coch.asp www.hearingloss.org
5. Name some areas that can be affected by a learning *disability*. 6. Tell some strategies that help children with auditory processing difficulties.	www.ldinfo.com www.ncld.org www.ldonline.org
7. What are the most common types of anxiety disorders in children?	www.mentalhealthamerica.net/go/get-info http://www.nimh.nih.gov/health/topics/index.shtml
8. Name some multimodal treatments for students with AD/HD.	www.chadd.org http://nichcy.org
9. What are the educational/employment implications for a child with Down syndrome?	http://nichcy.org www.ndss.org www.ndsccenter.org www.downsyndrome.com
10. Name some sensitivities that need to be exhibited toward children with Tourette syndrome.	www.tsa-usa.org www.tourettesyndrome.net
11. Why is self-determination an important outcome for people with intellectual *disabilities*?	www.thearc.org www.aamr.org (AAIDD)
12. What are some sports programs available to people with cerebral palsy?	www.ucpa.org

Directions: Now choose a topic and design your own curriculum Web search. A good way to design one is to first find appropriate sites and then work backwards and write questions.

Computer Certificates

Congratulations

You now understand more about _____

Name_____

Teacher_____

Date_____

Teachers can create certificates of praise on the computer as recognition for students' achievements. Simple phrases such as these validate learning strides:

Terrific math problem solving!

Excellent reading work!

Able to work well with peers!

Perfect science project!

Once students collect a certain number of these certificates, they can trade them in for an agreed-upon reward, such as lunch with the teacher, extra computer time, no-homework pass, teaching a lesson . . . or maybe just the attention itself is tangible enough!

Word Processing Programs and Computer Tools

Directions: Type the following paragraph on a word processing program, and then use the language tools of the thesaurus and spell check to revise your writing. The words with (sp) are *spelled incorrectly,* while the <u>underlined words</u> need to be replaced with a different or more exact word, *using the thesaurus* or your own replacement words to expand the thoughts. Check the Tools menu for other spelling and word options. Next, add another paragraph to this story, with specific details about your future plans. Afterward, use the language tools to revise that paragraph as well. After your story is completed, find and insert an appropriate graphic that tells about your future.

Skool (sp) is a <u>good</u> place for <u>good</u> students.

Classrooms <u>give</u> many <u>things</u> that will help you in lif (sp).

Practis (sp) <u>good</u> habuts (sp) now and you will benafit

(sp) when you <u>leave</u> skool (sp) and <u>pick</u> a fewchure (sp).

Prepair (sp) for laytor (sp).

Microsoft has downloads and many templates for teachers at www.microsoft .com/education. Students can also explore all types of writing genres such as creating graphic novels with software, e.g., *Comic Life* by Plasq.

More Educational Websites and Resources for Technological Information

Alliance for Technology Access (ATA)
2175 E. Francisco Blvd., Suite L
San Rafael, CA 94901
(415) 455-4575
TTY: (414) 455-0491
www.ataccess.org

IntelliTools
1720 Corporate Circle
Petaluma, CA 94954
(800) 899-6687
www.intellitools.com

Assistive Technology Industry Association
526 Davis St., Suite 217
Evanston, IL 60201
(877) 687-2842
www.ATIA.org

CAST (excellent UDL options)
Center for Applied Technology
40 Harvard Mills Square, Suite 3
Wakefield, MA 01880-3233
(781) 245-2212
TTY (781) 245-9320
www.cast.org

Family Center on Technology and Disability
www.fctd.info
National Early Childhood Technical Assistance Center
www.nectac.org

For Students

UpToTen.com
www.yahooligans.com
funbrain.com
www.ajkids.com
www.pbskids.org
www.KidsBank.com/
www.howstuffworks.com
www.kidsdomain.com

http://puzzlemaker.discoveryeducation.com

MiddleSchoolHub.org

www2.actden.com/writ_den

Typingpal.com

www.atomiclearning.com

www.brainpop.com, www.brainpopjr.com

www.webmath.com

www.aaamath.com

www.multiplication.com

www.aplusmath.com

www.allmath.com

www.poetry4kids.com

www.novelguide.com

www.English-Zone.com

www.questia.com

www.timeforkids.com

www.newseum.com

http://icom.museum/vlmp/

Excellent Video (shows how technology and personal perseverance help people with disabilities)

ABC News Home Video Library
At Home with Bob & Michelle
20/20 10/25/98, Segment 2
Item #T990528_01M
(800) CALL-ABC

Minnesota's Online Resource About Combined Vision and Hearing Loss
http://www.deafblindinfo.org/history/people

The University of Washington has this open-captioned and audio-described video about adaptive technology and computers: *Working Together: People With Disabilities and Computer Technology,* http://www.washington.edu/doit/Video/wt_dis.html

For Teachers

http://atto.buffalo.edu/registered/ATBasics.php

http://teachers.net

www.learningfirst.org

www.wikispaces.com

www.inspiringteachers.com

www.adl.org

http://rubistar.4teachers.org

http://eduplace.com

Community Learning Network, www.cln.org

www.interventioncentral.org

Educator's Reference Desk, www.eduref.org

U.S. Dept. of Education, www.ed.gov

Helping Teachers Use the Internet Effectively,
http://www.internet4classrooms.com

SCORE Cyber Guides

K–12, Schools of California Online Resources for Educators
www.score.k12.ca.us

Higher Achievement Through Better Nutrition and Health
www.dairycouncilofca.org

www.behavioradvisor.com

http://discoveryschool.com

www.learner.org

International Reading Association, www.reading.org

IEP Planner, www.visionplanet.com

National Staff Development Council, www.nsdc.org/

Gradebook.com

Council for Exceptional Children, www.cec.sped.org

Office of Special Education and Rehabilitative Services, www.ed.gov

NICHCY, www.nichcy.org

http://trace.wisc.edu/ resources/disability-resources.shtml

www.closingthegap.com

www.assistivetech.net

http://TeacherWeb.com

www.essentialschools.org

What Works Clearinghouse, http://ies.ed.gov/ncee/wwc

Reflecting as Classroom Practice

Without reflection, teaching is an impossible and stagnant endeavor. When teachers look back on their lessons, as educators they take many steps forward to assist their students and themselves to grow as learners. Quite often, more is learned from the lesson that did *not* go so well to ensure that the next go-around will be better. Teaching itself is forever changing with new research stepping forward. Although students themselves are perpetual variables, they must be seen as individual learners. Students with dis*abilities* are just that—individual students. Educators need to reflect on the ways that these students are included with appropriate strategies. Included in this chapter are ways that the students must also be reflective partners in their education to become self-regulated learners. The purpose of this chapter is to connect the learning by revisiting major points from prior chapters. Many activities, templates, resources, strategies, and reflections about students with special needs were discussed. But what does that mean to teachers in inclusive settings? This chapter serves as a textual conclusion to all that has been presented and a jumping-off point for all that will follow.

REVIEWING AND MAINTAINING SKILLS

How Much Do Students Remember?

Learning requires the implementation of a maintenance plan to guarantee that learning actually occurred, not just the memorization or the regurgitation of isolated facts. Teachers teach and then move on to the next topic. *Oops!* Many students forget those wonderfully designed but unmemorable lessons. Most educators can testify that what they thought they taught was only temporary learning.

Some questions to ponder:

- What about including the prior topic in the next one that is taught, or using project-based learning that allows students to demonstrate many related skills across interdisciplinary and thematic lessons?
- What about proactively including the outcomes as you design the objectives using a UbD (understanding by design) approach that expects accountability and outlines just what will be assessed from the lesson's outset?

- Can teachers check to see if students apply and generalize learning to a different situation or problem?
- Why does learning require periodic checkups?
- Can curriculum and textbook designers encourage teachers to narrow down topics, to pick and choose those that let students build upon prior knowledge while learning newer content?
- Can there be such a thing as learning weigh-ins?
- When is it appropriate to revisit information?
- Are basic skills being sacrificed in this age of knowledge explosion?
- How can we periodically weigh learning gains?

Even if learning is taught with a step-by-step method, establishing prior knowledge on a level that does not frustrate students, some students still do not retain information. Repetition means, "*Say it again!*" It is important that all learning is *over*learned. Teachers too often make remarks such as, "I know I taught this," while students frequently retort, "The teacher never said it." Who's right? For the sake of diplomacy, the jury is permanently out. Review is essential!

PRETEACH, TEACH, RETEACH

Veni, Vidi, Vici—Teacher Planner

Yesterday I taught

Today I'll review

Today I'll introduce

Homework practice:

Tomorrow I'll remind them

Next week I'll refresh memories about

Next month's learning will review

Future plans include

Self-Assessment Form

Directions: Answer the following two questions to reflect upon your learning.

1. Before I learned about _____, I thought _____.

2. Now, I know _____.

Reviewing Work*

"Play it again, Sam," is a famous line; no need to repeat what it means!

Directions: List five points about any two special education, dis*ability,* or inclusion topics previously reviewed.

Topic: _____		Topic: _____
1.		1.
2.		2.
3.		3.
4.		4.
5.		5.

---

*Review the TBC column on page 73, filling in answers to original questions you now know more about.

Shapely Review for Classroom Study

Directions: This template is used as a classroom review. Each column represents a different topic with accompanying questions. Students are divided into teams and earn points for correctly answered questions on *shapely* topics. As an alternative, cooperative classroom groups can think of their own topics and questions on any curriculum area, making their own game. The next page has questions about inclusion and disabilities. Disability tables and text can be reviewed for answers. Create your own curriculum-related games: http://www.superteachertools.com/jeopardy/

◯	▢	⬭	⬡	△
a	f	k	p	u
b	g	l	q	v
c	h	m	r	w
d	i	n	s	x
e	j	o	t	y

How Much Do You Remember?

Questions

Directions: Try to answer as many questions as possible, and then check the answers to see how much learning has occurred. Work cooperatively, collectively, in game format, or solo.

 **Name the Strategy**

a. Name for moving, feeling, or manipulating learning

b. Main tools you use to learn about the environment

c. Strategy that asks students to close their eyes and think about learning concepts

d. Term for visually separating information into boxes

e. These can be used to personalize learning

 **The 3 R's**

f. Vowel patterns, syllabication, context clues, structural analysis, dictionary

g. Reading comprehension technique that deletes key words, asking students to fill in appropriate words

h. Words the acronym "Ed's Car" stands for

i. Name of a program that makes students more aware of how to pronounce words they read

j. Mathematical term for a way to help students understand if computational answers make sense

 **Syndromes and Disorders**

k. Syndrome characterized by social impairment along with repetitive patterns of behavior, but no evidence of cognitive delays, and is often confused with autism

l. Neurological disorder that can include involuntary tics and vocalizations

m. Congenital defect with failure of the spine to completely close, resulting in possible muscle weaknesses or paralysis

n. Acquired and developmental injury to the brain caused by an external force

o. Symptoms of this may be similar to AD/HD, but it is not the result of a hearing loss

 **Disabilitrivia**

p. College where the huddle was invented

q. *Top Gun* actor who is an advocate, helping others develop literacy skills after his own struggle with dyslexia

r. Created by accident while trying to develop an amplification device for people who have a hearing impairment

s. Poverty rate for people 25 to 64 with a severe disability

t. Early 1900s baseball team that was the first to use hand signals

 **Legislative Issues**

u. 2001 revised version of 1965 Elementary and Secondary Education Act

v. Civil rights law from 1973 that stops discrimination against people with disabilities in public and private programs/activities that receive financial assistance

w. 1990 civil rights law that guarantees rights for people with disabilities in public accommodations, employment, transportation, and telecommunications

x. The disability categories protected under IDEA

y. Abbreviation for written plan for a child who is eligible for special education services

How Did You Do?

Answer Key for Shapely Review

 **Name the Strategy—Answers**

a. Kinesthetic learning

b. Modalities or senses

c. Visualization or imagining

d. Compartmentalization

e. Interest inventories

 **The 3 R's—Answers**

f. These are ways to help students identify unfamiliar words

g. The cloze technique

h. Expand, delete, substitute, combine, and rearrange

i. Readacognition

j. Estimation

 Syndromes and Disorders—Answers

k. Asperger syndrome

1. Tourette syndrome

m. Spina bifida

n. Traumatic brain injury

o. Auditory processing difficulties, or CAPD

 Disabilitrivia—Answers

p. Gallaudet University in Washington, D.C. Football plays, which were being signed, could be hidden from the opposing team.

q. Tom Cruise

r. The telephone. Discovery was by Alexander Graham Bell.

s. 26% (Source: http://www.disabledinaction.org/census_stats_print.html)

t. The New York Giants. There was a pitcher named Luther H. Taylor who was deaf and unable to communicate with his teammates. The manager of the Giants, John McGraw, required the entire Giants team to learn American Sign Language. William Ellsworth Hoy, who was also deaf, used hand signals when he played for the Cincinnati Reds. That's the origin of baseball hand signals today.

 Legislative Issues—Answers

u. No Child Left Behind

v. Section 504 of the Vocational and Rehabilitation Act

w. ADA, the Americans with Disabilities Act

x. Autism, visual impairment, deafness, speech/language, deafness/blindness, mental retardation, multiple disabilities, other health impaired, traumatic brain injury, specific learning disability, hearing impaired, emotional disturbance, orthopedic impairment

y. An IEP, Individualized Education Program, or "It's Educationally Prudent!"

Roundtable Discussion

Directions: This activity is a cooperative learning strategy—the roundtable. It allows for the simultaneous sharing of knowledge or opinions on varying topics and content areas, by using prompts. The group gets together and divides the given prompts. Each person writes the letter of a different prompt from the list below at the top of his or her own paper. The student writes a brief response, and then the student exchanges papers with someone and writes comments on another prompt, as the papers are passed around the table. Written comments on the prompts can then be collected for review or orally shared in class discussion.

Sample Roundtable Prompts

a. Children can benefit from inclusion.

b. Children with disabilities have difficulties with assignments.

c. Attitudes about disabilities vary.

d. Parental/family involvement can help.

e. Teachers need more support.

Prompt:	
Name	**Comment**

Reviewing Concepts With a Word Search

Directions: Use clues below to fill in missing words in sentences. Then locate the words in the word search. Students and teachers can design their own word searches and cloze exercises on a variety of topics, using the computer or even graph paper. It's a great way to study spelling words or review any subject!

```
S Y S J C K X K H R H K F W I G C J Q Q W F X T E
Q E W P Q J N G E W C I D B U N R P I D L D O F B
B T C Y J C Y P Z T P N Y O I I D R I G H T H S W
X F I N J U E R T W B E U S D N Z I D R Q S N D O
F G I C E T P L Y W L S R I V R N W V R E U O S Q
Q N A F I G B Y E W A T Q J Q A B V L I Y R G E G
J D Y T F Q I A Q I Z H I Y B E V R M Y D B M I Y
E O I H Y H I L Y J B E W A H L C T R X L U R T G
T O A R H Y W G L N N T N H T E E A W Q O D A I W
N B G R Q W X Q M E M I U D T V N P B V I Z P L E
S T S E R E T N I U T C O E W I R J V X V F M I S
N K H X O U E T Z T W N C U L T C O W B M A Z B I
E U H Z R E B J W V O Q I P B A M A E X V T E A Q
R L M O N A P Z F H B B I E V R F B B B G F Z J C
P I Z K E F A T D L Q C G R L E X D J U O L X G B
K Q D H J E L E C H S S J P U P F W I D W F W J A
N R W Z K D V L H I N R Z I B O I K T C T Q R S V
R U Z P E I A I D C G R H L U O L T U H F M D M H
L U B H Q I V R T J K P J P H C I J L N C L P I N
Y Y W F C Y E Y F I L S M F Y D W M B U C B R G N
G X M E I T N J K S S Z L I X W S Q T I M Q K B W
B J P R N O H A I I E O Y D K R O Z Z P X S M J Z
Q S Q I K V O Z M K P U P M K T X I K K E E H B V
V T M H P K B F A C O L L A B O R A T I O N J S I
N Z Y R Q N V X T B Z O N O D C A Y P G J X Y T P
```

ABILITIES

COLLABORATION

COOPERATIVE LEARNING

INDIVIDUALS

INTERDISCIPLINARY

INTERESTS

KINESTHETIC

MULTIPLE INTELLIGENCES

POSITIVE

REPETITION

RIGHT

SPECIAL

1. _____ education for all

2. _____ with Dis*abilities* Education Act

3. Essential ingredient for the retention of all learning matter

4. Noncompetitive teaching strategy

5. Type of reinforcement

6. "Touching" learning

7. More than one way of being smart

8. What a student likes

9. Two teachers working together

10. ____ angles of learning

11. Involving all subject areas when teaching

12. What people *can* do

SUMMING UP THE LEARNING

Simulations vs. Actualities

When students have problems with brain confusion, things do not make sense. In the activity below, the right part of the brain tries to say the shape, but the left brain wants to read the word. Remember that these are simulated problems, but some students face these types of difficulties on a daily basis. They do not always see things as they appear to others. Students with disabilities must solve problems that they did not create: social, cognitive, academic, or physical. Quite often, we do not pick our battles, nor do we always face the same choices in school. The *ins* and *outs* of life's daily occurrences can be filled with surprises and distortions.

What Do You See?

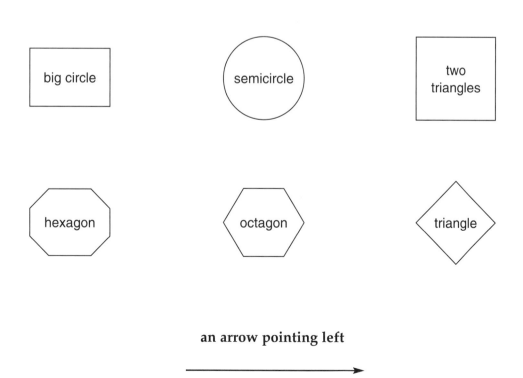

an arrow pointing left

COMBINING ELEMENTS

Closure/Periodic Table

The periodic table reminds us that students of all ages have different abilities in varying combinations. These include special strengths and intelligences. The elements of a periodic table are properly combined to create uniqueness, differences, and similarities with proportional bonding. For example, sodium and chlorine separately are both poisonous, yet people can safely place a combination of the two on their food (*NaCl* = table salt). Children can also be combined in *tasteful* ways. Given proper opportunities and interventions, today's classmates will be tomorrow's productive members of the community and the world.

Inclusion has its own set of formulas that work!

	IA																		0
1	1 H	IIA						Periodic Table of the Elements					IIIA	IVA	VA	VIA	VIIA		2 He
2	3 Li	4 Be												5 B	6 C	7 N	8 O	9 F	10 Ne
3	11 Na	12 Mg	IIIB	IVB	VB	VIB	VIIB	—— VIII ——			IB	IIB	13 Al	14 Si	15 P	16 S	17 Cl	18 Ar
4	19 K	20 Ca	21 Sc	22 Ti	23 V	24 Cr	25 Mn	26 Fn	27 Co	28 Ni	29 Cu	30 Zn	31 Ga	32 Ge	33 As	34 Se	35 Br	36 Kr
5	37 Rb	38 Sr	39 Y	40 Zr	41 Nb	42 Mo	43 Tc	44 Ru	45 Rh	46 Pd	47 Ag	48 Cd	49 In	50 Sn	51 Sb	52 Te	53 I	54 Xe
6	55 Cs	56 Ba	57 +La	72 Hr	73 Ta	74 W	75 Re	76 Os	77 Ir	78 Pt	79 Au	80 Hg	81 Tl	82 Pb	83 Bi	84 Po	85 At	86 Rn
7	87 Fr	88 Ra	89 +Ac	104 Rf	105 Ha	106 Sg	107 Ns	108 Hs	109 Mt	110 110	111 111	112 112	113 113					

*Lanthanide Series	58 Ce	59 Pr	60 Nd	61 Pm	62 Sm	63 Eu	64 Gd	65 Tb	66 Dy	67 Ho	68 Er	69 Tm	70 Yb	71 Lu
+Actinide Series	90 Th	91 Pa	92 U	93 Np	94 Pu	95 Am	96 Cm	97 Bk	98 Cf	99 Es	100 Fm	101 Md	102 No	103 Lr

Source: http://periodic.lanl.gov/default.htm. Public domain as per Los Alamos National Laboratory, Los Alamos, CA.

Inclusive Ingredients

Planning

Establishing Prior Knowledge

Learning About Abilities

Understanding Home Components

Awareness of Cultural Factors

Constructive Student Empowerment

Structured Classrooms

Repetition

Sensory Elements

Concrete Learning

Appropriate Accommodations and Modifications

Same Content, But Less Complex

Size

Amount

Student-Friendly Format

Authentic Assessments

UbD, Understanding by Design

UDL, Universal Design for Learning

Working With Parents, Guardians, and Families

Measuring Learning Ingredients

Cooperative Learning

Multiple Intelligences

Creating Self-Regulated Learners

Increasing Self-Awareness

Emphasizing the 3 R's

Using Technology

Interdisciplinary Approach

Step-by-Step Learning

Repetition

Positive Attitude!

Inclusive Environments

_____

_____

_____

Bottom Line: Successful Outcomes!

_____

Resource A
Disability Tables

The dis*ability* tables list possible causes of certain common disabilities/syndromes, characteristics of people who have these syndromes, educational strategies to use with these students, and resources to help you. As with all groups, please note that disabilities are heterogeneous and that each of these tables describes a syndrome, not a specific child. In addition, some characteristics and strategies may be shared and overlap with others. Remember that clinicians make diagnoses. The purpose of the information in the tables is to broaden knowledge, and it does not make anyone informed enough to diagnose. Diagnoses and labels are serious things! Information for the tables in Resource A was obtained from field experts, individual disability organizations listed, NICHCY, CEC, professional journals, and diagnostic criteria from *DSM-IV-TR. DSM-5,* due out in 2013, proposes a few changes which have yet to be finalized. These include folding the diagnosis of Asperger syndrome into a broader ASD category, adding a childhood disorder known as temper dysregulation disorder with dysphoria to account for too many children being diagnosed with bipolar who are prescribed medications, changing the term mental retardation to intellectual disability, adding a binge eating disorder, and adding measures of severity with types of anxiety or depression. View this site http://www.dsm5.org/Pages/Default.aspx for up-to-date information about all proposed labeling changes. Contact these references for additional personal and professional perspectives and more resources about specific dis*abilities.*

EATING DISORDERS

Anorexia Nervosa

Severely restricting food intake even if a person's body weight is way below normal

Causes

Low self-confidence

Possible genetic and environmental influences

Hormone imbalances or incorrect neurotransmitter levels

Possible Characteristics

Usually appears in early to mid-adolescence

Restriction of food intake, to the extreme that the person fears any weight gain and has a constant obsession with thinness

May even use excessive exercise, diuretics, and laxatives to prevent any weight gain

Muscle loss and weaknesses

Amenorrhea in women (cessation of normal menstrual cycle)

Unrealistic body image

Can fatally affect other body systems

Bulimia Nervosa

Disorder in which the person purges food consumed, in order to not gain any weight

Causes

May be unable to deal with emotional situations and uses food as a vehicle for control

Genetic and environmental influences

Possible Characteristics

A person with bulimia can eat large quantities of food within a short time frame and will then purge

May use exercise, laxatives, diuretics, or extreme diets to vigorously control weight

Purging is usually done secretively

Calluses on hands and fingers from sticking fingers down their throat

Fixation on body weight

May be depressed, but not necessarily

Can also have fatal results

Compulsive Overeating

Causes

Poor body image

General feelings of unhappiness

Environmental/genetic influences

May have conflicting and unsettling emotions in response

to stress, using food as a panacea to pacify those negative feelings, rather than eating from hunger

Possible Characteristics

Will usually be a *closet eater*

Binge eating is sometimes followed by guilt and depression for dietary overindulgences

Health complications may fatally spiral

Obesity among children today is of overriding concern. Children need to be encouraged to exercise more and learn about proper nutrition.

Contacts/Resources

National Eating Disorder Association (NEDA)
603 Stewart Street, Suite 803
Seattle, WA 98101

(206) 382–3587; (800) 931–2237
Web addresses: www
.nationaleatingdisorders.org,
www.bulimia.com

Kirberger, K. (2003). *No body's perfect.* New York: Scholastic. Web address: www.iam4teens.com

If left untreated, all three of these eating disorders may be fatal.

Treatments must involve proactive coordination between school, home, and community, while valuing opportunities for individual growth with realistic plans that include positive body image, diet, and proper amount of exercise. Replace fast foods and sedentary activities with better diets and more movement.

Private or group counseling sessions can help students deal with the underlying reasons for eating disorders, including counseling from a nutritionist for balanced, healthy diets. School psychologists and guidance counselors can establish personal and trusting relationships with students, providing a safe haven for open communication of both positive and negative emotions.

Educational programs must allow students to experience feelings of self-worth. Teachers can diminish academic pressures while health issues are of concern; establish individual plans with students that would increase their frequency of positive reflections to combat inadequacies. Encourage journal keeping for more introspection.

Regardless of their physique, students must feel like they belong to a nonjudgmental classroom environment that values them as contributing and successful individuals with promising futures.

EMOTIONAL DISTURBANCES

General Overview

Causes

Not determined

Contributing factors include the following:

- Heredity
- Brain disorder
- Diet
- Stress
- Family functioning

- Neurological impairment
- Brain injury
- Chemical imbalance
- Nutritional deficiency
- Alcohol or drugs used by the parents
- External factors such as divorce, death of a loved one, moving, and trauma are situational and do not cause the actual disturbance. Environment may contribute to diagnosis but does not justify the classification

Contacts/Resources

National Federation of Families for Children's Mental Health
9605 Medical Center Drive
Rockville, MD 20850
(240) 403–1901
Web address: www.ffcmh.org

National Alliance on Mental Illness
2107 Wilson Blvd., Suite 300
Arlington, VA 22201–3042
(888) 999–NAMI
Web address: www.nami.org

Dr. Mac's Behavior
Management Site
Web address:
www.behavioradvisor.com

Possible Characteristics

These behaviors are evidenced
over long periods of time:

- *Hyperactivity*—
Impulsiveness, short
attention span
- *Aggression/Self-Injurious
Behavior*—Acting out,
fighting
- *Withdrawal*—Excessive
anxiety, failure to initiate
interaction with others,
intimidated by social
interaction
- *Immaturity*—Poor coping
skills, inappropriate crying,
temper tantrums
- *Learning Difficulties*—
Academically performing
below grade level due to
behavior issues
- *More Severe Emotional
Disturbance*—Distorted
thinking, excessive anxiety,
bizarre motor acts,
abnormal mood swings; can
include schizophrenia

Educational Strategies

Behavior modification,
charting frequency of desired
behavior

Conflict resolution

Psychological/counseling
services

Coordination of services among
home, school, family, and
therapeutic community with
consistent communication

Help student develop
academic as well as social
skills

Establish rapport and trust
with the student by disliking
the behavior, not the child

Let the student know that you
are listening to him or her

Smile/praise

Eye contact

Structure with limits and
consequences

Yoga, breathing exercises

Constructive outlets such as art
or music

Find ways for students to feel
good about themselves

Promote more self-awareness/
evaluation with immediate
positive reinforcement

Bipolar/Manic Depressive Illness

Unusual and extreme shifts in
mood, energy, and behavior
that interfere with normal,
healthy functioning

Found in 25 to 35% of children
with AD/HD (National
Institute of Mental Health,
2000, Pub. No. 00–4778. Web
address: www.nimh.nih.gov)

Causes

Possible genetic predisposition
or chemical imbalance

Not caused by drugs,
medication, or bereavement

Contacts/Resources

Mental Health America
2000 N. Beauregard Street, 6th
Floor
Alexandria, VA 22311
Phone (703) 684–7722; (800)
969–6642
Web address: www.nmha.org

Child and Adolescent Bipolar
Foundation
820 Davis St., Suite 520
Evanston, IL 60201
(847) 492–8519
Web address: www.bpkids.org

Possible Characteristics

Children can have highly
volatile, short swings of mood;
adults can have mood
fluctuations that may last for
days or weeks.

Criteria for depression (when 5
or more symptoms are displayed
on an almost daily basis):

- Feel sad or irritable
- Diminished enjoyment in
formerly pleasurable
activities
- Weight loss or decrease of
appetite
- Insomnia or hypersomnia
- Restlessness
- Fatigue or lethargy
- Inappropriate guilt or low
self-worth
- Concentration difficulties or
indecisiveness
- Suicidal thoughts

Criteria for mania:

- Abnormally or persistently
elevated, expansive, or
irritable mood, lasting at
least 1 week (when 3 or
more symptoms are
displayed consistently)
- Inflated self-esteem
- More talkative, changes
topics frequently, cannot be
interrupted
- Racing thoughts
- Distractibility
- Decreased need for sleep
- Psychomotor agitation
- Increase in activities that
could be harmful
- Excessive pleasurable
activities (e.g., buying spree)

Signs of bipolar/manic depressive illness may include the following:

- School impairments in academics and social functioning with peers, along with home and family difficulties
- Increased energy with little sleep
- Physical complaints such as stomachaches, tiredness, headaches, or muscle pains
- Disruptive outbursts with sensitivity to failure or rejection, or may be overly silly or elated, talking excessively
- May evidence risk-taking behavior with alcohol, drugs, or by being sexually active
- If depressed, may show more sadness, with low tolerance for failure
- May also exhibit extremes with sleeping or eating

Educational Strategies

Psychiatrists, individual/group counseling with supportive nonjudgmental adults who demonstrate concern by listening to child

Behavioral intervention plans

Increase self-awareness

Awareness of prescribed medication

Individual educational support (tutoring)

Positive attention or rewards for appropriate behavior with programs to increase self-esteem and guided peer relationships

Obsessive-Compulsive Disorder (OCD)

Causes

- OCD has multiple types and causes:

Research is investigating neurobiological factors and environmental influences that contribute to this anxiety disorder.

OCD is not due to a substance disorder (medicine, alcohol, or drug) or other medical condition.

Genetic studies are being conducted to discover the molecular basis of OCD.

Sometimes linked with Tourette syndrome and AD/HD.

Positron emission tomography (PET) scanning involving brain imaging suggests different patterns of neurochemical activity in the brain.

National Institute of Health and other researchers believe strep throat and bacterial infections to be triggers of some types of obsessive-compulsive disorder as well as symptoms of Tourette syndrome, e.g., nervous tics.

Contacts/Resources

Obsessive-Compulsive Foundation
PO Box 961029
Boston, MA 02196
(617) 973–5801
Web address:
www.ocfoundation.org

Anxiety Disorders Association of America
8730 Georgia Avenue, Suite 600
Silver Spring, MD 20910
(240) 485–1001
Web address: www.adaa.org

Possible Characteristics

Repetitive, excessive, and unreasonable behavior (e.g., hand washing/fear of contamination, counting, rechecking, rearranging, repeated doubts)

Obsessions and compulsions cause marked distress and significantly impact functioning

Anxiety evidenced

Inability to control thoughts, worries, panic, and compulsiveness

Difficulty concentrating

Cannot effectively follow school schedules and transitions

Fear of contamination or a serious illness

Sometimes behavior is hidden in front of classmates due to embarrassment

May repeatedly erase and redo assignments, which can result in incomplete work

Educational Strategies

Communicate consistently with parents

Watch for side effects from some medication or drug combinations, such as nervousness or fatigue from insomnia

Use behavioral plans and progress reports to control impulsivity

Use cognitive behavioral therapy (CBT) to challenge and extinguish faulty compulsions

Increase self-awareness/ frequent and consistent self-monitoring

Cue students for key points and signal classroom changes

Establish an assignment book with a long-range calendar; use checklists to keep student organized

Provide a model of desired outcome

Have student repeat directions for understanding

Establish trusting relationship

Use cooperative learning

Educate other school personnel and help develop positive social interactions

Oppositional Defiant Disorder (ODD)

Caution should be exhibited in the ODD diagnosis, since oppositional behavior is frequently evidenced in preschool and adolescent children.

Causes

Uncertain

ODD is usually evident before age 8 and not later than early adolescence

Appears to be more common in families in which at least one parent has a history of mood, oppositional defiant, attention, or a substance-related disorder

Criteria for the diagnosis of this conduct disorder are met if behaviors cause significant impairment in social, academic, or occupational functioning

Contacts/Resources

Mental Health America
2000 N. Beauregard Street, 6th Floor
Alexandria, VA 22311
Phone (703) 684–7722; (800) 969–6642
Web address: www.nmha.org

American Academy of Childhood and Adolescent Psychiatry
3615 Wisconsin Avenue, NW
Washington, DC 20016–3007
(202) 966–7300
Web Address: www.aacap .org

Possible Characteristics

Negative behavior toward authority figures for at least 6 months

Deliberately doing things to annoy others

Blaming others for their mistakes

Easily annoyed by others

Resentment toward authority

Refusal to do school assignments or chores at home

Underachievement at school

Pouting, stubbornness, obstructive behavior (interfering with the plans and activities of others)

Easily frustrated

Loses temper frequently

Educational Strategies

Communication and consistency between home and school with parent management training (PMT) that advocates brief, nonaversive punishments

Listen to the student before giving a reaction

Avoid punitive patterns or negative attention for defiance; allow choices/ options under teacher's auspices (e.g., "pick 3 out of 5") to diminish power struggles and to build on positives

Give child meaningful responsibility in the classroom

Offer frequent praise and rewards for compliance and improvements, which can also be nonverbal, or even quietly whispered to the student

Develop individual goal chart or behavioral plan to decrease defiant behavior and increase self-awareness

School counseling or group therapy

Private discussions to predetermine rules and consequences

Opportunities for positive social interaction

Emphasis on problem-solving skills

Be aware of child's interests to increase the student's desire to learn

Establish an atmosphere of trust and calmness

Dislike the behavior, not the student

INTELLECTUAL DISABILITIES

Mental Retardation (MR)

Here is the IDEA definition: Significantly subaverage general intellectual functioning (measured by an intelligence test—usually below 70) existing concurrently with deficits in adaptive behavior (adjustment to everyday life), which are manifested during the developmental period, and adversely affects a child's educational performance

Causes

Chromosome abnormalities

Birth asphyxia (lack of oxygen when born or soon afterward)

Blood incompatibilities between the mother and the fetus or maternal infections such as rubella or herpes

Problems during pregnancy such as not eating right with extreme malnutrition, using certain drugs, alcohol, or smoking (e.g., FAS—fetal alcohol syndrome), exposure to poisons and environmental toxins such as lead or mercury

Down syndrome and Fragile X (with severe mutations) are known genetic causes

Malnutrition or inadequate medical care

Disease after birth that leads to brain damage, such as meningitis or encephalitis

More than half of MR cases are caused by environmental factors

Not a mental illness; cannot be cured

Contacts/Resources

The Arc
1010 Wayne Avenue, Suite 650
Silver Spring, MD 20910
(301) 565–3842; (800) 433–5255
Web address: www.thearc.org

American Association on Intellectual and Developmental Disabilities (AAIDD)
501 3rd Street, NW, Suite 200
Washington, DC 20001
(202) 387–1968; (800) 424–3688
Web address: www.aaidd.org; formerly www.aamr.org

Division on Developmental Disabilities, the Council for Exceptional Children
Web address: www.dddcec.org

Special Olympics—www.specialolympics.org

Best Buddies—www.bestbuddies.org

> The word *retarded* has developed such a negative connotation that some states and organizations use the term *intellectually disabled, cognitively impaired,* or *developmental disability* instead, even though IDEA still uses the term *mental retardation.* This might cause some confusion with other learning disabilities. However, it is not the label but the criteria and services rendered that matter.

Possible Characteristics

Low intellectual functioning (IQ) and poor adaptive behavior (skills to live independently); e.g., daily living skills, communication, social, self-help

Different academic, social, and vocational skills, depending on impairment level

Difficulties with the following areas:

- Learning in school, e.g., remembering things
- Communication, e.g., receptive and expressive language
- Social skills; consequences, rules
- Academic issues, e.g., thinking logically or solving problems
- Vocational concerns
- Personal needs, e.g., hygiene, dressing, eating
- Learning occurs, but at a slower rate
- Short-term memory impairment
- Unable to form generalizations

Educational Strategies

- Set realistic and functional goals with family support and coordination
- Use concrete, age-appropriate materials, avoiding totally abstract levels of presentation, but capitalize on student's interests and strengths
- Early infant stimulation, preschool intervention, neighborhood school programs, transitional services, opportunities for

schoolwork with emphasis on independent living skills
- Sensory educational considerations—more visuals, audios, hands-on (communication boards), interdisciplinary activities, and real-life situations (restaurant class, shopping in a store, community trips)
- Break down learning into smaller sequential steps with frequent review, going from simple to complex; honor each student's instructional level
- Use consistent, age-appropriate rewards
- Help students to generalize and apply learning from one situation to the next through teacher modeling with immediate realistic feedback
- Alternate means of assessment, more verbal and less written
- Teach memory strategies—chunking, association
- Offer lessons with functional skills infused, e.g., manners, conversation rules, safety, health, reading street signs

Traumatic Brain Injury (TBI)

Acquired injury to the brain caused by an external force; does not include congenital or degenerative brain injuries

Causes

Frequent causes of TBI are related to motor vehicle crashes, falls, sports accidents, physical abuse, assault, and other head injuries

Other causes include chemical (insecticides, carbon monoxide, lead poisoning), hypoxia (lack of oxygen), tumors

Types of injuries vary and can range from mild to severe

Sudden unexpected onset makes TBI differ from other disabilities since parents and children have not had time to emotionally deal with the disability and must suddenly learn how to manage and accept the changes.

Contacts/Resources

Brain Injury Association of America
1608 Spring Hill Road, Suite 110
Vienna, VA 22182
(703) 761–0750
Web addresses:
www.biausa.org;
www.traumaticbraininjury.com

Possible Characteristics

Symptoms vary depending upon the location and extent of the brain injury. Impairments can be

- *Physical*—Speech, vision, hearing, sensory impairments, headaches, difficulty with fine and/or gross motor, balance, and coordination
- *Cognitive*—Short- and long-term memory deficits, concentration problems, slowness of thinking/judgment, perceptual issues, disorganization with academic difficulties such as learning new information
- *Psychosocial, Behavioral, or Emotional*—Fatigue, mood swings, denial, self-centeredness, depression, inability to self-monitor, agitation, excessive laughing or crying, difficulty relating to others, poor impulse control

Educational Strategies

Schools need to have appropriate neurological, psychological, speech and language, and educational evaluations to determine accurate classification.

Careful planning for school reentry

Teach compensatory memory strategies

Repeated practice

Explain figurative language

Provide concrete examples to illustrate new concepts

Keep the environment as distraction-free as possible

Provide student with rest breaks if stamina is low

Family support and sharing of educational strategies for reinforcement at home

LEARNING/ATTENTION DISORDERS

AD/HD—Attention-Deficit/Hyperactivity Disorder

Causes

Exact cause is unknown; can be linked to a chemical imbalance in neurotransmitters (chemicals in the brain that help brain cells communicate with each other)

Differences in brain activity and structure that help control behavior and attention

Might be genetically transmitted (tends to run in families, but this could also be environmental)

Evidenced by both sexes; females are sometimes more inattentive than hyperactive

Theories exist about poor nutrition or diet

Contacts/Resources

CHADD (Children and Adults with Attention Deficit/Hyperactivity Disorder)
8181 Professional Place, Suite 150
Landover, MD 20785
(301) 306–7070; (800) 233–4050
Web addresses:
www.chadd.org,
www.cdc.gov/ncbddd/adhd

Possible Characteristics

May be predominantly inattentive:

- Daydreaming
- Inattentive to details
- Careless in schoolwork (e.g., sloppy handwriting, crumpled homework), forgetful, disorganized, may lose things
- Memory difficulties
- Distracted by extraneous stimuli
- Concentration and listening problems such as in attending to a teacher while trying to take notes
- Attention difficulties when initiating actions requiring foresight, sustaining concentration, inhibiting distractions and impulsive reactions, and shifting gears or transitioning to other tasks
- Difficulties following multistep directions

May be predominantly hyperactive-impulsive:

- Tendency to be in constant motion
- Might fidget with hands or feet (rocking in chair, twirling pencils)
- Misses social cues; may get into fights
- Difficulty in waiting turn— interrupts others
- Impulsivity such as blurting out answers
- May experience more accidents due to hyperactivity

Mixed-type symptomotology (may have symptoms of both inattention and hyperactivity–impulsivity)

Educational Strategies

Structured, predictable environment

Daily schedules and assignment pads

Clear, concise directions with routines announced and posted; remove all extraneous materials

Be aware of any medications as prescribed by child's physician, due to possible side effects

Establish eye contact

Have student rephrase or repeat directions

Teach organization such as using crates for extra texts from desks or student accordion files to hold notes and papers

Color code notebooks, folders, and text covers for different subjects

Reinforce study skills

Give frequent breaks, combined with stretching activities to channel motor excess

Write specific formal behavioral plans with clear expectations, immediate feedback, and rewards

Teach problem-solving, conflict resolution, and peer mediation skills

To increase self-awareness/self-discipline, have student keep a log of impulsive and quieter behaviors

Model with guided practice and application

Establish a nonthreatening classroom environment, using subtle cues for transitions

Be aware of *quiet noises* in the room. For example, a low humming from the heater or the sounds coming from a nearby classroom may be ignored by most, but distracting to a child with AD/HD

Dislike the behavior, not the child, using positives before negatives

Specific Learning Disabilities (SLD)

Causes

By clinical diagnosis, not primarily the result of visual, hearing, or motor disabilities; mental retardation, economic, environmental, or cultural factors

Varied spectrum of causes that may be linked to neurological or genetic factors

LD is a real disability, not laziness!

Contacts/Resources

LDA (Learning Disabilities Association of America)

4156 Library Road
Pittsburgh, PA 15234
(412) 341–1515
Web address: www.ldanatl.org

NCLD (National Center for Learning Disabilities)
381 Park Avenue South, Suite 1401
New York, NY 10016
(212) 545–7510; (888) 575–7373
Web Addresses: www.ncld.org; Council for Exceptional Children Division of Learning Disabilities, www.dldcec.org; LD Online, www.ldonline.org

Possible Characteristics

Wide range that can include difficulties with the following:

- Reading comprehension or word decoding
- Arithmetic calculations or concepts
- Spoken language
- Writing (spelling, creative expression, language mechanics or fine motor)
- Social skills
- Reasoning (getting thoughts together)

May also exhibit the following traits:

- Perceptual impairments
- Inattention
- Impulsiveness
- Low tolerance for frustration
- Poor organizational skills
- Dyslexia—reading difficulties
- Dysgraphia—writing difficulties
- Dyscalculia—math difficulties (These are discussed further on.)

Former criteria classification required a severe discrepancy model between measured achievement (which can include school performance) and ability (tested intelligence). IDEIA now says that the discrepancy criteria are not the sole criteria for placement, under an SLD definition. Response to intervention (RtI) is used to help students who have learning difficulties receive services in whole classrooms, smaller groups, or 1:1 without regard to tested intelligence. The evaluation procedure now allows states to review whether students are responding to the scientific research-based interventions, instead of exclusively using the severe discrepancy model (SDM).

Stress to students that intelligence is separate from achievement. They are not dummies just because they might read differently. Everyone is stronger or weaker in one thing or another.

Educational Strategies

Collaboratively design individualized education program (IEP) to address child's needs, with general education (GE) staff, special education (SE) staff, parents, families, and transitional services for age 16 and older children or younger, if appropriate, with administration's input

Use concrete, kinesthetic materials that students can see and touch

Break up learning into small bites and step-by-step lessons

Capitalize upon student's strengths, using multiple intelligences

Use redundancy—repeat, restate, reiterate, relate

Vary instruction and assessment with more active involvement and fewer lectures, allowing appropriate motoric releases

Offer immediate positive feedback without embarrassment

Emphasize consistent expectations with accountability

Use computers to help with reading, writing, and math issues

Shorten assignments based upon level of mastery

Instructional level should encourage independence with empowerment under teacher's auspices

Secure appropriate accommodations, based upon individual needs, but have weaning plans in place as well

Frequent home communication helps prevent misinformation.

Dyslexia

Causes

Genetic or neurological factors

Lack of cerebral dominance

Differences in brain function

Auditory language deficit

Contacts/Resources

The International Dyslexia Association
40 York Rd., 4th Floor
Baltimore, MD 21204
(410) 296–0232
Web address:
www.interdys.org

Recording for the Blind and Dyslexic
20 Roszel Road
Princeton, NJ 08540
(866) RFBD–585
Web address: www.rfbd.org

Academy of Orton-Gillingham Practitioners and Educators
PO Box 234
Amenia, NY 12501–0234
(845) 373–8919
Web addresses:
www.ortonacademy.org;
www.wilsonlanguage.com;
www.jollylearning.co.uk/
jp.htm; www.dyslexia.com

Possible Characteristics

Language-based learning disability; student may show difficulties in reading, and written and spoken language. Some need more help with spelling, grammar, textbooks, and writing essays

Sometimes have difficulties in use of numeric symbols in mathematics such as reversals of numbers or signs (+, –)

Visual problems (e.g., eye tracking, eye movements)

Lack of organization

Reversals of letters or mirror writing may be present

Confusing vowels or substituting one consonant for another

Clumsiness and awkwardness with hands

Often gifted in other areas that do not require strong language skills, such as art, computer science, math, music, sports, and electronics

Educational Strategies

Early diagnosis and interventions to improve phonemic awareness

Use multisensory channels to teach with a structured language approach that involves hearing, seeing, and touching (e.g., more manipulatives and kinesthetic approaches, visuals, and sounds to break words into phonemes and syllables)

Use colored overlays on texts

Use strengths to improve weaker areas

Computers (word processing programs and learning activities with sound animation)

Books on tape, along with alternate means of assessment, as needed

Orton-Gillingham approach, which is language-based, multisensory, sequential, structured, and cumulative. Students start by learning sounds in isolation, then blend sounds into syllables and words with all the elements of language, from consonants and vowels, to digraphs, blends, and diphthongs, and then syllable types

Teach structural analysis by breaking longer words into their parts, using index cards to separate syllables, root words, prefixes, and suffixes

Use graded, color-coded sight words/flashcards with student maintaining, adding, and reviewing alphabetical lists

Use structured reading, spelling, and phonics programs with controlled text that builds upon a hierarchy of skills, avoiding small print

Make modifications such as helping with note taking or allowing extra time to complete tests

Build self-esteem with more positive reflections, including dated portfolios of completed work

Allow older or adolescent students to use high-interest, controlled texts and age-appropriate words to practice reading, thereby honoring their dignity in the reading process, rather than belittling them!

Choral or echo reading for more difficult words within text not yet learned

> *Hyperlexia* is a disorder where students may have high word recognition levels and read at an early age, but limited comprehension and difficulty with verbal language and verbal issues and social skills (see www.hyperlexia.org).

Dysgraphia

Combination of fine-motor and eye–hand coordination problems, which can include improper pencil grip, confused hand dominance, poor wrist control, and illegible handwriting along with general difficulties putting thoughts into writings

Causes

May involve a brain dysfunction that includes translating mental thoughts into written language

Lack of hand strength developed early in infancy with incorrect kinesthetic memory, which led to incorrect motor routines and habits

Difficulties arising from dysgraphia are compounded by emotional factors if a child is pushed into using handwriting at an early age or overly criticized

Contact/Resources

Learning Disabilities
Web address: www.ldinfo.com

Handwriting Without Tears
Web address: www.hwtears.com

Possible Characteristics

Can include memory and attention difficulties or an inability to visualize letters and shapes

Written work may be illegible, with related difficulties in spelling, drawing, spontaneous expression, or simply copying letters

Writing hand may shake or cramp, with an awkward pencil grip, or slower fine-motor speed

Student may struggle with writing tasks, spending more time on how he or she forms the letters, rather than the writing content

Student dislikes writing tasks, showing tension when taking class notes or during other written assignments

May be a creative writer, but just dislikes the mechanics involved

Motor movements are unsequenced and not automatically learned

May complain of hand hurting or fatigue

Slowness in completing assignments involving writing due to difficulties forming letters, collecting thoughts, and organizing ideas

May omit words in sentences with poor syntax

Sometimes the student can't proofread own written work, since he or she is unable to read it

Educational Strategies

Multisensory approaches (using *multiple senses*)

Strengthen fine motor skills using various media (e.g., crayons, clay, tactile glue, games, toys, felt boards, sky writing, sorting objects, sponges, pipe cleaners, Legos, stringing beads, scissors, stencils, salt, pencil grips, tracing paper, yarn)

Verbalize letter-formation steps using configuration strategies, noticing the size, shape, and—later on, when ready—the slant of letters

Provide student with a sheet that matches and compares manuscript to cursive writing

Use purposeful writing such as labeling folders and other items in the classroom; making signs; writing letters, birthday cards, and thank-you notes; and designing bulletin boards

Establish rubrics with acceptable writing samples and encourage self-evaluation

Check how student is seated with emphasis on good posture, with paper correctly positioned and taped or Velcroed to desk

Have students use graphic organizers and computer templates to collect thoughts and minimize writing; use writing strategies that compartmentalize thoughts

Assign students a copying buddy who has carbon paper to share more legible notes

Audiotape lessons to play back at slower pace

Make use of technology: electronic spell checkers, keyboarding programs, laptop computers, or copies of notes off Smart Boards when available

Teach step-by-step ways to expand writing thoughts

Dyscalculia

Learning disability that affects ability to do math. Students may be *math phobic,* fearful of activities involving numbers such as computations requiring addition, subtraction, multiplication, or division. In addition, learning new mathematical concepts or problem solving may be stressful.

Causes

Can be based on prior negative experiences, poor self-confidence, instructional synapses, along with genetic or neurological factors

Brain imaging studies show different brain pulses in areas dealing with interpretation of numbers and spatial images

Contacts/Resources

Learning Disabilities Web site Web address: www.ldinfo.com; www.dyscalculia.org

Molko, M., Cachia, A., Rivière, D., Mangin, J., Bruandet, M., Le Bihan, et al. (2003). Functional and structural alterations of the intraparietal sulcus in a developmental dyscalculia of genetic origin. *Neuron, 40,* 847–858.

TouchMath
(888) TOUCHMATH
Web address:
www.touchmath.com

Abeel, S. (2003). *My thirteenth winter.* New York: Scholastic. (Memoir about dyscalculia)

Possible Characteristics

Weakness with visual processing and memory

Learning difficulties may be present in other content areas such as recalling important dates in social studies, or specific science and math formulas

May not spell well

May have poor fine-motor skills regarding size, spacing, organization, and alignment of letters and numbers

Sequencing difficulties

Limited organizational skills

Difficulty extracting information to solve word problems

Math test anxiety; may freeze, or forget what is taught and learned, evidencing a flawed test performance

If visual processing difficulties are the cause, reading comprehension and writing skills may be strengths, while spelling, applying phonetic rules, and sight-word development may be weaknesses.

Educational Strategies

Students need guided and systematic instruction to help them develop compensatory strategies to work with numbers

Use specific, step-by-step examples to both explain and review concepts

Teach new material, then review prior learning, consistently backtracking to maintain skills

Encourage students to peruse and develop helpful visual information such as graphs, charts, tables, and pictures to simplify word problems or computations

Allow students an opportunity to use an auditory approach, by listening to their own voices, music, computer programs, peers, or teachers as they work

Have students immediately apply skills; use less straightforward lecturing and more *student doing*

Use a variety of manipulatives and concrete materials to allow students to feel and internalize what they are learning, e.g., TouchMath, algebra tiles, hands-on equations

Try to make math fun by incorporating students' interests while meaningfully connecting mathematical skills and concepts to daily life (e.g., batting averages, weather, household products to learn about metrics; store circulars to teach comparison shopping)

Develop user-friendly, uncluttered worksheets

Allow students to hold lined paper horizontally to help keep the place value of numbers in columns

Deliver consistent praise

PERVASIVE DEVELOPMENTAL DISORDERS (PDD)

Diagnosis made from *DSM-IV* (*Diagnostic and Statistical Manual* of the American Psychiatric Association) identifying a cluster of disorders with developmental impairments in communication, language, and socialization. These include autism, Rett syndrome, pervasive developmental disorder not otherwise specified, Asperger syndrome, and childhood disintegrative disorder.

> Some researchers have changed the PDD umbrella to ASD (Autism Spectrum Disorder). However, *DSM-IV* (2000-TR) does not recognize that term. *DSM-5* does have some proposed changes that have not yet been finalized to fold Asperger syndrome under an ASD category. Pervasive developmental disorders generally show evidence of impairments affecting social interaction, communication, behavior, interests, and activities.

Asperger Syndrome

Causes

Criteria not met for any other pervasive developmental disorder or schizophrenia

Seems to be more prevalent in males

Increased frequency in families with members who have the disorder

Current research on neuroimaging shows that parts of the brain that control social processing differ in children with Asperger syndrome.

Contacts/Resources

MAAP Services for Autism and Asperger Syndrome Coalition of the United States (MAAP stands for More Advanced individuals with Autism, Asperger syndrome and Pervasive developmental disorder)
P.O. Box 524
Crown Point, IN 46307
(219) 662–1311
Web addresses:
www.asperger.org;
www.maapservices.org

Online Asperger Syndrome Information and Support (OASIS)
Web address: www.udel.edu/bkirby/asperger

Future Horizons Sensory Resources
Web address: www.fhsensory.com

Possible Characteristics

No delay in cognitive functioning, since IQ can range from normal to superior

Student displays age-appropriate behavior, language, self-help skills, and typical curiosity about the environment

Social impairment evidenced; can be unaware of how their behaviors might affect others (social reciprocity)

Difficulties sharing interests or enjoyment with others

Repetitive and stereotyped patterns of behavior, interests, and activities may be displayed, evidencing fascinations with own interests or idiosyncrasies, with possible preoccupation with parts of objects

Poor nonverbal behaviors, eye contact, facial expression; inappropriate body language

May have good logical skills, liking math and computers

Inflexible attachment to schedules and routines

Possible motor delays or clumsiness

Ineffective sensory processing

Usually recognized later than autism

Educational Strategies

Social behavior needs to be modeled, encouraged, practiced, and documented in school and at home with role-playing. Students can keep a social skills notebook or log and read guided social stories

Increase self-awareness with concrete rewards, verbal praises, and much patience

Adult and peer support needed to emphasize social appropriateness in academic settings, at first in a smaller setting. Then add more positive role models to increase interactions

Emphasis upon routine and structure to reduce stress; posting classroom routines; using outlines, planners, and monthly calendars to help students deal with transitions and daily happenings

If possible, give advance notice of changes in daily schedule, e.g., half day, assembly

Provide visual cues, sound signals, tactile learning, and handouts

Avoid sensory overstimulation

Allow for extra motoric movement

Be aware of students' likes and dislikes

Teach compensatory strategies

Use behavior modification program to reward more eye contact

Have instructional assistant shadow student, if necessary, but encourage independence

Educate other students and adults about the disorder

Provide a nurturing and accepting classroom and other quiet settings to channel behavior

Autism

Causes

Unknown

Theories:

- Biochemical imbalance in the brain
- Metabolic dysfunction of the brain
- Can be neurological damage
- Theories about environmental/toxic influences
- More common in males
- Not caused by psychological factors

Contacts/Resources

Autism Society of America
7910 Woodmont Avenue,
Suite 650
Bethesda, MD 20814
(800) 3–AUTISM

Web addresses: www.autism-society.org; www.autism.org

Possible Characteristics

Students will vary in abilities, intelligence, and behaviors. IQ is commonly in moderate range of an intellectual disability; autism may coexist and overlap with other disabilities, e.g., communication, social, behavioral. Cognitive skills are often uneven

Developmental—evidenced by the age of 3 (no big smiles or other expressions at 6 months and after; no babbling sounds, facial expressions, waving, or pointing by 12 months; no words by 16 months, which is sometimes mistaken for deafness by parents)

Children will display 6 or more of 12 symptoms listed across three areas:

- Social interaction: Difficulty relating to people; unusual play; appear unaware of others, affecting peer interactions and social reciprocity
- Communication difficulty: Hard time using and understanding language; may use repetitive speech (echolalia), nonspeech vocalization; receptive language is usually better than expressive language, but both verbal and nonverbal behavior is impacted
- Behavior: Can be ritualistic; unusual responses to lights, noises, textures; avoid eye contact; difficulty with abstract concepts

Educational Strategies

Early (preschool) diagnosis and educational intervention, including speech and language services with home coordination

Structured and predictable classroom with advance notice given for changes in routine

Direct social skill instruction and prompting with peers

Teach other ways to communicate if appropriate, such as communication boards, gestures, and music

Use of pictures to outline day's schedule

Visual and verbal presentation with concrete experiences (field trips, videos) and functional academics to enhance daily living

Tactile stimulation such as gentle pats or arm strokes; water therapy can also be soothing

Teach academics and socialization with step-by-step methods, focusing on strengths

Use behavioral analysis to improve and reward targeted behaviors and verbal behavior (see Association for Behavior Analysis International, www.abainternational.org; www.behavior.org/autism)

Rett Syndrome

Causes

Unknown; rare

Mutated gene for this disorder identified in 1999

Found almost exclusively in females; affects approximately 10,000 females in the United States

Some students are initially classified as having severe or

profound mental retardation, as it is associated with Rett syndrome

Contacts/Resources

Acton, O., Ellenburg, J., Katsiyannis, A., & Torrey, G. (2001). Addressing the needs of students with Rett's syndrome. *Teaching Exceptional Children, 33*, 74–77.

American Psychiatric Association. (2000). *Diagnostic and statistical manual of mental disorders (DSM-IV-TR)* (4th ed.). Washington, DC: Author. Web address: www.psych.org

National Institute of Neurological Disorders and Stroke
Web address: www.ninds.nih.gov/disorders/rett/detail_rett.htm

Possible Characteristics

Apparent normal development, with progressive slowing of head growth and loss of previously acquired social and hand skills, poor gait, and impaired language development

Loss of skills generally progressive

Physical difficulties include problems with digestion, apraxia (motor movements), spine curvature, poor gait, loss of functional hand skills, disorganized breathing, and seizures

Stereotypical hand movements can include wringing of hands and hand-washing gestures

Other behaviors can include body rocking, facial grimacing, teeth grinding, feeding difficulties, and self-injurious behaviors

May exhibit social withdrawal along with communication difficulties

Can be misdiagnosed as autism or cerebral palsy

Educational Strategies

Physical and occupational therapy to improve child's awareness and space in his or her environment (e.g., balancing and rotating activities, hydrotherapy)

Be aware that some nonverbal behaviors are attempts to communicate

Use of alternate communication (e.g., activation of switches, eye pointing, gestures) that require appropriate hand movement

Calming behavioral approaches

Feeding and nutritional guidance

Sensory input such as bright colors or reinforcing sounds to encourage student to use hands

Discrete task analysis to break up complex tasks

Frequent rewards

Social skill instruction

Parental support and training

PHYSICAL IMPAIRMENTS

Physical disabilities can affect a lot of different areas. Physical relates to the body and disability means not being able to do something. A child with a physical disability has a body that does not work in some way. A child's fine-motor skills can be affected, which means that he or she might not be able to hold things such as spoon, fork, or pencil. Gross-motor skills can also be affected when a child uses his or her feet for things such as walking or riding a bicycle. Communicating with others by moving the lips to talk can be difficult for a child with a physical disability.
The environment needs to be physically arranged for optimum usage by those with physical dis*abilities,* not for the convenience of others, e.g., the use of parking spots, dressing rooms, and bathrooms designed for those with disabilities. Some school arrangements and accommodations include

- Bathroom accessibility to maneuver a wheelchair to turn
- Lowered sinks, mirrors, and towel holders
- Wider classroom aisles
- Elevators for buildings with more than one floor, equipped with lights and bell signals, or tactile Braille for those with hearing and visual needs
- Structural accommodations to allow access to all facilities, from water fountains to meeting rooms
- Lowered windows that allow someone who uses a wheelchair to see outside
- TDD/TTY—telephone for someone who is deaf that

transcribes speech into text, with special equipment

- Positioning (e.g., raising or lowering) necessary adaptive equipment to facilitate student's independence
- Use of a Velcro mat on a student's desk to prevent books, papers, pencils, and other materials from slipping, or securing papers to the desk with tape
- Bean bag for student to sit on during floor activities to be on eye level with peers
- Occupational therapy can be a related school service, since fine/gross-motor training targets specific physical needs with additional training and practice

Enlist Help of Peers

- A classmate can make copies of notes or use carbon paper.
- Learning buddies can help students gather materials and assist with school or homework.
- Remember to try to be on eye level with someone in a wheelchair, so he or she does not strain his or her neck by looking up at you.
- Encourage students to exchange telephone numbers or email addresses to extend peer support and friendship outside of the school environment.
- Set tone in class by example; treat student socially and emotionally the same as you would a student without physical impairments, seeing the student as a child first, not only as a child with a disability.

Dynamics of Physical Disabilities

- Can be present at birth (spina bifida, cerebral palsy)
- May be caused by accidents (skiing, car injury, sports, spinal cord injury)
- Diseases can cause a physical impairment (polio, multiple sclerosis).
- Physical disabilities may increase with age as bone structure changes, and mobility can become limited.
- Remember that sensitivities and common sense always apply. Don't freeze up!
- Attitudes toward those with a physical impairment are still archaic, since some people inaccurately or subconsciously assume that someone who can't walk properly cannot have total usage of his or her brain. For example, a person with cerebral palsy can be just as intelligent as an able-bodied individual.
- Awareness about others is most important.

Organizations/Resources

Disabled Sports USA
451 Hungerford Drive,
Suite 100
Rockville, MD 20850
(301) 217–0960
Web address: www
.dsusa.org

Special Olympics
1133 19th Street, NW
Washington, DC 20036–3604
(202) 628–3630
Web address: www
.specialolympics.com

National Council on
Independent Living
1710 Rhode Island Avenue
NW, Fifth Floor
Washington, DC 20036
Voice: (202) 207–0334; TTY:
(202) 207–0340; Toll Free: (877)
525–3400
Web address: www.ncil.org

Goodwill Industries
15810 Indianola Drive
Rockville, MD 20855
(800) 741–0186; TTY: (301)
530–9759
Web address:
www.goodwill.org

Richard Simmons, *Sit Tight*
[Video]. Challenging workout
for those who cannot exercise
while standing up. It improves
stamina, endurance, and
energy levels.
Web address: http://www
.richardsimmons.com

Cerebral Palsy (CP)

Cerebral refers to the brain.
Palsy refers to muscle
movement that may be stiff,
uncontrolled, or unbalanced,
depending upon type of CP.

Causes

Rarely associated with
heredity, since the damage to
the brain usually occurs before,
during, or shortly after birth

Mother's illness during
pregnancy

Premature delivery

Lack of oxygen supply to the
baby or poor blood flow reaching
the fetal or newborn brain

Can be a result of accident,
lead poisoning, viral infection,
or child abuse

Might involve separation of the placenta, an awkward birth position, long labor, or interference from the umbilical cord

RH or A-B-O blood type incompatibility between parents may exist

Mother infected with German measles during pregnancy

Brain injury at birth

Contacts/Resources

United Cerebral Palsy
1660 L Street NW, Suite 700
Washington, DC 20036
(202) 776–0406; (800) 872–5827
Web address: www.ucpa.org

Possible Characteristics

Impairment may involve sight, hearing, and speech

Inability to fully control motor functions, ranging from mild to severe. *Not a disease;* it is a nonprogressive condition that is not contagious

There are three main types of cerebral palsy:
Spastic—Stiff and difficult movement
Athetoid—Involuntary and uncontrolled movement (facial grimaces, drooling)
Ataxic—Sense of balance and depth perception affected

Depending on which part of the brain has been damaged and the degree of central nervous system (CNS) damage, characteristics can include the following:

- Spasms
- Tonal problems
- Involuntary movements
- Seizures

- Disturbances in gait and mobility
- Abnormal sensation and perception
- Impairment of sight, hearing, or speech
- Mental retardation
- Normal or above-average intelligence

Educational Strategies

General or special education with equal academic opportunities

Technology with assistive equipment (e.g., book holder, pencil grip, word processor, tether ball)

Community integration opportunities

Recreation

Occupational therapy

Educate other students about misconceptions

Classroom assistance

Involvement and peer support in social and academic activities

Teach self-advocacy

Life-skills instructions with appropriate activities for daily living

Focus on strengths and interests

Provide opportunities for success

Allow more rest periods

Use communication boards if necessary

Transitional services

Epilepsy

Causes

Physical condition with sudden, brief change in how the brain works that in some cases happens for inexplicable reasons

Consciousness, movement, or actions are altered for a short time (epileptic seizure)

Repeated seizures can be caused by illness, brain damage, birth trauma, brain infection, head injury, metabolic imbalance in the body, drug intoxication, brain tumor, or disruption of blood to the brain

Environmental factors that might bring on a seizure include sudden lighting changes, flashing lights—e.g., photosensitivity—or loud noises

Some forms of epilepsy may be inherited

A single seizure does not mean that a person has epilepsy; seizures can be caused by fevers, imbalance of body fluids, or alcohol or drug withdrawal.

Contacts/Resources

Epilepsy Foundation of America
8301 Professional Place
Landover, MD 20785
(800) 332–1000
Web addresses: www.efa .org; www.epilepsyfoundation.org

Possible Characteristics

Types of seizures: Depends on which part of the brain is affected; types include general, partial, nonepileptic, and status epilepticus

- *Generalized-*—All brain cells are involved. Might involve a convulsion with a complete loss of consciousness or might look like a brief period of fixed staring
- *Partial*—Occurs when brain cells are not working properly and is limited to one part of the brain. May cause periods of automatic behavior and altered consciousness with repetitive behavior that is usually not remembered

Other possible symptoms:

- Involuntary movements of arms and legs
- Blackouts or periods of confused memory, with episodes of staring or unexplained periods of unresponsiveness. Teachers should keep an eye out for this inattentive behavior as being a possible sign of a seizure, if the child is known to have epilepsy
- Fainting spells with excessive fatigue following
- Odd sounds, distorted perceptions, and episodic feelings of inexplicable fear

Educational Strategies

Provide staff and students with information on seizure recognition and first aid with specific directions written into IEP (e.g., clear away dangerous objects, do not restrain the student, make the student comfortable by loosening clothing, never put anything in mouth—may bite hard)

Be aware of effects of antiseizure or anti-anxiety medications

Ensure good communication between school and home to gain more understanding for staff and parents

Teacher should observe and keep accurate anecdotal logs

Encourage other students/adults to treat someone with epilepsy with respect by educating them about possible behaviors

Provide student with downtime; he or she might be exhausted after a seizure

Help students lead independent lives by teaching transitional skills

Multiple Sclerosis (MS)

Causes

Neurological disorder

Multiple means many, while *sclerosis* means a thickening or hardening of tissue.

The majority of people are diagnosed between the ages of 20 and 50, but MS can also be found in the school-age population. Although no definitive cause is known, evidence suggests MS results from an autoimmune process in which immune cells (T cells) mistake *myelin,* the fatty coating around nerve cell fibers in the brain and spinal cord, for a foreign invader and attack it. Other theories of causation consider environment, infection, viruses, and genetics.

Contacts/Resources

National Multiple Sclerosis Society
(800) 344–4867

Web address:
www.nationalmssociety.org

Multiple Sclerosis International Foundation
Web addresses: www.msif.org; www.friendswithms.com

Possible Characteristics

Can impair movement, vision, coordination, and other functions

MS is categorized in the following ways, depending on type and severity:
Benign MS—Condition does not worsen over time, and there is little or no permanent disability. This type cannot be identified until 10 to 15 years after onset; otherwise it falls under relapsing–remitting type. Approximately 5% of the 20% initially diagnosed stay with this type.
Relapsing–Remitting—Episodes followed by remissions (accounts for about 25% of patients with MS). Disappearing and reappearing of neurological functioning
Primary-progressive or relapsing—(Affects about 15%). Continuous worsening with some variations in rate and progression, but no remissions
Secondary-Progressive—Type that half of people with relapsing–remitting experience within 10 years of initial diagnosis. Steady worsening with occasional flare-ups, and minor remissions or plateaus. About 40% occurrence, out of total diagnosed with MS

Many MS patients experience unpredictable day-to-day symptoms. Advances in treatment offer hope for future success in managing MS, especially when caught at an early stage.

Educational Strategies

Occupational therapy to help with daily living activities

Physical therapy to help patients with MS stand, walk, and maintain a range of motion with appropriate exercise

Educational support and awareness to give people with MS an opportunity to learn more about how to help themselves and how to gain support from others

Community–school connections and experiences

Individual educational programs to address present and future academic and social needs

Muscular Dystrophy

Neuromuscular disease that involves both the nerves and muscles

Causes

Can be X-linked recessive gene (female carriers) or autosomal dominant (defective gene is inherited from one parent's chromosomes in non-sex pairs 1 through 22)

Flaws in muscle protein genes

In general, genetic diseases can be related to these factors:

- *Types of Chromosomes*—(a) Autosomal (non-sex pairs 1–22) and (b) Sex-linked (X-chromosome)
- *Traits*—(a) Dominant (caused by genes from one parent) and (b) recessive

(caused by genes from both parents)

Source: National Library of Medicine National Institutes of Health, http://www.nlm.nih.gov; Muscular Dystrophy Association, http://www.mda.org/publications/fa-md.html

Contacts/Resources

Muscular Dystrophy Association USA National Headquarters 3300 East Sunrise Drive Tucson, Arizona 85718 (800) 572–1717 Web address: www.mda.org

Possible Characteristics

Onset can be from early childhood to adulthood

Severity and types vary from weakening and wasting of muscles in the hands, forearms, or lower legs to muscle cramps, twitches, or stiffness

Some progression is slow with periods of rapid deterioration

Can affect throat muscles or swallowing

May include weaknesses in leg, hip, shoulder, or respiratory muscles

Brain is sometimes involved with seizures, deafness, loss of balance and vision, and loss of lower cognitive abilities

May need a wheelchair at any time

May show signs of fatigue

May be frustrated by immobility

Educational Strategies

Emphasis on mobility and independent daily living

Accessibility to and inclusion in all school facilities and functions

Structured exercise program, with avoidance of intense physical demands

Be alert for any physical changes

Eliminate obstacles such as long note taking

Assign peer buddy to help with arduous physical tasks such as lifting heavy books or maneuvering about in crowded halls

Modified physical education program

Technology to augment educational strategies might include the following:

- Eye tracking to help those who lack physical power or dexterity to manually operate a keyboard or mouse (camera is employed to focus on the user's eye movement)
- Voice-recognition technology for word processing
- Cyberlink—Band strapped around the forehead, offering a hands-free, alternative, augmentative type of communication that can detect both muscle and brain impulses to operate a computer mouse, video games, and more

Staff should not lift or pull a student by the arms, since it could cause dislocation of limbs

Peer support system for academic help and social inclusion

Teach self-help skills

Transitional planning

Spina Bifida

Causes

Failure of the spinal cord to completely close up into one piece during early months of mother's pregnancy

Congenital defect

Affects newborns

Contact/Resources

Spina Bifida Resource Network
84 Park Avenue, Suite G-106
Flemington, NJ 08822
(908) 782–7475
Web addresses:
www.sbatsr.org;
www.spinabifida.org

Possible Characteristics

People born with spina bifida are not all alike.

Types of spina bifida include the following:

- *Spina Bifida Occulta* (meaning hidden)—Opening in one or more of the vertebrae (bones) of the spinal column, without apparent damage to the spinal cord
- *Closed Neural Tube Defects* with malformation of fat, bone, or membranes—Symptoms vary from few or none to incomplete paralysis with urinary and bowel dysfunction.
- *Spina Bifida Manifesta*—Includes the following two types:
  o *Meningocele*—Meninges (protective covering around the spinal cord) pushed out

through an opening in the vertebrae in a sac called the meningocele, but the spinal cord is intact and can be repaired with little or no damage to the nerve pathways
  o *Myelomeningocele*—Severe form in which the spinal cord itself is damaged

Nervous system (brain and spine) can be affected

Muscle weakness or paralysis below the area of the spine where the cleft (incomplete closure) occurs with weak bones and joints

Difficulty with bowel and bladder control in excretory system

May have buildup of fluid in the brain (hydrocephalus), which can be surgically drained with a shunt. Without a shunt implanted, the extra fluid can cause brain damage, seizures, or blindness

Attention difficulties

Need help with eye–hand coordination, e.g., perceptual activities

Language expression deficits

Varying academic, physical, and social needs, with characteristics dependent upon type and severity

Educational Strategies

Placement in the least restrictive environment with nondisabled peers

Adaptations in location and structure of the learning

environment to meet physical needs, including fine- and gross-motor ones

Early intervention for school preparation

Communication with teachers concerning catheterization needs (tube inserted to allow passage of urine), with development of a school bladder management program if necessary

Related services such as speech, physical, and occupational therapy

Address emotional and social development by involving student in positive peer relationships (e.g., cooperative learning, community integration)

Focus on positives and student's strengths

Transitional services

Communication Disorders

Communication is delayed when the child is noticeably behind peers in the acquisition of speech or language:

- Expressive Language Disorder (vocabulary, recall of words and sentences)
- Mixed Receptive–Expressive Disorder (expressive disorder along with difficulty understanding words and sentences)
- Phonological Disorder (speech sounds)
- Stuttering (fluency and patterning of speech is inappropriate)

- Communication Disorder Not Otherwise Specified (may include a voice disorder)

Speech is the production of sound; language is the message in speech. Communication disorders (including speech, language, and hearing disorders) affect an estimated 1 of every 10 people in the United States (www.psychologytoday.com/conditions/communication-disorders).

SENSORY INVOLVEMENTS

Communication Disorders

Causes

Acquired or developmental:

- Hearing loss
- Brain injury
- Drug abuse
- Physical impairments such as cleft lip or palate
- Vocal abuse or misuse
- Hearing loss
- Neurological disorder

Cause is frequently unknown

Some disorders are common in families

Apraxia is a motor-speech disorder in which child has difficulties saying sounds, syllables, and words with difficulties transmitting brain messages to body parts, e.g., lips, jaw, tongue

Language disorders can be related to or overlap with other disabilities, e.g., developmental, intellectual, autism, cerebral palsy.

Contacts/Resources

American Speech-Language-Hearing Association (ASHA)
2200 Research Boulevard
Rockville, MD 20850–3289
(301) 296–5700
Web address: www.asha.org

Division for Communicative Disabilities and Deafness (DCDD) of the Council for Exceptional Children (CEC)
Web address: www.dcdd.us

Possible Characteristics

Articulation:

- Distortions—"bud in yard" (bird)
- Additions—"brook I read" (book)
- Omissions—"we are see you" (seeing—can be ending sounds of words)
- Substitutions—"wabbit wunning" (rabbit running)

Voice quality:

- Intensity (softness or loudness)
- Resonance (nasality)
- Pitch (high or low tone)
- Dysfluency/Stuttering (rhythm and flow)
- Interjections (well, um, you know); repeats, hesitates, prolongs, or blocks sounds

Language disorders

- Impairment in understanding (receptive) and using/speaking (expressive) words in context
- Typically, receptive language is better than expressive
- Difficulties with word retrieval, expressing ideas, grammar, reduced vocabulary, following directions, understanding a word's meaning; improper usage of words

Educational Strategies

Timely intervention, since language and communication skills are easier to learn by age 5.

Speech counseling and coordination with classroom teacher to develop communication goals for class and home, with consistent practice

Communication boards with pictures; PECS—Picture Exchange Communication System

Technology for nonspeaking or severely disabled students

Computer programs to link speech with writing

Digital recorders

Let speech relate to children's experiences, with instruction through conversation as well

Mirrors

More visuals

Categorization of words

Modeling, since children learn from others

Patience (wait time)—Do not talk for the child

Praise for approximations

Deafness and Hearing Loss

Causes

Hereditary and environmental factors

Total deafness can be congenital.

Partial deafness may be attributed to loud noises, rubella, ear injury, or illness during pregnancy.

Types of hearing loss:

- *Conductive*—Caused by diseases or obstructions in the outer or middle ear
- *Sensorineural*—Results from damage to delicate sensory hair cells of the inner ear or the nerves
- *Mixed*—Combination of conductive and sensorineural loss (in both the outer or middle and the inner ear)
- *Central*—Loss results from damage or impairment to the nerves or nuclei of the central nervous system, either in the brain or its pathways

Possible Characteristics

Slight, mild, moderate, severe, or profound hearing loss

Conductive hearing loss is usually not severe and can be helped medically, surgically, or with a hearing aid.

Sensorineural losses range from mild to severe and can affect a person's ability to hear certain frequencies. Amplification does not help since a person might still hear distorted sounds. Hearing aids are also sometimes ineffectual.

Frustration from not hearing can lead to behavioral outbursts.

Contacts/Resources

Hearing Loss Association of America
7910 Woodmont Avenue, Suite 1200

Bethesda, MD 20814
(301) 657–2248
Web address:
www.hearingloss.org

Alexander Graham Bell Association for the Deaf
3417 Volta Place, NW
Washington, DC 20007
(202) 337–5220; TTY: (202) 337–5221
Web address: www .agbell.org

American Society for Deaf Children (ASDC)
3820 Hartzdale Drive
Camp Hill, PA 17011
(717) 703–0073; (800) 942–2732
Web address:
www.deafchildren.org

Educational Strategies

Sensitivity training for classroom peers with emphasis on social inclusion of students with hearing loss or deafness

Appropriate speech services by trained professionals

Amplification systems

Note takers, sticky notes, communication boards, Smart Boards

Favorable seating

Finger spelling or cued speech where hand signals and lip movements represent sounds

Captioned films, videos

Text telephones (TTY)

More visuals, handouts, and outlines

Interpreters (to bridge communication between people who do not share same language, e.g., using sign language for a

person who is deaf, then voicing it to a hearing person, such as with ASL—American Sign Language) or transliterators (to change one form of language to a different form of that same language, e.g., Cued Speech [see www.cuedspeech.org] with phonemes associated with language, or Conceptually Accurate Signed English, which uses ASL concepts to sign words in proper English language order)

Another type of communication is oral transliteration in which what is spoken is silently mouthed to person with hearing loss or deafness, along with hand gestures and facial expressions. People should communicate with each other, not with the oral interpreter or transliterator, establishing eye contact and body language between parties having a conversation.

C-print, a translation of classroom lecture in which instructional assistant, aide, or even an assigned classmate types the lecture/notes on a computer in the back of the room that is then immediately sent to and read by the student at his or her own desk/laptop computer, can be a way to see the words.

Language development (help with idiomatic expressions, vocabulary, and grammar) with frequent monitoring

Face the student when reading and giving directions, speaking slowly and clearly in conversational voice, not overemphasizing lip reading

Eliminate background noises

Processing Disorders: Auditory

Causes

Not a result of hearing loss

Possible Characteristics

Symptoms similar to AD/HD; must distinguish between the two

Trouble hearing similarities and differences in sounds

Blending word parts/decoding/phonics

Expressive and receptive language difficulties

Difficulties with any or all of the following:

- Listening to lectures
- Grammatical structure
- Oral directions
- Understanding music and lyrics
- Spelling

May involve the following:

- Auditory discrimination (hearing whether sounds of letters are the same or different)
- Auditory memory (repeating a clapped sequence, following a band's rhythm, remembering sounds of familiar objects, following more than one direction)
- Auditory localization (determining the source or direction of a sound)
- Auditory figure-ground (paying attention in a noisy room)

Contacts/Resources

Bellis, T. J. (2002). *When the brain can't hear: Unraveling the mystery of auditory processing disorder.* New York: Atria.

National Coalition on Auditory Processing Disorders
Web address:
www.ncapd.org/php

Educational Strategies

Give brief, concise directions, at a student's level of comprehension

Accompany verbal directions with written ones

Use more gestures when speaking

Intermittently check student's understanding by asking simple questions, or request him or her to repeat or paraphrase what was said; use appropriate grade-level vocabulary

Reduce the amount of background noises—place old cut-up tennis balls on bottom of desk and chair legs

Ask school nurse to check student's hearing to rule out any medical concerns

Increase student's self-awareness of type of mistakes made with words

Make more eye contact with student before speaking

Teach the student how to take notes while listening for main ideas presented; give the student a graphic organizer to follow

Use more technology that offers audible learning, such as word processing programs with speech capabilities

Have student connect with a partner or peer who can model and consult

Utilize speech/language therapy

Teach phonetic rules vs. just sight-word programs or strict memorization to develop automaticity with linguistic skills

---

Central auditory processing disorder (CAPD) occurs when a child has normal hearing, but an area of the brain where auditory analysis occurs is not obtaining meaning from sounds and stimuli. It can affect memory, speech, language, and reading. Students have difficulties discriminating phonemes that are the basic building blocks of language and specific consonants, such as *b, d,* and *p.* They can confuse these sounds while reading. More strategies are also listed under the auditory processing heading: More visuals, repetition of directions, teaching configuration of words, strengthening expressive and receptive language skills, encouraging more self-awareness, and continual praise is crucial.

Source: Shprintzen, R. (2000). *Syndrome identification for speech-language pathology: An illustrated pocket guide.* New York: Singular.

Processing Disorders: Visual Impairments

Can include disorders that lead to vision impairments such as retinal degeneration, albinism, cataracts, glaucoma, corneal disorders, diabetic retinopathy, infections, muscular problems that result in visual disturbances, and other congenital disorders

Causes

Environmental or genetic

Birth injuries, heredity, illness with fever, muscle problems

Contacts/Resources

American Foundation for the Blind
11 Penn Plaza, Suite 300
New York, NY 10001
(800) AF–BLIND; (800) 232–5463
Web address: www.afb.org

Recording for the Blind and Dyslexic
20 Roszel Road
Princeton, NJ 08540
(866) RFBD-585
Web address: www.rfbd.org

Concordia Learning Center at St. Joseph's School for the Blind
761 Summit Avenue
Jersey City, NJ 07307
Web address: www.sjsnj.org

Possible Characteristics

Vary with the age of onset, severity, type of loss, and overall functioning of the child

May not explore things in the environment and may miss opportunities to imitate social behavior or understand nonverbal skills

May involve difficulties with the following:

- Easily understanding and remembering what is seen
- Picturing words or concepts in their heads
- Matching like shapes
- Doing art activities
- Reproducing patterns
- Working on puzzles
- Noticing the differences between objects, words, numbers
- Spelling accurately
- Poor handwriting
- Organizational or neatness issues
- Accurate proofreading of writing, checking accuracy of computational problems, aligning columns in math, writing words and letters on lines

Dislikes learning when seeing it alone as the only method of presentation; students need kinesthetic (body) and tactile (touch) connections along with auditory input

May involve the following:

- Visual motor (may work close to a paper or desk)—Rotate papers and books
- Visual figure-ground (completing work on crowded pages)
- Visual discrimination (matching shapes or forms, or distinguishing similar words, such as *hundreds* and *hundredths*)
- Visual closure (doing simple puzzles)—Not able to see objects or their functions in their entirety
- Visual memory (for example, retelling three visual acts in sequence: close a door, sharpen a pencil, sit down)

Terminology:

- *Hyperopia*—Farsightedness, when a person sees far away objects better than objects that are nearby
- *Myopia*—Nearsightedness, when objects close by can be seen, but there is difficulty seeing objects at a distance
- *Strabismus*—Eyes are not straight; each eye sends a different message to the brain
- *Astigmatism*—Blurred or distorted images
- *Ocular motor*—Muscles of the eye working together, e.g., fixate, follow, converge
- *Partially Sighted (Visually Impaired)*—Some type of vision problem with sight ranging from 20/70 to 20/200 after correction with glasses. Signs of eye trouble include blinking a lot, rubbing eyes, squinting, shutting or covering one eye, red or swollen watery eyes, and headaches
- *Low Vision*—Severe visual impairment
- *Legally Blind*—Less than 20/200 vision in better eye or limited field of vision
- *Totally Blind*—Complete darkness

Educational Strategies

Support visual information with verbal instructions

Reduce amount of work on pages, or block off part of the work

Use stronger modalities (auditory, or kinesthetic-tactile paired with auditory)

Strengthen memory by associating how and where students originally saw learning material

Use highlighters on worksheets and colored overlays on texts

Compartmentalize information in student-friendly graphic organizers that visually separate information

Provide more manipulatives such as puzzles, tangrams, geoboards, sorting activities such as categorizing words on index cards into syllable types

Reduce clutter in the room, including extra materials by student's desk

Use copiers to enlarge print

Gradually increase time and difficulties of visual tasks

Praise accomplishments

Early intervention programs

Technology—using computers with talking text programs

Low-vision and optical aids for the partially sighted

Magnification pages

Books on tape

Large-print materials; Braille books

Interdisciplinary approach, with learning through all subjects taught using more auditory and kinesthetic-tactile presentations

Emphasize independent daily living and self-care skills, e.g., hygiene, mobility training, using kitchen tools, and following routines

Participation in regular classroom activities with appropriate support, understanding, and encouragement

Adaptations in lighting

Encourage positive peer social interactions

Processing Speed

Can affect memory, writing, reading, speaking, word retrieval, any type of timed activity, focusing while working independently, and staying on task for any reasonable time period

Selective Mutism

Child does not speak in select social settings, not because the child is unable, but because of internal feelings.

Causes

Possibly a psychiatric disorder, related to anxiety

Noncommunication is not caused by any other disorder, including a communication disorder

Definitive cause unknown; can start at a young age, usually before age 5

Rare; fewer than 1% of children have selective mutism

Slightly more common in girls than boys

Contacts/Resources

Selective Mutism Group, part of Childhood Anxiety Network Web addresses: www .selectivemutism.org; www

.social-anxiety.com (site also addresses social/public speaking anxieties)

Possible Characteristics

No language or speech difficulties

Consistent failure to speak in some social situations such as school, but willingness to speak in other situations such as home environment

Language impairment with duration lasting more than a month

Difficulty with relationships

Problem may be related to anxiety or a social phobia, since the children have the ability to both speak and understand language, but fail to use this ability

Social isolation/withdrawal

Clinging behavior; compulsiveness; negativism; temper tantrums with controlling or oppositional behavior, especially at home

Can become peer scapegoat

Usually lasts for only months, but can continue for years

Educational Strategies

Speech and language therapy with encouragement for family and child

Be patient and calm

Do not speak for the child!

Socially include the child as an integral part of the classroom, regardless of lack of vocalizations

Introduce other forms of communication (gestures,

signs, written expression, communication board)

Include more nonspeaking activities such as writing, using the computer, drawing, or silent reading

Reward small steps whenever the child makes sounds or words

Digitally record and note when child speaks, to gain more understanding of speech patterns

Have child speak in smaller setting (e.g., one to one, with a speaking buddy, or into a digital recorder) and then gradually add more people to conversations

Keep a chart of gains that can be coordinated with a reward system in home and school environment, involving parents and families. Gradually phase out rewards as child speaks more

SYNDROMES

Angelman Syndrome (AS)

Causes

Genetic disorder with a deleted region of genes on chromosome 15

Children with AS were formerly called *puppet children*, named after an oil painting (*Boy With a Puppet*) seen by Dr. Harry Angelman, which depicted a boy with similar characteristics as his patients. The name was later changed to Angelman syndrome

Estimate of 1 in 15,000 to 1 in 30,000 are affected; exact numbers are unknown

AS appears equally among all races and in both sexes

Contact/Resources

Angelman Syndrome Foundation Web address: www .angelman.org

Possible Characteristics

Not usually detected at birth or in infancy, since there are nonspecific developmental delays

Usual age of diagnosis is when features and characteristic behaviors become most evident (ages 3 to 7)

Range of gait disorders with uncoordinated movements that affect walking, feeding, and reaching for objects

Hypermotoric activity with short attention span

Difficulty attending to social cues

Excessive, often contagious laughter, with lots of smiling and a happy disposition

Difficulty with conversational speech, along with varying nonverbal skills

Skin and eye *hypopigmentation* (no pigment in the retina)

Strabismus (eye coordination problem in which eyes do not concurrently focus on the same point, but may look in different directions)

Sleep disturbances

Educational Strategies

Early training and enrichment programs

Physical therapy for gross-motor difficulties

Occupational therapy for oral-motor and fine-motor control

Structured classroom design and environment to accommodate hypermotoric needs

Speech and communication therapy including augmentative aids such as communication boards and more visuals

Individualization with flexibility

Behavior modification

Peer support and awareness of syndrome

Training of all staff working with children

Home-to-school communication with coordination of physical, academic, and behavioral programs

Down Syndrome

Causes

Chromosomal disorder, which occurs from an accident in cell development that leaves 47, instead of the usual 46, chromosomes. Determined by a *karyotype* (visual chromosome study)

Most people with Down syndrome have an extra No. 21 chromosome

Uncertain what causes this extra genetic material that happens at conception

One of the leading clinical causes of mental retardation

Does not correlate to race, nationality, or socioeconomic status

Higher incidence for mothers who give birth over age 35

Contacts/Resources

National Down Syndrome Congress
1370 Center Drive Suite 102
Atlanta, GA 30338
(800) 232–NDSC
Web address: www.ndsccenter.org

National Down Syndrome Society
666 Broadway, 8th Floor
New York, NY 10012–2317

Goodwin Family Information and Referral Center
(800) 221–4602
Web address: www.ndss.org

The Arc
1010 Wayne Avenue, Suite 650
Silver Spring, MD 20910
Web address: www.thearc.org

Down Syndrome Internet Social Network
Web address: www.downsyndrome.com

Possible Characteristics

Slower physical and intellectual growth

Health-related problems could include heart defects, gastrointestinal tract problems, visual and hearing impairments (crossed eyes, far- or nearsightedness, mild to moderate hearing loss), speech difficulties, atlantoaxial instability (misalignment of top two vertebrae of the neck), and respiratory difficulties since they might have a lower resistance to infection. Need cardiogram at birth to identify heart concerns and appropriate medical care

Physical signs can include a smaller head; slanting eyes (epicanthal folds); short, broad hands, feet, and toes; flat bridge of the nose; short neck; low-set ears; and poor muscle tone (hypotonia). Wide range of mental abilities, from mild to severe cognitive impairments

Difficulties understanding directions and abstract concepts

Receptive language better than expressive language (understanding more than communicating through speech)

Memory affected

Educational Strategies

Early educational and developmental services and therapies beginning in infancy

Speech therapy

Nutritional/hygiene counseling

Peer education and sensitivity to reinforce acceptance, since children all have certain social/emotional needs in common. Necessary whether or not children are placed in inclusive classrooms

Increase usage of visuals, manipulatives, and concrete learning experiences

Physical exercise program, including more wrist- and finger-strengthening activities such as cutting and sorting as well as activities to strengthen individual stamina

Teach in a step-by-step manner with consistent positive feedback, drill, and repetition

Encourage independence under teacher's auspices with realistic but high expectations

Concentrate on potentials, not limitations

Consistent family communication of progress with home reinforcement of learned academic/social skills

Transitional plans with planned community involvement and functional training for daily living skills with participation in supported employment with job shadowing and mentoring

Relate new content to previously learned subjects and real-life situations

Prader-Willi Syndrome (PWS)

Complex genetic disorder that can cause cognitive disabilities, behavior problems, short stature, poor muscle tone, incomplete sexual development, and a chronic hungry feeling that if uncontrolled may lead to excessive eating and life-threatening obesity.

Causes

Genetic cause is loss of unidentified genes (defect of

chromosome 15), contributed by the father, that occurs at or near time of conception for unknown reasons

DNA analysis confirms PWS diagnosis

Prevalence: 1 in 12,000 to 15,000 (both sexes, all races). One of the most common conditions seen in genetic clinics and leading genetic cause of obesity

PWS-like disorder can occur after birth if the hypothalamus portion of the brain is damaged during surgery or injured

Contacts/Resources

Prader-Willi Syndrome Association (USA)
8588 Potter Park Drive, Suite 500
Sarasota, FL 34238
(800) 926–4797
Web address:
www.pwsausa.org

Possible Characteristics

Excessive or rapid weight gain between ages 1 and 6 with possibility of obesity if not vigilantly monitored and nutritionally controlled

Short stature by age 15

Range of IQ from 40 to 105, with learning problems evident in those with average IQ

May have short-term auditory memory problems, attention difficulties, and weak abstract thinking

Good visual perception skills, long-term memory, reading ability, and receptive language

Deficits in speech articulation, motor coordination, strength, and balance

Habit of skin-picking

Younger children usually do not exhibit behavioral problems, but most older children and adults with PWS have difficulties regulating behavior and dealing with transitions and unexpected changes

May have outbursts of stubbornness; may steal money or items to buy/trade food; may be prone to lying

Sleep disorders/fatigue

Educational Strategies

Behavior plans that emphasize positive rewards, clear rules, limits, structure, and daily routines

Physical and occupational therapies

Exercise and sports-related activities that are less competitive (to accommodate poor muscle tone and fatigue)

Social skills training

Speech therapy

Early infant stimulation

Full range of appropriate services in least restrictive environment

Peer support system

Communicate with family to coordinate behavioral plans

Food restriction plan in school and home; structured diet plan and lifelong diet supervision

Transitional plans with preparation for adult living and maximum community involvement based upon varying cognitive levels

Tourette Syndrome (TS)

Causes

Genetic predisposition

Neurological disorder

Abnormal metabolism of neurotransmitters (chemicals in the brain), which might cause the tics

Early diagnosis and treatment, since some children require medication

Contacts/Resources

Tourette Syndrome Association
42–40 Bell Boulevard
Bayside, NY 11361–2874
(718) 224–2999; (800) 237–0717
Web address: www. tsa-usa.org

Tourette Syndrome Plus
Web address: www
.tourettesyndrome.net/

> tic = sudden, rapid, recurrent, nonrhythmic, stereotyped motor movement or vocalization

Possible Characteristics

Symptoms include involuntary tics and rapid motor or vocal movements that can range from simple to complex. Onset is before the age of 18 with most cases being mild. Symptoms can decrease as children mature (late teens, early twenties) with possible remission of tic symptoms

There are two types of Tourette syndrome:
Simple—Motor: eye blinking, facial grimaces, shoulder shrugs, head jerking; Vocal: noises such as tongue clicking, and other throat sounds
Complex—Motor: twirling, jumping, touching possessions of others, and—rarely—self-injurious behavior; Vocal: coprolalia (use of obscene language, e.g., derogatory remarks, swearing), which is present in less than 15% of the TS population

Associated with impulsivity and attention problems (AD/HD), and with learning or perceptual difficulties

Easily frustrated

Misbehavior due to neurobiological disturbances

Educational Strategies

Give the student more opportunities for movement, with frequent breaks outside of the classroom setting

Involve school psychologist

Educate peers and other staff (e.g., bus drivers, lunch aides, special subjects teachers)

Reduce—break down, sequence, and color-code assignments

Avoid front seating since tics can be embarrassing; even

allow student a place to work outside of the classroom

Try to seat student away from visual distractions

Encourage use of a word processor, or allow alternatives to written assignments

Allow extra time for class work or shorten assignments based on level of mastery

Provide outlines and study guides

Cue student about learning expectations before a new lesson; have student repeat directions for a task, and signal student for transitional activities

Watch for side effects from medication

Resource B

Organizations

Academy of Orton-Gillingham Practitioners and Educators—PO Box 234, Amenia, NY 12501–0234, (854) 373–8919, www.ortonacademy.org

Alexander Graham Bell Association for the Deaf—3417 Volta Place, NW, Washington, DC 20007, (202) 337–5220, TTY: (202) 337–5221, www.agbell.org

American Alliance for Health, Physical Education, Recreation, and Dance (AAHPERD)—1900 Association Drive, Reston, VA 20191, (800) 213–7193, www.aahperd.org

American Association on Intellectual and Developmental Disabilities (AAIDD)—501 3rd Street, NW, Suite 200, Washington, DC 20001, (202) 387–1968 or (800) 424–3688, www.aaidd.org, www.aamr.org

American Foundation for the Blind—11 Penn Plaza, Suite 300, New York, NY 10001, (800) AFB–LINE or (800) 232–5463, www.afb.org/afb

American Society for Deaf Children—820 Hartzdale Drive, Camp Hill, PA 17011, (800) 942–ASDC, 2732 V-TTY, www.deafchildren.org

American Speech-Language Hearing Association—2200 Research Boulevard, Rockville, MD 20850–3289, 301–296–5700, Members: (800) 498–2071, Non-Members: (800) 638–8255, TTY: (301) 296–5650, www.asha.org

Angelman Syndrome Foundation—www.angelman.org

Anxiety Disorders Association of America—8730 Georgia Avenue, Suite 600, Silver Spring, MD 20910, (240) 485–1001, www.adaa.org

The Arc—1010 Wayne Avenue, Suite 650, Silver Spring, MD 20910, (301) 565–3842, 800–433–5255, www.thearc.org

The Association on Higher Education and Disability (AHEAD)—107 Commerce Center Drive, Suite 204, Huntersville, NC 28078, (704) 947–7779, www.ahead.org

Attention Deficit Disorder Association (ADDA)—PO Box 7557, Wilmington, DE 19803–9997, (800) 939–1019, www.add.org

Autism Society of America—7910 Woodmont Avenue, Suite 300, Bethesda, MD 20814, (301) 657–0881 or (800) 3–AUTISM, www.autism-society.org

Brain Injury Association of America—1608 Spring Hill Road, Suite 110, Vienna, VA 22182, (703) 761–0750, Brain Injury Information: (800) 444–6443, www.biausa.org

CAST-Center for Applied Technology—40 Harvard Mills Square, Suite 3, Wakefield, MA 01880–3233, (781) 245–2212, TTY (781) 245–9320, www.cast.org

Center for Applied Linguistics—4646 40th Street, NW, Washington, DC 20016–1859, (202) 362–0700, www.cal.org

The Center for Effective Collaboration and Practice: Improving Services for Children and Youth with Emotional and Behavioral Problems—U.S. Dept. of Education, Office of Special Education and Rehabilitative Services (OSERS), http://cecp.air.org

Child and Adolescent Bipolar Foundation—820 Davis St., Suite 520, Evanston, IL 60201, (847) 492–8519, www.bpkids.org

Children and Adults with Attention Deficit Disorder (CHADD)—8181 Professional Place, Suite 150, Landover, MD 20785, (301) 306–7070 or (800) 233–4050, www.chadd.org

The Children's Museum Kits Program—300 Congress Street, Boston, MA 02210, (800) 370–5487, (617) 426–6500, www.bostonkids.org/kits

College Board Services for Students with Disabilities—PO Box 6226, Princeton, NJ 08541–6226, (609) 771–7137, TTY: (609) 882–4118, www.collegeboard.com/ssd/student/index.html

The Council for Exceptional Children (CEC)—1110 North Glebe Road, Suite 300, Arlington, VA 22201, (703) 620–3660, (888) CEC-SPED, TTY: (866) 915–5000, www.cec.sped.org

Disabled Sports USA—451 Hungerford Drive, Suite 100, Rockville, MD 20850, (301) 217–0960, www.dsusa.org

Division for Communicative Disabilities and Deafness (DCD), for Council for Exceptional Children, 1920 Association Drive, Reston, VA 22091, http://www.dcdd.us

Down Syndrome on the Internet, Social Networking—www.downsyndrome.com

The Early Childhood Research Institute on Culturally and Linguistically Appropriate Services (CLAS)—http://clas.uiuc.edu

The Educator's Reference Desk—Lesson plans, with links to online education information and resource guides, www.eduref.org

Epilepsy Foundation of America—8301 Professional Place, Landover, MD 20785, (800) 332–1000, www.efa.org, www.epilepsyfoundation.org

Federation of Families for Children's Mental Health—9605 Medical Center Drive, Rockville, MD 20850, (240) 403–1901, www.ffcmh.org

Hearing Loss Association of America—7910 Woodmont Avenue, Suite 1200, Bethesda, MD 20814, (301) 657–2248, www.hearingloss.org

HEATH Resource Center at George Washington University, National Clearinghouse on Postsecondary Education for Individuals with Disabilities—2134 G Street, NW, Washington, DC 20052, (800) 544–3284, www.heath.gwu.edu

The International Dyslexia Association—40 York Rd., 4th Floor, Baltimore, MD 21204, (410) 296–0232, www.interdys.org

International Reading Association Headquarters—800 Barksdale Rd., PO Box 8139, Newark, DE 19714–8139, (800) 336–7323, www.reading.org

Intervention Central—www.interventioncentral.org

Jolly Phonics-Jolly Learning Ltd—50 Winter Sport Lane, Williston, VT 05495–0020, (800) 488–2665, www.jollylearning.co.uk

Just One Break—570 Seventh Avenue, New York, NY 10018, (212) 785–7300, TTY: (212) 785–4515, www.justonebreak.com

The Kids on the Block, Inc—9385-C Gerwig Lane, Columbia, MD 21046, (800) 368–KIDS (5437), www.kotb.com

Learning Disabilities Association of America (LDA)—4156 Library Road, Pittsburgh, PA 15234, (412) 341–1515, (412) 341–8077, (888) 300–6710, www.ldanatl.org

Learning Disabilities Info—www.ldinfo.org

MAAP Services for Autism and Asperger Syndrome—PO Box 524, Crown Point, IN 46307, (219) 662–1311, www.maapservices.org

The Math Forum at Drexel Math Library—www.mathforum.org

Mayer-Johnson LLC—2100 Wharton Street, Suite 400, Pittsburgh, PA 15203, Toll Free: (800) 588–4548, www.mayer-johnson.com

Mental Health America—2000 N. Beauregard Street, 6th Floor, Alexandria, VA 22311, (703) 684–7722, (800) 969–6642, TTY: (800) 433–5959, www.nmha.org

Multiple Sclerosis International Foundation—www.msif.org, www.friendswithms.com

Muscular Dystrophy Association USA, National Headquarters—3300 East Sunrise Drive, Tucson, AZ 85718, (800) 572–1717, www.mdausa.org

National Alliance on Mental Illness (NAMI)—2107 Wilson Blvd., Suite 300, Arlington, VA 22201–3042, (703) 524–7600, Member Services: (888) 999–NAMI (6264), www.nami.org

National Association for Bilingual Education—1313 L Street NW, Suite 210, Washington, DC 20005, (202) 898–1829, www.nabe.org

National Association for Down Syndrome (NADS)—PO Box 206, Wilmette, IL 60091, (630) 325–9112, www.nads.org

National Association for Gifted Children (NAGC)—1707 L Street, NW, Suite 550, Washington, DC 20036, (202) 785–4268, www.nagc.org

National Association for Music Education—1806 Robert Fulton Drive, Reston, VA 20191, (800) 336–3768, www.musicfriends.org, www.menc.org

National Association for the Education of Young Children (NAEYC)—1313 L St. NW, Suite 500, Washington, DC 20005, (202) 232–8777, (800) 424–2460, www.naeyc.org

National Center for Educational Statistics—Institute of Education Sciences, U.S. Dept. of Education, 1990 K Street, NW, Washington, DC 20006, (202) 502–7300 www.nces.ed.gov

National Center for Family Literacy—325 West Main Street, Suite 300, Louisville, KY 40202, (877) FAMLIT–1, (502) 584–1133, www.famlit.org

National Center for Learning Disabilities (NCLD)—381 Park Avenue South, Suite 1401, New York, NY 10016, (212) 684–5536, (888) 575–7373, www.ncld.org

National Center on Disability and Journalism (NCDJ), ASU Walter Cronkite School of Journalism and Mass Communication—www.ncdj.org

National Council of Learning Disabilities—http://www.ncld.org as cited in http:www.idea-data.org

National Council of Teachers of English—1111 Kenyon Road, Urbana, IL 61801, (217) 328–3870 or (877) 369–6283, www.ncte.org

National Council of Teachers of Mathematics (NCTM)—1906 Association Drive, Reston, VA 20191–1502, (703) 620–9840, www.nctm.org

The National Council on Independent Living—1710 Rhode Island Avenue Northwest, 5th Floor, Washington, DC 20036, (202) 207–0334, TTY: (202) 207–0340, Toll Free: (877) 525–3400, www.ncil.org

National Dissemination Center for Children with Disabilities (NICHCY)—PO Box 1492, Washington, DC 20013, V-TTY: (800) 695–0285, www.nichcy.org

National Down Syndrome Congress—1370 Center Drive, Suite 102, Atlanta, GA 30338, (800) 232–NDSC, www.ndsccenter.org

National Down Syndrome Society—666 Broadway, 8th Floor, New York, NY 10012–2317, Goodwin Family Information and Referral Center, (800) 221–4602, http://ndss.org

National Eating Disorder Association (NEDA)—603 Stewart Street, Suite 803, Seattle, WA 98101, (206) 382–3587, www.nationaleatingdisorders.org

National Institute on Deafness and Other Communication Disorders, National Institutes of Health—31 Center Drive, MSC 2320, Bethesda, MD 20892–2320, www.nidcd.nih.gov/index.asp

National Multiple Sclerosis Society—(800) Fight–MS, (800) 344–4867, chapters listed at www.nmss.org

National Reading Conference—7044 S. 13th St., Oak Creek, WI 53154, (414) 908–4924, www.nrconline.org

National Rehabilitation Information Center (NARIC)—8201 Corporate Drive, Suite 600, Landover, MD 20785, (800) 346–2742, (301) 459–5900, TTY: (301) 459–5984, www.naric.com

Obsessive-Compulsive Foundation (OCF)—PO Box 961029, Boston, MA 02196, (617) 973–5801, www.ocfoundation.org

Office of Special Education and Rehabilitative Services (OSERS), U.S. Department of Education—400 Maryland Ave., SW, Washington, DC 20202–7100, (202) 245–7468; OSEP Office of Special Education Programs: (202) 245–7459, www.ed.gov/about/offices/list/osers/osep/index.html

Online Asperger Syndrome Information and Support (OASIS)—www.udel.edu/bkirby/asperger

Parent Advocacy Coalition for Educational Rights (PACER)—8161 Normandale Blvd., Minneapolis, MN 55473–4826, (800) 537–2237, (952) 838–9000, TTY: (952) 838–0190, www.pacer.org; National Technical Assistance Center at PACER Center: (888) 248–0822, www.taalliance.org

People Living Through Cancer—3401 Candelaria Blvd, Suite A, Albuquerque, NM 87107, (505) 242–3263, www.pltc.org

The Prader-Willi Syndrome Association—8588 Potter Park Drive, Suite 500, Sarasota, FL 34238, (800) 926–4797, (941) 312–040, www.pwsausa.org

Project Zero—Harvard Graduate School of Education, 124 Mount Auburn Street, 5th Floor, Cambridge, MA 02138, (617) 496–7097, www.pzweb.harvard.edu

PTA National Headquarters—541 N. Fairbanks Court, Suite 1300 Chicago, IL 60611–3396, (312) 670–6782, Toll-Free: (800) 307–4PTA (4782), www.pta.org, www.ptacentral.org

Recording for the Blind & Dyslexic—20 Roszel Road, Princeton, NJ 08540, (609) 452–0606, (866) RFBD–585, www.rfbd.org

Respect Diversity Foundation—2808 West Lexington Way, Edmond, OK 73012, (405) 359–0369, www.respectdiversity.org

St. Joseph's School for the Blind at Concordia Learning Center—761 Summit Avenue, 253 Baldwin Avenue, Jersey City, NJ 07307, (201) 876–5432, www.sjsb.net

Selective Mutism Group—www.selectivemutism.org, www.social-anxiety.com

Sensory Resources at Future Horizons—721 W. Abram Street, Arlington, TX 76013, (800) 489–0727, www.fhsensory.com

Services for Students with Disabilities (SAT)—PO Box 6226, Princeton, NJ 08541–6226, (609) 771–7137, TTY: (609) 882–4118, www.collegeboard.com/ssd/student/index.html

Southern Poverty Law Center, Teaching Tolerance—400 Washington Avenue, Montgomery, AL 36104, www.tolerance.org/teach

Special Olympics—1133 19th Street, NW, Washington, DC 20036–3604, (202) 628–3630, (800) 700–8585, www.specialolympics.com

Spina Bifida Association of America—4590 MacArthur Boulevard, NW, Suite 250, Washington, DC 20007, (202) 944–3285, (800) 621–3141, www.sbaa.org

Sports and Recreational Activities for Children with Physical Disabilities, Cure Our Children Foundation—www.cureourchildren.org/sports.htm

Tangrams—www.curiouser.co.uk/tangram/template.htm

TASH—1025 Vermont Avenue, NW, Suite 300, Washington, DC 20005, (202) 540–9020, www.tash.org

Teaching LD, Division of Learning Disabilities (DLD) of the Council for Exceptional Children—http://www.teachingld.org

TouchMath, Innovative Learning Concepts—6760 Corporate Drive, Colorado Springs, CO 80919, (800) 888–9191, www.touchmath.com

Tourette Syndrome Association—42–40 Bell Boulevard, Bayside, NY 11361–2874, (718) 224–2999, (800) 237–0717, www.tsa-usa.org

Tourette Syndrome Information—www.tourettesyndrome.org

United Cerebral Palsy—1660 L Street, NW, Suite 700, Washington, DC 20036, (202) 776–0406, (800) 872–5827, www.ucpa.org

What Works Clearinghouse, U.S. Dept. of Education, Institute of Education Sciences—PO Box 2393, Princeton, NJ 08543–2393, (866) 503–6114, http://ies.ed.gov/ncee/wwc

Wilson Language Training—47 Old Webster Road, Oxford, MA 01540, (800) 899–8454, www.wilsonlanguage.com

Resource C

Bibliography

ABC News Home Video Library. (1998, October 25). At home with Bob & Michelle [Video]. *20/20*, Segment 2, Item #T990528_01M.

Acton, O., Ellenburg, J., Katsiyannis, A., & Torrey, G. (2001). Addressing the needs of students with Rett Syndrome. *Teaching Exceptional Children, 33,* 74–77.

Allsopp, D., Kyger, M., Lovin, L., Gerretson, H., Carson, K., & Ray, S. (2008). Mathematics dynamic assessment: Informal assessment that responds to the needs of struggling learners in mathematics. *Teaching Exceptional Children, 40*(3), 6–16.

American Psychiatric Association. (2000). *Diagnostic and statistical manual of mental disorders* (4th ed.). Washington, DC: Author.

Anderson, O., Marsh, M., & Harvey, A. (1999). *Learn with the classics.* San Francisco: Lind.

Armstrong, T. (1994). *Multiple intelligences in the classroom.* Alexandria, VA: Association for Supervision and Curriculum Development.

Armstrong, T. (2000). *Multiple intelligences in the classroom* (2nd ed.). Alexandria, VA: Association for Supervision and Curriculum Development.

Armstrong, T. (2003a). *The multiple intelligences of reading and writing.* Alexandria, VA: Association for Supervision and Curriculum Development.

Armstrong, T. (2003b). *You're smarter than you think: A kid's guide to multiple intelligences.* Minneapolis, MN: Free Spirit.

Association for Supervision and Curriculum Development. (2002). *ASCD education update.* Alexandria, VA: Author.

Auer, C., & Blumberg, S. (2006). *Parenting a child with sensory processing disorder: A family guide to understanding and supporting your sensory-sensitive child.* Oakland, CA: Harbinger Publications.

Baker, J. (2001). *The social skills picture book: Teaching play, emotion, and communication to children with autism.* Arlington: TX: Future Horizons.

Baker, J. (2005). *Preparing for life. The complete guide to transitioning to adulthood for those with autism and Asperger's syndrome.* Arlington, TX: Future Horizons.

Banks, J. (1999). *An introduction to multicultural education.* Boston: Allyn & Bacon.

Beattie, J., Jordan, L., & Algozzine, B. (2006). *Making inclusion work: Effective practices for ALL teachers.* Thousand Oaks, CA: Corwin.

Bellis, T. J. (2002). *When the brain can't hear: Unraveling the mystery of auditory processing disorder.* New York: Atria.

Berninger, V., & Wolf, B. (2009). *Helping students with dyslexia and dysgraphia make connections: Differentiated instruction lesson plans in reading and writing.* Baltimore: Paul H. Brookes.

Bloom, B. S. (Ed.). (1956). *Taxonomy of educational objectives: Cognitive domain.* New York: David McKay.

Bos, C., Nahmias, M., & Urban, M. (1999). Targeting home–school collaboration for students with ADHD. *Teaching Exceptional Children, 31,* 4–11.

Browder, D. (2006). *General curriculum: How to access the content and assess achievement tor students with disabilities.* Retrieved October 2, 2007, from http://acressped.org/conference/2006/docs/Diane_Browder_Generai_Curriculum_06.pdf

Burke, K., & Sutherland, C. (2004). Attitudes toward inclusion: Knowledge vs. experience. *Education, 125*(2), 163–172.

Callahan, J. (1990). *Don't worry, he won't get far on foot.* New York: Vintage.

Campbell, L., Campbell, B., & Dickinson, D. (2004). *Teaching and learning through multiple intelligences.* Boston: Pearson Education.

Canfield, J., Hansen, M., & Kirberger, K. (1997). *Chicken soup for the teenage soul.* Deerfield Beach, FL: Health Communications.

Cassidy, J. (1994). *A kid's geography museum in a book.* Palo Alto, CA: Klutz Press.

Chambers, C. (2008). Trends in special education. *District Administrator, 44*(4), 3.

Chapman, C., & Gregory, G. (2002). *Differentiated instructional strategies: One size doesn't fit all.* Thousand Oaks, CA: Corwin.

Chorzempa, B., & Lapidua, L. (2009). To find yourself, think for yourself: Using Socratic discussions in inclusive classrooms. *Teaching Exceptional Children, 41*(3), 54–59.

Cisneros, S. (1984). *The House on Mango Street.* New York: Vintage.

Council of Administrators of Special Education. (1999). *Section 504 and the ADA, promoting student access: A resource guide for educators* (2nd ed.). Albuquerque, NM: CASE.

Craig, A., & Rosney, C. (1993). *The Usborne science encyclopedia.* Tulsa, OK: EDC.

Cramer, S. (2006). *The special educator's guide to collaboration: Improving relationships with co-teachers, teams, and families.* Thousand Oaks, CA: Corwin.

Crawford, G. (2004). *Managing the adolescent classroom: Lessons from outstanding teachers.* Thousand Oaks, CA: Corwin.

Cummings, R., & Fisher, G. (1991). *The school survival guide for kids with LD.* Minneapolis, MN: Free Spirit.

Cunningham, P., & Allington, R. (1994). *Classrooms that work: They can all read and write.* New York: HarperCollins.

Cunningham, P., & Hall, D. (1994). *Making big words.* Redding, CA: Good Apple.

Cybele, R. C. (2003). *Young children's emotional development and school readiness.* Champaign, IL: ERIC Clearinghouse on Elementary and Early Childhood Education.

Dailey, D., & Zantal-Wiener, K. (2000). *Reforming high school learning: The effect of the standards movement on secondary students with disabilities.* Alexandria, VA: Center for Policy Research.

Damasio, A. (2003). *Looking for Spinoza: Joy, sorrow, and the feeling brain.* New York: Harcourt.

Discovery Education's *Puzzlemaker*—http://www.puzzlemaker.com

Edwards, B. (1989). *Drawing on the right side of the brain* (Rev. ed.). New York: Tarcher.

Edwards, B. (1999). *The new drawing on the right side of the brain.* New York: Putnam.

Elias, M. J., Zins, J. E., Weissberg, R. P., Frey, K. S., Greenberg, M. T., Haynes, N. M., et al. (1997). *Promoting social and emotional learning.* Alexandria, VA: Association for Supervision and Curriculum Development.

Elliott, J., & Thurlow, M. (2000). *Improving test performance of students with disabilities.* Thousand Oaks, CA: Corwin.

Erikson, E. (1968). *Identity, youth, and crisis.* New York: Norton.

Forte, I., & Schurr, S. (1987). *Science mind stretchers.* Nashville, TN: Incentive Publications.

Frender, G. (1990). *Learning to learn.* Nashville, TN: Incentive Publications.

Friend, M., & Bursuck, W. (1996). *Including students with special needs.* Boston: Allyn & Bacon.

Friend, M., & Cook, L. (2003). *Interactions: Collaborative skills for school professionals* (4th ed.). New York: Longman.

Fry, E., Kress, J., & Fountoukidis, D. (1993). *The reading teacher's book of lists.* Upper Saddle River, NJ: Prentice Hall.

Frymier, J. (1992). Children who hurt, children who fail. *Phi Delta Kappan, 74*(3), 257–259.

Gardner, H. (1993). *Creating minds.* New York: Basic Books.

Gehert, J. (1991). *Eagle eyes: A child's guide to paying attention.* New York: Verbal Images Press.

Gelb, M. (1998). *How to think like Leonardo da Vinci.* New York: Random House.

Gess, D., & Livingston, J. (2006). *Teaching writing: Strategies for improving literacy across the curriculum.* New York: Write Track. (800) 845–8402, http://www.thewritetrack.com

Getskow, V., & Konczal, D. (1996). *Kids with special needs.* Santa Barbara, CA: The Learning Works.

Gore, M. (2003). *Successful inclusion strategies for secondary and middle school teachers: Keys to help struggling learners access the curriculum.* Thousand Oaks, CA: Corwin.

Graham, S., & Harris, K. (2005). *Writing better: Effective strategies for teaching students with learning difficulties.* Baltimore: Paul H. Brookes.

Grandin, T. (1986). *Emergence: Labeled autistic.* New York: Warner.

Grandin, T. (1995). *Thinking in pictures and other reports from my life with autism.* New York: Vintage.

Greenspan, S. (1998). *The child with special needs.* Boulder, CO: Perseus.

Hallahan, D., & Kaufman, J. (1997). *Exceptional learners.* Needham Heights, MA: Allyn & Bacon.

Hallowell, E., & Ratey, J. (1994). *Driven to distraction.* New York: Touchstone.

Hammeken, P. (2007). *The teacher's guide to inclusive education: 750 strategies for success.* Thousand Oaks, CA: Corwin.

Handley, P. (2002). Every classroom teacher's dream. *Educational Leadership, 59,* 5.

Hardman, M., Drew, C., & Egan, M. (1996). *Human exceptionality.* Boston: Allyn & Bacon.

Harwell, J. (1989). *Complete learning disabilities handbook.* New York: Center for Applied Research in Education.

Havasy, R. (2001, November 7). Getting a clue. We need a revolution in the way we teach science. *Education Week,* 49.

Heintzman, L., & Hanson, H. (2009). *RTI & DI: The dynamic duo* [DVD]. Port Chester, NY: National Professional Resources, Inc.

Hirsch, E. D., Kett, J., & Trefil, J. (2002). *The new dictionary of cultural literacy.* Boston: Houghton Mifflin.

Holler, R., & Zirkel, P. (2008). Section 504 and Public Schools: A national survey concerning "Section 504-only" students. *NASSP Bulletin, 92*(1), 19–43.

Hyde, A. (2007). Mathematics and cognition. *Educational Leadership, 65*(3), 43–47.

James, P. (1983). *Teaching art to special students.* Portland, ME: J. Weston Walch.

Jenkins, J., Antil, L., Wayne, S., & Vadasy, P. (2003). How cooperative learning works for special education and remedial students. *Exceptional Children, 69*(3), 279–292.

Jensen, E. (2000). *Learning with the body in mind.* San Diego, CA: The Brain Store.

Jensen, E. (2005). *Teaching with the brain in mind* (2nd ed.). Alexandria, VA: Association for Supervision and Curriculum Development.

Johnson, D., & Johnson, R. (1975). *Learning together and alone.* Englewood Cliffs, NJ: Prentice Hall.

Johnson, J. (2003, November). What does the public say about accountability? *Educational Leadership, 61*(3), 39.

Jolivette, K., Stichter, J., & McCormick, K. (2002, January 1). Making choices—improving behavior—engaging in learning. *Teaching Exceptional Children, 34*(3), 24–30.

Kagan, S. (1994). *Kagan cooperative learning.* San Juan Capistrano, CA: Kagan Cooperative Learning.

Kagan, S. (2000). *Silly sports & goofy games.* Bellevue, WA: Kagan.

Karten, T. (2007a). *Inclusion activities that work!* Workbooks, K–2, 3–5, 6–8. Thousand Oaks, CA: Corwin.

Karten, T. (2007b). *More inclusion strategies that work! Aligning student strengths with standards.* Thousand Oaks, CA: Corwin.

Karten, T. (2008a). *Embracing disabilities in the classroom: Strategies to maximize students' assets.* Thousand Oaks, CA: Corwin.

Karten, T. (2008b). *Facilitator's guide to more inclusion strategies that work!* Thousand Oaks, CA: Corwin.

Karten, T. (2008c). *Inclusion succeeds with effective strategies* [Laminated reference guides], Grades K–5, 6–12. Port Chester, NY: Dude Publishing.

Karten, T. (2009). *Inclusion strategies that work for adolescent learners!* Thousand Oaks, CA: Corwin.

Karten, T. (2010). *The inclusion lesson plan book for the 21st century.* Port Chester, NY: Dude Publishing.

Kasser, S. (1995). *Inclusive games.* Champaign, IL: Human Kinetics.

Katz, I., & Rivoto, E. (1993). *Joey and Sam.* Northridge, CA: Real Life Storybooks.Reallifestories .com

Kehert, P. (1996). *Small steps: The year I got polio.* Morton Grove, IL: Whitman.

Kent, D., & Quinlan, K. (1996). *Extraordinary people with disabilities.* New York: Children's Press.

Keyes, D. (1959). *Flowers for Algernon.* New York: Harcourt Brace.

Key Math Diagnostic Arithmetic Test by American Guidance. 4201 Woodland Road Circle Pines, MN 55014, (800) 328–2560.

Klass, P., & Costello, E. (2003). *Quirky kids: Understanding and helping your child who doesn't fit in— When to worry and when not to worry.* New York: Random House.

Klein, S., & Schive, K. (2001). *You will dream new dreams.* New York: Kensington Books.

Kleinert, H. L., Green, P., Hurte, M., Clayton, J., & Oetinger, C. (2002). Creating and using meaningful alternate assessments. *Teaching Exceptional Children, 34*(4), 40–47.

Kniveton, B. (2004). A study of perceptions that significant others hold of the inclusion of children with difficulties in mainstream classes. *Educational Studies, 30*(3), 331–343.

Konigsburg, E. L. (1996). *The view from Saturday.* New York: Aladdin.

Kranowitz, C. (1998). *The out-of-sync-child: Recognizing and coping with sensory integration dysfunction.* New York: Perigee.

Kriegsman, K., Zaslow, E., & Zmura-Rechsteiner, J. (1992). *Taking charge: Teenagers talk about life & physical disabilities.* Bethesda, MD: Woodbine House.

Lamorey, S. (2002). The effects of culture on special education services: Evil eyes, prayer meetings, and IEPs. *Teaching Exceptional Children, 34*(5), 67–71.

LeDoux, J. (2002). *Synaptic self: How our brains become who we are.* New York: Viking.

Lessenberry, B., & Rehdfeldt, R. (2004). Evaluating stress levels of parents of children with disabilities. *Exceptional Children, 70*(2), 231–244.

Levy, S., & Chard, D. J. (2001). Research on reading instruction for students with emotional and behavioral disorders. *International Journal of Disability, Development and Education, 48,* 429–444.

Littky, D. (2004). *The big picture: Education is everyone's business.* Alexandria, VA: Association for Supervision and Curriculum Development.

Loechler, K. (1999). Frequently asked questions about ADHD and the answers from the Internet. *Teaching Exceptional Children, 31*(6), 28–31.

Macysyn, C. (1996). *It's your life—live it to the max! A self-determination manual for youth with disabilities.* New Jersey Department of Education-Partnership for Transition. (609) 984–0905.

Marzano, R. (2000). *Transforming classroom grading.* Alexandria, VA: Association for Supervision and Curriculum Development.

Marzano, R. (2007). *The art and science of teaching.* Alexandria, VA: Association for Supervision and Curriculum Development.

Matlin, M. (2002). *Deaf child crossing.* New York: Simon & Schuster.

McCarney, S., Wunderlich, K., & Bauer, A. (2006). *The teacher's resource guide* (2nd ed.). Columbia, MO: Hawthorne Educational Services. (800) 542–1673.

McKinley, L., & Stormont, M. (2008). The school supports checklist: Identifying support needs and barriers for children with ADHD. *Teaching Exceptional Children, 41*(2), 14–19.

McLaughlin, M. (2000). *Reform for EVERY learner: Teachers' views on standards and students with disabilities.* Alexandria, VA: Center for Policy Research.

McLesky, J., & Waldron, N. (2002). Inclusion and school change: Teacher perceptions regarding curricular and instructional adaptations. *Teacher Education and Special Education, 25*(1), 53.

McNary, S., Glasgow, N., & Hicks, C. (2005). *What successful teachers do in inclusive classrooms: 60 research-based strategies that help special learners succeed.* Thousand Oaks, CA: Corwin.

Merrow, J. (1996, May 8). What's so special about special education? *Education Week, 15,* 33.

Meyer, D., & Vadasy, P. (1996). *Living with a brother or sister with special needs: A book for sibs.* Seattle: University of Washington Press.

Mitchell, M. (2009). *Physical activity may strengthen children's ability to pay attention.* Urbana-Champaign: University of Illinois News Bureau.

Molko, M., Cachia, A., Rivière, D., Mangin, J., Bruandet, M., Le Bihan, D., et al. (2003). Functional and structural alterations of the intraparietal sulcus in a developmental dyscalculia of genetic origin. *Neuron, 40,* 847–858.

Mooney, J., & Cole, D. (2000). *Learning outside the lines.* New York: Fireside.

Mostert, M., & Crockett, J. (1999–2000). Reclaiming the history of special education for more effective practice. *Exceptionality, 8*(2), 133–143.

Muldoon, K. (1989). *Princess Pooh.* Morton Grove, IL: Whitman.

National Easter Seal Society. (1990). *Disability awareness program for elementary students* [videotape]. Chicago: Friends Who Care. (800) 221–6827. Online updated version available at http://www.easterseals.com/friendswhocare

National Institute on Deafness and Other Communication Disorders. (n.d.). *How loud is too loud?* Retrieved July 15, 2009, from http://www.nidcd.nih.gov/health/hearing/ruler.asp

Nevin, A., Cramer, E., Voigt, J., & Salazar, L. (2008). Instructional modifications, adaptations, and accommodations of co teachers who loop. *Teacher Education and Special Education, 31*(4), 283–297.

New roles in response to intervention: Creating success for schools and children. (2006, November). A collaborative project with the American Speech-Language-Hearing Association and others. Retrieved June 30, 2009, from http://www.nasponline.org/advocacy/New%20Roles%20in%20RTI.pdf

Noonan, D. (2004, May 3). Don't we call them quirky? *Newsweek, 143*(18), 51–52.

Norris, D., & Schumacker, R. E. (1998, January 22). *Texas special education effectiveness study.* Paper presented at the Southwest Educational Research Association Conference, Houston, TX. Retrieved June 21, 2009, from http://www.eric.ed.gov:80/ERICDocs/data/ericdocs2sql/content_storage_01/0000019b/80/17/46/d3.pdf

O'Brien, J., & Forest, M. (1989). *Action for inclusion: How to improve schools by welcoming children with special needs into regular classrooms.* Toronto, Ont., Canada: Inclusion Press.

Office of Special Education Programs. (2005, June 27). *Memorandum from Troy Justesen.* Accessed May 4, 2009, from http://www.k12.wa.us/specialEd/pubdocs/wac/federal/OSEP%2005-09%20private%20schools.pdf

Okimoto, J. (1993). *A place for Grace.* Seattle, WA: Sasquatch Books.

Opitz, M., & Rasinski, T. (1998). *Good-bye round robin: 25 effective oral reading strategies.* Portsmouth, NH: Heinemann.

Orelove, F., & Sobsey, D. (1996). *Educating children with multiple disabilities: A transdisciplinary approach.* Baltimore: Paul H. Brookes.

Owens, R. (1995). *Language disorders: A functional approach to assessment and intervention.* Boston: Allyn & Bacon.

Ozuru, Y., Dempsey, K., & McNamara, D. (2009). Prior knowledge, reading skill, and text cohesion in the comprehension of science texts. *Learning and Instruction, 19*(3), 228–242.

Packer, A. (2002). *The dive from Clausen's Pier.* New York: Alfred Knopf.

Piaget, J. (1952). *The origins of intelligence in children.* New York: International University Press.

Pipher, M. (1994). *Reviving Ophelia.* New York: Random House.

Pisha, B., & Stahl, S. (2005). The promise of new learning environments for students with disabilities. *Intervention in School & Clinic, 41*(2), 67–75.

Popham, J. (2001). *The truth about testing.* Alexandria, VA: Association for Supervision and Curriculum Development.

Ratey, J. (2008). *SPARK: The revolutionary new science of exercise and the brain.* New York: Little, Brown.

Reeve, C. (1998). *Still me.* New York: Ballantine.

Reeve, C. (2002). *Nothing is impossible: Reflections on a new life.* New York: Random House.

Rothstein-Fisch, C., & Trumbull, E. (2008). *Managing diverse classrooms: How to build on students' cultural strengths.* Alexandria, VA: Association for Supervision and Curriculum Development.

Rubio, G. (1998). *Icy sparks.* New York: Penguin.

Rubric site—http://www.rubrics.com http://rubistar.4teachers.org

Russo, C., Tiegerman, E., & Radziewicz, C. (2009). *RTI guide: Making it work, Strategies = Solutions.* Port Chester, NY: National Professional Resources.

Sacks, O. (1985). *The man who mistook his wife for a hat.* New York: Touchstone.

Sacks, O. (1995). *An anthropologist on Mars.* New York: Vintage.

Salend, S. (2005). *Creating inclusive classrooms: Effective and reflective practices for ALL students* (5th ed.). Columbus, OH: Pearson.

Sanchez, I., & McGinnis, R. (2003). *Art and the alphabet: A tactile experience.* Humacao, Puerto Rico: Creative Creativo, Inc.

Savard, J. (n.d.). *Braille alphabet.* Available at http://www.quadibloc.com/crypto/intro.htm

Schemo, D. (2004, June 7). States' end run dilutes burden for special ed. *New York Times.* Retrieved October 13, 2009, from http://www.nytimes.com/2004/06/07/education/07CHIL.html

Seuss, Dr. (1989). *The Sneetches and other stories.* New York: Random House.

Shanker, A. (1994–1995). Full inclusion is neither free nor appropriate. *Educational Leadership, 52*(4), 18–21.

Shelly, G., Cashman, T., & Gunter, R. G. (2002). *Integrating technology in the classroom* (2nd ed.). Cambridge, MA: Course Technology.

Shriver, M. (2001). *What's wrong with Timmy?* Boston: Little, Brown.

Simmons, R. (n.d.). *Sit tight* [Video]. Available at http://www.richardsimmons.com

Simon, R. (2002). *Riding the bus with my sister.* Boston: Houghton Mifflin.

Siperstein, G. N., Parker, R. C., Bardon, J. N., & Widaman, K. F. (2007). A national study of youth attitudes toward the inclusion of students with intellectual disabilities. *Exceptional Children, 73*(4), 435–455.

Skiba, R., Simmons, A., Ritter, S., Gibb, A., Rausch, M. K., Cuadrado, J., et al. (2008). Achieving equity in special education: History, status, and current challenges. *Exceptional Children, 74*(3), 264–288.

Slavin, R. E. (1990). *Cooperative learning: Theory, research, and practice.* Englewood Cliffs, NJ: Prentice Hall.

Smith, J. D. (2003). *Stories of disability in the human family: In search of better angels.* Thousand Oaks, CA: Corwin.

Snowman, J., McCown, R., & Biehler, R. (2009). *Applying psychology to teaching* (12th ed.). Boston: Houghton Mifflin.

Sobsey, D. (1978). *Special Eddy* [online]. Available at http://www.our-kids.org/Archives/Spec_eddie.html

Sousa, D. (1995). *How the brain learns.* Reston, VA: National Association of Secondary School Principals.

Sousa, D. (2007). *How the special needs brain learns.* Thousand Oaks, CA: Corwin.

Sprenger, M. (1999). *Learning and memory: The brain in action.* Alexandria, VA: Association for Supervision and Curriculum Development.

Steele, M. (2007). Methods and strategies: Science success for students with special needs. *Science and Children, 45*(2), 48–51.

Steen, L. (2007). How mathematics counts. *Educational Leadership, 65*(3), 8–14.

Steinbeck, J. (1993). *Of mice and men.* New York: Penguin. (Original work published 1937)

Stemkowski, L. (n.d.). *Tangrams* [online]. Available at http://www.Dartmouth.edu

Storey, K. (2007). Combating ableism in schools. *Preventing School Failure, 53*(1), 56–58.

Study of Personnel Needs in Special Education—http://www.spense.org

Sylwester, R. (2000). *A biological brain in a cultural classroom.* Thousand Oaks, CA: Corwin.

Symeonidou, S., & Phtiaka, H. (2009). Using teachers' prior knowledge, attitudes, and beliefs to develop in-service teacher education courses for inclusion. *Teaching and Teacher Education: An International Journal of Research and Studies, 25*(4), 543–550.

Teaching Tolerance [magazine]. 400 Washington Avenue. Montgomery, AL 36104.

Thurlow, M. L. (2003, February). *Linking standards, assessments, and instructional practices.* Presentation at the Pacific Rim Conference, Waikiki, HI. National Center on Educational Outcomes. Retrieved February 3, 2008, from http://cehd.umn.edu

Tomlinson, C. (1999). *The differentiated classroom.* Alexandria, VA: Association for Supervision and Curriculum Development.

Tomlinson, C. (2001). Grading for success. *Teaching Exceptional Children, 58,* 12–15.

Tomlinson, C. (2008). The goals of differentiation. *Educational Leadership, 66*(3), 26–30.

Tomlinson, C., & McTighe, J. (2006). *Integrating differentiated instruction and understanding by design: Connecting content and kids.* Alexandria, VA: Association for Supervision and Curriculum Development.

Torbert, M. (n.d.). *Follow me: A handbook of movement activities.* P.L.A.Y. (Positive Learning Activities for Youth). mtorbert@thunder.ocis.temple.edu

Tramer, H. (2007). Awareness of disability law up among lawyers, families. *Cleveland Business, 28*(15), 15.

Trout, A. L., Epstein, M. H., Nelson, R., Synhorst, L., & Hurley, K. D. (2006, Winter). Profiles of children served in early intervention programs for behavioral disorders: Early literacy and behavioral characteristics. *Topics in Early Childhood Special Education, 26*(4), 206–218.

Tyen, W. D. (n.d.). *E-Medicine clinical knowledge base.* Retrieved June 24, 2004, from http://www.emedicine.com/PED/topic2791.htm

U.S. Department of Education. (1998). *Twentieth annual report to Congress on the implementation of the Individuals with Disabilities Education Act.* Washington, DC: Author (Writers of the modules included OSEP personnel and staff from OSEP-funded research and technical assistance projects.). Available at http://www.ed.gov/offices/OSERS/OSEP/Research/OSEP98 AnlRpt/index.html

Vaughn, S., Bos, C., & Schumm, J. (2002). *Teaching exceptional, diverse, and at-risk students in the general classroom* (3rd ed.). Boston: Allyn & Bacon.

Villa, R. A., & Thousand, J. S. (Eds.). (1995). *Creating an inclusive school.* Alexandria, VA: Association for Supervision and Curriculum Development.

Vision Management Consulting. (n.d.). *IEP Planner: A compendium of educational and behavior goals and objectives.* Retrieved November 11, 2003, from http://www.visionplanetcom

Walter, J. (2006). The basic IDEA: The Individuals with Disabilities Act in your classroom. *Teaching Music, 14*(3), 22–26.

Warner, F. (1997). *Dis "ability" joke book.* Palmetto, FL: Author. Available at http://disabilityjokebooks.50megs.com

Welton, E. (1999). How to help inattentive students find success in school. *Teaching Exceptional Students, 31,* 12–18.

West, C. (1999). *First person plural.* New York: Hyperion.

Westbridge Young Writers Workshop. (1994). *Kids explore the gifts of children with special needs.* Santa Fe, NM: John Muir Publications.

Wiener, D. (2005). *One state's story: Access and alignment to the GRADE-LEVEL content for students with significant cognitive disabilities* (Synthesis Report 57). Minneapolis: University of Minnesota, National Center on Educational Outcomes. Retrieved September 15, 2007, from http://education.umn.edu/NCEO/OnlinePubs/Synthesis57.html

Wiggins, G., & McTighe, J. (2005). *Understanding by design* (2nd ed.). Alexandria, VA: Association for Supervision and Curriculum Development.

Williams, K. (1998). *Disability awareness: 24 lessons for the inclusive classroom.* Portland, ME: J. Weston Walch.

Willingham, D. (2004, Spring). Practice makes perfect—But only if you practice beyond the point of perfection. *American Educator,* 31–33, 38–39.

Willis, C. (2009). *Creating inclusive learning environments for young children: What to do on Monday mornings.* Thousand Oaks, CA: Corwin.

Winebrenner, S. (1992, rev. 2001). *Teaching gifted kids in the regular classroom* (Rev. ed.). Minneapolis, MN: Free Spirit.

Wissick, C., & Gardner, E. (2000). Multimedia or not to multimedia? That is the question for students with learning disabilities. *Teaching Exceptional Children, 32*(4), 34–43.

Wolfe, P. (2008). *Brain-compatible practices for the classroom: Grades K–6* [DVD]. Port Chester, NY: National Professional Resources.

Wood, J. (1995). *The man who loved clowns.* New York: Hyperion.

Woodward, J., & Cuban, L. (Eds.). (2001). *Technology, curriculum, and professional development.* Thousand Oaks, CA: Corwin.

Yenawine, P. (1991). *Shapes.* New York: Delacorte.

Young, S. (1994). *Rhyming words.* New York: Scholastic.

Zipprich, M., Grace, M., & Grote-Garcia, S. (2009). Building story schema: Using patterned books as a means of instruction for students with disabilities. *Intervention in School & Clinic, 44*(5), 294–299.

Zirkel, P., & Richards, D. (1998, April/May). The new disorder maze. *Teaching Exceptional Children, 30*(5), 2.

Zubov, L. (2007, September). *IDEA Updates, Current Legislative Action, & Advocacy* Presentation at the CEC Western Carolina Regional Conference, Appalachian State University, Boone, NC.

Resource D

Alphabetized Acronyms

AA-AAS—Alternate Assessment based upon Alternate Academic Achievement Standards

AA-MAS—Alternate Assessment based upon Modified Academic Achievement Standards

ABA—Applied Behavior Analysis

ABOWA—Assessment by Observation and Walking Around

ADA—Americans with Disabilities Act

ADAAA—Americans with Disabilities Act Amendments Act

AD/HD—Attention-Deficit/Hyperactivity Disorder

AEIOU's of Study Skills—Attitude, Effort, Involvement, Organization, Understanding

ARC—The ARC

ASD—Autism Spectrum Disorder

AYP—Adequate Yearly Progress

BIP—Behavior Intervention Plan

BOE—Board of Education

BOSE—Beginning of Special Education

BP—Bipolar or Be Positive!

CA—Chronological age

CAPD—Central Auditory Processing Disorders (APD)

CAST—Center for Applied Special Technology

CBA—Curriculum-Based Assessments

CBT—Cognitive Behavioral Therapy

CEC—Council for Exceptional Children

CHADD—Children and Adults with Attention Deficit Disorder

CI—Communication Impaired

CNS—Central Nervous System

CP—Cerebral Palsy

CRAFT—Communication, Resourcefulness, Accommodations, Flexibility, Training

CSI—Common Sense Interventions (for inclusion)

CST—Child Study Team

DA—Dis*ability* Awareness

DD—Developmental Dis*ability*

DOE—Department of Education

DRA—Developmental Reading Assessment

DSM-IV—Diagnostic and Statistical Manual of Mental Disorders

DVRS—Division of Vocational and Rehabilitation Services

EIS—Early Intervening Services

EBP—Evidence-Based Practice

ED'S CAR—Expand, Delete, Substitute, Combine, and Rearrange

ELL—English Language Learner

EPA'S of Grading—Effort, Progress, Achievement, Self-Awareness

ESEA—Elementary and Secondary Education Act

ESL—English as a Second Language

ESY—Extended School Year

FAPE—Free Appropriate Public Education

FBA—Functional Behavioral Assessment

FERPA—Family Education Rights and Privacy Act

FSA—Family Support Act

GE—General Education

HEATH—Higher Education and Training for People with Disabilities

HI—Hearing Impaired

IAES—Interim Alternative Educational Setting

IDEA—Individuals with Disabilities Education Act

IDEIA—Individuals with Disabilities Education Improvement Act

IEP—Individualized Education Program (or It's Educationally Prudent!)

IES—Institute of Education Sciences

IFSP—Individualized Family Service Plan

IHE—Institutes of Higher Education

ILP—Independent Living Plan

ITIP—Instructional Theory into Practice

JOB—Just One Break

LDA—Learning Disabilities Association of America

LD—Learning Dis*ability* or Learning Differences

LEA—Local Education Agency

LRE—Least Restrictive Environment

MAAP—More Advanced Individuals with Autism, Asperger Syndrome, and Pervasive Developmental Disorder

MDT—Multidisciplinary Team

MI—Multiple Intelligences, or Massive Initializations

MS—Multiple Sclerosis, or Master of Science, or both!

NAEP—National Assessment of Educational Programs

NCES—National Center for Education Statistics

NCLB—No Child Left Behind

NCLD—National Center for Learning Disabilities

NICHCY—National Dissemination Center for Children with Disabilities

NIMAS—National Instructional Materials Accessibility Standard

OCF—Obsessive–Compulsive Foundation

OCR—Office of Civil Rights

ODD—Oppositional Defiant Disorder

OH—Orthopedically Handicapped

OHI—Other Health Impairment

OSEP—Office of Special Education Programs, U.S. Department of Education

OSERS—Office of Special Education and Rehabilitative Services

OT—Occupational Therapy

PANDAS—Pediatric Autoimmune Neuropsychiatric Disorders Associated with Streptococcal Infections

PDD—Pervasive Developmental Disorder

PECS—Picture Exchange Communication System

PET—Positron Emission Tomography, or Pupil Evaluation Team

PL—Public Law

PLAAFP—Present Level of Academic Achievement and Functional Performance

PT—Physical Therapy

RtI—Response to Intervention (or Remember to Include!)

SAT—Scholastic Aptitude Test

SDM—Severe Discrepancy Model

SE—Special Education

SEA—State Education Agency

SI or SID—Sensory Integration Dysfunction

SLD—Specific Learning Disability

SLP—Speech Language Pathologists

SOARing—Scanning, Outlining, Analyzing, Reading

SPED—Special Education

TAG—Talented and Gifted

TBI—Traumatic Brain Injury

TDD—Telecommunication Devices for the Deaf, and Test Driven Development

TGIF—Thank Goodness Inclusion's Feasible!

TIPS—Topic, Individuals, Planning, Setting

TLC—Tender Loving Care: What students in every classroom need!

TPP—Transition Planning Process

TS—Tourette syndrome, or Transitional Services

TTY—Text Telephone

UbD—Understanding by Design

UDL—Universal Design for Learning

VAKT—Visual, Auditory, Kinesthetic, Tactile

VI—Visually Impaired

VOIP—Voice Over the Internet Protocol

WWC—What Works Clearinghouse

WWCI—Ways We Can Include!

Consulted sources for some of the above abbreviations: http://ericec.org/fact/acronyms.html, http://www.ode.state.or.us/search/page/?id=293

Index

CORWIN
A SAGE Company

The Corwin logo—a raven striding across an open book—represents the union of courage and learning. Corwin is committed to improving education for all learners by publishing books and other professional development resources for those serving the field of PreK–12 education. By providing practical, hands-on materials, Corwin continues to carry out the promise of its motto: **"Helping Educators Do Their Work Better."**